S0-AVW-941

RACIAL THINKING
in the United States

African American Intellectual Heritage Series

PAUL SPICKARD

General Editor

RACIAL THINKING
in the United States

UNCOMPLETED INDEPENDENCE

EDITED BY
PAUL SPICKARD &
G. REGINALD DANIEL

University of Notre Dame Press • *Notre Dame, Indiana*

305.8009 R121 2004

Racial thinking in the
United States.

Copyright © 2004 by University of Notre Dame
Notre Dame, Indiana 46556
www.undpress.nd.edu
All Rights Reserved

Manufactured in the United States of America

Library of Congress Cataloging-in-Publication Data
Racial thinking in the United States : uncompleted independence / edited
by Paul Spickard and G. Reginald Daniel.
    p.   cm. — (African American intellectual heritage series)
  Includes bibliographical references and index.
  ISBN 0-268-04103-2 (cloth : alk. paper)
  ISBN 0-268-04104-0 (pbk. : alk. paper)
  1. United States—Race relations.   2. United States—Race relations—
Public opinion.   3. Race awareness—United States.   4. Racism—
United States.   5. Ethnicity—United States.   6. Racially mixed
people—Race identity—United States.   7. Social movements—United
States.   8. United States—Intellectual life.   9. Public opinion—United
States.   I. Spickard, Paul R., 1950–   II. Daniel, G. Reginald, 1949–
III. Series.
  E184.A1R3235   2004
  305.8'00973—dc22

2004011377

∞ *This book is printed on acid-free paper.*

To Patrick Miller, estimable scholar, patient friend

CONTENTS

ACKNOWLEDGMENTS

The editors owe debts to several people and institutions connected with the making of this book. The Collegium for African American Research (CAAR), an esteemed body of European scholars of African America, provided the occasion for most of the volume's contributors to gather in March 1999 in Münster, Germany, and share their ideas. Special thanks are due to the leaders of CAAR, especially Maria Diedrich and Carl Pedersen. The University of California, Santa Barbara, provided travel funds, a wonderful library, and a stimulating intellectual environment for the editors. Barbara Hanrahan at the University of Notre Dame Press was steadfast in her encouragement and insightful in her commentary. Sheila Berg was an exemplary copyeditor. Patrick Miller, of CAAR and Northeastern Illinois University, helped us to conceive the idea for this book, brought to our attention scholars who could contribute, read drafts of chapters, and goaded us genially to complete the work. Thanks to them all.

INDEPENDENCE POSSIBLE

PAUL SPICKARD *&*

G. REGINALD DANIEL

Five metanarratives frame American history: democracy, capitalism, colonialism, misogyny, and racism. Almost everything that has happened in the past four centuries on the North American continent can be interpreted with reference to one or more of these themes. The creation and development of U.S. political institutions can be understood primarily with reference to the course of democracy and secondarily with reference to the other four metanarratives. The industrial revolution and the postindustrial age are founded on capitalism but deeply affected by each of the other themes offered here. The march across the continent, and then across the Pacific, is mainly a product of the career of colonialism, although racist, capitalist, and other themes play their parts. Slavery and the Civil War were founded on racism and capitalism. America's rise to world military and political dominance can be understood as the interplay of aspirations and compulsions that relate to democracy, capitalism, and colonialism. And so on and on.

The topic of this book is the fifth of these metanarratives, racism. As W. E. B. Du Bois famously declared a century ago, "The problem of the twentieth century is the problem of the color line." More recently, John Hope Franklin concluded, "The problem of the twenty-first century will be the problem of the color line. . . . By any standard of measurement or evaluation the problem has not been solved in the twentieth century, and thus becomes a part of the legacy and burden of the next century."[1] By "color line," Franklin and Du Bois meant race generally and the racial relations between Black and White Americans specifically. Both men were right. No problem in America and the world was more powerful in the twentieth century than race. Other themes competed on the world stage in that period—tyranny, technology, entropy, ecology, to name just a few—but none stood larger than race in shaping the life chances of humans. And Franklin's point, that racial hierarchy and privilege, domination and oppression, are with us still and will be so for a very long time, is true as well.

What is not quite clear, as the century of which Du Bois spoke has turned to the next, is what precisely has been meant by "race." That turns out to be a slippery idea. Are there two races in America, Black and White, or are there many? If the latter, how many, and what makes them races? Is this a biological business, or is it constrained, even initiated by social dynamics? Are races discrete entities, or do they mix? Does race make politics, or does politics make race? These and many other questions about race have found quite different answers in different social, cultural, and political contexts over the course of the past two centuries.

Racial Thinking in the United States is a critical study of ideas about race in American history. Make no mistake about our intentions. We are here to enlist the reader in the antiracist struggle and to provide tools for that encounter. The essays herein investigate the creation of racial ideas and systems in the United States in the context of slavery and colonialism and the subsequent revisions of those ideas and systems in later eras. At the broadest level, the thesis of this book is that racial thinking was historically bound to slavery and to colonialism and that, although slavery was formally ended and colonialism was revised, racial thinking has not yet been emancipated. We do not claim to have a detailed road map; instead we hope to point in some directions that may ultimately prove emancipatory and to help us all avoid some dead ends.

In preparation for the analyses that will follow, we wish to make some summary theoretical comments about race from several interpretive angles. First, we examine some features of the two dominant schools of thought regarding race—the biological and the sociocultural. Then we turn to racialization theory for a set of ideas that we hope will take us beyond biological essentialist thinking, and also beyond some difficulties that arise when attending only to socio-cultural themes. Then we contemplate the relative usefulness of talking about race, ethnicity, and culture. Finally, this introduction lays out the argument of the book as a whole.

The Biologic of Race

For much of modern history, as G. Reginald Daniel describes in chapter 2, discussion of race has been dominated by the idea that race is a biological thing. In what ways and to what extent may that be an accurate characterization? Genetic, archaeological, and linguistic evidence suggests that the first human communities evolved in Central Africa millennia ago. Between 90,000 and 180,000 years ago, these populations began to spread throughout Africa, Asia, Europe, and the Pacific. Perhaps as early as 30,000 years ago, and at least as early as 15,000 years ago, they migrated to the Americas. As a result of adaptation to various environments, they evolved into geographic population aggregates displaying differences in various bodily features. Some of the externally visible features of such difference—skin color, hair color and texture, facial morphology—are commonly referred to as "racial traits." These physical differences (phenotypes) reflect some of the difference in genetic information (genotypes) that is transmitted through one's ancestors and duplicated by sexual reproduction. So there are in fact human populations that, taken as aggregates, exhibit higher incidences of particular genotypical and phenotypical traits than do other human populations, taken as aggregates.

Nevertheless, despite such commonly observed differences, it is important to remember that all human beings, as members of the same species, *Homo sapiens sapiens,* share 90 percent to 95 percent of their genes.[2] Geno-phenotypical diversity in the form of racial traits is a biological fact, yet the boundaries delineating racial subgroupings are not concrete, discrete, or fixed. The different population aggregates probably were never completely separate and "pure." In any case, their boundaries have been constantly under erosion by contact—through migrations, trade, war, and so on. Over time, this contact has leveled out any actual absolute differences by diffusing common genetic information—and ultimately common phenotypical traits—

throughout the general population where no forces have intervened to prevent the process. Consequently, the 5 percent to 10 percent of total genetic information determining phenotypical traits associated with racial differentiation is itself the product of millennia of genetic blending.[3] Considering how long *Homo sapiens sapiens* has inhabited the planet Earth, a "multiracial" lineage is the norm rather than the exception among humans. In short, although we recognize certain phenotypical features as marking off population aggregates as different from one another, in fact everyone is mixed. There are no pure races.[4]

In general, there is a statistical relationship between the proportion an individual has of any given ancestry and the number of genes he or she is likely to inherit from that ancestry. Yet the belief that individuals will inherit a genotypical blueprint in direct proportion to their fraction of a specific ancestry is inaccurate. Genes are randomly distributed in individuals so that, for example, an individual who is the offspring of one European and one West African parent in fact might not inherit any genes from West African forebears (although that would be highly unlikely). More likely, such a person would have a mix of European and West African genetic material, although the exact proportion of genotype inherited from each group could vary widely.

There are cases in which an individual's known ancestry is three-fourths or even one-half West African and in which that individual is phenotypically able to pass as European. In such cases the number of African-derived genes is presumably less than the proportion of known African ancestry.[5] Such individuals, despite substantial West African ancestry, are rarely if ever phenotypically distinguishable from Europeans despite their partial ancestral and genotypical links to Africanity. In these cases, the illusion of complete Whiteness is attributable to the fact that the human visual system is unable to perceive information at the genetic level except by technological means. It is at the genetic level where one could perceive the DNA inherited from both African and European ancestors.[6]

Yet the United States has a one-drop rule (sometimes referred to as the "rule of hypodescent"). This rule uses social knowledge about ancestry, not genotype or even phenotype, to arrive at racial designations. By the one-drop rule, all individuals of any traceable West African ancestry ("one drop of blood") are designated African American—and would generally identify themselves as such—irrespective of their genotypical or phenotypical situation.[7] That is, this social device necessitates that they identify as Black if anyone knows they have Black ancestors, irrespective of their actual genetic inheritance. At the same time, the idea that race is a biological thing continues to have power. Hence, an essentially social definition (the one-drop rule) is invested with scientific authority as a biological essence.

The Sociocultural Logic of Race

There are some who have seen this racial business from a very different angle, not as biological fact but as social myth. The concept of biological race attempts to explain geno-phenotypical differentiation as perceived visually and interpreted by one's consciousness. The elusive nature of racial boundaries, however, in conjunction with the fact that individual phenotypical traits vary independently—rather than being transmitted in genetic clusters—has led some to assert that there is no such thing as race. Those who maintain this race-as-illusion position view race as an unfortunate legacy of the past five hundred years of human history. Accordingly, they recommend that we discard the concept of race altogether.[8]

Others argue that even if there is not a scientific reality to race, there is nonetheless a social reality that is equally powerful. Those who support this race-as-social-construction position point out that race has been a powerful tenet of Western behavior and thought and that it is embedded in the structure of society's institutions. Even those individuals who maintain the race-as-illusion stance are cognizant of the social reality of race and their inability to avoid the term even as they deny its existence.[9]

Scholars, as well as the larger educated community, have reached no consensus regarding definitions of race. There is widespread agreement, however, that the concept itself should be regarded as a neutral classificatory term. Race, in this interpretation, is simply one of myriad categories of differentiation, along with sex or gender, socioeconomic class, and other factors that influence the human experience. Therefore, one could argue not that we need to dispense with the concept of race (i.e., ignore geno-phenotypical diversity) but that we should transcend essentialized notions of racial boundaries and categories, as well as deal more forthrightly with racism and racial inequality. These phenomena, which reflect odious forms of human thought and behavior such as domination, discrimination, and hatred, have less to do with the concept of race and more to do with abuses and atrocities that have been committed in the name of race. In short, the problem is not racial thinking but racial hierarchy and oppression.

Any attempt to use the term "race" in an objective, scientific, and functionally neutral manner is fraught with unavoidable contradictions. Despite its supposed neutrality as a biological concept, race has historically been (and continues to be) inextricably intertwined with inequality in the distribution of wealth, power, privilege, and prestige. Moreover, in the national consciousness of the United States (and other societies with systems of social inequality) race is a major mode of social differentiation that has historically cut across and taken priority over socioeconomic class, sex, gender, age, and other factors. Accordingly, race has become a convenient code word that has served to disguise, or deflect attention from, other types of social division. This, in turn, has resulted in a chasm of social distance expressed explicitly and implicitly in all kinds of social intercourse and, ultimately, has had a vastly more deleterious effect on the social order than any biological concept of race.[10]

RACIAL FORMATION: AN ATTEMPT AT SYNTHESIS

One goal of social scientific studies of race relations is to explain the sociopolitical reality of race, quite apart from its use as a concept in the biological sciences and distinct from whether those disciplines reach any consensus on a definition. Accordingly, racial formation theory challenges the race-as-illusion position, which contends that race is something we can and should move beyond. It also rejects the race-as-objective-reality position, the essentialist formulation that views race as absolutely fixed in biological data. The racial formation paradigm embraces the race-as-social-construction position. Racial formation thinking notes that the concept of race invokes biologically based human characteristics but that the selection of specific human features for purposes of racial signification has changed over time and that selection is necessarily a sociohistorical process.[11]

This process, called "racialization," delineates the different phenotypical embodiments into presumed exclusive groupings and imposes on them attributes and features according to the ideological and social values of the specific culture within which racial categories are being defined. These categories, in turn, signify social conflicts and interests, which determine how a given society allocates wealth, power, privilege, and prestige. Equally important, in such an analysis, racial categories are seen as unstable complexes of sociocultural meanings that are continuously being created, inhabited, contested, transformed, and destroyed.[12]

Racial formation thus plays an important role in structuring and representing the social world, despite the unavoidable contradictions inherent in the concept of race and the elusive and somewhat arbitrary nature of biophysical racial groupings and boundaries—not to mention the abuses and genocidal practices that have been committed in their name. Race may be thought of, not only as an element of social structure, but also as a dimension of human cultural representation and signification, rather than as an illusion. In addition, race in this interpretation is at once a micro-level phenomenon of the individual psyche and interpersonal relations and a macro-level component of collective identities from the intrapsychic to the supranational.[13]

By recognizing race as a sociohistorical construct, a racial formation orientation makes it possible to analyze the process by which a society determines racial meanings and assigns racial identities. At any given juncture in time and space, there are many interpretations and reinterpretations of the meaning of race in the form of what racial formation theorists call "racial projects." On the one hand, every racial project is necessarily a discursive or cultural initiative. This involves an interpretation, representation, or explanation of racial dynamics by means of identity politics that attempts to rescue racial identities from their distortion and erasure by the dominant society. On the other hand, a racial project is also a political initiative whose goal is to organize and redistribute resources, a process in which the state is often called on to play a significant role. This is a logical and critical strategy, given that the state is composed of institutions, policies, conditions, and rules that support and justify these conditions, as well as the social relations in which they are embedded. Equally important, the state has historically exercised power not only in the politics of racial exclusion (and inclusion) but also in enforcing racial definition, classification, and, ultimately, identification.[14]

Racial formation theory suggests that the articulation and rearticulation of racial meanings is a multidimensional process of competing projects, which may stem from a variety of sources. These may include subjective phenomena such as racial identities, religion, and popular and elite culture. They may also involve social structural phenomena such as political movements (e.g., the civil rights movements of the 1950s and 1960s), political parties (e.g., the Know-Nothing Party of the mid-nineteenth century, the Black Panther Party and La Raza Unida Party of the late 1960s), state institutions (the Bureau of the Census, the Immigration and Naturalization Service), state policies (Jim Crow segregation, the Chinese Exclusion Act, the Civil Rights Act), and market process (labor, capital, and consumption of goods).

The pattern of racial meanings and identities, the racial dimensions of social inequality, and the degree of political mobilization based on race, therefore, all display instability and flexibility such that the logic of race is multiply determined at any given historical moment. At a particular moment, or in a given society, race may be simply a matter of common sense. Accordingly, racial identities are reproduced by their own taken-for-grantedness in the daily lives and conversations of the society. Under these circumstances, racial conflict would be minimal, or at most, limited to a few marginalized racial projects such as the period from the end of Reconstruction to the end of World War I. At another moment, or in another social context, race may be highly politicized and the occasion of significant social mobilization, as was the case with the mass-based racial movements spanning the period of the 1950s through the early 1970s. In this situation, there would most likely be a high degree of racial conflict. This would not only generate a large-scale national debate about race but also foster a great deal of popular uncertainty about the significance of race in everyday life.

RACE, CULTURE, AND ETHNICITY

Some scholars, as well as many members of the public, regard ethnicity as a less problematic concept than race—less burdened with the weight of old oppressions and biologistic explanations—and, therefore, a suitable substitute. "Ethnicity," in such constructions, generally refers to a segment or subset of a larger society whose members are thought by themselves or others to share a common culture (beliefs, values, customs, artifacts, shared fields of meaning) that sets them off from other groups in the society. These individuals also share a common ancestry or origin (real or imagined)—and thus may have similar or common geno-phenotypical traits—that distinguish them from other members of society as well. In addition, they may participate more or less in shared activities in which that common origin and culture are significant ingredients.[15]

Considering that ethnicity includes notions of both race and culture, it might seem more appropriate in this book to use the terms "ethnic" rather than "racial" and "multiethnic" rather than "multiracial." This would seem to facilitate a nuanced discussion of identity, that is, an individual's sense of personal spatiotemporal location in relation to other points of reference. Nonetheless, we choose to use the terms "race" and "multiracial"—not out of perversity on our part, but out of an understanding that the dynamics of which the racialization school speaks are especially important for understanding the history of the American social system.

The notion of ethnicity experienced as culture—the culturalization of ethnicity—is in important senses different from the experience that involves notions of race or geno-phenotypical and ancestral differentiation—the racialization of ethnicity. This does not mean that ethnocultural differences between groups that are thought to be ethnoracially similar (e.g., English Americans and Irish Americans) have not been the source of negative societal biases similar to those attached to groups that are thought to be ethnoracially different (e.g., English Americans and African Americans). It means, rather, that the overriding structural wedge in the United States, in terms of the distribution of wealth, power, privilege, and prestige, has been based primarily on notions of ethnoracial difference and secondarily on differences of an ethnocultural nature. This issue is taken up in greater detail by Paul Spickard in chapter 10.

Finally, the issues surrounding racial categories and identities in the United States are by no means limited to the experience of individuals of predominantly African and European descent. The Native American component is a key part of any discussion of racial issues, from the colonial period to the present, and Latinos and Asians have been part of the picture for most of that time. During recent decades, as we hope to show, the adequacy of the Black-White paradigm for understanding the history, the present, and particularly the future of race relations generally has incurred myriad challenges from all quarters. Race in America has never been about White and Black only. Nonetheless, most formal racial thinking and much racial acting in America, historically and in the present, have begun from the White-Black nexus, and so that is where we begin also.

THIS BOOK

Part 1. The essays in part 1 describe the setting up of a binary racial system, Black and White, in North America in the eighteenth and nineteenth centuries. G. Reginald Daniel describes the making of a racial system in the minds of Euro-Americans as part of the modernist intellectual outworking of the Enlightenment. A key development was the creation of a dichotomous racial worldview, which Daniel refers to as the Law of the Excluded Middle. By the late nineteenth century, with a few exceptions, the North American racial system had room only for White and Black, with the former dominant, people of mixed racial origins consigned to the lower group, and people without Black or White ancestry ignored altogether. The contexts that created this system were slavery and colonialism.

Stephen Small investigates the racial system that emerged in Jamaica in the same period. There, unlike in most of North America, some racially mixed people attained a racial status intermediate between Black and White. But Small describes the racial situation of those marginally privileged mixed people with less sanguine eyes than do many interpreters. Further, he argues that most people of mixed ancestry were consigned to slavery and did not enjoy significant privileges despite their mixedness. He finds that the critical differences are the wealth and class connections of the mixed people in question. Hence Small calls them, not "multiracial people," as does Daniel, but "Blacks of mixed origins." This is a terminological difference, but it highlights a difference of interpretation as well.

Both Daniel and Small draw lessons from their respective histories for the situation of racially mixed people in the United States today. Daniel is hopeful that the racial hierarchy that was built in slavery and colonialism can begin to be undone by recognizing and affirming the mixedness of multiracial people. Small argues that multiracial identity is a luxury item to be pursued mainly by racially mixed people of means, and so is far less hopeful.

Part 2. The White-over-Black racial binary that existed in North America was never so simple as the rules said; there were always anomalies. The essays in part 2 describe three such anomalies in the first half of the twentieth century. Hannah Wallinger describes the literature and lives of people of multiracial ancestry who passed as White. Engaging the life and writings of Alice Dunbar-Nelson, Wallinger portrays the complex ways in which Dunbar-Nelson and others dealt with their racial ambiguity, including occasional acts of passing for White even as they maintained a formal Black identity.

Wallinger and Paul Spickard also investigate the racial identities of multiracial people who passed as Black. Spickard tells the stories of several people of racially mixed origins who identified with the African American community and one who chose a Black identity for a while before crossing to the White side. W. E. B. Du Bois, Walter White, Jean Toomer, and Frederick Douglass all were widely recognized as leaders of Black America, yet all of them had mixed ancestry. He finds all these people to have acknowledged, even embraced, their multiple ancestries, at the same time that they existed in a binary racial system that required they choose allegiance to only one. They lived in a time when they could acknowledge the fact of their racial mixedness but were still constrained by the one-drop rule to adopt a functional Black identity, as if they were unmixed.

Finally, Lori Pierce explores a setting, Hawai'i, where race operated, not according to a binary model, but in a multiple-sided way. There, in a classical colonial setting, Haoles (Whites) built a racial order with themselves at the top and used what Pierce calls the "discourse of Aloha" to mask their racial privilege behind an ideology of mixing. Nonetheless, Hawai'i was a place where race had not two but four, five, or more sides: Haole, Hawaiian, Japanese, Chinese, Local, and so on.[16] Each of the episodes recounted in these chapters represented an anomaly in the national binary racial hierarchy, however, not a challenge to that system.

Anomalies such as the ones that Pierce, Spickard, and Wallinger describe had the potential to subvert the racial system, but they turned out to be anomalies only. Regionally specific in the Hawaiian case, or cast in binary terms even as they expressed multiplicity in the case of multiracial people of White and Black ancestry, they did not succeed in undermining the Black-White national understanding of race. Hence, the racial ideology that had been built in slavery and colonialism was left without successful challenge.

Part 3. Then the system's foundations began to shake. The remainder of this book looks at the second half of the twentieth century, at a series of challenges that have been mounted to the binary system of racial hierarchy. First came monoracial challenges. The Black civil rights movement challenged White privilege but not the idea of race. It had its echo in civil rights movements by Asians, Chicanos, and Native Americans. They not only challenged White supremacy but also pointed out stridently that America was not—indeed, had never been—just Black and White. It had always been Red, too, and now it was also Yellow and Brown.[17] Ralph Armbruster-Sandoval describes one such monoracial challenge, the Chicano movement, and offers criticisms of both it and its Black model for the things that they might have done and did not.

William Wei summarizes the main features of the Asian American movement. This political movement of the 1960s and 1970s, an echo of the Black movement for civil rights, created an Asian American pan-ethnicity where none had existed before, for the purpose of working on behalf of the interests of a variety of peoples whom non-Asians had commonly labeled "Orientals" but who in fact had little in common theretofore. First on West Coast college campuses, then in West Coast communities, and finally spreading across the country, the Asian American movement redrew the racial map of America and brought people whose ancestry harked back to Asia into the American political system as a common group with consolidated goals and organizational identities. The Asian American movement was an effective attack on the racial binary, in that it brought to the attention of many Americans the fact that America was more than just White and Black. Further, it acted effectively on behalf of many Asian communities. Still, it did not undermine the system of racial ideas that was established in the eighteenth and nineteenth centuries.

Reginald Daniel asks whether Afrocentricity constitutes a challenge to the racial binary and offers a novel vision for how the Afrocentric ideal might best be achieved. He explores the roots and course of the Afrocentric position in twentieth-century American intellectual history and argues that it has not yet lived up to its potential for combating racial hierarchy. He argues further that a particularly valuable way for the Afrocentric school to proceed would be to acknowledge, embrace, and explore the subtle meanings of multiracial identity for Africanity.

Paul Spickard asks whether White studies, an ethnic studies subfield that burgeoned in the late 1990s, constitutes a challenge to racial hierarchy or just another means of expressing White dominance. A horde of humanists and social scientists turned to studying the racial experiences of White people in the same kinds of terms that many of them had studied populations of color in the preceding third of a century. Spickard finds a worthy goal at the foundation of this movement and describes several instances in which the study of White privilege and White group making is very helpful. But he also finds a great deal of White self-indulgence, even closet racism, in this new movement, and so questions its usefulness in overturning racial hierarchy.

Part 4. The essays in part 4 address a significant revision in American racial thinking: the rise of a multiracial movement in the waning years of the twentieth century. Daniel tells the story of the multiracial movement and its quest to have multiplicity of identity recognized in the U.S. census and society at large. The 2000 census was the first in U.S. history that diminished the power of the binary vision: for the first time, respondents were encouraged to check all categories that applied rather than having to choose one from among their racial ancestries. Michael Thornton reviews the same movement with a more critical eye. Zipporah Glass, assuming the new embrace of multiplicity, shows how it is critical to the tasks of contemporary African American theology. Each of these authors, in various ways, contends that the idea of admitting racial multiplicity tends to destabilize the very notion of race and hence the power relationships that were set up in slavery and colonialism. Thus some may argue that the multiracial movement represents the first real opportunity to begin to emancipate American racial ideas from the forces that made them in slavery and colonialism.

The Way Out Is Through

Not all readers may go so far as to support that conclusion. At least two contributors to this volume (Stephen Small and Michael Thornton) argue that while claiming a multiracial identity may be an attractive option for some individuals, its widespread embrace might have deleterious effects for a monoracially defined minority group such as African Americans or Latinos. Each of these writers suggests it might be better to maintain the idea that African Americans are a mixed multitude, people with a unitary political identity, while acknowledging but not emphasizing their multiple ancestry.

At the other end of the spectrum, there are some people who simply want race to go away. Dinesh D'Souza, for example, proclaims "the end of racism" without a shred of evidence that racism is, in fact, in significant decline. He suggests that not only is race a myth but also that "'racism' is a social construct," an idea that should simply be abolished. If we ignore it, it will go away. He then strides on to the perverse notion that government in particular should get out of the business of doing anything about racist actions: "What we need is a long-term strategy that holds government to a rigorous standard of race neutrality, while allowing private actors to be free to discriminate as they wish."[18] We understand Newt Gingrich to be in sympathy with such a position when he says, "[A] complicated set of Government rules and regulations were developed in almost every area of life, the intent of which was to eliminate discrimination. Yet the cruel fact has been that Government has brought about nearly as much discrimination as it has eliminated—just in different forms—and has masked the real problems that still exist."[19] In an essay with a similar tone, Nancie Caraway writes, "Isn't everyone hapa [a Hawaiian term for racially multiple] to some extent? 'Mixed,' composed of many intersecting circles of culture, ethnicity, region and familial affiliations? Isn't the struggle about transcending punishing ideas of race anyway?"[20]

The editors of this book work daily toward the goal suggested by Caraway's last sentence—getting past the pains of race—but we could not disagree more with the means she (and Gingrich and D'Souza) advocate.[21] We find no reason for the sanguine belief that ignoring racial hierarchy and oppression will drive them out of existence. Instead, in this book as in our lives, we are working toward the goal of lessening racial divisions, animosities, and oppressions. But we believe that the way out of a racist social structure is not by running away from race. Rather, it is by embracing racial and cultural difference and maximizing racial and cultural contact and knowledge. The way out is through. That is to say, the eradication of racism and the achievement of racial equality will best be served not by denying the existence of race or ignoring its continuing significance. Rather, these goals will best be achieved by going to the heart of race-making, understanding as much as possible about racial processes, and deploying what we understand in the task of liberating racial thinking from racial essentialism and dichotomous racial hierarchies.

It is in this spirit that we put forward the suggestion that the acknowledgment and embrace of racial multiplicity may be steps toward dismantling the monoracial idea system that was created as a prop to slavery and colonialism. We are emphatically *not* arguing that multiraciality solves the problem of race. Yet we do not believe that the idea systems created by the eighteenth- and nineteenth-century racist colonial project must be clung to for all time. We believe that acknowledging and exploring racial multiplicity may contribute over the long haul to undermining racism by undermining its very categories of understanding.[22] As Zipporah Glass demonstrates in this volume's final essay, the multiracial idea offers hope for some real steps forward toward dismantling racism's evils.

NOTES

1. W. E. B. Du Bois, *The Souls of Black Folk* (Greenwich, Conn.: Fawcett, 1961; orig. 1903), 23; John Hope Franklin, *The Color Line: Legacy for the Twenty-First Century* (Columbia: University of Missouri Press, 1993), 5.

2. Philip V. Tobias, "The Meaning of Race," in *Race and Social Difference,* ed. Paul Baxter and Basil Sansom (London: Penguin, 1972), 19–43.

3. Jack D. Forbes, "The Manipulation of Race, Caste, and Identity: Classifying Afro-Americans, Native Americans, and Red-Black People," *Journal of Ethnic Studies* 17.4 (1990): 1–52. Jonathan Marks takes up the complex and variable business of calculating genetic commonality and difference in *What It Means to Be 98 Percent Chimpanzee: Apes, People, and Their Genes* (Berkeley: University of California Press, 2002). See also Jonathan Marks, *Human Biodiversity: Genes, Race, and History* (New York: Aldine de Gruyter, 1995); and

Joseph L. Graves Jr., *The Emperor's New Clothes: Biological Theories of Race at the Millennium* (New Brunswick, N.J.: Rutgers University Press, 2001).

4. Forbes, "Manipulation of Race, Caste, and Identity"; Marks, *Human Biodiversity.*

5. F. James Davis, *Who Is Black? One Nation's Definition* (University Park: Pennsylvania State University Press, 1991), 19–23.

6. Admittedly, even what constitutes "African" genes and "European" genes is an arbitrary, time-bound designation, resting on a high pile of assumptions.

7. See chapter 2 for the reasons for choosing one drop as the threshold.

8. Michael Omi and Howard Winant, *Racial Formation in the United States from the 1960s to the 1990s,* 2d ed. (New York: Routledge, 1994), 54–60.

9. Paul Spickard and W. Jeffrey Burroughs, eds., *We Are a People: Narrative and Multiplicity in Constructing Ethnic Identity* (Philadelphia: Temple University Press, 2000); Omi and Winant, *Racial Formation,* 54–55; Audrey Smedley, *Race in North America: Origin and Evolution of a Worldview* (Boulder, Colo.: Westview Press, 1993), 18–21.

10. Smedley, *Race in North America,* 20–21; Elaine K. Ginsberg, "Introduction: The Politics of Passing," in *Passing and the Fictions of Identity,* ed. Elaine K. Ginsberg (Durham, N.C.: Duke University Press, 1996), 8. The disruptive power of race is perhaps most apparent in the formation of labor, women's, and gay and lesbian movements. Such social movements have historically been plagued and riven with racial divisions that have made it difficult to mobilize respectively around questions of class, gender, and sexual orientation.

11. Omi and Winant, *Racial Formation,* 55–56; Robert Miles, *Racism after Race Relations* (New York: Routledge, 1993).

12. Smedley, *Race in North America,* 21. For detailed examples of this process at work, see chapters 2 and 3 in this volume.

13. Omi and Winant, *Racial Formation,* 56–60; Lisa Lowe, *Immigrant Acts* (Durham, N.C.: Duke University Press, 1996).

14. Omi and Winant, *Racial Formation,* 83.

15. Spickard and Burroughs, *We Are a People,* 1–14; J. Milton Yinger, *Ethnicity: Source of Conflict? Source of Strength?* (Albany: State University of New York Press, 1994), 3–4, 16, 25.

16. Neil Foley and Tomás Almaguer do something similar in *The White Scourge* (Berkeley: University of California Press, 1997) and *Racial Fault Lines* (Berkeley: University of California Press, 1994), respectively. The former is Foley's study of the racial system that developed in the central Texas cotton region from the late nineteenth century to the mid-twentieth. Almaguer's book describes racial hierarchy in California in the nineteenth century. Both works illuminate the ways that race was created and maintained, in a system where

race had not two but three or four sides: Black, White, Mexican, and, in California, Asian. They find Mexicans in both places and Asians in California negotiating third spaces for themselves, not between Black and White, but off at a third point on the racial map.

17. Gerald Horne suggests that people in the American West have long been more sensitive to the multiracial character of American society and less trapped in a Black-White binary understanding than have people who live in the East; "America's New Racial Divide Is East-West, not North-South," *Los Angeles Times*, August 24, 1997, M1, M6.

18. Dinesh D'Souza, *The End of Racism* (New York: Free Press, 1995), 448, 544.

19. *New York Times*, June 15, 1997.

20. Nancie Caraway, "Identity Redux," *Honolulu Weekly*, June 7–13, 2000, 7–8.

21. We suspect that Caraway may have benign intentions in this matter; we suspect that Gingrich and D'Souza do not. More in sympathy with our antiracist project than any of these is Gregory Stephens. He seems to take seriously the problem of racism but believes "that the problems of race [cannot] be solved with the language of race" (*On Racial Frontiers: The New Culture of Frederick Douglass, Ralph Ellison, and Bob Marley* [Cambridge: Cambridge University Press, 1999], 1). Our disagreement with Stephens is over strategy, not goals.

22. For suggestions as to how this might work, see Paul Spickard and Rowena Fong, "Pacific Islander Americans and Multiethnicity: A Vision of America's Future?" *Social Forces* 73.4 (1995): 1365–84; Paul Spickard and Rowena Fong, "Undermining the Very Basis of Racism, Its Categories," *Social Work* 40.5 (1995): 581–84.

PART I

*Creating Racial Hierarchy in
Slavery and Colonialism*

2

EITHER BLACK OR WHITE

Race, Modernity, and the Law of the Excluded Middle

G. REGINALD DANIEL

WHITE OVER BLACK: EUROCENTRISM AND THE MASTER RACIAL PROJECT

Race, Modernity, and the Rise of the West

Racial formation is a specifically modern phenomenon that coincided with the colonial expansion of various western European nation-states—Spain, Portugal, Italy, France, Germany, Holland, Denmark, and England—beginning in the late fifteenth and early sixteenth century. It was an outgrowth of encounters between Europeans and populations that were very different from themselves culturally and, above all, phenotypically as they established colonial empires in the New World, Asia, the Pacific, and, eventually, Africa. More important, racial formation was a catalyst in the creation of and justification for a unique form of slavery. Although expansion, conquest, exploitation, and enslavement had been a part of human history for millennia, none of these phenomena were supported by ideologies or social systems based on race.[1]

The rising competitiveness among European nation-states, as well as the awareness of their power to dominate others, influenced European perceptions of all non-Europeans and ultimately laid the foundation for the formation of the concept of race. Although racial formations differed among the various colonizing powers, none of the populations that came under European domination either participated in originating or contributed to formulating the racial classifications created for and imposed on them even as they inherited and internalized these systems of racial division.[2]

A corollary to the rise of European nation-states to global dominion was a Eurocentric worldview. Eurocentrism, as a way of encompassing a broader paradigm of western European reflection, emerged during the Renaissance in the fifteenth century, reached maturity during the Enlightenment in the eighteenth century, and has been a dominant mode of consciousness in Western civilization for the past several hundred years. Accordingly, Eurocentrism is the leading self-definition of the historical period encompassing what is generally referred to as modernity. It is a form of knowledge that views Europe as a self-contained entity, as an enclosure sufficient unto itself, and as a transcendental nexus of all particular histories by virtue of its unprecedented accomplishments in the realms of materialist rationalism, science, and technology and the extremes to which it thus progressed into the outer reaches of modernity. Consequently, Europe became the unquestioned and dominant center of a global civilization from which emanated an encompassing universalism in the form of colonialism and imperialism directed outward to exploit and dominate the non-Western Other, as well as force the latter to adopt European norms.

The epistemological underpinnings of the Eurocentric paradigm, and ultimately the entire modern worldview, originated in what the sociologist Pitirim Sorokin calls "the sensate" sociocultural mode. This paradigm of consciousness has supported the belief that the external world has a logical order and is the interplay of calculable forces, discernible rules, and measurable bodies—the materialist rationalist view of nature. Mechanical principles that the human consciousness could comprehend through the senses working in tandem with the intellect were seen to govern the structure and movement of the planets, the changes on Earth, and the structure of the smallest insects alike. Once grasped, these laws also could be manipulated for human profit and gain.[3]

This materialist rationalist conception of the cosmos represents a fundamental reorientation toward ultimate reality. It was a radical shift away from the spiritual and metaphysical beliefs that prevailed during the medieval era when the religious authority of the church was seen to prevail over natural knowledge. During that period, supersensory and intuitive types of mentation originating in what Sorokin calls "the ideational" sociocultural mode gave rise to the conviction that the structure of the universe was of a profoundly divine order.[4] Consequently, the physical world was viewed as having a moral plan. All entities from the smallest particle up through humanity and beyond to the heavens and the Godhead had their fixed and "natural" place in a hierarchy.

Although the heavenly bodies were considered of a "higher" order than terrestrial ones in this Great Chain of Being, all of creation was linked in a tightly knit world that displayed a careful graduation of ranks accompanied by a detailed catechism of instructions governing mutual responsibilities and obligations.[5] The social imperative included Christian cooperation with one's neighbors in the commune and fealty to the Godhead's representatives, which in descending order were the pope, the monarch, and the lord of the manor. Security in this world depended on human beings faithfully playing the roles that Providence had assigned to them in the grand hierarchy. By faithfully exercising their obligations and duties in this world, medieval women and men could rest assured that everlasting life would be theirs in the otherworld to come.[6]

In this medieval worldview there could be no ultimate distinction between or dichotomization of physical events, truths, and spiritual experiences. It was understood that changes undergone by bodies on Earth were parallel to and controlled by movements in the heavens above. By contrast, the Renaissance worldview—embodied in the sensate mode (and represented in the persons of Galileo and Francis Bacon)—dichotomized the spiritual or metaphysical universe and the natural or physical world into somewhat mutually exclusive if not antagonistic phenomena. The natural environment and the physical world, which previously had been experienced as an organic and direct unity of spirit and matter, were now viewed as a composite of lifeless material bodies, acted upon by immaterial forces and energies that were distinct from humanity. Taken to its logical conclusion, the natural and physical worlds ceased to be an "inspirited" domain with which humans felt a sacred kinship. Instead, they were reduced to a secular terrain subject to objective laws. The latter were to be discovered by logical deduction and careful empirical observation and testing repeatable at will by others.[7]

The humanity that knew and worked to discover these laws was a dematerialized mind distinct from the body and the rest of the objective world it observed. This shift was accompanied by the further detachment of humanity (the creature of reason and intellect) from nature (that which the Godhead controlled), although it was man (and not woman, parenthetically) who had been provided with intellect and reason in order to serve as the Godhead's manager of the Earth's resources and make the fullest use possible of the gifts of nature. Nature, along with woman (as well as human traits such as feeling and intuition, which were deemed more reflective of the female value sphere), was to be dominated and rendered submissive to the rational will of man (and, indirectly, the Godhead).[8]

The "City of God" and the "City of Man"[9]

The growth of Western science and technology, a catalyst for the rise of sensate sociocultural dominance, was the result of a combination of favorable factors. For example, western Europe had certain ecological advantages lacking in most other regions. Rainfall was evenly distributed throughout the year such that extreme periods of dryness and flooding were rare. Because it was unnecessary to maintain complex irrigation systems, the economy was much less dependent on effective political rule to maintain prosperity. European farmers not only were spared many tropical diseases that attacked their herds, but once livestock were built up and farmers developed the technology to plow the heavy and moist soils, agricultural improvements were made. Correspondingly, European farmers could produce a relatively large agricultural surplus that could feed urban specialists.

Moreover, a secure and growing urban merchant tradition, coupled with enormous religious doubt, and a multiplicity of political units and classes fighting with each other for supremacy—particularly feudal lords, centralizing kings, and the church—thwarted political unity and provided comparatively more leeway for commerce and independent urban life. Urban merchant cities could bargain for considerably greater freedom and self-government than elsewhere, which in turn provided more room and greater reward for independent thinkers. In no region outside of western Europe was this combination of circumstances more favorable for the development of a somewhat autonomous rational urban tradition whose practitioners were allowed to pursue their work with comparable intensity. Materialist rationalism, science, and a new kind of philosophical speculation were more valued and encouraged such that the sensate sociocultural mode became deeply rooted.[10]

The paradigmatic shift to the sensate sociocultural mode in Western consciousness, having separated the physical and mundane worlds from the moral world, led to a decline in the church's authority, which ultimately served as a catalyst for the disintegration of the relationship between church and state. This was paralleled during the Reformation in the sixteenth century by a breaking away of the religiously deviant and defiant—particularly the Protestants of the Anglo-Germanic cities of northern Europe. These individuals pushed this rationalization the farthest and eventually broke with the authority of the Mother (Catholic) Church of Rome.[11] This in turn helped to nurture the belief that the entire history of Europe necessarily led to the blossoming of capitalism—the ultimate economic expression of the sensate mode—to the extent that Christianity, particularly Protestantism, was more favorable than other religions to the flourishing of individual over collective concerns.[12]

Indeed, the relationship between Protestantism and the evolution of capitalism was reciprocal. Both displayed a mutual desire to apply the same calculating rationalization and ethic of individual responsibility to faith and government that they used in the world of work. More important, in the more highly urbanized southern Europe and the Low Countries of northern Europe, this legitimized the values and socioeconomic status of the increasingly powerful and wealthy class of merchants, bankers, and small manufacturers. Whereas the European nobility received much of its status and prestige through landownership and "divinely granted" titles originally given to them (at least indirectly) by the pope, this mercantile class was completely divorced from any relationship with the land. Instead, it achieved its wealth, power, and status strictly from opportunities created by material wealth, particularly through trade in spices, exotic goods, and, increasingly, slaves.[13]

The feudal order began to weaken as early as the thirteenth century, after the Crusades and after the discovery of new markets in China following the journeys of Marco Polo. By the end of the fifteenth century, feudal laws or rules of mutual obligation no longer restricted social relations. Commercial or fiduciary relations originating in the new money economy and mercantile classes were replacing them. In addition, merchants, bankers, and manufacturers were no longer tied to local markets but instead were free to make the entire world their domain.[14] These forces would culminate during the eighteenth century in the Enlightenment and subsequently the French, American, and, eventually, industrial revolutions. In these social upheavals, the merchant class and the larger bourgeoisie would replace the nobility and hereditary monarchies with the principles of liberal democracy. This was the ultimate political expression of the sensate mode, as was Protestantism its religious expression and the capitalist mode of organization its expression in the economic sphere.

Yet capitalism encouraged an unbridled passion for profit and would take acquisitive property-based individualism and freedom in the marketplace to unprecedented extremes. The capitalist orientation would involve the investment of capital in an enterprise that was the production of commodities for the market, with profits created by extracting surplus from labor by having laborers work longer hours than was necessary for their own subsistence. Consequently, more often than not, capitalism would undermine the egalitarian principles of democracy and become a mechanism for the exploitation of the weak by the powerful in both the economic and the political domain.[15] Under feudalism, the pursuit of profit was somewhat constrained by a sense of mutual obligation, by notions of community, and by charity and cooperation. With the decline of feudalism these cherished virtues were supplanted by a new social order dominated by an unrestrained passion for profits. Everything, including human life, was subordinated to the quest to extract value, exchange commodities, and accumulate wealth that could be transformed into commodities sold on the market for profit.[16]

Afro-Eurasia and the "Rebirth" of the West

As the epitome of an almost sacred Law of the Excluded Middle, the rise of sensate sociocultural dominance in modern western European consciousness has perpetuated an either/or mode of thinking that differentiates things into dichotomous and hierarchical categories of experience, studies things in isolation and in parts, and acknowledges no shades of gray.[17] Before the Renaissance (and its companion piece, the Reformation), the European world, however, had maintained a cosmovision in which the ideational and sensate modes were viewed as comparatively more reciprocal and complementary rather than antithetical and dichotomized opposites.[18]

It should not be assumed, however, that conflicts between the two modes, and their various sociocultural embodiments, had never existed before. Ever since humanity crossed the threshold of city or "civilized" life, all humans to some extent have been confronted with the various embodiments of the schism between the sensate and ideational modes. The sensate mode has historically sought to push humans toward a seemingly progressive if not always certain future. It has been responsible for developments in communications and transportation, the growth of leisure and luxury, and the achievement of private property, individualism, and autonomy, as well as a host of ills stemming from rampant alienation, isolation, and anarchy that have plagued the urban environment. The ideational mode, in response to this malaise, has often sought to pull humans back to a certain but irrevocably lost past, to recapture those elements that made "precivilized" life appear comparatively warmer and more humane. Yet, it has often overlooked the high rate of certain diseases, infant mortality, and shorter life expectancy, as well as the endless fear of natural forces that plagued the earliest human communities.[19]

The increasing dominance of the sensate over the ideational mode, a dynamic seemingly inherent in the civilization process itself, made a first major inroad at the height of Greco-Roman Hellenism.[20] Whereas science for the early Greeks had been mainly a theoretical pursuit, the Hellenistic world put theory into practice. With the exception of optics, the major areas of development were utilitarian: mechanics, pneumatics, hydrostasis, medicine, geography, and mechanical devices.[21] The remnants of Greco-Roman knowledge in the West were smothered beneath the ideational shroud of Christianity that dominated its landscape during the medieval period from the fall of the Roman Empire through the end of the first millennium.[22]

Yet Byzantine thinkers in eastern Europe and particularly Islamic and Jewish scholars in the Afro-Eurasian world became the direct heirs of ancient Hellenistic learning—as well as the learning from India, China, and the Far East. At the time western Europe was still relatively cut off by Moslem forces from contact with urban centers in that region. Later, when western Europe was just recuperating from its "dark ages," a juncture between civilizations in the Afro-Eurasian world had already led to a flourishing exchange of knowledge. This included not only eastern Europe and parts of the Near East (Byzantine) and the Far East but also West Africa as far south as the Senegal and Niger Rivers to North Africa and southern Europe (Islamic Spain, Portugal, and Sicily).[23]

In addition, the absorption of the Hellenistic culture by Byzantine civilization was more thorough such that differences between Hellenism and Christianity assumed the character of a genuine dialogue concerning common problems. Islamic civilization, although much more influenced by sensate culture than was Christian western Europe at the time, nevertheless remained comparatively more balanced in its consciousness due to the strong moral tenets of the Moslem faith.[24] Yet, whereas the spiritual, and most often tyrannical, authorities of Western Christendom spurned much of the learning amassed by pre-Christian civilizations, Islamic (and Byzantine Christian) influences allowed for the continued development of sensate culture without at the same time eclipsing the ideational. Consequently, Arabic-speaking scholars took this knowledge as legitimate spoils of wars won by Moslem armies.[25] Also, there was a notable absence of ecclesiastical authority in the Islamic faith paralleling the medieval Christian church in its preoccupation with competing heresies. Islamic absorption of new knowledge was a judicial rather than a theological question. The issue was whether "new and alien sciences" interfered with beliefs prescribed by law as defined by jurists. Islamic culture, largely through translations into Arabic, now began the absorption of the more developed scientific and philosophical thought of antiquity.[26]

During this period, western European knowledge of antiquity and the contemporary African and Asian worlds declined dramatically. The decline and absence of urban centers in western Europe and the geographic isolation of western Europeans from other centers of civilization, along with the subsequent colonization of the Mediterranean area by Islamic civilization, proved catastrophic for their knowledge of populations beyond the eastern fringes of the European peninsula. The ancient civilizations of the Old World, in Asia as well as in Africa, became legends, preserved primarily in the obscure histories of biblical narrative. As knowledge became more and more a monastic preserve, secular knowledge and renderings of the non-European world became increasingly rare as the church was committed to the interpretation of history in accord with its perceptions of divine revelation and will.[27] European ethnocentrism, legitimated by church authorities as well as by ignorance, became the sources of medieval knowledge and understanding of the world. Ultimately, with the evolution of Christian ideology into the dominant worldview in Europe, it was sufficient enough to know that humanity was divisible into two dichotomous collectives: the forces of Light and the forces of Darkness. The former was the domain of the Godhead and personified by Europeans; the latter belonged to the world of Satan and was represented for the time being by the rest of humanity.[28]

If Christian Europe viewed itself as morally superior to the darker-skinned Asian and African Moslem infidels, it also displayed an uncomfortable awareness of its own technical, material, and cultural inferiority as compared to Islamic civilization. This sentiment pervaded much of western European consciousness until the rediscovery of Eastern Christianity and Hellenistic thought in the West gave birth to Christian Scholasticism, which, ironically, was spurred on through trade and other contacts with the Islamic world.[29] Considering that Western consciousness was dominated by the ideational mode until the eleventh century, this ancient Greco-Roman knowledge was necessarily rediscovered through the mediation of the Islamic metaphysical construct.[30]

In addition, Western medieval Scholasticism took shape beginning in the twelfth century, not by chance in regions in close contact with the Islamic world: the Iberian Peninsula and Sicily.[31] (It was only later that the West learned that Hellenistic thought was preceded by that of classical Greece, whose very existence was largely unknown until that time.) Medieval Scholasticism—which represented a fragile synthesis of ideational and sensate mentalities expressed respectively in the Christian faith and Aristotelian empiricism—originated in the need to reconcile the realities of the burgeoning economic prosperity of the physical world with the metaphysical tradition.

By giving birth to a new world largely freed from the domination of metaphysics, medieval Scholasticism laid the intellectual foundation for the Renaissance, the Reformation, and thus the "rebirth" of the West.[32] This sensate ideal truly blossomed in the eighteenth century during the Enlightenment (represented in the personages of Descartes and Newton). This rise of sensate dominance, and the subsequent meteoric ascent of secularism, materialism, scientific rationalism, and technology—along with the growth of acquisitive property-based individualism—catapulted Europe onto the stage of modernity by freeing it from the comparatively more ideational and communalistic values and constraints of the past. This in turn would serve as the basis for notions of Europe's superiority and would justify its secular and religious colonization of the non-European world. The underlying dual purpose of the colonial project was to awaken these traditional societies from their primordial slumber as a beneficial "civilizing" process and to exploit them in order to accrue wealth to the various emerging European nation-states.[33]

FROM EUROCENTRISM TO WHITE RACISM: ESTABLISHING THE DICHOTOMOUS RACIAL HIERARCHY

By the fifteenth century the growth of sensate culture and the drive to accumulate wealth had reached the point where Western civilization was coming to view the entire world, including human beings, as objects to be used to create wealth, or to be disposed of if they stood in the way of acquiring it. Never before had the opportunity for seemingly unlimited wealth and resources seemed so great as during Europe's imperialist expansion. The conquest of the Americas was of particular importance. The New World exceeded the wildest dreams of European explorers and merchants seeking new venues for trade.[34]

But the New World—like Africa, Asia, and the Pacific Islands—contained not only natural resources to exploit but human populations as well, populations that were culturally and above all phenotypically different from themselves. Indeed, the fact that sensate culture spread so rapidly as a dominant mode throughout Europe, in conjunction with the light complexion of many Europeans, allowed for an ideology that would grant preferential valuation to somatic Whiteness and other European phenotypical traits. The cultural, scientific, and economic revolution of the modern world thus laid the foundation for the ranking of all societies on the basis of the European phenotypical and cultural norm images.[35]

These differences between Europeans and Others challenged European understandings of the origins of the human species and raised disturbing questions as to whether strange peoples could even be considered part of the same human family. Perhaps the differences of these Others—not only the physical but also the cultural ones— could justify their exploitation and even enslavement. Of course, these questions presupposed a "worldview in which Europeans, as the children of God, as full-fledged human beings," were distinguished from Others.[36] Given the scope of the European onslaught—the Europeans' advantages in military technology, their religious conviction of their own righteousness, and their lust for new goods and new markets—the division between the "civilized" world of White European culture and the "primitive" world of Red, Black, and Brown "savages," seemed a "natural" consequence.[37]

The breaking of the "oceanic seal" separating the Old and the New Worlds, which began with the European "discovery" of the Americas, was paralleled by a break with the previous "protoracial awareness" by which Europe had contemplated Others.[38] The conquest of the Americas was not simply an epochal historical event; it also marked the beginning of modern racial awareness and formation. This awareness was first expressed in religious terms, and soon also in political and scientific ones, as a rationale for the exploitation, appropriation, domination, and dehumanization of people of color and was sanctioned by the state.[39]

Racialized thinking originating in Eurocentric discourse was grounded in and used to justify oppressive and exploitative economic relations. Racial formation thus emerged in the twin policies of extermination of Native Americans and enslavement of Africans. It also served as a justification for the conquest and direct settlement and control of Others in the manner of colonialism, particularly in terms of occupation of their land—through the distant control of resources and of direct settlement.[40] Consequently, the significance of racial formation was by no means limited to the Western Hemisphere but rather initiated a process whereby Europe was constituted as the center of a group of empires that viewed the entire globe as a domain for its expansionist ideals. Eurocentric consciousness represented this new structure as a struggle between "civilization" and "barbarism."[41]

In sum, Eurocentrism comprised the master racial project from which all other racial projects originate. Eurocentrism, and its companions White racism and White supremacy, differ significantly from the longer-standing identification of distinctive human groups and their association with differences in physical appearances. It is not merely a form of ethnocentrism—that is, racial and cultural chauvinism in which one's own group is considered the standard against which all others are measured—which exists in almost every culture that has ever existed. Eurocentrism is more extreme than the mere racial and cultural chauvinism that applies almost universally, because it is based on a more systematic, comprehensive, integrated, and reciprocal set of ideological beliefs, which had their genesis in the late fifteenth and early sixteenth century. All of the major European philosophies, social theories, and literary traditions of the modern age have been implicated in this system. Even the antagonism that Christian Europe displayed toward the two most significant non-Christian Others—the Moslem and Jewish populations—cannot be considered more than a "dress rehearsal" for racial formation.[42] Despite the chauvinism and atrocities of the Crusades, these hostilities were universally interpreted in religious terms even when they had racial metaphors.

"Devout" Christians and Moslem "Infidels"

Indeed, the primary distinction Europeans initially made between themselves and those who diverged from the European norm image—in terms of superiority versus inferiority—was that of Christian versus Moslem. This was "natural" when making a distinction between believers and nonbelievers of any faith. However, it was exacerbated by the fact that substantial portions of Christian territory in southwestern Europe were primarily under the control of African Moslems. Thus, this distinction based on religious differences was amplified to ideological warfare that accompanied the actual physical warfare that took place during the Crusades, and the Christian "reconquest" of southern Spain and Portugal as well as Sicily from Islam. Throughout this period, the enslavement of Africans in Europe was not an uncommon occurrence. African Moslems captured in battle were enslaved by European Christians (and vice versa). The Catholic Church in the course of "just wars" against the "Moslem infidels" sanctified this long-held and fairly universal tradition of enslaving enemies captured in warfare.[43]

Portugal regained complete control of its southern Iberian territory from Moslem forces in 1250, approximately two hundred fifty years before Spain reclaimed its territory in 1492. In 1415 the Portuguese invaded and began occupying Islamic territory in northwestern Africa as a continuation of the Christian routing of Islamic forces from continental Europe. They also maintained the practice of enslaving infidel Moslems as prisoners of war. However, the populations that Europeans encountered as they progressed farther down the West African coast in the fifteenth century were not adherents of Islam. Technically, they were not infidels and therefore could not justifiably be enslaved. They were, however, contingents of the Old World, the world of antiquity and the world of the Bible, which for more than a millennium should have been known to them as the sacred text of the one true faith. The Africans' apparent lack of allegiance to the Christian Godhead was an indication in the European mind of their inferiority and a justification of their enslavement as a means of leading them to the true faith and putting them on the road to heaven.[44]

This also implied their predestination to slavery, whether Moslem or pagan, as long as their souls had not been set free by faith but did not necessarily mean manumission once they were Christianized; Portuguese merchants viewed these captives with eyes significantly different from the church. They realized that they could enrich themselves by capturing Africans and selling them as slaves. Spain, initially through Islamic and then Portuguese intermediaries, followed suit. African slaves on the Iberian Peninsula were used primarily as domestic servants and artisanal helpers in urban areas. With the notable exceptions of sugar plantations in the Algarve of southern Portugal and the Azores and Madeira islands (Portugal), as well as in the Canary Islands (Spain), they were not used extensively in agricultural labor. This was primarily because African slaves were expensive, especially as compared to the ready local supply of unpaid serf and peasant labor.[45]

As the Portuguese continued down the coast of Africa, capturing (and trading for) slaves, they maintained the just war rationale, no matter how loosely it was interpreted, as a justification for the enslavement of West Africans. As they began requiring ever-larger quantities of slave labor, particularly for their offshore African sugar-plantation islands of Cape Verde and São Tomé—and eventually in the Americas—this rationale for African enslavement became increasingly inadequate. Yet the powerful mercantilists in Lisbon (and their financiers in the northern Italian city-states and the Low Countries of northern Europe) had become too dependent on the massive profits of the sugar-slave trade to give everything up so easily.[46] Therefore, a new rationale for the enslavement of Africans was in the making.

White Racism and the "Blackening" of Sub-Saharan West Africa

Western Europeans and West Africans began their encounter in the fifteenth century as different but equal in terms of sociocultural development. Indeed, the urban centers of Africa and Europe had much more in common with each other than with the rural areas of their respective continents. That coastal West Africans lived in densely populated and highly organized agrarian communities initially precluded their massive enslavement. Although they were comparatively less technologically "advanced" than Renaissance western Europe—particularly in terms of military technology—West Africans could not be overwhelmed by armies or by masses of European colonists spreading through their lands. In fact, had it not been for Moslems folding back on West African soil after their defeat in Europe—a major factor in the sacking, breakdown, and literal physical destruction of medieval West African civilizations such as Ghana, Gao, and Songhay—Africans might have been an even more formidable force to be reckoned with. Yet faced with the awesome brutality of retreating Islamic forces, large portions of those populations had fled, and cities, built mainly of timber and clay, were abandoned for the jungle inhabited by less urbanized populations and left to crumble.[47]

In addition, West African contact with Europeans was confined to small groups of professional traders and missionaries, clustered in vulnerable forts along the coast and subject to the rules and restrictions of the well-defined commercial system. When the chieftain of a semifeudal society sold Africans to a European trader, he was following a practice long established with Islamic markets to meet the demand for domestic slaves, particularly women to fill harems and eunuchs to tend the latter.[48] Neither African chieftains nor local traders, however, envisioned that the colonization of the Americas would transform the nature of this trade into the massive deportation of millions of their kinsmen and kinswomen.[49]

The influx of European goods, particularly firearms used in the slave trade, further disrupted the equilibrium of West African societies that already had been weakened by the Moslems. To Europe, improved technology brought power and material wealth, but to Africa, it brought only a more efficient means of capturing slaves for the New World market. Furthermore, the religious and political power structure of West Africa was peculiarly susceptible to the corrosive effects of the slave system. Priests, who traditionally imposed heavy fines on individuals who offended an oracle, found it relatively easy to cite and justify an increasing number of offenses, which could be expiated only by a payment in slaves, who could then be sold profitably to European traders. Communities driven by kinship and religious loyalties looked upon each other as contemptible heretics who deserved death or slavery; accordingly, their religious wars were well adapted to procuring captives who could be exchanged for guns.[50]

If the religious and political power structure of West Africa was complicit in justifying the slave trade, the Judeo-Christian explanation for the Blackening and banishing of Noah's son Ham and his offspring provided the ultimate and most extreme rationalization. This "curse of Ham" began as an innocuous anecdote (Noah curses a son of Ham, making him and his progeny "a servant of servants" for looking at him in his nakedness while he was drunk). The myth did not draw its inspiration from the Christian Bible, as some contemporary theologians thought. Rather, it originated in an arbitrary interpretation of the biblical story of Ham, which appeared in the Talmud, a collection of Jewish oral traditions, in the sixth century A.D. The descendants of the son of Ham, according to this interpretation of the story, were Africans and Egyptians (who at the time the myth began to circulate had fallen from their pinnacle of power).[51]

What began as a seemingly harmless if humorless anecdote grew into a destructive racial myth that affected all subsequent histories of Africa and individuals of African descent. The curse of the son of Ham, ordained by the Godhead as an eternal punishment for his disobedience, was said to be the curse of Blackness, which in turn was the badge of slavery. The symbology of Blackness was significantly intensified when Europeans observed that Africans did not cover their bodies and behaved more freely toward them. From the European perspective, the Africans' nakedness, their sexual mores, and above all their Blackness, served to set them off as a profoundly distinct form of humanity, if they were human at all. That all too human anthropoid apes were found inhabiting Africa certainly did nothing to diminish this image.[52]

Africa, a hostile world of disease, dangerous animals, and bloodthirsty Black warriors and cannibals, in sum, the "Dark Continent," defied penetration. Its people were Black, naked, and pagan, and therefore were cursed.[53] Evil forces, and whatever was forbidden and horrifying in human nature, were personified as black and could be projected onto the African whose dark skin remained as a constant symbolic reminder. Death and the unconscious were Blackness, and so were Africans: if not absolutely so, they were close enough. The Godhead (or nature) had conveniently seen to it that Africans came to represent blackness, darkness, and the unconscious that would become the "nuclear fantasy," or nightmare, of its polar opposite, whiteness, lightness, and the conscious that were personified by Europeans.[54]

With the rise of western European domination in the sixteenth century—particularly the growing need for a cheap dependable source of plantation labor after the "discovery" of the Americas—the notion of the Black Hamite, and its religious association with the punishment suffered by Ham's descendants, gradually became an accepted part of secular culture. It was used to support the legal justification for the enslavement of an entire people simply because of their Blackness. Although some form of color prejudice against Blacks had appeared in various places since antiquity, where it was present, it was not institutionalized in systems of racialized slavery. More important, it was not justified by an elaborate racialized ideology of White superiority and Black inferiority. In addition, captivity was not in perpetuity as was the case with African enslavement. It was rather a temporary condition after which former slaves were generally granted the same rights accorded other citizens. Also, color (or phenotype) was not the crucial factor determining an individual's social location and mobility in the society.[55]

Now, however, Black Africans were seen as descendants of Ham, bearing the eternal ancestral and phenotypical stigma of Noah's curse, a view that was compatible with the various economic, political, and religious interests extant at the time. On the one hand, this belief left the exploitation of Blacks for economic gain undisturbed by moral concerns. On the other hand, identifying Africans as Hamites kept them within the human family, which had the advantage of keeping

Christian cosmology intact according to the biblical story of creation.[56] Thus the Africans' moral value as human beings became subsumed under the Europeans' technical value of material wealth as they established the institution of chattel slavery. In the process, the European slavers did not come to merely own the body of the Black slave. They went one step further and reduced him or her to a body without a mind, then from a body to a black thing. By dehumanizing and ultimately objectifying Black slaves, European slavers made them quantifiable and more easily absorbed into a rising world of productive exchange. This meant that Black slaves were virtually the same, in certain key respects, as the rest of the soulless or mindless universe of objectified matter, all of which had come under the domination of the Eurocentric worldview.[57]

In its progressive evolution toward enlightenment and thus modernity, western Europe deemed anything that smacked of humanity's primal and premodern origins inferior and to be safely guarded against lest it topple the rational world that had been so painstakingly created. Whatever was forbidden and horrifying in human nature could be designated as "black" and projected onto the African whose dark skin and "uncivilized" ways remained as a constant symbolic reminder. Accordingly, it was considered an act of humanity to remove Black Africans from their harsh world of sin and darkness. Blacks were better off in Christian lands, even as slaves, than living like beasts in Africa. With this view of servitude as a reciprocal relationship between loving master and quiescent slave institutionalized by the Godhead for the better ordering of a sinful world, bondage appeared to balance natural freedom and worldly fate, human authority and the equality of all individuals under the supreme rule of God.[58]

Yet, always mindful of the possibility that religious instruction might succeed in restoring that part of the conscious that understood injustice, the church's program, conforming to the Christian ideal of servitude, did not necessarily intend for Blacks to be baptized and instructed in the faith. Rather, their purpose was to instill in Blacks the Christian precepts of patience, willing obedience, and humility. This would make it possible for masters to rule by love rather than by force, irrespective of the mounting empirical cruelties of slavery that eclipsed this ideal. Nevertheless, the ideal of the contented slave in a benevolent Christian society, the remoteness of Africa, and the fact that as the slave trade progressed larger numbers of slaves were derived from the bush societies of forest regions behind the coastal cities—which were truly "uncivilized"—made it easier to disassociate African servitude from the act of enslavement and to justify an institution vital to the economy of Europe and essential to the Americas. In the end, the decision to enslave Africans had the dual benefit of profiting both the spiritually minded church fathers in search of lost souls and the more enterprising colonists in search of a cheap labor force.[59]

From White Racism to White Supremacy: Consolidating the Binary Racial Project

White Supremacy and the One-Drop Rule

The U.S. racial order, like other racial orders in the Americas, originated in the Eurocentric paradigm. Consequently, Blackness and Whiteness represent the negative and positive designations, respectively, in a dichotomous hierarchy grounded in African and European racial and cultural differences. Racial formation in Latin America, particularly in places like Brazil, however, has been characterized by a more attenuated dichotomization of Blackness and Whiteness—and thus a more mitigated implementation of the Law of the Excluded Middle—than that in the United States. This is reflected in the region's pervasive miscegenation and the validation of this blending by the implementation of a ternary racial project that differentiates the population into Whites, multiracial individuals, and Blacks. In addition, Blackness and Whiteness have represented merely polar extremes on a continuum where physical appearance, in conjunction with class and cultural, rather than racial, signifiers per se, has come to determine one's identity and status in the social hierarchy.

By virtue of this dynamic, select "visibly" multiracial individuals, for reasons of talent, education, and behavior, historically have been allowed vertical socioeconomic mobility and integration into the middle class, and thus the status of situational Whiteness, in accordance with their approximation to the dominant psychosomatic norm image. In its broadest sense, this phenomenon, which Degler calls the "mulatto escape hatch," has made it possible over time for other millions of individuals whose ancestry has included African forebears, but who are phenotypically White or near-White, to become officially White.[60] This has led to a notable fluidity in racial-cultural markers and has been accompanied by the conspicuous absence of legalized barriers to equality in both the public and private spheres.

The social construction of racial Whiteness in Latin America is thus more inclusive as compared to the United States. In addition, the social positioning of those individuals designated as multiracial is intermediate in the racial hierarchy. Yet collectively, their location is much closer to the subordinate Blacks than to the dominant Whites. Therefore, in keeping with Eurocentric dynamics, the primary racial divide in terms of the distribution of wealth, power, privilege, and prestige is between Whites and non-Whites and only secondarily between the Black and multiracial populations in the manner of inegalitarian pluralism.[61]

The U.S. racial order is also based on the dichotomization and hierarchical valuation of Blackness and Whiteness in the manner of inegalitarian pluralism. Yet U.S. Anglocentrism is an extreme form of Eurocentrism that has recognized no intermediate or multiracial identity and status, in contrast to the ternary racial project in Latin America, although both patterns of race relations originate in the Eurocentric paradigm. Rather, the United States perpetuates a binary racial project based on the one-drop rule of hypodescent that designates as Black all individuals of African descent. Accordingly, this binary racial project necessitates individual identification as either African American or European American.[62]

It should be pointed out, however, that rules of hypodescent in the United States have been applied to the first-generation offspring of interracial unions between dominant European Americans and other subordinate groups of color (e.g., Native Americans, Asian Americans, Pacific Islander Americans, Latina/o Americans). The dominant European Americans implemented this mechanism to maintain social distinctions between themselves and the subordinate groups of color. Accordingly, racial group membership has historically been assigned to these first-generation offspring of interracial unions based exclusively on the subordinate "background of color." Generally, successive generations of individuals who have a background of color and a European American background have not been designated exclusively, or even partially, members of the group of color if that background constitutes less than one-fourth of their lineage. Furthermore, self-identification with that background has been more a matter of choice.[63] However, for individuals of African American and European American descent the one-drop rule has ensured that not only first-generation but also later-generation offspring have experienced the most restrictive rule of hypodescent. This mechanism, the one-drop rule, designates as Black everyone with traceable African American descent. It thus precludes any notion of self-identification and ensures that all future offspring of African American ancestry will be socially designated Black.

The one-drop rule that emerged in the late seventeenth and early eighteenth century underpinned legal prohibitions against interracial sexual relations, specifically, interracial marriages, as a means of preserving White racial and cultural "purity." It also served to increase the number of slaves and exempt White landowners (particularly slaveholders) from the legal obligation of passing on inheritance and other benefits of paternity to multiracial offspring that were born of their sexual relations with African American slave women. Moreover, the rule helped to maintain White racial privilege by supporting other legal and informal barriers to racial equality in most aspects of social life. These barriers have existed in public facilities and areas of the public sphere (e.g., political, economic, educational) as well as in the private sphere (e.g., residential, associational, interpersonal), particularly the realm of miscegenation.[64] By the late nineteenth century, this culminated in Jim Crow segregation.

The one-drop rule did not, however, become a normative part of the legal apparatus in the United States until the early twentieth century. By that time, it had gained currency as the customary social and informal, that is, "commonsense," definition of Blackness. And by the 1920s the one-drop rule had become an accepted part of the fabric of the United States.

White Supremacy and the "Aryanization" of Greece

According to the Swedish social scientist Gunnar Myrdal, the racist attitudes and practices that systematically excluded African Americans from having contact with European Americans as equals in most aspects of social life—and that were buttressed by the one-drop

rule—constituted a racial creed that was a flagrant breach of what
he defined as the American creed. The latter was based on the egalitarian principles set forth in the Declaration of Independence, the
United States Constitution, and the Bill of Rights and upheld by the
Supreme Court. It proclaimed that all individuals were born equal
with inalienable rights to life, liberty, and the pursuit of happiness.[65]

The tension and contradiction between the American and racial
creeds were heightened over the course of the eighteenth and nineteenth centuries with the increasing demand for cheap labor and the
expansion of African slavery to meet these needs. If, however, racial
differences were indicative of different species of humans, rather
than merely superficial geno-phenotypical variations within a single
species—with individuals of African descent classified as a lower species
that did not share all the human characteristics—then it could be
argued that the American creed and its promise of constitutional
equality did not apply to them.[66]

To support these arguments a number of prominent European
American thinkers sought to prove that Africans were a subhuman
species. They became part of a larger concerted effort among Western intellectuals that sought to replace the doctrine of monogenesis
with the theory of polygenesis in explaining human origins. According to the former, all individuals were equally human, if not equal
in stature and ability, and constituted one integrated species. The
latter was premised on the inegalitarian pluralist creation of races that
deemed Africans and Africans American a separate, different, and
inferior species.[67]

As the debate raged on over whether Africans were to be included
in the human species, European and European American thinkers
were especially concerned with distancing the origins of Western civilization from any association with individuals of African descent.
Egypt became a focal point of this debate by virtue of its location
on the African continent and its long history of racial and cultural
contact with Europe and Asia. More important, it had given rise to
one of the earliest civilizations, if not the first. In addition, the conventional view in antiquity (Bernal's Ancient Model) stated that
Greek culture was not merely influenced significantly by Egypt but
actually had arisen around 1500 B.C. as the result of Egyptian and
Phoenician colonization. This rendering of Greek history was derived

from the writings of Greek philosophers, particularly Herodotus and Deodorus, who obtained their information largely from the oral accounts of Egyptian priests.[68]

During the eighteenth and early nineteenth century, Greece came to be viewed as not only the epitome of Europe but also its pure childhood and the homeland of the West. The ancestral connection with Greece supposedly predisposed western Europe to rationality (the sensate mode), which in turn became the cornerstone of modernity, whereas the Afro-Asian world never succeeded in going beyond metaphysics (the ideational mode).[69] The conspicuous advances of contemporary natural science in western Europe seemingly confirmed the truth of this belief.[70]

Bernal argues that with the concomitant expansion of African slavery during the same period, it became increasingly unacceptable that Greek civilization could have been the result of the blending of indigenous Europeans, Africans, and Semites. Accord   the Ancient Model was eclipsed by the penetration of racism into the writing of European history. To support the belief in the autonomous, "immaculate" conception and purity of Western origins, many individuals replaced the Ancient Model of Greek history with what Bernal calls the "Aryan Model" (the currently accepted version of Greek history).[71] The notion of the Greek ancestry of western Europe—which underlies the Eurocentric paradigm—thus performed an essential function in the emergence of Europe's sense of superiority over Africans and Others. Accordingly, Greece became the source of rational philosophy, the development of thought free from religious constraints, the birth of humanism, and the triumph of reason (the sensate mode).[72]

However, to incorporate Greece fully into western Europe's lineage it was imperative to accentuate differences between Greece and the ancient Afro-Asian world. Furthermore, to support the notion that the ancestral connection with Greece predisposed western Europe to rationality, it became necessary to emphasize if not invent commonalities with these Greeks—who were highly "civilized" at a time when most western Europeans were still "barbarians." In addition, those who supported this historical revisionism resolved the contradiction between anecdotal accounts of Egyptian colonization and their own more scientific chronicles by treating the former as flights from reason in otherwise rational Greek thought and attributing this to "Egyptomania."[73] This delusion supposedly prompted Egyptian priests and Greek thinkers respectively to enhance Egypt's reputation and Greece's prestige by linking the latter with the impressive accomplishments of the ancient civilization of the former. More important, these accounts were therefore considered fanciful notions that were as much an offense to the canons of science as the Greek myths of sirens and centaurs.[74]

The interpretation of the history of Christianity, itself a long and complicated process, suffered a fate similar to that of Greece. Since Christianity was Afro-Eurasian in origin the historical formation of the religion has been rendered in such a way as to imbue it with particular and exclusive virtues that made it possible to become part of the basis of Europeanness and the principal factor for the maintenance of European cultural unity. In fact, the West has so completely emphasized Christianity's European origins and erased its Afro-Asian lineage that in vernacular culture, as well as in official religious iconography, the holy family is presented as blue-eyed and blond.[75] Greek Hellenism and Christianity were not only severed from the very milieu in which they unfolded but were also employed to account for the superiority of the West—"the Occident"—and its conquest of the globe. A vision of Africa, the Near East, and the more distant Far East was constructed on these same racialized and dichotomous premises and resulted in the creation of the artificial, antithetical construct of the (Afro-)"Orient."[76]

White Supremacy and the "Aryanization" of Egypt

Before the nineteenth century western European thinkers generally located Egypt in Africa but appear to have been uncertain about the exact phenotype of the Egyptians.[77] It was not until the rediscovery of ancient Egypt in the early nineteenth century, after Napoleon's expedition into North Africa, that Europeans uncovered the splendors of an ancient civilization that antedated Greece. More important, scholars such as Vincent Denon, who accompanied Napoleon, noted a substantial Africoid phenotypical and ancestral presence in this highly evolved and impressive civilization that was said to have contributed so much to Europe.[78] Consequently, Denon came to the same startling conclusions about Egypt as had Count Volney, a French traveler who earlier visited Egypt and Syria.[79]

The discovery of the antiquity of Egyptian civilization, and that Africans could have contributed significantly to its development, was a major obstacle to the claim that Africans had always been inferior. Although nineteenth-century European scholars may have been secure in their belief that Greek civilization was essentially self-generated and owed nothing to Egypt, they could not, however, convincingly argue their thesis of the inherent and permanent biological inferiority of African-descent individuals as long as Egypt remained an African civilization.

Christian theologians began to argue, therefore, that Noah had only cursed Canaan, one son of Ham. Correspondingly, the curse lay only on his progeny, which included all of Black (sub-Saharan) Africans and their descendants. Another son, Mizraim, had not been cursed and was the progenitor of the gifted dark-skinned Caucasian Egyptians, the creators of possibly the earliest civilization.[80] In this way a population that was Afro-Eurasian in ancestry—and in many respects predominantly African in origin—was given a berth among the Aryan races, not in first class, but in the escape hatch section reserved for dubious Whites. The creation of two lineages—a servile cursed Africoid branch and a gifted blessed Europid branch—thus neatly resolved the problem of the Hamitic curse and allowed the Christian conscience to rest peacefully once again.[81]

This "Whitening" of Egypt in the context of nineteenth-century Anglo–North American racial theory was an attempt to justify and rationalize slavery in the years leading up to the Civil War and the ruthless segregation of Blacks from Whites through the installation of Jim Crow segregation afterward. Consequently, it was in the United States where the most concerted "scientific" effort took place to prove that Egyptian civilization had not been African in origin.[82] The primary focus was on the question of miscegenation and the potentially deleterious effects it could have on precipitating the decline of Anglo–North American civilization. Throughout the nineteenth century European and European American savants, along with the scientific establishment, tried to prove that the Egyptians were and always had been White and that Africans had no connection whatsoever with the development of Egyptian civilization. To achieve this goal, phrenological researchers selectively measured and classified skeletal material from Egypt. They concluded that Blacks were numerous in Egypt, yet they also argued that their social position in ancient times was the same as it was at that time, that of servants and slaves, whereas the kings, priests, and military—the elite—were Caucasian.[83]

Accordingly, Egypt served as an ancient historical precedent for a White society with Black slaves, which justified the "natural" place of Blacks in the U.S. South. Researchers used this evidence to support not only claims that the races were permanently different and mutually antagonistic but also public policy recommendations that would maintain their permanent separation. That the contemporary Egyptian population was clearly made up of a blend of Arabs, Africans, and Afro-Arabs, therefore, was held not to disprove the Caucasian thesis but rather to explain Egypt's long decline. Aryans alone created Egyptian civilization, and the subsequent blending of the races brought about its degeneration, infertility, barbarism, and, ultimately, its fall.[84]

Correspondingly, it was maintained that any breakdown of the social divisions between Blacks and Whites in the United States—which it was always feared would lead inevitably to widespread interracial unions—would result in the eventual extermination of the entire nation. Those who supported this belief argued that the different racial groups represented different species of humans and that these differences are permanent. Moreover, this permanence is preserved through the laws of hybridity by the degeneration and eventual infertility of the mulatto offspring that results from any hybrid crossing between them.[85] The focus was primarily on the idea that miscegenation between Anglo–North Americans and African-descent Americans would cause Whites as a race to decline and literally die out altogether. These arguments were in no small part supported and justified by the founding fathers of the Anglo–North American school of anthropology, Josiah Nott and George Gliddon. From the 1840s onward these individuals and others were instrumental in promoting in Europe and the United States the Anglo–North American ideology of race and presenting their claims as scientific truth.

White Supremacy and the Meaning of Race

The meaning of race is not fixed in the geno-phenotypical features of differing populations, nor is it a unitary phenomenon. It is, rather, a synthesis of various elements originating in popular beliefs that when combined culminated in a new way of viewing human differences.[86] As a cultural initiative the concept of race had no basis in natural science or naturalistic studies. The naturalists wrote in Latin, classifying specimens in terms of classes, orders, genera, and species—but not races.[87] Yet as the scientific orientation gained in confidence and the authority of the Old Testament as history declined, people looked for a more systematic and scientific understanding of the natural order.[88]

Beginning in the mid- to late eighteenth century, therefore, the concept of race was embraced by naturalists and other learned individuals who gave it legitimacy as a supposed product of scientific investigation. In this intellectual climate, "race" increasingly came to designate a biologically defined group. The concept of race became so widely used that it began to replace other classificatory terms. Indeed, had the concept of race never been invented it is likely that the people would have continued to be identified by their own name for themselves or by other categorizing terms such as people, group, society, and nation, or by labels derived from the geographic region or locales they inhabited.[89]

Racial formation not only underpins a social order that has historically divided the world's peoples into biologically discrete and exclusive groups; it also became a way of categorizing what were already conceived as inherently unequal populations. More important, racial formation supports the notion that these groups are by nature unequal and can be ranked on a continuum of superiority and inferiority. Differentiation, in combination with notions of inequality, therefore, was central to the meaning of race. In addition, racist ideology was so universal and infinitely expandable that by the nineteenth century, all human groups of "varying degrees of biological and/or cultural diversity could be subsumed arbitrarily into some 'racial' category, depending upon the objectives or goals of those establishing the classifications."[90]

By borrowing the methods of animal classification and transferring them from Linnaeus and Cuvier to Darwin, Gobineau, and Renan, nineteenth-century European and European American savants contended that the genetic variants of the human species called races inherited innate characteristics that transcended social evolution. "Races" were accordingly conceived as "naturally" immutable and heritable status categories linked to visible physical markers. Racial formation not only served to justify the dominance of certain socioeconomic classes or ethnic elements but also became a new dimension of social differentiation that superseded socioeconomic class.[91]

Races, which were formed by the landscape and climate of their homelands, retained permanent and pure essences, even though they took on new forms in each new era. History became the biography of races and consisted of the triumph of strong and vital populations over weak and feeble ones.[92] Victors were seen as more advanced than and thus superior to the vanquished. It was self-evident that the greatest race in world history was the European or Aryan one. It alone had and always would have the capacity to conquer all other peoples and to create advanced and dynamic civilizations. Once structured in the form of a dichotomous hierarchy of inequality, different racial pluralities became socially meaningful wherever the term was used and to whatever groups it could be applied. European identity, constructed to distinguish it from the identity of Others, led necessarily to a ranking among Europeans themselves based on their closeness to or distance from the western European ideal.[93]

Racial formation reached maturity as the European nation-states reached positions of economic, military, political, and cultural domination globally in the eighteenth and nineteenth centuries.[94] Racialized thinking thus served as a justification not only for African slavery but also for the conquest and direct settlement and control of Others in the manner of colonialism, particularly in terms of occupation of their land—through both the distant control of resources and direct settlement. During the second half of the nineteenth and early part of the twentieth century, these forces culminated in European justifications for dividing their "spoils" in Africa, as well as in Asia and the Pacific. They would serve as the underpinning of similar justifications not only for the Anglo–North American annexation and incorporation of Mexican territory into the United States but also for expansion into the Philippines and the Pacific, as well as into Latin America and the Caribbean through the implementation of "free trade" hegemony or Monroe Doctrine–style military interventions.[95]

White Supremacy and the Contours of Racist Ideology

From its inception race was a product of popular beliefs about human differences that evolved from the sixteenth through the nineteenth centuries. By the early decades of the nineteenth century, the concept of race generally contained several ideological ingredients—beliefs, values, and assumptions generally unrelated to empirical facts—that served to guide individual and collective behavior.[96] The first and most basic ingredient of "race" was the universal classification of human groups as discrete, mutually exclusive biotic pluralities. Racial classifications were based not on objective variations in culture but on subjective and arbitrary judgments that reflected superficial assessments of phenotypic and behavioral variations. The second ingredient was an inegalitarian ethos that ranked these biotic pluralities hierarchically, with Aryan Europeans at the top of the pyramid.[97]

The third ingredient was the belief that superficial physical characteristics reflected behavioral, intellectual, temperamental, moral, and other qualities. It followed that the culture of any given "race" was a reflection of its biophysical form. The fourth ingredient was the notion that biophysical characteristics, behavioral attributes and capabilities, and social status were inheritable.[98] Fifth, and perhaps most important, was the belief that each exclusive racial plurality was created by God or nature as unique and distinct from all others. Imputed differences could never be altered, bridged, or transcended. Christians saw racial inequalities as divinely ordained, and the nonreligious rationalized them as the product of natural laws. "Scientific" inquiry confirmed the inequalities between races in a way that supported Europeans' conviction of their own superiority. And the state ultimately gave this structural inequality official sanction. White racism and White supremacy were institutionalized as systematic components of social structure.[99]

In the United States, these beliefs were buttressed by antimiscegenation sentiments and occupied a core position in the covert defense of African slavery and the segregation of African Americans during the era of Jim Crow segregation. In addition, these sentiments were perhaps the clearest indication of the gradual broadening of the ideology of White racism that originally had been used to support African enslavement and the systematic subordination of Blacks afterward. During the nineteenth century, it had expanded to include notions of White supremacy, which were grounded in "scientific" arguments perpetuating notions of the primordial and permanent genetic superiority of Europeans and the genetic inferiority of Blacks to maintain White racial and cultural "purity," as much as to preserve White privilege.

The strict enforcement of the one-drop rule furthered these goals. It buttressed the institution of slavery and the systematic exclusion of African Americans from having contact with European Americans as equals in most spheres of society. Furthermore, the system of slavery not only placed White men in control of the productive labor of African American men, it also gave them authority over the productive and reproductive labor of both African American and European American women.[100] More important, these dynamics assured that most miscegenation in the United States would tend to be one-directional: from European American men to African American women, and from multiracial individuals to Blacks. The Anglo–North American patriarchy thus established an economic and political system and a cultural ideology that maintained a fundamentally racist and sexist hierarchy of wealth, power, privilege, and prestige. Accordingly, the one-drop rule became the ideal solution to the Anglo–North American patriarchy's labor needs as well as their extracurricular and inadmissible sexual desires. More important, this device supported their obsession with maintaining White racial and cultural "purity" and solved the problem of maintaining, at least in theory, absolute dominance, superiority, and social control.

While U.S. law and public policy have been preoccupied with race in general, the specificity of the one-drop rule in U.S. jurisprudence, in conjunction with the legacy of slavery and Jim Crow segregation, makes an examination of the social construction of Blackness particularly significant. Despite the limitations of the Black-White paradigm for understanding the history, the present, and especially the future of racial formation in the United States generally, the nation's historic treatment of African Americans has been the touchstone for its treatment of all racialized Others. The one-drop rule, as the ultimate expression of the Law of the Excluded Middle, is the linchpin of U.S. racial formation and has provided the larger context in which those Other experiences have historically been grounded and the construct in which they have historically been (and continue to be) framed.

NOTES

This chapter, as well as chapters 9 and 11, borrows from G. Reginald Daniel, *More Than Black? Multiracial Identity and the New Racial Order* (Philadelphia: Temple University Press, 2002).

1. Carter A. Wilson, *Racism: From Slavery to Advanced Capitalism* (Thousand Oaks, Calif.: Sage, 1996), 37–47; Audrey Smedley, *Race in North America: Origin and Evolution of a Worldview* (Boulder, Colo.: Westview Press, 1993), 14–16.

2. Smedley, *Race in North America,* 14–16.

3. Pitirim Sorokin, *Social and Cultural Dynamics: The Study of Change in Major Systems of Art, Truth, Ethics, Law and Social Relationships,* rev. and abr. (Boston: Porter Sargent Books, 1957), 15, 226–30.

4. Thomas Goldstein, *The Dawn of Modern Science: From the Arabs to Leonardo da Vinci* (Boston: Houghton Mifflin, 1980), 191–98; Ankie M. M. Hoogvelt, *The Sociology of Developing Societies,* 2d ed. (London: Macmillan, 1978), 41; Sorokin, *Social and Cultural Dynamics,* 226–30, 272–75.

5. Bruce Mazlish, *A New Science: The Breakdown of Connections and the Birth of Sociology* (New York: Oxford University Press, 1989), 24–26, 32. In actuality the underlying principles of the Great Chain of Being have much more in common with what Ken Wilber has defined as holarchy, rather than hierarchy. Differential function, responsibility, and/or rank are not inherently and necessarily equivalent to differential value and worth. In other words, the Great Chain viewed virtually all growth processes, from matter to life to mind, as occurring via holarchies, or orders of increasing holism and wholeness; wholes then become parts of new wholes, each of which transcends and includes its predecessor. To say that the whole is greater than the sum of its parts means that the whole is at a higher or greater or deeper level of organization than the parts alone. Ken Wilber, *The Eye of the Spirit: An Integral Vision for a World Gone Slightly Mad* (Boston: Shambhala, 1996), 38–51.

6. Jeremy Rifkin, *Biosphere Politics: A Cultural Odyssey from the Middle Ages to the New Age* (San Francisco: Harper, 1991), 15.

7. Samir Amin, *Eurocentrism* (New York: Monthly Review Press, 1989), 79; Hoogvelt, *Sociology of Developing Societies,* 41.

8. Mazlish, *A New Science,* 3–9, 12–14; Brian Easlea, *Witch-Hunting, Magic, and the New Philosophy* (Sussex: Harvester Press, 1980), 201, 216–18, 241–42; Amaury de Riencourt, *Sex and Power in History* (New York: David McKay, 1974), 262–63; Bryce Little, "Rationalism and the Rise of the Sensate," unpublished ms., 1989.

9. The term "Man" is not being used here generically to refer to both men and women. Rather, it is deliberately used to emphasize the increasing patriarchal domination that accompanied the detachment of humanity from nature.

10. Daniel Chirot, *How Societies Change* (Thousand Oaks, Calif.: Pine Forge Press, 1994), 66–67.

11. Ibid.

12. Amin, *Eurocentrism*, 71–76, 85.

13. Chirot, *How Societies Change*, 66–67, 74–77; Smedley, *Race in North America*, 45–52; Little, "Rationalism and the Rise of the Sensate"; Mazlish, *A New Science*, 3–9; 12–14.

14. Wilson, *Racism*, 37–47.

15. Ken Morrison, *Marx, Durkheim, Weber: Formations of Modern Social Thought* (Thousand Oaks, Calif.: Sage, 1995), 6–16; George Ritzer, *Sociological Theory*, 5th ed. (New York: McGraw Hill, 2000), 6–7.

16. Wilson, *Racism*, 6, 18–19, 43–44.

17. Mazlish, *A New Science*, 3–9, 12–14; Easlea, *Witch-Hunting*, 201, 216–18, 241–42; de Riencourt, *Sex and Power in History*, 262–63.

18. Amin, *Eurocentrism*, 60–67; Sorokin, *Social and Cultural Dynamics*, 15, 226–30.

19. W. Warren Warger, *World Views: A Study of Comparative History* (Hinsdale, Ill.: Dryden Press, 1977), 1–14.

20. Goldstein, *The Dawn of Modern Science*, 45–46.

21. Cedric Robinson, *Black Marxism: The Making of the Black Radical Tradition* (London: Zed Books, 1991), 111–13, 118.

22. Goldstein, *The Dawn of Modern Science*, 55–58.

23. Other startling and more controversial evidence—which continues to be largely dismissed—suggests that before the Renaissance, Afro-Islamic civilization in West Africa may have had empirical knowledge of the Americas, particularly the Mesoamerican area. This information itself may have been responsible in part for Portugal's "accidental" discovery of the New World, considering southern Portugal's intimate contact with the latest navigational wisdom, cartographic, astronomical, and geographic knowledge available through Islamic civilization with which parts of West Africa were closely linked. Phillip Foner, *History of Black Americans: From Africa to the Emergence of the Cotton Kingdom* (Westport, Conn.: Greenwood Press, 1975), 34–47, 95; Ivan Van Sertima, *They Came before Columbus: The African Presence in Ancient America* (New York: Random House, 1976), 19–107, 180–231.

24. Sorokin, *Social and Cultural Dynamics*, 150–53.

25. Robinson, *Black Marxism*, 111–13, 118.

26. Goldstein, *The Dawn of Modern Science*, 97–98; Robinson, *Black Marxism*, 111–12.

27. Robinson, *Black Marxism*, 110–11.

28. Ibid.

29. Goldstein, *The Dawn of Modern Science*, 92–129, 130–33; Sorokin, *Social and Cultural Dynamics*, 268–72.

30. Amin, *Eurocentrism*, 53, 56.

31. Goldstein, *The Dawn of Modern Science*, 92–96.

32. Sorokin, *Social and Cultural Dynamics*, 268–75; Roland N. Stromberg, *An Intellectual History of Europe*, 2d ed. (Englewood Cliffs, N.J.: Prentice-Hall, 1975), 4, 10, 14–16.

33. Amin, *Eurocentrism*, 71–76.

34. Michael Omi and Howard Winant, *Racial Formation in the United States from the 1960s to the 1990s*, 2d ed. (New York: Routledge, 1994), 61–62.

35. Amin, *Eurocentrism*, 77.

36. Omi and Winant, *Racial Formation*, 62.

37. Ibid.

38. Ibid.

39. Omi and Winant, *Racial Formation*, 61–62.

40. Colonialism was a specific phase in the history of Western imperialism, although the latter is frequently limited to the period between 1870 and 1914. At that time conquest of territory became linked to a systematic search for markets and an expansionist exporting of capital. In a broader sense this included the expansion of a First World capitalist mode of production and mass culture, as well as the concomitant destruction of pre- or noncapitalist forms of social organization. Ella Shohat and Robert Stam, *Unthinking Eurocentrism: Multiculturalism and the Media* (London: Routledge, 1994), 1–54; Patrick Williams and Laura Chrisman, "Colonial Discourse and Post-Colonial Theory: An Introduction," in *Colonial Discourse and Post-Colonial Theory: A Reader*, ed. Patrick Williams and Laura Chrisman (New York: Columbia University Press, 1994), 1–19; Helen Tiffin, "Introduction," in *Past the Last Post: Theorizing Post-Colonialism and Post-Modernism*, ed. Ian Adam and Helen Tiffin (Calgary: University of Calgary Press, 1990), vii–xvi.

41. Omi and Winant, *Racial Formation*, 61–62.

42. Ibid., 62.

43. Little, "Rationalism and the Rise of the Sensate." Eurocentrism has obscured the West's indebtedness to this Asian, and Near Eastern, not to mention North and West African, influence that is often concealed in the rather ambiguous term "Moor." The latter in and of itself simply refers to the inhabitants of Mauritania (current Morocco), but became associated in the European mind with the invading Islamic forces who entered the Iberian Peninsula from North Africa. Many of these individuals were in fact Moors and a substantial number were culturally Arab, if not from the Arabian Peninsula. However, the use of the terms "Arab" and "Moor" by European historians has often obscured, sometimes deliberately, the fact that many of these so-called Moors or Arabs, like their more distant Egyptian neighbors, were phenotypically Africoid or Eurafricoid and largely a racial and cultural blend of European, Asian, and African ancestries and heritages. Foner, *History of Black Americans*, 85–86, 88.

44. Little, "Rationalism and the Rise of the Sensate"; Jean Devisse and Michel Mollat, "Africans in the Christian Ordinance of the World (Fourteenth to Sixteenth Century)," trans. William Granger Ryan, in *From the Early Christian Era to the "Age of Discovery."* vol. 2. pt. 2 of *The Image of the Black in Western Art*, ed. Ladislas Bugner (New York: William Morrow, 1979), 154–60; David Brian Davis, *The Problem of Slavery in Western Culture* (Ithaca: Cornell University Press, 1967), 186.

45. A. C. de C. M. Saunders, *Social History of Black Slaves and Freedmen in Portugal, 1441–1555* (New York: Cambridge University Press, 1982), 84–88, 110, 176–77. Foner, *History of Black Americans*, 94–97; Little, "Rationalism and the Rise of the Sensate"; Herbert S. Klein, African Slavery in Latin America and the Caribbean (New York: Oxford University Press, 1986), 18–19.

46. Little, "Rationalism and the Rise of the Sensate"; Foner, *History of Black Americans*, 94–97.

47. Davis, *The Problem of Slavery in Western Culture*, 181–82; Foner, *History of Black Americans*, 34–47.

48. Foner, *History of Black Americans*, 35, 93.

49. Davis, *The Problem of Slavery*, 180–82.

50. Ibid.

51. Van Sertima, *They Came before Columbus*, 108–10; Edith Sanders, "The Hamitic Hypothesis: Its Origin and Function in Time Perspective," *Journal of African History* 10 (1969): 521–32; Anton L. Allahar, "When Black First Became Worth Less," *International Journal of Comparative Sociology* 34, nos. 1–2 (1993): 39–55; Kathryn A. Manzo, *Creating Boundaries: The Politics of Race and Nation* (Boulder, Colo.: Lynn Rienner, 1996), 46–53.

52. Davis, *The Problem of Slavery*, 186.

53. Ibid.; Winthrop Jordan, *Black over White: American Attitudes toward the Negro, 1550–1812* (Chapel Hill: University of North Carolina Press, 1968), 3–43.

54. St. Claire Drake, *Black Folk Here and There* (Los Angeles: UCLA Center for African American Studies, 1987), 1:31, 62–75; Frantz Fanon, *Black Skin, White Mask* (New York: Grove Press, 1967), 167, 177, 188–92; Jordan, *Black over White*, 248, 253; Joel Kovel, *White Racism: A Psychohistory* (New York: Columbia University Press, 1970), 14–20, 62–64.

55. Wilson, *Racism*, 37–40.

56. Sanders, "The Hamitic Hypothesis," 524.

57. Kovel, *White Racism*, 16–19.

58. Davis, *The Problem of Slavery*, 186.

59. Ibid.

60. The escape hatch allows vertical mobility primarily in terms of phenotypical, that is, somatic, approximation to the dominant European norm image as defined by Hoetink. However, somatic (external) characteristics of a

cultural and economic nature (e.g., speech, mannerisms, attire, occupation, income) and psychological (internal) factors (e.g., beliefs, values, attitudes) are also taken into consideration. Consequently, a few exceptional Blacks have gained vertical mobility in accordance with their socioeconomic and sociocultural if not phenotypical approximation to the dominant Whites.

61. G. Reginald Daniel, "Multiracial Identity in the United States and Brazil," in *We Are a People: Narrative and Multiplicity in the Construction of Ethnic Identity,* ed. Paul Spickard and W. Jeffrey Burroughs (Philadelphia: Temple University Press, 2000), 153–78; Carl N. Degler, *Neither Black nor White: Slavery and Race Relations in Brazil and the United States* (Madison: University of Wisconsin Press, 1986).

62. The differences between the binary U.S. and ternary Latin American racial projects were closely tied to if not determined respectively by the ratio of European men to women and Whites to Blacks. In Brazil and other areas of Latin America—including parts of "Latin" North America (or the U.S. lower South) such as the lower Mississippi Valley, the Gulf Coast, and South Carolina—the colonizing Europeans were a minority and most were single men. Africans constituted a majority of the colonial population. Rape, fleeting extramarital relations, and extended concubinage and common-law unions between White men and women of African descent, therefore, were more or less approved if not encouraged by the prevailing unwritten moral code. There were legal barriers to interracial marriages during most of the colonial period, however, and formidable social prejudice against these relationships that remained in place long afterward. Nevertheless, the absence of the possible numerical self-perpetuation of the White family led to permissive attitudes toward miscegenation and the informal legitimization of the interracial family, as well as the social differentiation of mulatto offspring from both Whites and Blacks.

As slaves, these mulatto offspring were often assigned more exacting tasks that symbolized greater personal worth and required greater skill (e.g., domestics and artisans). Moreover, the pronounced scarcity of White women mitigated or prevented significant opposition from the legal wife. This enhanced the likelihood of socially tolerated demonstrations of affection, economic and educational protection, and the preferential liberation of mulatto offspring and slave mistresses. These comparatively more favorable attitudes toward the emancipation of multiracial individuals over Blacks, who overwhelmingly were slaves, resulted in the disproportionate numbers of mulattos among Free Coloreds, as compared to their numbers among slaves. Therefore, the mulatto's intermediate phenotypical and ancestral markers emerged as signifiers of an intermediate socioeconomic status, just as European and African phenotypical and ancestral markers emerged as signifiers of the dominant and subordinate social locations respectively of White masters and Black slaves.

Colonial race relations in the U.S. North and upper South ("Anglo" North America) differed markedly from those in South America, Central America, and the Caribbean, as well as "Latin" North America. The comparatively early balance between European men and women in North Carolina and the area northward made possible the reestablishment of European patterns of domestic life. Consequently, the White family formed by legal marriage remained the standard social unit and precluded the development of permissive attitudes toward miscegenation typified by Latin America. This was particularly true of New England. In that region, Europeans not only emigrated with families, but if they were single men, they found a sufficient number of women, as parity between the sexes was established quickly and continued throughout the colonial period.

As African slavery became entrenched in society over the course of the seventeenth century, the population of African descent expanded to meet these needs. Consequently, slavery and African ancestry not only become inextricably intertwined in the European American mind but also became necessary to ensure White dominance over individuals of African descent. The newly established slave system could hardly be maintained unless the barriers between African Americans and European Americans, particularly indentured or formerly indentured White servants, were maintained and strengthened. Subsequently, codes were promulgated to solidify the distinction between slave and free, which ultimately came to belie the distinction between Black and White. Simultaneously, the southern colonies, and some northern colonies, began enforcing laws that criminalized sexual relations and intermarriages between Whites and Blacks. Although Free Coloreds in Anglo North America tended to be disproportionately multiracial as was the case in Latin America and performed an important role in the artisanal and skilled trades, there was generally an abundant supply of Whites—particularly impoverished European immigrants—who could fill interstitial roles in the economy. These same factors also obviated the social differentiation of multiracial individuals from Whites and Blacks.

Distinctions between Black and multiracial individuals have existed in the United States. Yet, unlike Latin America, these distinctions have historically been more semantic than social. European Americans have had little inclination to make social distinctions—particularly formal ones—among individuals of African descent based on the degree of phenotypical approximation to and divergence from the European American somatic norm image.

63. U.S. attitudes toward the offspring of unions between African Americans and other groups of color (e.g., Native Americans) have varied. More often than not, these individuals have been subject to the one-drop rule. There has been greater ambivalence toward offspring whose ancestry has combined other backgrounds of color (e.g., Mexican American–Asian American; or Native

American–Mexican American). Some of this is due to the fact that these other groups of color occupy a more ambiguous position than do Blacks in the U.S. racial hierarchy. Also, membership in these groups—except perhaps in the case of Native Americans—has been less clearly defined in U.S. law. Consequently, the racial subordination of Americans of color by European Americans, while similarly oppressive, has not been exactly the same. This makes it more difficult to assess intragroup relations among groups of color in terms of the one-drop rule.

64. The term "miscegenation" is said to have originated in the mid-nineteenth century during the Democratic Party's campaign for the presidency and was coined in a pamphlet entitled *Miscegenation: The Theory of the Blending of the Races* that was published anonymously in 1864, although authorship has been attributed to David Croly and George Wakeman (William Lee Miller, *Arguing about Slavery: The Great Battle in the United States Congress* [New York: Alfred A. Knopf, 1996], 12; Kenneth James Lay, "Sexual Racism: A Legacy of Slavery," *National Black Law Journal* 13, nos. 1–2 [spring 1993]: 165). To keep Whites, particularly White women, free from contamination by the "Black peril" that would arise from racial blending, racial stereotypes and fears were central to gaining support for the continued enslavement of African Americans as well as the segregation, or repatriation to Africa, of those who were free. Consequently, racial blending between Blacks and Whites was considered the genetic crossing of different species that are in fact merely geno-phenotypical variations of the same species, *Homo sapiens sapiens*. Because of this history of negative attitudes toward racial blending, many individuals have assumed erroneously that the etymology of *miscegenation* is the same as that of words such as *misbehave*, *mistake*, and *mishap*, which are derived from the Anglo-Germanic prefix *mis*, meaning *ill*, *wrong*, or simply *negating*. However, *miscegenation* is actually derived from the Latin words, *misce(re)* [to mix] + *gen(us)* [race or stock].

65. A lengthier discussion of this topic can be found in Gunnar Myrdal's *An American Dilemma* (New York: Harper and Brothers, 1944).

66. Robert Young, "Egypt in America," in *Racism, Modernity, and Identity*, ed. Ali Rantansi and Sallie Westwood (Cambridge, Mass.: Polity Press, 1994), 160–65.

67. Robert Young, *Colonial Desire: Hybridity in Theory, Culture, and Race* (New York: Routledge, 1995), 118–41; Sanders, "The Hamitic Hypothesis," 521–32.

68. Martin Bernal, *Black Athena: The Afroasiatic Roots of Classical Civilization*, vol. 1 (New Brunswick, N.J.: Rutgers University Press, 1987), 1–2, 29.

69. Ibid.

70. Ibid., 7–8.

71. Bernal's Revised Ancient Model accepts the invasions from the north by Indo-European speakers but also supports the stories of Egyptian and

Phoenician colonization of Greece set out in the Ancient Model, although he sees them as beginning somewhat earlier, in the first half of the second millennium B.C. Bernal, *Black Athena,* 2.

72. Amin, *Eurocentrism,* 77, 90–92.

73. Ibid.

74. Some recent scholarship acknowledges Egyptian influence on Greece and vice versa but continues to challenge, as did nineteenth-century historiographers, the accuracy of the Ancient Model's claims of Egyptian colonization. By virtue of the lack of direct empirical evidence and incontrovertible historical proof, this scholarship also rejects the anecdotal accounts passed on orally to Greek thinkers by Egyptian priests claiming that Greek philosophers such as Plato and Aristotle studied in Egypt (Mary Lefkowitz, *Not Out of Africa: How Afrocentrism Became an Excuse to Teach Myth as History* [New York: Basic Books, 1996], 53–90, 134–54). Other scholars argue that from the pre-Christian seventh century on, Egyptian law, science, art, architecture, religion, and philosophy had a dramatic impact on Greek civilization as well as vice versa. Yet the extent to which these and other areas in which Egyptian influence made itself felt on Greek civilization needs to be further explored. This is particularly the case given the paucity of definitive sources and questionable reliability of some evidence (Robinson, *Black Marxism,* 108).

75. Amin, *Eurocentrism,* 89–100.

76. Ibid.; David Slater, "Exploring Other Zones of the Postmodern: Problems of Ethnocentrism and Difference across the North-South Divide," in *Racism, Modernity, and Identity,* ed. Ali Rattansi and Sallie Westwood (Cambridge, Mass.: Polity Press, 1994), 101–3.

77. Bernal, *Black Athena,* 30–33.

78. Many scholars argue that it was in Mesopotamia where what we call civilization was first assembled. However, all the elements of which Mesopotamian civilization was composed—cities, agricultural irrigation, metalworking, stone architecture, wheels for both vehicles and pot making, long-distance trade, and writing—had existed in some combination before and elsewhere. Certainly, this assemblage, when capped by the phonetic alphabet, as opposed to the pictorial hieroglyphics of Egyptian script, allowed a great social, cultural, economic, and political accumulation. Peter Farb, *Humankind* (New York: Houghton Mifflin, 1978), 162–63. Egyptian civilization is clearly based on the rich predynastic cultures of Upper Egypt and Nubia, whose African origin is uncontested. In addition, the great extent of Mesopotamian influence, evident from predynastic and First Dynasty remains, leaves little doubt that the unification and establishment of dynastic Egypt around 3250 B.C. was in some way triggered by developments to the east. The cultural blend was further complicated by the fundamental cultural links between Egypt and the basically Semitic component of Mesopotamian civilization.

79. According to popular African American tradition, the Africoid phenotype of the Sphinx was apparently so disturbingly obvious that Napoleon's soldiers allegedly took special cautions to cover this up by shooting off the statue's flattened nose. It is unclear where and when this belief originated. However, Minister Louis Farrakhan's address at the Million Man March on October 16, 1995, and poet Amiri Baraka's speech at a rally at a Washington, D.C., high school the day before the march contained the most recent charges against Napoleon for having shot off the Sphinx's nose. Drake, *Black Folk Here and There,* 130–35; Robert Girardi, "Nose Job: Farrakhan, Napoleon, and the Sphinx," *New Republic* (November 13, 1995): 14; Sanders, "The Hamitic Hypothesis," 526–27; Van Sertima, *They Came before Columbus,* 119. However, Chiekh Anta Diop, a Senegalese authority on Egyptian origins, states that the nose actually fell to the ground during an expedition and was collected and deposited in the British Museum. Although he attributes the Sphinx's current facial physiognomy to the effects of centuries of erosion, he also adds that Egypt could very well ask to have the nose returned but suggests that the Sphinx would thus have a typically Africoid visage, a fact that would be most unsettling to Eurocentric claims of Egyptian "Whiteness." Ivan Van Sertima and Larry Williams, eds., *Great African Thinkers* (Journal of African Civilizations) (New Brunswick, N.J.: Transaction Books, 1986), 333; George F. Will, "Intellectual Segregation," *Newsweek* (February 19, 1996): 78. In truth, the defacing of the Sphinx, along with the mutilation of many other important Egyptian antiquities, appears to have been carried out by Islamic conquerors who began invading Egypt in A.D. 693, long before Napoleon's arrival, as well as by the Ottoman Mamelukes who were dominating Egypt at the time of his expedition.

80. Sanders, "The Hamitic Hypothesis," 521–32.

81. Drake, *Black Folk Here and There,* 132–37.

82. John S. Haller Jr. *Outcasts from Evolution: Scientific Attitudes of Racial Inferiority, 1859–1900* (Urbana: University of Illinois Press, 1971), 72.

83. Van Sertima, *They Came before Columbus,* 108–10.

84. Young, "Egypt in America," 163–68.

85. In popular thought, "mulatto" is said to have evolved from the Portuguese word for mule (*mulo*) as an epithet. It referred to the fact that the latter was the sterile offspring of a donkey and a horse. The mulatto, as the multiracial offspring of a Black and a White, was imagined to be degenerate and at least low in fertility if not actually sterile, like its zoological counterpart. There is enough linguistic evidence, however, to argue that as a legacy of the Islamic occupation of the Iberian Peninsula, the Arabic word used to refer to blended individuals of African/Arab descent, *muwallad,* actually may have evolved into the Portuguese word *mulato* to refer to Afro-Europeans (or Eurafricans). *Mulatto* can be used with derogatory connotations, yet it is more often used simply as a designation for individuals of blended African and European backgrounds.

Jack D. Forbes, *Black Africans and Native Americans: Color, Race and Caste in the Evolution of Red-Black Peoples* (London: Blackwell, 1988), 131–50.

86. Michael Barton, "The Idea of Race and the Concept of Race," in *Race, Education, and Identity,* ed. Gajendra K. Verma and Christopher Bagley (New York: St. Martin's Press, 1979), 17; Smedley, *Race in North America,* 14–18.

87. Baton, "The Idea of Race and the Concept of Race," 17.

88. Ibid.

89. Smedley, *Race in North America,* 14–18, 25–29.

90. Ibid.

91. Ibid.

92. Bernal, *Black Athena,* 31–33.

93. Amin, *Eurocentrism,* 94–97.

94. Ibid.

95. Young, "Egypt in America"; Shohat and Stam, *Unthinking Eurocentrism,* 1–54; Williams and Chrisman, "Colonial Discourse and Post-Colonial Theory"; Tiffin, "Introduction," vii–xvi.

96. Smedley, *Race in North America,* 26–27.

97. Ibid.

98. Ibid.

99. Ibid.

100. Elaine K. Ginsberg, "Introduction: The Politics of Passing," in *Passing and the Fictions of Identity,* ed. Elaine Ginsberg (Durham, N.C.: Duke University Press, 1996), 5.

3

MUSTEFINOS ARE WHITE BY LAW

Whiteness and People of Mixed Racial Origins in Historical and Comparative Perspective

STEPHEN A. SMALL

One of the most distinctive characteristics of the societies established by Europeans throughout the United States, the Caribbean, and South America is the elaborate and intricate system of racialized differentiation and stratification developed to define legally and socially the status of different population groups.[1] This system distinguished, broadly, those who were European, Christian, and, increasingly, defined as White from those who were African, heathen, and, increasingly, defined as Black (or for Native Americans, indigenous and savage). Although increasingly codified notions of race were at the forefront of this system, it was never contingent on color or phenotype alone but was intricately shaped by a series of cultural factors, including nativity, gender, religion, language, and wealth. This range of factors came into play in ways such that there developed an extensive and elaborate range of racialized categories along the space between the presumed binaries of White and Black. These categories varied temporally and spatially, not surprisingly, given the involvement of numerous European nations in this process, given that legally slavery lasted from the 1490s to the 1880s, and given that the territories under the purview of European enslavers were as far afield as Brazil and Ecuador and those that became New England and Canada.

The island of Jamaica was the jewel in the crown of the British Caribbean empire: more persons were enslaved there than on any other island controlled by the British; more profits were wrenched from the laborers on its sugar plantations than from laborers in crops on any other island; and the plantations were larger there, and the planters richer, than on any other British island.[2] Among these British colonial possessions, Jamaica also revealed one of the clearest and most elaborate systems of racialized classifications for defining the range of "Blacks of mixed origins" who resided on the island.[3] The specific terms used to describe people of mixed origins depended on their parentage. In Jamaica at the start of the nineteenth century, racialized categories were explicitly and systematically defined by law. "Mustefinos"—who had the least African ancestry—were white by law, whereas all other Blacks of mixed origins were legally considered "mulattoes."[4]

Elsewhere, I ask whether during the nineteenth century, Blacks of mixed origins were better off in the Caribbean than in the United States, and if so, why?[5] The usual characterization in most of the literature is that in the Caribbean enslaved persons of mixed origins enjoyed preferential job allocations, acquired better material goods (such as food, clothing, and medicine), were more likely to become literate, had higher social status in the eyes of White people, and over-all had a better quality of life. They were also more likely to attain legal freedom and to become socially mobile once legally free.[6] This was particularly the case if they were the children or the sexual partners of White master-enslavers.[7] In contrast, it is suggested that in the United States Blacks of mixed origins were subject to the one-drop rule and treated as if they were the same as Blacks.[8] The explanation usually offered for this divergence is demographic and attitudinal: where Blacks outnumbered Whites, an intermediate racialized category was developed as a buffer group by the White planter elite, and Whites preferred to assist people who looked physically like them. I reject this broad characterization. I have demonstrated that similar patterns of differentiation and stratification existed in each territory, and I argue that in Jamaica the extent of privilege and advantage conferred on Blacks of mixed origins has been greatly exaggerated and the mechanisms by which these privileges were secured neglected or misunderstood. The majority of Blacks of mixed origins remained enslaved in both territories and occupied far more common ground with Blacks believed to be "pure African" than has been acknowledged; those who did well were overwhelmingly a tiny group of legally free, elite people who had rich White fathers and distant African ancestry. The diverse institutional structures of slavery—demographic ratios, plantation size, the work processes associated with different crops, and ideologies of White racism—did not allow for the magnitude of unfettered privilege for Blacks of mixed origins suggested by the prevalent characterizations.[9]

Using data from my earlier study, I review here the historical record on people of mixed origins in Jamaica to challenge some common misconceptions, including the belief that the majority of Blacks of mixed origins had wealthy White fathers who privileged them while enslaved and legally freed them; and I interrogate the tendency to treat all people of mixed origins as if they were a largely homogeneous group, possessing similar phenotypical features and expressing largely homogeneous attitudes (i.e., "light-skinned," self-hating, and covetous of White values). I also question the tendency to take the experiences of a tiny minority as indicative of the experiences of the majority. These tendencies are common in both academic literature and popular culture.[10]

The fact is that in Jamaica Blacks of mixed origins found themselves in extremely diverse legal, social, and occupational circumstances (with widely varying consequences), had distinctive patterns of parentage, possessed diverse physical appearances, and reflected a multiplicity of identities.[11] Recognition of this can provide us with better insight into the range of circumstances and outcomes for these groups under slavery and with a number of conceptual clues about the circumstances of racialized intermediate populations in the contemporary United States. In particular, it offers a number of insights into the processes out of which racialization—in this instance, Blackness, intermediate racialized categories, and Whiteness—are constituted in broad social terms, including demographic, political, legal, and economic. Or more precisely, it offers insights into the dynamics of color differentiation and stratification of which Whiteness is a part. This offers a way to sharpen our analytic tools and unearth the necessary evidence that will help us to address the uncompleted independence that is the subject of this volume.

RACIALIZED CATEGORIES UNDER SLAVERY IN JAMAICA

Jamaica was colonized by the Spanish at the end of the fifteenth century, and for a period of approximately 150 years, they ravished the island and decimated the indigenous Arawak population.[12] When the British captured the island from the Spanish in 1655, they developed a large-scale commercial enterprise based on monocrop plantation agriculture and enslaved African labor. The main crops were sugar and coffee, and by the 1830s there were more than 155,000 enslaved persons working in sugar agriculture (i.e., almost 50 percent of the enslaved) and about 45,000 working in coffee cultivation (just over 14 percent of the enslaved). The remainder worked in livestock pens and in the few towns on the island.[13] The British maintained uninterrupted control of the island for the next two centuries. In 1807 they abolished the slave trade, and in 1833–38 slavery was legally abolished.[14] During the period of slavery, the island's population was systematically differentiated in a number of ways. Given that the Spanish had almost decimated the entire indigenous population by the time the British took control, the primary groups were Europeans (who were always free) and Africans (who were presumed enslaved and usually were) and their descendants (who were subject to a range of legal and social categories, described below). Most estimates of Blacks of mixed origins indicate that by 1817 they were about 10 percent of the enslaved population and 80 percent of the legally free population.[15] With an enslaved population of 345,252 and a legally free population of 31,000 in 1817, that would amount to 34,525 enslaved persons of mixed origins and 24,800 legally free persons of mixed origins (for a total of 55,800 Blacks of mixed origins). At the same time there were about 30,000 Whites. That means that 311,000 enslaved persons and about 6,200 legally free persons were Black.[16] When slavery was legally abolished in the 1830s there were just over 310,000 enslaved persons on the island.[17]

Whites, Blacks, and Blacks of mixed origins in Jamaica believed that they were different races, with different abilities, both physical and mental. Generally, Blacks of mixed origins were people with any known African ancestry, however remote, and they were seen by Whites as an intermediate group of biological degenerates, as well as immoral offspring. There existed a range of terms to differentiate Blacks of mixed origins of varying physical appearance, legal and social standing, and wealth. They may have had one White parent (almost invariably a man), but the majority of them had two parents of color.[18] Blacks of mixed origins were commonly called "mongrels" and "mungrels."[19] As one contemporary observed:

> A Mongrel is any thing that is engendered or begotten between different kinds, and resembles neither in nothing but form; such as a mule that is begot between an ass and a mare; or in the human species, a Sambo that is begot by a Mulatto and a black; a Mulatto, that is begot by a white and a black; a Mestee, that is begot between a white and a Mulatto; a Quadroon, that is begot between a white and a Mestee, &c. &c.[20]

The offspring of a "mestee" and a "white" was a "mustefino," who was White by law. A law of 1733 proclaimed:

> No Person who is not above Three Degrees removed in lineal Descent from the Negro Ancestor exclusive, shall be allowed to vote or poll in Elections; and no one shall be deemed a Mulatto after the Third Generation, as aforesaid, but that they shall have all the Privileges and Immunities of His Majesty's white Subjects of this Island, provided they are brought up in the Christian Religion.[21]

If there is any doubt that mustefinos were White by law, it can easily be put to rest. Using data from four parishes in the Returns to the Registration of Slaves for 1817, I undertook a count of more than 90,000 enslaved persons, including over 7,000 Blacks of mixed origins. These numbers amounted to more than 25 percent of all enslaved persons on the island at the time and more than 20 percent of all enslaved Blacks of mixed origins. Among that number I did not find a single enslaved person defined as "mustefino."[22]

These views were propounded by all Whites, especially those in power, and were explained or rationalized via reference to the Bible, that is, God's curse on the descendants of Ham; or by reference to the emerging beliefs on biology. In addition to the range of terms used to differentiate each racialized category—White, negro, mulatto, quadroon, mustee, mustefino—there were other color categories, especially colloquially, including mestizo, yellow, and red. Many of the views expressed by Whites on the island were influenced by the so-called scientists of the day.[23] These attitudes constitute what has come to be called "biological racism."[24] The terminology was inextricably gendered, with men and women of mixed origins being regarded as possessing different characteristics. For example, Black women were regarded as physically stronger than Black women of mixed origins and more likely to survive the rigors of field labor and childbirth, whereas women of mixed origins were regarded as more intelligent and more physically attractive.[25] The majority of Whites generally expressed the view that distance from African ancestry made one less African and hence more White (biologically, mentally, culturally). But there were, too, some extremists who felt that anyone tainted by African blood could never truly be White.[26] These views, and the language and concepts used to articulate them, have filtered down into both the common currency of racialized discourse at the popular level and the academic literature, in which words such as *miscegenation* are used as if they are neutral or have some analytic value.[27]

Blacks of mixed origins occupied a range of legal and occupational positions. Let us first consider those who were legally free and then those who were enslaved. There were extensive differences in the socioeconomic positions and in the legal and political rights enjoyed by legally free Blacks of mixed origins. The first distinction was between those who were born legally free and those who were manumitted or who purchased their legal freedom. Blacks of mixed origins were overrepresented in both groups, but they were also distinguished into several categories. A small number of legally free people of mixed origins, those who were the lightest in skin color, that is, phenotypically closest to Europeans, were the beneficiaries of individual petitions and the wealthiest. They were known as the "whites by law."[28] They were not given benefits collectively but comprised a group after they received benefits individually. They included people such as James Rowe Williamson, Daniel Saa, and the England-educated and wealthy master-enslavers James Swaby and Thomas Drummond.

Swaby and Drummond were generally accepted as White. Among the 24,800 legally free Blacks of mixed origins, only a tiny minority, no more than a couple of hundred, were in this circumstance.[29] Most petitions for better treatment were offered on the grounds that individuals were educated and wealthy and accepted by Whites. Given the nature of gender power inequalities, although the majority of legally free Blacks of mixed origins were women, far fewer women became Whites by law.[30] These individuals were distant from African ancestry, had phenotypical attributes comparable to Whites presumed to be entirely European, and, if they had wealth, were usually treated as tantamount to Whites. Many attended school in England and sent their children to be educated in England or in White schools in Jamaica. Only a tiny number of individuals, the Whites by law, had full rights. Even fewer of these individuals passed, often unrecorded, into the White population, especially if they supported the system. Overall, Blacks of mixed origins had far more wealth, better jobs, and greater advantages than did Blacks both of whose parents were Black.

The rights of legally free Blacks of mixed origins were not coterminous with the rights of Whites. Of the 128 bills that petitioned for legal rights for free people of color in the eighteenth century, "[o]nly 4 . . . provided for the grant of all the rights of white men, including suffrage and office holding (subject, as in the case of whites, to property and religious qualifications)."[31] The Jamaica House of Assembly introduced statutes on several occasions to restrict the inheritance of property by free people of color, who almost invariably were women of mixed origins who had married White men. To gain benefits for their children, people of mixed origins had to marry Whites. Legally free people of color in general enjoyed certain privileges that were completely denied to the enslaved, for example, jury duty, court testimony, the possession of firearms, reading, and writing.[32] And they had legal access to jobs that no enslaved person could obtain, for example, in the military. In practice such rights were limited, and only a minority were able to benefit from them.

Although the wealth of legally free Blacks of mixed origins as a group was noteworthy, compared to that of Whites it paled into insignificance. In 1761 the Jamaica House of Assembly discovered that property bequeathed to legally free people of color (including

Blacks and Blacks of mixed origins) amounted to 200,000 to 300,000 pounds, including "four sugar estates, seven pens, thirteen houses, besides other lands unspecified."[33] A bill was passed to prevent this from continuing and to limit bequests to 2,000 pounds. Other writers have detailed the nature of such wealth.[34] Sheila Duncker says people of color paid less than one-thirty-fourth in taxes of what Whites paid. Others add that successful people of mixed origins were a very small proportion of the total group.[35] Part of the wealth and property owned by legally free people of color was in the form of enslaved persons. In 1826, for example, these people owned 50,000 of a total of 310,368 enslaved persons.[36] In 1823 it was pointed out that the amount of taxes paid by this population was less than 3 percent of that of Whites.

The more fortunate among legally free people of color occupied the limited number of middlemen roles between Whites and the enslaved, many of them as artisans. An influx of people of color from Haiti increased the range of skilled jobs available to them, and by the nineteenth century some were clerks and schoolmasters. But most did the same work as the enslaved—servants and porters—and the vast majority of them were at the lower end of the occupational and economic ladder. The majority of all legally free people of color were poor. In 1825 it was estimated that 400 of the free people of mixed origins were "rich," 5,500 were in "fair circumstances," and 22,900 were "absolutely poor."[37] Many people of mixed origins lived in degraded conditions, in the towns.[38] A contemporary commented about the "free browns," "[F]ew of them are industrious enough to increase their possessions by any honest exertions of their own," even if left estates by their White fathers; and the free Blacks "are almost uniformly lazy and improvident, most of them half-starved, and only anxious to live from hand to mouth. . . . [F]ew of them ever endeavour to earn their livelihood creditably."[39] Moreover, he said, they are beggars and vagrants or keep "miserable stalls with rancid butter, damaged salt pork, and other such articles."[40] Attempts to mobilize legally free people of mixed origins and Blacks were hindered by their "apathy and indifference . . . caused by years of degradation and hopelessness."[41] Legally free people of mixed origins went to separate churches, often attended separate schools, and sat separately from Whites in theaters. Only the richest sent their children to White schools. Legally free Blacks of mixed origins kept their own balls and forbade entrance not only to Blacks but also to Whites. M. G. Lewis was allowed to observe one, as a "spectator," in Falmouth.[42]

But the majority of Blacks of mixed origins remained enslaved. Among the enslaved, people of mixed origins frequently worked in trades and in domestic service, both in rural and urban areas. But it was also common for them to work in sugar and coffee fields, or in animal pens and related crops. And whereas many of them enjoyed privileges, many did not. If they had a wealthy White father, lived on a large plantation with the father present and his White wife absent, and were significantly outnumbered by Blacks—so that Blacks could be placed exclusively in field labor and Blacks of mixed origins in domestic labor and trades—they usually did well. This is the most common representation of Blacks of mixed origins under slavery, and there is substantial evidence to support it. For example, records from Old Montpelier Plantation in 1825 reveal that all of the "mulattoes," quadroons, and mustees on the plantation were found in privileged occupations, while the seven sambos were in trades or supervisory roles. The same was true at Worthy Park Plantation.[43]

But the many Blacks of mixed origins, perhaps even the majority, who had no White father or a poor White father (especially one who had abandoned them) and who lived on large plantations in significant numbers were just as likely as Blacks to be working in the fields. In Jamaica it is estimated that about 58 percent of Blacks of mixed origins had White fathers, and thus 42 percent did not.[44] Therefore, of the 34,525 enslaved persons of mixed origins, about 14,500 did not have White fathers (while about 20,000 did). Most of these White fathers were certainly poor. In 1820, of the 5,349 properties on the island, only 1,189 had one hundred enslaved persons or more.[45] At the same time, there were five thousand merchants, the majority of whom were likely to be wealthy. But there were also twenty-four thousand Whites working in a variety of jobs (including 3,000 troops) who were not wealthy. And these White men were notorious for their sexual abuse of women of color. White men's promiscuity was pervasive on the island. As L. J. Ragatz points out, "[C]omparatively few wives were brought out and concubinage was universal."[46] One contemporary noted, "Every unmarried white man, and of every class, has his black or his brown mistress, with whom he lives openly; and of so little consequence is this thought, that his white female friends and relations think it no breach of decorum to visit his house."[47] The majority of these White men were reckless and irresponsible; they saw women of color as an opportunity for their own pleasure, and they frequently fathered children and abandoned them.[48] Plantation owners frequently dismissed the offenders, but because of the high demand for White workers, it was not difficult for them to find employment on another plantation and do the same thing over and over again.

Blacks of mixed origins were especially likely to work in the fields, especially at an agricultural unit where they outnumbered Blacks and where the imperatives of harvesting required that all enslaved persons do so at least some of the time. At a small number of plantations, more than 50 percent of the enslaved workforce was of mixed origins, and in these circumstances, given the economic imperatives, the owners had little choice but to put them in the fields, where they labored alongside Blacks. As Edward Long pointed out, "[T]he lower class of these mixtures, who remain in the island, are a hardy race, capable of undergoing equal fatigue with the Blacks."[49] He continued: "And as for the lower rank, the issue of casual fruition, they, for the most part, remain in the same slavish condition as their mother; they are fellow-labourers with the Blacks, and are not regarded in the least as their superiors."[50]

There were hundreds of agricultural units with house servants and artisans on which there were no Blacks of mixed origins. Of the 3,700 owners of enslaved persons whom I counted in the four parishes, about 2,500 (67.5 percent) owned at least one person of mixed origins (totaling about 7,500 Blacks of mixed origins), while 1,200 owners had none (32.5 percent). Of the 7,500 Blacks of mixed origins, at least 2,000 were defined as "sambo," that is, the child of a Black parent and a mulatto parent. This means that on the 1,200 agricultural units with no Blacks of mixed origins present, all the jobs, good and bad, went to enslaved Blacks. These facts challenge the view that most of the house servants and artisans were Blacks of mixed origins.

It was not unusual for a wealthy White father of a Black of mixed origins to abandon the child, and if he had a White wife present, she might persecute the child. Mary Seacole commented on these conditions, especially among domestic servants.[51] In the most extreme instances, there was incest, whereby a White man, having had sex with a woman of color, then raped the daughter who resulted from this intercourse.[52] Even when Blacks of mixed origins worked in trades or domestic labor, they did not enjoy the benefits that some have claimed: they worked longer days, were more directly under the vigilant and vengeful eyes of Whites, and were more readily and frequently the victims of sexual abuse. The presence of large numbers of Blacks of mixed origins in these circumstances among the enslaved—with whom they ate and slept, socialized and prayed, worked and died in the sun—attests that Whiteness on its own (phenotypically, that is) was no guarantee of privilege. And it raises many questions for which we have little evidence about how common circumstances, family, and kinship gave rise to common outlooks and a shared identity.

Under slavery in Jamaica, then, only the legally free, elite Blacks of mixed origins could benefit from the opportunity to enjoy the "wages of whiteness."[53] The few people of mixed origins who rose in the social and economic hierarchy did not constitute a challenge to the racial basis of the system, which held to the distinctions between all Whites and all people of color. This was because while Whites believed there were significant differences between Blacks and people of mixed origins, they regarded "miscegenation" with repugnance, and they always saw fundamental differences between themselves and all people of color. Furthermore, this was possible in large part because the social context of Jamaica—the massive demographic imbalance in favor of enslaved Blacks (Whites were outnumbered more than eleven to one by people of color), which meant that Whites felt under constant threat—was conducive to it. Though there were many instances of people of African origin being treated in this way in the United States, the practice was far less frequent. In this respect, demography was decisive.[54]

Nor were Whites and Blacks homogeneous groups. Whites were "people from Europe or of patently unmixed European descent—in Jamaica, mainly English, Scots and Irish."[55] The more than one thousand wealthy Portuguese Jews in Jamaica faced discrimination, although they were considered White. Among the 30,000 Whites, Edward Brathwaite says, there were 1,100 planters, 5,000 merchants and professionals, 3,000 troops, and the rest, 21,000 or so, in various occupational positions, on plantations, in towns, on the wharves.[56] Europeans were thus differentiated by nationality, religion, and class, and the vast majority of them did not own enslaved persons.[57] This fact immediately poses the question, how did the minority of planters keep the allegiance of the majority of Whites in a system that permitted the latter group limited wealth and power? The short answer is that they were rewarded with the wages of Whiteness, wages that included ideology, psychology, and material gain. The wages of Whiteness were racialized purity. Poor Whites were promised the opportunity to become rich, because only they, by virtue of their White skin, could become plantation owners. That is, you may be poor, but at least you're pure, and because you're pure, you will soon be rich. This was an opportunity denied to those who, by virtue of African ancestry, were not pure. There is a Jamaican folk expression, often found in reggae music, that says, "A promise is a comfort to a fool!" The promise of richness was such a comfort because poor Whites were not soon rich; more often they were soon dead (from malaria and other tropical diseases), or soon gone (absconded to the United States in search of better opportunities for landownership), or remained poor until their dying days.

Given that the enslaved greatly outnumbered Whites, Whites found it necessary to manipulate divisions between Blacks and Blacks of mixed origins. Powerful Whites offered the latter better jobs, allowed them to live in certain areas, encouraged them to distance themselves from the former.[58] Whites separated legally free Blacks and people of mixed origins into distinct militia companies (despite the absence of formal legal distinctions), a measure designed to promote maximum rivalry.[59] They offered those who were closest in phenotypical appearance to themselves the opportunity to pass for White. White men married women of mixed origins, especially those who were mustefinos, or more distant from African ancestry.[60] Among the enslaved, they encouraged status distinctions. Long felt that the distinctions between mixed and unmixed Blacks should be promoted at all levels, so that there could be three ranks of men: Whites at the top, Blacks of mixed origins in the middle, Blacks at the bottom. If Blacks of mixed origins could be retrieved "from profound ignorance," he said, and afforded "instruction in Christian morals and . . . a regular apprenticeship to artificers and tradesmen," then they would become "orderly subjects and faithful defenders of the country."[61] Many other Whites promoted similar views in the final decades of slavery.[62] In these various ways they encouraged and rewarded the identification and persistence of color differences among those of mixed and unmixed African ancestry. More generally, Whites in power encouraged and rewarded Blacks of mixed origins for embracing Whiteness—that is, speaking, acting, behaving, and dressing like Whites in power and supporting the political and social status quo of slavery. Usually, opportunities and rewards were more forthcoming for the children of wealthy planters, in keeping with the patriarchal system, but most could benefit.

Restrictions and constraints on opportunities for legally free people of color often changed as a result of changing circumstances (e.g., the threat or actuality of revolt or of invasion) or pressures from legally free people of color themselves. For example, after the 1760 slave rebellion on the island a series of laws were introduced that not only imposed stricter constraints on the enslaved but also restricted the rights of free people of color.[63] Similar actions were taken at other historical junctures, particularly at the start of the nineteenth century, when the legally free Browns were pushing for equality with Whites.[64] Legally free Blacks of mixed origins got full legal rights in the 1830s. Restrictions were occasionally rescinded, if powerful Whites felt it prudent due to pressure or fear, as in 1823 when many of the legal disabilities against free people of color were repealed. To take another example, between 1772 and 1796, there were special petitions granted to 90 "mustees," 245 "quadroons," 176 "mulattoes," and 1 "negro." But between 1802 and 1823 not a single one was granted, because of fear of foreign invasion and of the Haitian revolution.[65]

The changing contours of opportunity and privilege reflected the ambivalence Whites felt toward Blacks of mixed origins. While many felt that the growth of an intermediate group would benefit White control of the island, there were others who saw in such growth the seeds of revolt (in which Blacks of mixed origins were seen as spies for the enslaved) or the decline of slavery as an institution (given the stereotype that Blacks of mixed origins could not labor in the fields with the same endurance of Blacks). For example, in 1813, as a result of pressures from England and demands by free people of color, several restrictions on court evidence and deficiency were lifted. These restrictions and constraints were imposed even though many privileged legally free people of color were more educated than many Whites, had adopted European values, and had rejected links with the enslaved and with Africa.

What all this highlights is a context in which racialized identity (who was Black, Black of mixed origins, or White) was not a free-flowing consequence of natural or biological differences, or the unique domain of individual choice, but rather the consequence of social factors, social relationships, and collective decisions. In other words, racialized identity is a social relationship, not a characteristic of individuals or a consequence of individual decisions alone. Laws decided who was enslaved and who was legally free, who could be charged with rape and who could not, what the status of a child born to an enslaved person would be. Clearly, gender was central here, as White men maintained their patriarchal relationships. The identity of Blacks of mixed origins was highly influenced by the responses of those around them. If they were legally free, light-skinned, educated, and associated with Whites, then they might be accepted as White—but only with the approval and support of powerful Whites. However, if they were enslaved, worked in the fields, and maintained close relationships with their Black family members, then a Black identity was far more likely. Central to this is the fact that race and race mixture, Blackness and Whiteness, existed along a continuum rather than being divided into a binary system. In other words, there was no despotic dualism—no dualism that proclaimed all people of African ancestry as negro, no matter how far removed they might be from their African ancestry and no matter how close their phenotype might be to that associated with Europeans.

CONCLUSION

I have been concerned here with documenting the rich texture of the diverse experiences of different racialized populations, in order that we might understand their unique experiences in a far more comprehensive way. I have sought to challenge our current understanding and impressions of the historical record on people of mixed origins under slavery in Jamaica. I have highlighted the variety of circumstances in which they found themselves and the structural, institutional, and ideological factors that shaped their experiences. A greater appreciation of these variations and the factors that cause them is indispensable to a more complete understanding of the location, experiences, and attitudes of people of mixed origins and of those presumed to be of unmixed origins. I want such an understanding to help us to pose new questions and collect new evidence in order to arrive at a more complete picture.

STEPHEN A. SMALL

In Jamaica, I have argued, the extent of privilege and advantage enjoyed by Blacks of mixed origins has been exaggerated, the varied means through which such privilege was secured have been misunderstood, and the fact that large numbers of Blacks of mixed origins remained in desperate circumstances has been neglected. I argue that the diverse institutional structures of slavery—demographic ratios, plantation size, the work processes associated with different crops, and ideologies of White racism—did not allow for the magnitude of unfettered privilege for Blacks of mixed origins suggested in most of the literature and in much popular culture. The most successful Blacks of mixed origins were a minuscule group who had White fathers who actively supported them and who helped one another through collective efforts. The majority of Blacks of mixed origins remained enslaved and in circumstances similar to those of Blacks believed to be "pure African"—working in the fields, sharing kin networks, and abandoned by their White fathers (if they had a White father at all). And even if they had jobs in domestic service, they faced particular problems of constant vigilance by Whites and incessant work routines, and, if women, they were subject to sexual abuse. Whether enslaved or legally free, Whites often encouraged and sought to entrench divisions between Blacks and Blacks of mixed origins, offering rewards and punishments as they saw appropriate. Such rewards were more forthcoming for the children of wealthy planters, in keeping with the patriarchal system. By exploring the contours of racialized mixture and Whiteness among the elite, legally free Blacks of mixed origins in Jamaica, we can see how racialized identity in general and Whiteness in particular are not characteristics of Europeans or of a self-defined in-group; rather, they arise from relationships between groups as well as between individuals. They are organized in routinized ways that preclude exclusively individual decisions.

What happened in Jamaica was common across the British Caribbean and across the United States.[66] In the Caribbean, Blacks of mixed origins experienced a variety of circumstances: the majority remained enslaved and often in dire circumstances; a minority were successful, because they had close family kinship to powerful Whites and embraced the status quo and White values. In the United States, Blacks and Blacks of mixed origins were differentiated from one another: the majority remained enslaved, often in dire circumstances; and the successful ones—those in New Orleans, Charleston, and Richmond—

maintained close relationships with powerful Whites.[67] There were no common circumstances shared by all or most people of mixed origins. People with known African ancestry could become legally and socially White but only if they were legally free, had high social status and wealth, were phenotypically similar to Whites, and adopted the social and behavioral patterns of powerful Whites. Nor were these individual decisions alone; the state introduced or withdrew status at its own choosing, opportunities for entrance into White society were severely restricted by gender and class, and racist ideology prevailed. At the same time, people of color worked collectively to circumvent or subvert state power and hegemony. Although individuals certainly exercised choices, they did not do so in circumstances of their own choosing. I have sought to emphasize the systemic and institutionalized patterns of these processes under slavery, and to suggest that any analysis of race mixture will be seriously deficient if it focuses only on a minority of people of mixed origins, if it focuses on the individual level and individual choices alone or primarily, and if it fails to locate intermediate racialized populations in a broader context of racialization.

NOTES

1. The difference between "racial" and "racialized" is not merely semantic; rather, it reflects a conceptual framework of fundamentally different assumptions. I prefer to use the term "racialized" because it rejects the notion that there are real biological races, and racial identities associated with them, and it highlights the active, always-in-process character of how identities called Black, White, Asian, and Latino are socially constructed and always in flux. For details, see Stephen Small, *Racialized Barriers: The Black Experience in the United States and England in the 1980s* (London: Routledge, 1994); Robert Miles, *Racism* (London: Routledge, 1989).

2. Orlando Patterson, *The Sociology of Slavery* (Kingston: Sangsters Book Stores, 1973).

3. In place of the conceptually misleading term "mixed-race," I prefer "Blacks of mixed origins," which refers to all persons who are known to have some African ancestry but who are not believed to be of exclusively African origin. For an elaboration of the concepts of race and race mixture, see Stephen Small, "Concepts and Terminology in Representations of the Atlantic Slave

Trade," *Museum Ethnographers Journal* (December 1994): 1–14. As can be seen from other chapters in this volume, the language and terminology for describing people of mixed origins remains highly variable. For details of the system in Jamaica, see Patterson, *Sociology of Slavery;* Edward Brathwaite, *The Development of Creole Society in Jamaica, 1770–1820* (Oxford: Clarendon Press, 1971).

4. Edward Long, *The History of Jamaica* (1774), 321; James M. Phillipo, *Jamaica: Its Past and Present State* (London, 1843), 144. See also Gad Heuman, *Between Black and White: Race, Politics and the Free Coloreds in Jamaica, 1792–1865* (Westport, Conn.: Greenwood, 1981), 16.

5. The book is tentatively entitled *Inside the Matrix of Miscegenation: Blacks of Mixed Origins under Slavery in Jamaica and Georgia in the Nineteenth Century,* forthcoming, New York University Press, 2004. For an introduction to the broad theoretical and conceptual issues covered, see Stephen Small, "Racial Group Boundaries and Identities: People of 'Mixed-Race' in Slavery across the Americas," *Slavery and Abolition* 15, no. 3 (December 1994): 17–36.

6. It is misleading to call people of color who were not enslaved "free," as if they had the same civil and social rights as White people. Their rights were legally and socially curtailed at all times. I use the term "legally free" in preference to "free" to mark their difference in legal status from those who were enslaved and their difference in social status from Whites, who enjoyed all the rights and privileges of freedom.

7. The notion "slave master" suggests an uncritical acceptance of the status of the enslaved person and of the person who had enslaved him or her. I prefer the term "master-enslaver," which suggests a more active relationship, and one under constant tension and negotiation.

8. The "one-drop rule" refers to the practice of treating anyone with any African ancestry, that is, anyone with a single drop of Black blood, as if they were "negro." See Joel Williamson, *"New People": Miscegenation and Mulattoes in the United States* (Baton Rouge: Louisiana State University Press, 1995). Tannenbaum maintained that in Brazil "both negro and mulatto had access to the culture and a role in social life unknown in the United States and an acceptance unthinkable in the American scene." Harris argued that because they recognized the threat of slave insurrections "the white slave-owners had no choice but to create a class of free half-castes." Degler argued that "[i]n Brazil the mulatto is not a Negro, whereas in the United States he is." Frank Tannenbaum, *Slave and Citizen: The Negro in the Americas* (New York: Knopf, 1947); Marvin Harris, *Patterns of Race in the Americas* (New York: Walker, 1964); Carl N. Degler, *Neither Black nor White: Slavery and Race Relations in Brazil and the United States* (New York: Macmillan, 1971). See also David W. Cohen and Jack P. Greene, eds., *Neither Slave nor Free: The Freedmen of African Descent in the Slave Societies of the New World* (Baltimore: Johns Hopkins University Press, 1972).

9. See Winthrop Jordan, *White over Black: American Attitudes towards the Negro, 1550–1812* (Chapel Hill: University of North Carolina Press, 1968); Mavis Campbell, *The Dynamics of Change in a Slave Society: A Sociopolitical History of the Free Coloureds of Jamaica, 1800–1865* (Rutherford, N.J.: Fairleigh Dickinson University Press, 1976).

10. See Jordan, *White over Black*. See also the movies *Get on the Bus* (1996) and *Sankofa* (1997).

11. These facts have been acknowledged in some of the literature, usually in passing, but I want to incorporate them more fully into this analysis. For example, see Douglas Hall, "Jamaica," in Cohen and Greene, eds., *Neither Slave nor Free*, 193–213

12. Bryan Edwards, *The History, Civil and Commercial, of the British Colonies in the West Indies* (London: J. Stockdale, 1794); Long, *History of Jamaica;* W. J. Gardner, *A History of Jamaica* (New York: Appleton & Company, 1909).

13. Data are from Barry Higman, *Slave Population and Economy in Jamaica, 1807–1834* (Jamaica: University Press of the West Indies, 1995), 16.

14. L. J. Ragatz, *The Fall of the Planter Class in the British Caribbean, 1763–1833* (New York, 1928).

15. George W. Roberts, *The Population of Jamaica* (Cambridge: Conservation Fund of the University Press, 1957); Brathwaite, *Development of Creole Society;* Higman, *Slave Population and Economy.*

16. Returns to the Registration of Slaves, 1817, Spanish Town Archives, Spanish Town, Jamaica. See also Higman, *Slave Population and Economy,* 256.

17. Higman, *Slave Population and Economy,* 256.

18. The best data indicate that 58 percent of enslaved Blacks of mixed origins had a White father. Birth records for legally free people of color indicate that most of them had two parents of color. See Higman, *Slave Population and Economy.*

19. J. B. Moreton, *Manners and Customs in the West India Islands* (London, 1790).

20. Ibid., 123.

21. Winthrop Jordan, "'American Chiaroscuro': The Status and Definition of Mulattoes in the British Colonies," *William and Mary Quarterly* 19 (1962): 198.

22. Returns to the Registration of Slaves, 1817, Spanish Town Archives, Spanish Town, Jamaica. The four parishes were St. Elizabeth, St. James, Trelawny, and Westmoreland.

23. These included Buffon and others. We must be skeptical of calling them "scientists" because they lacked the training, resources, or rigor of scientists of today. See Stephen Jay Gould, *The Mismeasure of Man* (Harmondsworth: Penguin, 1984).

24. Michael Banton, *The Idea of Race* (London: Tavistock, 1977).

25. See Long, *History of Jamaica*.

26. Ibid; Edwards, *The History;* Moreton, *Manners and Customs*.

27. For a critique of this language, see Small, "Concepts and Terminology,"

28. Samuel J. Hurwitz and Edith F. Hurwitz, "A Token of Freedom: Private Bill Legislation for Free Negroes in Eighteenth-Century Jamaica," *William and Mary Quarterly* 24.3 (1967): 423–31.

29. Hall, "Jamaica"; Campbell, *Dynamics of Change;* Heuman, *Between Black and White*.

30. Ibid.

31. Hurwitz and Hurwitz, "A Token of Freedom," 425.

32. Phillipo, *Jamaica*, 145. See also Hall, "Jamaica," 205.

33. Long, *History of Jamaica*, 323.

34. See Brathwaite, *Development of Creole Society*.

35. Sheila Duncker, "The Free Coloured and Their Fight for Civil Rights in Jamaica, 1800–30" (M.A. thesis, University of London, 1960). See also David Brion Davis, *The Problem of Slavery in Western Culture* (Ithaca, N.Y.: Cornell University Press, 1966).

36. Campbell, *Dynamics of Change*.

37. Heuman, *Between Black and White*, 10.

38. Campbell, *Dynamics of Change*, 57.

39. M. G. Lewis, *Journal of a West Indian Proprietor* (London, 1834), 154.

40. Ibid.

41. Campbell, *Dynamics of Change*, 57. See also Hall, "Jamaica," 205.

42. Lewis, *Journal*, 87.

43. Old Montpelier Estate Account book, cited in Higman, *Slave Population and Economy*, 210; Michael Craton and James Walvin, *A Jamaican Plantation: A History of Worthy Park, 1670–1970* (London, 1970).

44. Higman, *Slave Population and Economy*.

45. Brathwaite, *Development of Creole Society*, 121.

46. Ragatz, *Fall of the Planter Class*, 33.

47. J. Stewart, *An Account of Jamaica and Its Inhabitants* (London 1808), 173–74.

48. Michael Craton, *Searching for the Invisible Man* (Cambridge, Mass.: Harvard University Press, 1978), 250.

49. Long, *History of Jamaica*, 332.

50. Ibid.

51. Mary Seacole, *The Wonderful Adventures of Mrs. Mary Seacole in Many Lands*, ed. Z. Alexander and A. Dewjee (Bristol: Falling Wall Press, 1984; orig. pub. 1887).

52. Patterson, *Sociology of Slavery*, indicates that incest was rampant among the Spanish before the British arrived.

53. See David R. Roediger, *The Wages of Whiteness: Race and the Making of the American Working Class* (London: Verso, 1991).

54. See Ira Berlin, *Slaves without Masters* (New York: Knopf, 1974). The practice varied considerably across the United States.

55. Brathwaite, *Development of Creole Society,* 105.

56. Given the lack of a census until after slavery was abolished, estimates of the White population necessarily vary. For a discussion, see Roberts, *Population of Jamaica;* Higman, *Slave Population and Economy.*

57. See estimates in Long, *History of Jamaica.*

58. Campbell, *Dynamics of Change.*

59. Heuman, *Between Black and White,* 27; Campbell, *Dynamics of Change,* 44.

60. Gad Heuman, "White over Brown over Black: The Free Coloureds in Jamaica Society during Slavery and after Emancipation," *Journal of Caribbean History* 14 (1981): 46–69.

61. Long, *History of Jamaica,* 333.

62. Heuman, "White over Brown over Black."

63. Ibid.

64. Fernando Henriques, *Children of Conflict: A Study of Interracial Sex and Marriage* (New York: Dutton, 1975), 104.

65. Hall, "Jamaica," 201.

66. Patterns were different in South America; in many nations the majority of people of mixed origins were legally free. See Degler, *Neither Black nor White.*

67. For the Caribbean, see Cohen and Greene, *Neither Slave nor Free;* for the United States, see Berlin, *Slaves without Masters.* Also see Michael P. Johnson and James L. Roark, *Black Masters: A Free Family of Color in the Old South* (New York: Norton, 1984).

PART 2

Anomalies in the Racial Binary

4

NOT COLOR BUT CHARACTER

*Alice Dunbar-Nelson's
Uncompleted Argument*

HANNA WALLINGER

In a 1904 article in the *Voice of the Negro* Nannie H. Burroughs (1879–1961), prominent African American clubwoman, journalist, and public lecturer, treated the topic of intraracial color prejudice harshly. In the article, "Not Color but Character," Burroughs accused many of her race of having "colorphobia as badly as the white folk have Negrophobia."[1] Her accusation was directed mainly against the colored man who preferred to marry a light-colored girl: "The white man who crosses the line and leaves an heir is doing a favor for some black man who would marry the most debased woman, whose only stock in trade is her color, in preference to the most royal queen in ebony."[2] She was very direct: "The man who puts color as the first requisite in his choice of an associate invariably gets nothing but color, but the man who puts character first, always gets a woman."[3] Her hope lay in the abandonment of this color prejudice: "Let character, and not color, be the first requisite to admission into any home, church or social circle, and a new day will break upon ten million people."[4]

From Burroughs's standpoint the positions were clear-cut: If you were not White by legal or social definition, your solidarity must extend to all other non-White people. She was probably motivated to make her statement about colorphobia by the many cases in turn-of-the-century and early-twentieth-century society in which light-colored African Americans formed their own "blue vein societies" or "upper 400" or other associations that restricted access to African Americans of light color, good education, wealth, or prominent family background. Despite the many attempts to define race along biological and scientific lines, real-life racial identity has always been much more complicated. Evelyn B. Higginbotham defined race in allegiance with gender and class as "a social construction predicated upon the recognition of difference and signifying the simultaneous distinguishing and positioning of groups vis-à-vis one another."[5] She brought into consideration the power constructions deriving from racial identification when she said that "race is a highly contested representation of relations of power between social categories by which individuals are identified and identify themselves."[6] Whereas Burroughs called for solidarity based on race and not on any other possible category, such as class, region, or gender, Higginbotham correlated her experience with a larger theoretical explanation: "Race not only tends to subsume other sets of social relations, namely, gender and class, but it blurs and disguises, suppresses and negates its own complex interplay with the very social relations it envelops. It precludes unity within the same gender group but often appears to solidify people of opposing economic classes. Whether race is textually omitted or textually privileged, its totalizing effect in obscuring class and gender remains."[7]

Race, class, and gender were thus for Higginbotham social constructions that helped to form group identities but did not automatically function as such when one or the other of the differentiating factors were not clearly definable, outside an accepted norm or category.[8] How did the sort of criticism that Nannie Burroughs uttered affect a woman who was rather light-colored and of mixed racial origin and who was married to a darker-skinned man? What problems did she encounter when she was accused of trying to pass but identified herself closely with African American society? This is the situation confronted by Alice Dunbar-Nelson, one of the few early-twentieth-century authors articulate about colorphobia from the standpoint of the light-colored woman. She was born Alice Ruth Moore in 1875 in New Orleans to a mixed, mainly Creole family and married the much darker Paul Laurence Dunbar in 1898. The couple separated in

1902, but there was no divorce. Dunbar died in 1906. In 1916 Alice Moore Dunbar married the journalist Robert J. Nelson, a marriage that lasted until her death in 1935.

Dunbar-Nelson addressed the issue of passing and the intraracial color prejudices in her essays, her diary, some plays, and some of her later short stories; her first two volumes of short stories, *Violets and Other Tales* (1895) and *The Goodness of St. Rocque and Other Stories* (1899), and most of her poetry treated this topic in a more oblique manner. The color question was also prominent, at least to outside observers, in her short and stormy marriage to Dunbar, whose fame as a writer eclipsed hers. It is interesting to note that her diary as well as her later short stories and plays remained largely unpublished in her lifetime. I want to argue that her private acts of passing, as they are recorded in the diary, and her most prominent statement about herself as a light-colored woman in her essay "Brass Ankles Speaks" have to be seen as conscious acts of crossing the color line that were relatively free from feelings of guilt and betrayal. The issue that I address here is that although racial thinking determined the public utterances and creative writing of many prominent African Americans—Charles Chesnutt, Wallace Thurman, Langston Hughes, Hallie E. Queen, and Josephine and Senator Blanche Bruce, in addition to Dunbar-Nelson—it did not determine their personal lives to an exclusive degree.

On September 6, 1921, Alice Dunbar-Nelson bought orchestra seats for a matinee in the Globe theater in Atlantic City for herself, her niece Elizabeth, and her stepdaughter, Ethel. When she approached the ticket taker, she felt a pounding in her throat: "Suppose he should not let us take our seats? Suppose the ticket seller had sold the seats to me thinking I was white, and seeing Elizabeth and Ethel should make a scene. I choked with apprehension, realized that I was invoking trouble and must not think destructive things, and went on in. Nothing happened. How splendid it must be never to have any apprehension about one's treatment any where?"[9] This incident is one of several recorded in her diary that reflect the attitude of Dunbar-Nelson, who was easily able to pass as White, about the convenience of occasionally crossing the color line. The pleasure might be marred by anxiety and apprehension, but in most cases the advantages, better seats in the theater and a more convenient mode of transportation, outweighed the fear of detection. She wrote about her sister Leila "travelling au fait" while her daughter Pauline "gave her away by running up the gang plank kissing her in full view of the horrified passengers, who probably thought the brown skin young woman very impertinent to be kissing the white lady."[10] She wrote in a matter-of-fact tone about Leila, Pauline, and herself trying to get lunch in Philadelphia: "Go to Horn and Hardart's on Market opposite 16th. Are not served. Sit and wait—no one comes to take our order. Go to the Roadside where a honky-tonky band is playing and get a sandwich and coffee for Leila and coffee for Polly and me."[11] Frequently she referred to Jim Crow laws that enforced racial segregation in public transportation, education, performance halls, eating places, and so on. She mentioned, for example, a segregated boat ride—"It was lovely on a boat J[im] C[row] notwithstanding"—or cited the fact she "did not go J.C."[12] Gloria T. Hull, editor of Dunbar-Nelson's diary, explained "that she indulged in this bit of occasional 'passing' for white for the traveling convenience."[13] Later Dunbar-Nelson said that she did "get by" at a beauty parlor and so could record: "Nice place. Nice girls. Beauty problem solved."[14]

Dunbar-Nelson was aware of her privileged position as a light-colored African American and recorded with commiseration and bitterness her friend Edith's attempt to attend a performance at the Little Theatre in Philadelphia: "Edith did not get into the Little Theatre. They drew the [color] line on her. I shall not recommend any more theatres to her; every time I do, she has an uncomfortable experience. Poor kid! She does have the rottenest times!"[15] Once she commented on her friend Edna's decision not to go on a boat ride: "I don't blame her. In that aggregation of blondes and high browns, she would have looked like a fly in a flour barrel."[16]

With the publication of three volumes of Dunbar-Nelson's work in the Schomburg series, Nineteenth-Century Black Women Writers, under the expert editorship of Gloria T. Hull, and with the personal record of part of her career in *Give Us Each Day: The Diary of Alice Dunbar-Nelson,* also edited by Hull, a comprehensive evaluation of her writing is now possible. Critics tend to point out an ambivalence in Dunbar-Nelson's writing between her private and her public selves. I would say that this ambivalence has to be seen as the necessary result of the nation's equivocal attitude toward color: the one-drop rule rendered it virtually impossible to recognize race from outward appearance and led to great difficulties for those whose lives and appearances did not correspond to clear-cut categories. What has been seen as two conflicting attitudes in the private and public utterances of Dunbar-Nelson must be judged as inevitable and unavoidable parts of one personality at a time when social forces and individual preferences dictated a clash between private life and public performance. It is an uncompleted argument because, as she could not publish most of her thinking on this subject, there is little recorded response to her, and an argument needs some proof or rebuttal to be effective.

Throughout the diary Dunbar-Nelson conveys the feeling that she enjoyed the moments of occasional passing and refused to put too much emphasis on them. However, she felt a need to record and comment on them. Her passing was restricted mainly to transportation, eating places, and performance halls, the major areas in which segregation went hand in hand with severe personal inconvenience. In most other areas of her life, she never seriously considered her place in the African American community. Although her mother objected to her marriage to the much darker Dunbar and old Mrs. Dunbar was not overly happy about the union, Alice Dunbar-Nelson never regretted their marriage on the grounds of color differences.[17]

In two stories, "The Decision," written between 1902 and 1909, and "No Sacrifice," written between 1928 and 1931, Dunbar-Nelson fictionalized her marriage to Dunbar. Neither of the stories was published during her lifetime, probably because they contained thinly disguised critiques of her late husband's alcoholism, tendency to violence, and womanizing. In "The Decision," the brilliant but vulgar Burt Courtland committed "a deed that even Marion [his wife] could not bear,"[18] and it was primarily the husband's love affair that alienated the couple in "No Sacrifice." The remarkable fact about both stories is the absence of a color problem in the relationship between the couples, Marion and Burt Courtland in "The Decision" and Aline and Gerald Kennedy in "No Sacrifice." One can argue, however, that Dunbar-Nelson left it out of these semiautobiographical stories because she did not want to touch on a delicate subject, but why, then, did she include references to Dunbar's alcohol and drug problems, his occasional brutality, and his extramarital affairs, all of them issues that were equally sensitive breaches of genteel behavior? It is class, or more clearly an upper-class ideal of marital fidelity, dedication to hard work, proper social behavior, and a distinguished outward appearance, more than race, that is at issue here. Hull argued that in the later short stories class functions as "a signifier for race,"[19] which introduces the enticing idea that for a writer of Dunbar-Nelson's age and time, it might have been easier to concentrate on class because it offered less obvious pitfalls. In both stories, Courtland/ Kennedy was presented as a gifted writer whose lionization led to a distorted view of reality, health problems, and an eventual breakdown. (The real Dunbar developed a lung condition and died of tuberculosis aggravated by lack of rest and proper treatment.)

In both stories, as in real life, the wife separated from the husband but did not ask for divorce; Marion Courtland inherited a large fortune, and Aline Kennedy became a professional woman and then inherited a fortune. In both cases the wife had to decide between the husband and the money. Twice Dunbar-Nelson envisioned her alter ego forsaking the fortune and staying with a husband who, a reformed rake, fell severely ill and needed her care. The relationship now was one in which the returned wife possessed the more powerful position. In real life, the couple separated, and after Paul's death, Alice remarried twice. She never gave up her first husband's name and was regarded as Paul's widow throughout her lifetime. This provided her with some income from lectures and readings but it did not help her own career as a writer. It can be assumed that her eventual reunion with the husband as portrayed in the stories represents a sort of wishful thinking that if she could start over again, she would find a way to reform him and live with him happily ever after.

It has to be emphasized that Alice Dunbar-Nelson did not see herself as a "tragic mulatto." In her diary there is no record that she was suffering only because of her color. Her one striking record of fear in her diary was reserved for concern about the future because of financial problems. When her salaried position at the American Friends Inter-Racial Peace Committee was about to end, she wrote: "Fear, fear, fear—it haunts me, pursues, dries my mouth, parches my lips and shakes my knees, nauseates me. Fear! And no money—yet."[20] Of course, we can argue that she had financial problems because of her race, but this would stretch the argument too far considering the dismal economic circumstances of the 1920s and early 1930s. Her frequent references to depression centered on these financial worries, her health problems, her longing for a decent home, her occasional failure to deliver a successful lecture, and her inability to "produce literature" and then to publish what she had managed to write despite a lack of time and encouragement. In contrast, her record of high times centered on travels, moments of happiness with her third husband, Bobbo, and, most prominently, her friendship and close relationship with women. I do not see the problem of color as the tragedy of her life but rather the fact that she was old and in ill health when wealth finally came to her through her husband's well-paying position. Now that she could afford a congenial lifestyle she had no time left to enjoy it.

In many documented cases, light skin color afforded "greater access to wealth, power, privilege, and prestige."[21] The case of Alice Dunbar-Nelson proves that this did not happen automatically. Throughout her life, Dunbar-Nelson craved the attributes of affluence, but she could not achieve them. Her family background, her education, her gifts as teacher and writer—all seemed to predestine her to wealth, privilege, and prestige. Several facts of her life and individual choices, however, prevented her rise in society. First, there was a rumor about her birth that hinted at illegitimacy,[22] and, in addition, the Moores were rather poor—a setback to the accepted notion of class. Second, she married the much darker and also very poor Paul Laurence Dunbar, a choice that did not always meet with understanding, just as her occasional acts of passing must not have done. This was a setback to the accepted notion of race. Third, there were hints at homosexual tendencies, which were a setback to the notion of gender. Together, these facts led, at times, to bitterness, despair, and depression. Taking class, race, and gender as social constructions, as Higginbotham suggested, Dunbar-Nelson did not fit neatly into any of the accepted categories.

Dunbar-Nelson's is the rare case of an early-twentieth-century African American writer whose diary and, thus, private thoughts are available. In most other cases, scholars are restricted to published autobiographies or other published material. In many other prominent writers, a similar dichotomy between public and private writings can be detected. For example, Helen Chesnutt wrote about her father's mostly public life, quoting at length from letters he wrote and received, but she offered the reader a view of Charles Chesnutt that was carefully filtered through the loving and uncritical eyes of a daughter. Chesnutt was first of all associated with the development of the stereotype of the "tragic mulatto." Like many other writers, Chesnutt felt he had to portray the tragic aspects of a character, such as Rena Walden in *The House behind the Cedars* (1900), who could not reconcile the dichotomy between her White exterior and her identification as a Black woman. Like many other heroes and heroines, she died desolate, in despair, and lacking a positive view of herself.

When Chesnutt sent the story that was later to become this novel to *Century Magazine,* he received a letter from George Washington Cable, in which Cable said that Richard Watson Gilder, editor of the magazine, found the story's sentiment "amorphous." It should be noted that Chesnutt was corresponding with a writer famous for his Southern stories depicting quaint Creole figures, the kind of depictions that Dunbar-Nelson well knew and reacted against. Chesnutt responded to Gilder, "I suspect that my way of looking at these things is 'amorphous' not in the sense of being unnatural, but unusual. There are a great many intelligent people who consider the class to which Rena and Wain belong as unnatural."[23] Chesnutt felt he, of mixed-race origin himself, had to defend this class against stereotypes. He also felt he had to justify his own preference not to write about "Negroes[,] . . . blacks, [and the] full-blooded," whose "chief virtues have been their dog-like fidelity to their old master, for whom they have been willing to sacrifice almost life itself,"[24] the type of old-fashioned and loyal African American that peopled much of Cable's fiction. Chesnutt remained faithful to the other, amorphous type that he saw as unpopular at his time.

Like Dunbar-Nelson, Chesnutt dropped out of the public limelight after 1905 and was unable to get his work published. And yet what Helen Chesnutt remembered about her father was by no means the prototype of a tragic man who suffered only because he was a person of mixed race. In a 1917 episode, for example, the entire family was sitting in a restaurant in Gettysburg when the son suddenly started to speak French: "Edwin explained in French that when the hostess had seated them, the manager had appeared on the far side of the room and after some discussion was bearing down on them. They were very much shocked, for they had not had this particular kind of experience before. But they rose to the occasion and were vivaciously conversing in French when the manager and hostess neared the table. That was enough! The relief on the woman's face was comical."[25] Here is a recorded incident of passing that is devoid of feelings of guilt or shame. In much of his writing, however, Chesnutt chose to point out the tragic aspects of passing.

A light-colored woman who spoke up for herself and recorded having suffered from the prejudice of her contemporaries was rare. Alice Dunbar-Nelson left one of the few accounts of this. In "Brass Ankles Speaks," she pointed out color distinctions in the public school she attended from age six to twelve that went so far that she was vaccinated against her will when the teacher would not grant the exemption her mother had requested. In the private school she attended after recovering from the long illness contracted after this vaccination, she felt more at ease. But even there she was rebuffed. For example, she fell in love with a brilliant, very dark boy who, she recalls, "would not demean himself by walking with a mere golden butterfly."[26] Later, as a public school teacher and as a student in the North, she was confronted with subtle insinuations that she tried to set herself apart from other African Americans in her choice of housing, churches, and associates and that she treated darker children unfairly. Dunbar-Nelson recalled ridiculous situations: on train rides she was put off the Jim Crow cars because she looked White, yet she was refused food in the dining car because the colored waiters "'tipped off' the white stewards."[27]

She wanted to publish "Brass Ankles Speaks" anonymously. But her editor refused to do so, and it remained in the closet. One of the reasons for its refusal was her frankness about unfair treatment and lack of solidarity: "I have been turned down by my own race far more often than many a brown-skinned person has been similarly treated by the white race. I have been snubbed and ostracized with subtle cruelties that I am safe to assert have hardly been duplicated by the experiences of dark people in their dealings with Caucasians."[28] "Brass Ankles Speaks" was written in 1929[29] when Dunbar-Nelson was working for the American Friends Inter-Racial Peace Committee, a job she obtained years after she was dismissed as a schoolteacher from Howard High School in Wilmington, Delaware, for being too radical. This was a very busy year in her life, one beset by financial problems that resulted from the loss of her salaried position as a schoolteacher. The essay is highly personal and reflects her anger and growing feeling of failure as a writer and journalist and what she calls "her loss of social touch."[30] Dunbar-Nelson, now fifty-four, had difficulty selling her stories. Sometimes her frequent lectures did not go well, as on January 7 of that year: "My talk on the 'Negro's Literary Reaction to American Life' apparently appreciated, but of course, they would want to hear dialect Dunbar [Dunbar's poetry was written in "Negro dialect"] at the end. Makes me sick."[31] She recorded that at a National Association for the Advancement of Colored People (NAACP) ball, she felt she was snubbed by several famous writers: "Find a curious selfishness on the part of the Jim Johnsons and the Walter Whites and have my usual loneliness in the crowd. Oh, so pitiful!"[32] Several times in her diary she wrote about being depressed and feeling the blues. All this certainly contributed to the bitter and accusing tone of the essay. It remained a private ventilation of her anger, barred from publication because it would not fare well with the public.

Despite her private misgivings, she remained an articulate spokeswoman for her race throughout her life. She was actively involved in the Federation of Colored Women's Clubs, the League of Colored Republican Women, Delta Sigma Theta Sorority, and other organizations. In many of her editorials and journalistic essays she berated racism, especially when it came from prominent White leaders. In an editorial for the Washington *Eagle* of October 26, 1928, she railed against the negative publicity engendered by accusations that presidential candidate Herbert Hoover had "call[ed] upon and danc[ed] with a colored woman."[33] When his assistant, George Akerson, denied the accusation by dubbing it "'the most indecent and unworthy statement in the whole of a bitter campaign,'"[34] Dunbar-Nelson responded in bitterness: "And in so doing he hurls the vilest of insults in the face of every Negro in the United States. He wipes mud in their teeth, and he utterly destroys whatever lingering belief in the decency of the Republican party might have been left in the mind of the Negro."[35]

More outspoken than other writers, Dunbar-Nelson addressed the schizophrenia that came easily to light-colored African Americans who were forever in between two races: "There are a thousand subtleties of refined cruelty which every fair colored person must suffer at the hands of his or her own people."[36] All these people, she said, "must bear the hatred of their own and the prejudice of the white race."[37] There was no easy way, it seems, to avoid being trapped one way or the other. To be fair, however, it has to be observed that

Dunbar-Nelson reserved her bitterest outbreaks against this unfair situation for her diary and clearly did not intend them to be published. She wrote, for example, in 1921 out of a mood of despair about the dire financial situation of her husband Bobbo's newspaper: "Then I got *mad. Mad.* I rose in my rage and I swore I *wouldn't* be beaten. The nasty bitter niggers have tried to ruin me. But I won't be downed. I rose and damned them all to hell and back again. I would live in this town and make the *Advocate* a success, and put Bobbo in a big position and make them all cringe and fawn to me yet."[38] On another occasion, in 1928, she ridiculed the usual "'cullud' affair": "Freebies as usual. My expenses. That's all. The older I grow and the more I do, the cheaper I get."[39]

Dunbar-Nelson also wrote about the humorous aspects of passing. For example, we get the sense that she and her colleagues at the Inter-Racial Peace Committee, most of whom were White, were playing a joke on a White visitor in 1928: "The little Quaker lady from the Swarthmore meeting came into the office and added considerably to the gayety of nations by her stringent objections to the Negro in general and Negroes in Quaker meetings in particular. Her aspersions and complaints could not have been more bitter if she had come from Georgia. 'I've had colored servants etc. etc.' We all had a good laugh after she had gone. If she had known I was colored she would have died."[40]

In modern terms, one can say that Dunbar-Nelson was not "politically correct" in her language. When she demanded race solidarity despite color and not because of it, she must have offended all those race leaders and concerned African Americans who felt that solidarity should first and foremost be extended to those who bore the burden of visible Blackness and were affected by discrimination in so many more ways than their light-colored contemporaries. In fact, she demanded of others that they put character over color, thus applying Nannie Burroughs's admonishment to all people, including light-colored women.

The more common interpretation of this admonition, however, came from writers such as Wallace Thurman. In his greatly successful novel, *The Blacker the Berry*, the heroine, Emma Lou, the dark child of a light-colored family, suffered immensely from imaginary and real discrimination at the hands of her lighter friends and family. Early in her life, after experiencing many unconscious acts of unfriendliness and discrimination, she was determined: "She would show all of them that a dark skin girl could go as far in life as a fair skin one, and that she could have as much opportunity and as much happiness. What did the color of one's skin have to do with one's mentality or native ability? Nothing whatsoever. If a black boy could get along in the world, so could a black girl, and it would take her, Emma Lou Morgan, to prove it."[41] As Therman B. O'Daniel said in his introduction to the 1970 reprint, the novel was successful but embarrassed many African Americans: "What irked them most of all was that one of their sacred principles had been violated—namely, that although a well-known, unbecoming and embarrassing racial problem might be privately admitted, it should never be publicly discussed."[42] This observation can be applied to Dunbar-Nelson's failed attempts to discuss this "unbecoming and embarrassing racial problem" of intraracial color prejudice. While Thurman's heroine was at least suffering and lonely, albeit rather silly, Dunbar-Nelson went further and spoke from the position of the privileged woman.

The sort of critique of colorphobia more typical of the time came from Langston Hughes, who saw the snobbery of the so-called better society from his point of view: "[T]he 'better class' Washington colored people, as they called themselves, drew rigid class and color lines within the race against Negroes who worked with their hands, or who were dark in complexion and had no degrees from colleges. These upper class colored people . . . were on the whole as unbearable and snobbish a group of people as I have ever come in contact with anywhere. They lived in comfortable homes, had fine cars, played bridge, drank Scotch, gave exclusive 'formal' parties, and dressed well, but seemed to me altogether lacking in real culture, kindness, or good common sense."[43] Hughes's statement would be a case in point to prove Higginbotham's theory that race often obscured class differences, because what Hughes mainly complained about were rich people who happened to be African American. Their failure to show "real culture, kindness, or good common sense" was more a sign of their upper-class status than their race. Hughes understood the kind of reservation people had about the depiction of characters such as in *The Blacker the Berry*. African Americans were especially sensitive about depictions of their race in books that Whites were likely to read: "They had seen their race laughed at and caricatured so often in stories like those by Octavus Roy Cohen, maligned and abused so often in books like Thomas Dixon's, made a servant or a clown always in the movies, and forever defeated on the Broadway stage, that when Negroes wrote books they wanted them to be books in which only good Negroes, clean and cultured and not-funny Negroes, beautiful and nice and upper class were presented."[44] As Dunbar-Nelson found out, the acceptable image also excluded intraracial critique.

Real-life experiences of colored people in the early twentieth century revealed the damage to a person's sense of belonging and feeling at ease from prejudice and discrimination. In the *Colored American Magazine*, Hallie E. Queen wrote an article entitled "I Am a College Negro Problem," which is one of many examples of the difficulties of making one's way through college as a colored person. Queen was not allowed to live in a house built for poorer students; she was not invited to festivities that involved a social gathering of both men and women. Queen also mentioned the several girls who "passed": "There was not absent from the university the small quota who bearing slight traces of Negro blood said nothing about their racial connections. I distinctly remember that I came into daily contact with a girl whom I knew to be colored, but who at the university was 'passing' as white. She was very popular and lived in the most exclusive society house."[45] Queen here addressed the remarkable social advantages open to African Americans light enough to pass.

In *Aristocrats of Color,* Willard B. Gatewood corroborated Dunbar-Nelson's experience by citing the life story of a prominent light-colored African American woman, Josephine Bruce (1852–1923), wife of Senator Blanche K. Bruce (1841–98). Josephine Bruce was an extraordinarily beautiful woman whose familial background and education distinguished her from most other African American families as to style, income, and color.[46] Gatewood used the careers of the Bruce family as exemplary of color distinctions. He argued that Josephine Bruce "epitomized the moral rectitude, polished manners, and social grace associated with the genteel lady at the turn of the century."[47] Yet even her very fair skin classified her: "No matter how fair her complexion or how completely she conformed to the image of an ideal Victorian lady, she was still a Negro, the wife of a black senator whose skin color was only a shade darker than hers."[48]

The Bruces were aware of the criticism directed at them for disdaining their poorer and darker contemporaries and failing to understand their problems. Despite all this, Josephine Bruce was a founding member of the Colored Women's League in 1892,[49] worked in numerous social clubs and racial uplift organizations, and was Lady Principal of Tuskegee Institute from 1899 to 1902. But when she applied for the presidency of the National Association of Colored Women (NACW) in 1906, "she, or rather her color, became the center of the only serious dispute at an otherwise harmonious convention, for opposition to her candidacy centered on the fairness of her skin."[50] Bruce withdrew her candidacy. Gatewood also emphasized that "complaints about the color consciousness of light-complexioned aristocrats surfaced regularly. The charge was that any drawing of the color line within the black community undermined racial unity and therefore weakened movements to combat the proliferation of restrictions and proscriptions."[51] Many educated and wealthy colored people with good family backgrounds would judge themselves by class rather than color, an attitude that regularly met with opposition in the media.

Josephine Bruce, Walter White, Jean Toomer, Charles Chesnutt, Mary Church Terrell, and the many others who could pass more or less easily often did so for the simple and practical reason that they could. Dunbar-Nelson was pragmatic about this: "[A] purely practical standpoint . . . is the real reason why the so-called 20,000 who 'pass' each year would tell you, if they dared be vocal. 'It was more comfortable to live as a white woman, to receive the homage paid a handsome white woman. . . . She could live more comfortably as a white woman, she could go where she chose, she could earn more money.' "[52] However, not all who could pass did so or wanted to. As Walter White said, "Large as is the number of those who have crossed the line, they form but a small percentage of those who might follow such an example but who do not."[53] In *Who Is Black?* James Davis wrote, "The pain of this separation, and condemnation by the black family and community, are major reasons why many or most of those who could pass as white choose not to. Loss of security within the minority community, and fear and distrust of the white world are also factors."[54] Dunbar-Nelson complained that many of her friends, meeting her on the street, automatically assumed that she was passing and did not talk to her: "I have had my friends meet me downtown in city streets and turn their heads away, so positive that I do not want to speak to them. Sometimes I have to go out of my way to pluck at their sleeves to force them to speak. If I do not, then it is reported around that I 'pass' when I am downtown—and sad is my case among my own kind then."[55]

All these people knew that passing involved some tangible and real risks. The fear of discovery, therefore, often outweighed the advantages. Many legal cases, most of them much publicized and commented on, prove this thesis. The Rhinelander case, for example, centered on the marriage of the prominent and rich Kip Rhinelander and Alice B. Jones, a mixed-race chambermaid, on October 14, 1924. A month after the wedding, Kip Rhinelander filed suit for annulment because he claimed that his wife had deceived him about her racial identity. For a good year the suit instigated controversy and commanded headlines. Alice Rhinelander even had to strip in court to show the color of her body. In 1925 the New York State Supreme Court jury "ruled that Alice Rhinelander had not deceived her husband."[56] There were more suits for separation later on the part of Alice Rhinelander, and she brought suit against her father-in-law for alienating her husband from her and for payments for the divorce in 1930. As Mark J. Madigan argued, the Rhinelander case "provided a ready context for the discussion of similar cases."[57] Nella Larsen, for example, referred to this case in her novel, *Passing*. And Dunbar-Nelson satirized the case in one of her serialized "From a Woman's Point of View" articles on January 2, 1926: "Now after the stench of the Rhinelander case has died down, we will have to carry the burden of owning the Artful Alice with her bared romance and still more bared back, who married a man so dumb that he thought a girl with a brown skin father, a black brother-in-law, and a golden body was a white woman. Though she repudiated her race, it must bear her on its aching shoulders."[58] Dunbar-Nelson here reminds us indirectly of the dire consequences of passing.

Werner Sollors mentions court cases in which couples were separated or weddings prevented because it was discovered that one of them was passing.[59] William E. Jackson, for example, a construction company owner, Columbia University graduate, and former member of the university's football team, was forced to describe himself as colored, although his fiancée, Helen Burns, a White woman, had urged him to say he was White. Immediately after this he was threatened by the Ku Klux Klan.[60] Even in 1982, as Samira Kawash reported, "Susie Guillory Phipps lost her suit against the Louisiana Bureau of Vital Records to change her racial classification from black to white. A 1970 state law defined anyone with at least ⅟₃₂ 'Negro blood' to be black. Under this law, Phipps' one slave ancestor made her legally black, even though she had been living all her 46 years as a white woman."[61] These legal cases highlight the real-life background of the innumerable accounts in fiction of passing, trying to pass, or concealing part of one's identity.

One more example might suffice to prove that Dunbar-Nelson thought about this matter in various ways. She never offered the easy way out, and she always claimed that life had to be accepted as it was. There was no possibility of escape, as Victor Grabert in her story "The Stones of the Village" or Allan in her play *Gone White* attempted to do by passing. Her story "The Pearl in the Oyster" began with the graduation of the light-colored Creole Auguste Picou and his dark friend Frank Boyer. Picou was persuaded by the dark-skinned Boyer, who was not an acceptable friend in the eyes of his family, to go to school at an "institution for the higher education of Negro youth,"[62] a move that met with a great deal of criticism in the Creole community. The graduation ceremony was a moment of high significance for the young people who harbored high hopes about their future careers. But as in other stories by Dunbar-Nelson and other writers, these hopes fell to pieces. Auguste Picou ended up in a billiard hall and soon came into contact with local politicians who did not know about his racial background. Picou began to see the advantages of passing, for example, taking privileged seats in the theatre. He married a light-colored Creole woman and moved uptown with her. He was extremely busy with political work, but she grew silent and unhappy because her downtown family rarely visited and her new friends were shallow and not interested in her. While for the husband, passing entailed a gain in social position, for the wife it meant a loss of security following on the severance of family ties. This gendered view of the subject was, however, not explored fully in this story.

When after the election Picou did not receive his just reward in the form of a government position, he and his wife decided to move back downtown, and he became a letter carrier. There he found that his friends and family deeply resented his "former defection"[63] and were bitter about his having now returned. Picou still wanted the proverbial pearl in the oyster, "power, political preferment, position, recognition,"[64] and was prepared to work hard for it. His attitude toward his own people became clear when he dropped the following racist remark, "'Better to be a king among dogs than a dog among kings.'"[65] He still passed when it suited him and retained much of his former disdain for African Americans. After the election was lost, he was dismissed from his position as a letter carrier and finally realized with "wonder and shame and resentment"[66] that he would have no future in that region of the United States. He decided to take his family west: "[W]e will go away somewhere where we are not known, and we will start life again, but whether we decide to be white or black, we will stick to it."[67] Their leaving repeats the common ending in most stories involving "tragic mulattoes": death or expatriation, usually in Europe.

Alice Dunbar-Nelson stayed it out in America, through difficult periods of public neglect, financial worries, and frustrating efforts to get published. Nannie Burroughs called for a consideration of the innate values of a person, not his or her outward appearance; Dunbar-Nelson wished for a fulfillment of this admonishment, although she looked at this problem in a way that was different from Burroughs. Dunbar-Nelson's argument had to remain fragmentary and uncompleted because of the simple fact that she could not resolve the central dichotomies of her time, a racial binary that put people into categories but neglected, as Higginbotham argued, class and gender distinctions. Of necessity, a writer such as Dunbar-Nelson, who was seen as in-between by others, saw herself as a complete, albeit complex human personality with a place in society that she occupied because of her family background, her education, her artistic gifts, and the individual choices in marital relationships. She was not more tragic than any other person whose innermost wishes were not fulfilled.

NOTES

1. Nannie H. Burroughs, "Not Color but Character," *Voice of the Negro* 1 (July 1904): 277.

2. Ibid.

3. Ibid., 278.

4. Ibid., 279.

5. Evelyn Brooks Higginbotham, "African-American Women's History and the Metalanguage of Race," *Signs* 17.2 (1992): 253.

6. Ibid.

7. Ibid., 255.

8. As many recent studies have shown, the fundamental issue at stake here is that of race itself, including Whiteness as a supposedly superior and non-questionable category. To adopt Toni Morrison's phrase, the "unspeakable things unspoken" challenged the established nature of progress, civilization, manhood, or virtue usually accepted as the privilege of the so-called dominant race. "Passing" in its broad sense of negotiating the boundaries between races, nations, classes, and occasionally even genders has come to stand for the unsettling state of modern-day life in general. See Toni Morrison, "Unspeakable Things Unspoken: The Afro-American Presence in American Literature," in *Criticism and the Color Line: Desegregating American Literary Studies*, ed. Henry B. Wonham (New Brunswick, N.J.: Rutgers University Press, 1996), 16–29. In addition to Wonham's collection, studies about passing, miscegenation, and mixed-race people have increased considerably over recent years. See, for example, G. Reginald Daniel, *More than Black? Multiracial Identity and the New Racial Order* (Philadelphia: Temple University Press, 2002); M. Giulia Fabi, *Passing and the Rise of the African American Novel* (Urbana: University of Illinois Press, 2001); Grace Elizabeth Hale, *Making Whiteness: The Culture of Segregation in the South, 1890–1940* (New York: Pantheon, 1998); Dana D. Nelson, *National Manhood: Capitalist Citizenship and the Imagined Fraternity of White Men* (Durham, N.C.: Duke University Press, 1998); Werner Sollors, *Interracialism: Black-White Intermarriage in American History, Literature, and Law* (New York: Oxford University Press, 2000); Paul R. Spickard, *Mixed Bloods: Intermarriage and Ethnic Identity in Twentieth-Century America* (Madison: University of Wisconsin Press, 1989).

9. Alice Dunbar-Nelson, *Give Us Each Day: The Diary of Alice Dunbar-Nelson* (New York: Norton, 1984), 69. This chapter is based on a paper presented at a conference of the Collegium for African American Research in Münster. It was published as "Alice Dunbar-Nelson and the Color Line," in *Black Liberation in the Americas*, ed. Fritz Gysin and Christopher Mullvey (Hamburg: Lit, 2001), 121–32.

10. Dunbar-Nelson, *Give Us Each Day*, 114.

11. Ibid., 237.

12. Ibid., 240, 354.

13. Ibid., 354.

14. Ibid., 430.

15. Ibid., 306f.

16. Ibid., 54.

17. See Violet Harrington Bryan, "Race and Gender in the Early Works of Alice Dunbar-Nelson," in *Louisiana Women Writers: New Essays and a Comprehensive Bibliography*, ed. Dorothy H. Brown and Barbara C. Ewell (Baton Rouge: Louisiana State University Press, 1992), 123.

18. Alice Dunbar-Nelson, "The Decision," in *The Works of Alice Dunbar-Nelson*, vol. 3, ed. Gloria T. Hull (New York: Oxford University Press, 1988), 199.

19. Gloria T. Hull, Introduction to *The Works of Alice Dunbar-Nelson*, 3 vols. (New York: Oxford University Press, 1988), xxxix.

20. Dunbar-Nelson, *Give Us Each Day*, 424.

21. G. Reginald Daniel, "Beyond Black and White: The New Multiracial Consciousness," in *Racially Mixed People in America*, ed. Maria P. P. Root (Newbury Park, Calif.: Sage, 1992), 337.

22. See Gloria T. Hull, *Color, Sex and Poetry: Three Women Writers of the Harlem Renaissance* (Bloomington: Indiana University Press, 1987), 34f.

23. Helen M. Chesnutt, *Charles Waddell Chesnutt: Pioneer of the Color Line* (Chapel Hill: University of North Carolina Press, 1952), 57. In his *House behind the Cedars*, Wain became "Walden."

24. Chesnutt, *Charles Waddell Chesnutt*, 57.

25. Ibid., 274.

26. Alice Dunbar-Nelson, "Brass Ankles Speaks," in *The Works of Alice Dunbar-Nelson*, 2:315.

27. Ibid., 320.

28. Ibid., 319.

29. See Hull, *Color, Sex and Poetry*, 101.

30. Dunbar-Nelson, *Give Us Each Day*, 283.

31. Ibid., 303.

32. Ibid., 313.

33. *The Works of Alice Dunbar-Nelson*, 2:278.

34. Ibid., 278.

35. Ibid., 279.

36. Dunbar-Nelson, "Brass Ankles," 320.

37. Ibid., 321.

38. Dunbar-Nelson, *Give Us Each Day*, 128; original emphasis.

39. Ibid., 224.

40. Ibid., 258.

41. Wallace Thurman, *The Blacker the Berry* (New York: Collier Books, 1970), 39.

42. Therman B. O'Daniel, Introduction to Thurman, *The Blacker the Berry*, x.

43. Langston Hughes, *The Big Sea: An Autobiography* (New York: Hill and Wang, 1984), 206f.

44. Ibid., 267.

45. Hallie E. Queen, "I Am a College Negro Problem," *Colored American Magazine* 17 (July 1909): 31.

46. See Willard B. Gatewood, *Aristocrats of Color: The Black Elite, 1880–1920* (Bloomington: Indiana University Press, 1990), 4.

47. Ibid., 37.

48. Ibid., 33.

49. See ibid., 143.

50. Ibid., 142.

51. Ibid., 50.

52. *The Works of Alice Dunbar-Nelson*, 2:248.

53. Walter White, "The Paradox of Color," in *The New Negro*, ed. Alain Locke (New York: Touchstone, 1992), 365f.

54. James F. Davis, *Who Is Black? One Nation's Definition* (University Park: Pennsylvania State University Press, 1991), 15.

55. Dunbar-Nelson, "Brass Ankles," 320.

56. Mark J. Madigan, "Miscegenation and the 'Dicta of Race and Class': The Rhinelander Case and Nella Larsen's *Passing*," *Modern Fiction Studies* 36, no. 4 (1990): 526.

57. Ibid., 528.

58. *The Works of Alice Dunbar-Nelson*, 2:108.

59. See Werner Sollors, *Neither Black nor White Yet Both: Thematic Explorations of Interracial Literature* (New York: Oxford University Press, 1991), 280f.

60. See Sollors, *Neither Black nor White Yet Both*, 507 n.125.

61. Samira Kawash, *Dislocating the Color Line: Identity, Hybridity, and Singularity in African-American Literature* (Stanford: Stanford University Press, 1997), 233, n.16.

62. "The Pearl in the Oyster," in *The Works of Alice Dunbar-Nelson*, 3:52. This story was published in the *Southern Workman* in 1900.

63. Ibid., 60.

64. Ibid.

65. Ibid., 61.

66. Ibid., 63.

67. Ibid., 64.

5

THE POWER OF BLACKNESS
Mixed-Race Leaders and the Monoracial Ideal

PAUL SPICKARD

Four of the most prominent African American political and cultural leaders of the last half of the nineteenth century and the first half of the twentieth—W. E. B. Du Bois, historian, sociologist, cofounder of the NAACP, editor of *The Crisis,* and pan-Africanist leader; Jean Toomer, herald of the Harlem Renaissance; Walter White, novelist and NAACP executive secretary; and Frederick Douglass, antislavery firebrand and African America's first national leader—had mixed racial ancestry, at least Black and White and perhaps also Native American. They were members of what one might call the "beigeoisie"— that coterie of light-skinned, multiracial people who formed an elite upper class within African American society in the generations after slavery.[1] All of them but Douglass might have passed for White had they chosen to do so. Instead, all—with the revealing exception of Jean Toomer—consistently chose to pass for Black. I use the phrase "pass for Black" purposely. Reginald Daniel, in chapter 2 of this volume and elsewhere, argues that passing was a strategy used by people of mixed ancestry to take advantage of their phenotypical ambiguity to acquire a measure of White privilege—to "pass" for White. That is the sense in which the term "passing" has ordinarily been used. But people of mixed ancestry who presented themselves in public as Black were passing, too.[2] This chapter is a meditation on why some multiracial people made the choice to adopt a Black social and political identity—to pass for Black—and what implications their choice has for the construction of race (at least, of Black and White) in this period in American history.[3]

A few matters should be clarified at the outset. One concerns the issue of choice. Often a choice is not entirely freely made. To what extent did these individuals choose a public racial identity, and to what extent was their choice constrained by circumstance? Passing for White may have been a choice, but it came with a cost. One had to be wealthy enough or desperate enough to move away from family and friends, or else risk exposure and collapse of the life one was attempting to build. One had to be psychologically strong enough or scarred enough to abandon a former identity, the comforts of kin, and familiar surroundings. One had to have the education or the skill or the luck to be able to make a living in the world of White people. Passing for Black was the choice dictated by the dominant racial ideology. The power of racial ideologies lies in their very ability to deny us absolutely free choices. Each of the persons discussed in this chapter made a choice to identify as Black. For some, this was an act with a substantial element of freedom; they could have made another choice. For others, the choice was constrained. In each case, I have examined the writings of the individual and the work of their biographers to try to ascertain the pattern in their choosing of public and private racial identities.

Second, it is important to note that there has been a long history of racial mixing in the United States. Several historians have observed that during the early colonial period there was more interracial mating than at any later time in American history. White slave masters took Black slave concubines, Black freemen married White women, and so forth. Such practices continued, often without widespread public acknowledgment, throughout the slave period.[4] Some have asserted that early in U.S. history the lines of race and class were not so rigid as they later became. For example, it has frequently been alleged that Alexander Hamilton was of mixed Black and White descent. Hamilton was born to a White mother, the product of an adulterous affair, on the West Indian island of Nevis in 1755. When Hamilton rose to the heights of government in the early years of the Republic, his political opponents alleged that his mother's paramour had been Black or mulatto in an attempt to discredit Hamilton in a White-dominated society, a difficult charge to refute given the blurred racial lines in the islands in the era of his birth. If indeed Hamilton had African ancestry, then he was a racially mixed person who reached the highest levels of society as White.[5]

Whatever the merits of the stories about Hamilton's parentage and however flexible was the racial system of the eighteenth century, it is clear that by the end of the nineteenth century the options afforded a multiracial person were more limited. Many authors have observed that there were places in the South under slavery where elements of racial mixedness were recognized.[6] Yet, as Joel Williamson argues convincingly, in the 1850–1915 period American society at large embraced that peculiarity, the one-drop rule (see chapter 2). To ensure racial hierarchy as slavery came under attack and was eclipsed, White people began to reckon as Black any person who had known African ancestry, no matter how remote, and free people of mixed race were pushed into an externally undifferentiated Black class. Williamson asserts:

> The period between 1850 and 1915 marked a grand changeover in race relations in America. . . . A long-running intolerance of miscegenation and mulattoes among whites in the upper South joined with the rising and crystallizing intolerance among whites in the lower South to exert tremendous pressures upon both whites and mulattoes. Whites who mixed found themselves abused and ostracized. Under heavy fire from a seemingly universal racism, the previous ambivalence of mulattoes toward both whites and blacks turned during the Civil War toward a steadily growing affinity with blacks. . . . [T]he engagement of mulattoes and blacks was firmly cemented, though obvious vestiges of a preference for lightness lingered for two or three generations. By the 1920s the great mass of mulattoes saw their destiny as properly united only with that of their darker brothers and sisters. They saw themselves as fusing with blacks and together forming a whole people in embryo. . . . Negroes accepted the blackness of the seemingly pure white . . . and of others strikingly light—they too accepted the one-drop rule.[7]

Over those decades, this binary, Black-White construction hardened and was a keystone of the ideology of White supremacy. The creation of the one-drop rule required a substantial assault on what might have been known about people's genealogies. The U.S. population, despite the monoracial labels attached to various groups, was in fact a mixed multitude, with a substantial amount of mixing between White and Black and between both of those and native peoples. But multiracial ancestry was a fact that White supremacists wanted to forget and one whose memory they strove to eradicate. The notion became entrenched, across the color line, that place in society was bound to race and that racial difference was timeless and immutable. Not only the European Americans who asserted dominance but also the people of African ancestry who were dominated by the system came to view it, not as a political construction, but as an unquestioned biological fact: White people were agreed by all to be unmixed; mixed people were deemed to be Black. This taking on of the dominant group's racial ideology by the subordinate people is an example of what Antonio Gramsci termed "hegemony"—domination so thorough that one knows not one is dominated but thinks it the natural order of things.[8]

Nearly all of the people who informed W. E. B. Du Bois's notion of the talented tenth and who populate Willard Gatewood's study of aristocrats of color fell into this category: Black-identified people of mixed European and African (and perhaps Native American) ancestry, many of whom could have passed for White had their Black ancestry not been known and had they chosen to do so.[9] This chapter makes a start at understanding how the *multiracial fact* (their ancestry) encountered the *monoracial fact* (their identity) in the lives and the minds of some such people, who were prominent Black intellectuals and political leaders.[10] Here, then, are their stories and some observations.

W. E. B. Du Bois

William Edward Burghardt Du Bois was one of the most famous African Americans of the dawn of the twentieth century and is the figure most admired by the past two generations of intellectuals. Du Bois was racially mixed, although the mixing had taken place some generations back. Du Bois's forebears were Africans, French Huguenots, and Hudson Valley Dutch. His father, Alfred, born in Haiti, was so light and smooth-haired as to be able to live as White.

In *Dusk of Dawn,* one of several autobiographies, Du Bois wrote fondly of his childhood in Great Barrington, Massachusetts, where his playmates were White, where he attended a White church, and where he was culturally "quite thoroughly New England," unconscious of race. "Living with my mother's people I absorbed their culture patterns and these were not African so much as Dutch and New England. The speech was an idiomatic New England tongue with no African dialect; the family customs were New England, and the sex mores."[11] In *The Souls of Black Folk,* he wrote that a schoolhouse snub by a White girl brought him to a sudden consciousness of his Blackness: "Then it dawned upon me with a certain suddenness that I was different from the others; or like, mayhap, in heart and life and longing, but shut out from their world by a vast veil. I had thereafter no desire to tear down that veil, to creep through; I held all beyond it in common contempt." He vowed to spend his life outdoing those who lived beyond.[12] When Du Bois, still a proud son of New England, applied for admission to Harvard College he was turned down. He went instead to Fisk University, a Black college in Nashville that then was mainly engaged in turning out teachers for Black schools in the rural South. Du Bois was one such teacher in his college summers. In other autobiographical writings Du Bois located the critical era of his development of a Black consciousness in his years at Fisk.[13]

Whenever Du Bois's Black monoracial consciousness emerged, his biographers described him as remaining in conflict about his racial identity even while he proclaimed his Blackness. Citing Rayford W. Logan and E. Franklin Frazier, two Du Bois disciples, David Levering Lewis wrote:

> Du Bois insisted . . . that he had embraced his racial identity only at Fisk. "Henceforward I was a Negro," Du Bois would proclaim, and then soar into a grand vision of his place in the race, knowing full well that Anglo-Saxon America was objectively blind by custom and law to intermediate racial categories. Logan always said that Du Bois's claim of belated racial self-discovery was a polemical contrivance to give greater punch to his writings about

race relations. To claim that his identity as a Negro was in some sense the exercise of an option, an existential commitment, was to define Willie's celebration of and struggle for his people as an act of the greatest nobility and philanthropy. He was a Negro not because he had to be—was born immutably among them—but because he had embraced the qualities of that splendid race and the moral superiority of its cause. . . . Willie's feelings about race in these early years were more labile or tangled, not to say conflictive, than his public professions revealed. . . . [He wrote] diary entries flashing over Franco-Caribbean roots like far-off lightning, enhancing a lordly sense of self. Willie's racial shape in his last year at Fisk was still congealing, and it would always be an alloy, never entirely pure. . . . Willie's ambivalence endowed him with a resilient superiority complex, and . . . his lifelong espousal of the "Darker World" was an optional commitment based above all upon principles and reason, rather than a dazzling advocacy he was born into.[14]

The most famous passage from Du Bois's writings expresses ambivalence about mixedness:

[T]he Negro is a sort of seventh son, born with a veil, and gifted with second-sight in this American world—a world which yields him no true self-consciousness, but only lets him see himself through the revelation of the other world. It is a peculiar sensation, this double-consciousness, this sense of always looking at one's self through the eyes of others, of measuring one's soul by the tape of a world that looks on in amused contempt and pity. One ever feels his twoness—an American, a Negro; two souls, two thoughts, two unreconciled strivings; two warring ideals in one dark body, whose dogged strength alone keeps it from being torn asunder. The history of the American Negro is the history of this strife—this longing to attain self-conscious manhood, to merge his double self into a better and truer self.[15]

Formally, this passage is about the tension between a unitary African American racial identity and an ambiguous civic identity as an American whose citizenship is not fully credited. Here Du Bois does not speak directly to the racial ambiguity his other writings reveal. Yet might it be that behind the veil of that formal duality, Du Bois was also questioning monoracial Blackness? Could his sensitivity to "this longing . . . to merge his double self into a better and truer self" have been shaped by a racial double consciousness? I have not yet located the private documents that would settle this question definitively, yet certain published writings are suggestive.

Throughout *Dusk of Dawn,* which Du Bois revealingly subtitled *An Essay toward an Autobiography of a Race Concept,* he was careful to note both African and White ancestries and mark the color of each character. Othello Burghardt was his "very dark grandfather," his grandmother Sally Burghardt "a thin, tall, yellow, and hawk-faced woman." His mother, Mary Sylvina, "was brown and rather small with smooth skin and lovely eyes, and hair that curled and crinkled." His father, Alfred, was "a light mulatto." Stories and an elaborate genealogical chart laid out all Du Bois's known ancestors and highlighted the race of the White ones.[16]

Du Bois elaborated his thinking about racial construction and mixedness in a chapter titled "The Concept of Race."[17] As he did in much of his writing, here Du Bois presented his personal struggles as emblematic of the struggles of the African American people. He proclaimed the racial binary: "I was born in the century when the walls of race were clear and straight; when the world consisted of mutually

W. E. B. Du Bois in Sisters
Chapel, Spelman College,
February 1938.
Courtesy of Special Collections
and Archives, W. E. B. Du Bois
Library, University of
Massachusetts,
Amherst.

exclusive races; and even though the edges might be blurred, there was no question of exact definition and understanding of the meaning of the word." Yet most of his discussion surrounding that proclamation is not binary; it is, rather, an embrace of multiplicity. He goes on at length about his White ancestry. He notes his cousins who lived as White. And in the same sentence where he makes his strongest affirmation of solidarity with Africa, he also asserts that "this heritage binds together not simply the children of Africa, but extends through yellow Asia and into the South Seas."[18]

Surely, no African American intellectual was more unambiguously Black than W. E. B. Du Bois. And none more clearly expressed multiplicity. Yet recent generations of readers and writers see in Du Bois only the monoracial Black and not the embrace of multiplicity. This monoracial assumption has gone so far that often paintings and photographs of Du Bois are darkened and stylized to emphasize African-derived features and minimize the European-derived aspects of Du Bois's countenance. The first picture (p. 109) shows Du Bois untinted: a beige man who could easily pass for Italian or Spanish. The second, a portrait of Du Bois by Laura Wheeler Waring, shows the same angular features but kinkier hair and sepia skin tones, high-

W. E. B. Du Bois.
Portrait by Laura Wheeler Waring.
Courtesy of Special Collections
and Archives, W. E. B. Du Bois
Library, University of
Massachusetts, Amherst.

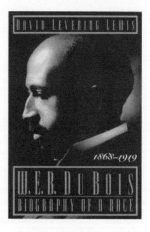

W. E. B. Du Bois.
Portrait by Addison N.
Scurlock. Courtesy of the
National Portrait Gallery,
Smithsonian Institution.

lighting a stylized Africanity. The third, very dark indeed, is from the cover of Lewis's Pulitzer Prize–winning biography. It is as if Du Bois, in order to stand in the role of honored Black intellectual and political forebear, must be presented as darker than he was in life.[19]

JEAN TOOMER

Jean Toomer was an icon of Blackness who embodied racial multiplicity—indeed, who changed his race, more than once. No more powerful or controversial figure exists in Black letters. Born Nathan Pinchback Toomer in 1894, he grew to adolescence in the Washington home and psychic shadow of his grandfather, P. B. S. Pinchback. Pinchback served as governor and was elected U.S. senator in Louisiana during Reconstruction. He won on the strength of Black votes and his constitutents' understanding that, though born the free son of a White planter, he possessed slave ancestry.[20]

Toomer's identity was flexible. Born Nathan, he changed his name to Eugene in childhood and Jean later. He attended high school among Washington's light, bright, and almost White African American upper class. The young Jean Toomer identified as Black but traveled socially on the White side of the line nearly as much as on the Black. He then flitted through several colleges without telling anyone about his African ancestry. His life from beginning to end was personalist, a spiritual search for the center of himself, and through that center for the universally human. Because of his grandfather's prominence and because of the racial angle of his own first coming to public notice, race was always part of that search, and he resented it.

For a brief time in the early 1920s Jean Toomer was a writer and a Black American. His spiritual search and the need for employment led him to live briefly in rural Georgia and to write about the experience. *Cane,* a jumble of prose, poetry, drawings, and a novella disguised in play form, ignited the imaginations of the makers of the Harlem Renaissance of the 1920s and two generations later the makers of the Black Revolution. Toomer thought he was drawing from a dying well of Black peasant culture with which he had only the most tenuous personal connection. Readers, by contrast, from Langston Hughes to Alice Walker, found the well Toomer tapped deep, rich, and ever self-renewing.[21]

PAUL SPICKARD

Jean Toomer, early 1920s.
From the Marjorie Toomer
Collection. Copyright
Estate of Marjorie Content.

Within a year of *Cane*'s publication, Toomer was off on his spiritual quest, leaving behind both the New York intellectual world to which he had briefly aspired and the Black identity he had tried on. He became successively a disciple of the mystic Georges Gurdjieff, an itinerant teacher, a seldom-published philosopher, a Quaker leader, and a recluse. He died in 1967, just before his masterwork was republished and spoke to a new generation of monoracial African Americans.

Black critics saw and valued the powerful talent at work in the making of *Cane,* as well as the celebration of Black peasant life and the horrifying account of White racial oppression. But they tended to see Toomer the man as racially confused. Alice Walker confessed to "feelings of disappointment and loss":

> Disappointment because the man who wrote so piercingly of "Negro" life in *Cane* chose to live his own life as a white man, while [Langston] Hughes, [Zora Neale] Hurston, Du Bois, and other black writers were celebrating the blackness in themselves as well as in their work. Loss because it appears this choice undermined Toomer's moral judgment: there were things [White racism] in American life and in his own that he simply refused to see.[22]

This account suggests that, whatever Toomer's talent and contribution, he did not know who he really was, a Black man in a racist nation. Indeed, Walker's assessment might imply self-hatred on Toomer's part, the internalization of White America's contempt for Black people. It is clear that Walker thinks Du Bois and the others made a nobler choice when they embraced an unambiguous Black identity.

Yet, in addition to the remarkable sensitivity to the Black folk portrayed in *Cane*, Toomer's writings show that he saw things differently from the way Walker understood him. He thought he knew who he was—not simply a monoracial Black man, but a man of multiple ancestries and identities in a nation that did not yet recognize multiplicity. Many decades before others took up the theme, Toomer asserted the constructedness of race and proclaimed a vision of a society that went beyond race. He believed he was a universal man—not, as Walker would have it, a Black man who eschewed Blackness for Whiteness, but a man who did not fit in racial boxes, whose very existence challenged monoracial categories and, behind them, the viciousness of racism. Thus, he could write in later years:

> I would liberate myself and ourselves from the entire machinery of verbal hypnotism. . . . I am simply of the human race. . . . I am of the human nation. . . . I am of Earth. . . . I am of sex, with male differentiations. . . . I eliminate the religions. I am religious. . . . What then am I?
>
> I am at once no one of the races and I am all of them.
>
> I belong to no one of them and I belong to all.
>
> I am, in a strict racial sense, a member of a new race. . . .
>
> I say to the colored group that, as a human being, I am one of them. . . . I say to the white group that, as a human being, I am one of them. As a white man, I am not one of them. . . . I am an American. As such, I invite them [both], not as [colored or] white people, but *as Americans,* to participate in whatever creative work I may be able to do.[23]

Toomer's was a personal vision, born out of mystical seeking, written into a vague program for humankind. It spoke in no concrete way to the needs of people in America who were marked off by color for domination and abuse. Rather, it was a psychological vision of a person who knew his mixedness and his wholeness, and who believed them to be more important than group strivings. Ultimately, neither White nor Black America in the first half of the twentieth century had room for a racially multiple man like Jean Toomer, at least not for public recognition of his multiplicity. Perhaps now, in a new century, there is room.

WALTER WHITE

Walter White was the Whitest and the Blackest of the multiracial people I discuss in this chapter. Physically, he was short, blond, and blue-eyed. By history and by choice, he was Black. Like Toomer, White grew up in a nearly White family on the margin between African American and European American social circles, in his case in Atlanta. Unlike Toomer, his family was not wealthy or well connected. His father carried the mail. Both the elder White and his wife were light-skinned enough to pass for White, but either they chose, or circumstances forced them, to remain on the Black side of the racial margin.

In middle age White declared his racial allegiance, with none of the ambivalence of Du Bois or Toomer. Perhaps it was because he did not come from the interstitial class and color position of the mulatto elite, or perhaps it was that by midcentury the one-drop rule imposed by Whites had so taken hold among African-derived people that they could imagine no other. Or maybe it was his personal history that led Walter White to make such an unequivocal statement of his identity.

> I am a Negro. My skin is white, my eyes are blue, my hair is blond. The traits of my race are nowhere visible upon me. Not long ago I stood one morning on a subway platform in Harlem. As the train came in I stepped back for safety. My heel came down upon the toe of the man behind me. I turned to apologize to him. He was a Negro, and his face as he stared at me was hard and full of the piled-up bitterness of a thousand lynchings and a million nights in shacks and tenements and "nigger towns." "Why don't you look where you're going?" he said sullenly. "You white folks are always trampling on colored people." Just then one of my friends came up and asked how the fight had gone in Washington—there was a filibuster against legislation for a per-

Walter White.
Photo by Al Grann,
Detroit. Poppy Cannon
Collection. Courtesy of Holt
and Rinehart.

manent Fair Employment Practices Committee. The Negro on whose toes I stepped listened, then spoke to me penitently:

"Are you Walter White of the NAACP? I'm sorry I spoke to you that way. I thought you were white."

I am not white. There is nothing within my mind and heart which tempts me to think I am. Yet I realize acutely that the only characteristic which matters to either the white or the colored race—the appearance of whiteness—is mine. There is magic in a white skin; there is tragedy, loneliness, exile, in a black skin. Why then do I insist that I am a Negro, when nothing compels me to do so but myself? . . .

There is no mistake. I am a Negro. There can be no doubt.[24]

The dawning of this monoracial, one-drop consciousness came suddenly to young White. In August 1906, when he was thirteen, a race riot struck Atlanta. When the rioters came to the White family's house, the racial line was forever drawn.

A voice which we recognized as that of the son of the grocer with whom we had traded for many years yelled, "That's where that nigger mail carrier lives! Let's burn it down! It's too nice for a nigger to live in!" In the eerie light Father turned his drawn face toward me. In a voice as quiet as though he were asking me to pass him the sugar at the breakfast table, he said, "Son, don't shoot until the first man puts his foot on the lawn and then— don't you miss!"

In the flickering light the mob swayed, paused, and began to flow toward us. In that instant there opened up within me a great awareness; I knew then who I was. I was a Negro, a human being with an invisible pigmentation which marked me a person to be hunted, hanged, abused, discriminated against, kept in poverty and ignorance, in order that those whose skin was white would have readily at hand a proof of their superiority. . . .

Yet as a boy there in the darkness amid the tightening fright, I knew the inexplicable thing—that my skin was as white as the skin of those who were coming at me. . . . I was gripped by the knowledge of my identity, and in the depths of my soul I was vaguely aware that I was glad of it. I was sick with loathing for the hatred which had flared before me that night and come so close to making me a killer; but I was glad I was not one of those who hated; I was glad I was not one of those made sick and murderous by pride. . . .

It was all just a feeling then, inarticulate and melancholy, yet reassuring in the way that death and sleep are reassuring, and I have clung to it now for nearly half a century.[25]

The monoracial identification was reinforced when Walter White's father died in 1931 after being hit by a car. He was taken by the car's White driver to the city hospital, where he was placed in the White ward. Neighbors who had witnessed the accident told Walter White's darker-skinned brother-in-law that the elder White was in the hospital. He went looking in the Black ward and did not find him. When he looked in the White ward, the hospital workers realized they were tending a Black-identified man in the wrong ward. Horrified at having sullied their pristine Whiteness, they delivered White Senior to the Black ward across the street. There, as Walter White recounted the story, in a dirty, vermin-infested, densely packed facility, his father died.[26]

Walter White's vision, then, was purely monoracial. He worked for the NAACP, the premier Black organization, for thirty years,

twenty of them as executive director. Yet he had his multiracial moments, too. His masterwork as a novelist, *Flight*, is a tale of color and
passing. This is as close as White came to contemplating the constructedness of racial categories in print. In 1949 White divorced his
African American wife of more than twenty years and married a White
woman, Poppy Cannon, who was several shades darker than he.
There was a great hue and cry in both Black and White circles. In the
former, White was accused of having sold out his race for a piece of
White flesh, and Cannon, of having seduced one of Black America's
most beloved leaders. Some White segregationists leered that this
proved that all Black men wanted was to bed White women.[27]

Only in the final chapter of his autobiography did Walter White
confess to some feelings of racial multiplicity and then only in the
context of a starry-eyed paean to interracial harmony:

> Yet I know, I know, I know that there is no reason for this
> killing, this hatred, this demarcation. There is no difference be-
> tween the killer and the killed. Black is white and white is
> black. . . .
> I am one of the two in the color of my skin; I am the other
> in my spirit and my heart. It is only a love of both which binds
> the two together in me, and it is only love for each other which
> will join them in the common aims of civilization that lie before
> us. . . .
> I am white and I am black, and know that there is no dif-
> ference. Each casts a shadow, and all shadows are dark.[28]

Granted that Walter White adopted a formal monoracial identity,
the degree to which observers have credited monoracial Blackness to
him is still remarkable. The cover of the recent reprint of his autobiography, *A Man Called White*, bills it as "the life story of a man
who crossed the color line to fight for civil rights." By that the pub-
lishers mean, it turns out, not that a phenotypically White man crossed
the color line to identify himself as Black and fight racism for decades
but rather that on one brief occasion in 1918 the Black man Walter
White posed as a White man in order to investigate a racist group.
Surely, vital though that was as a political moment, it was the less
significant color line crossing in White's personal life.

In choosing a monoracial Black identity, Walter White was making a personal response to a political situation, conforming his personal racial decision to his politics. He did not sustain this monoracialism in all aspects of his life. Nonetheless, a monoracial, essentialist Blackness is the main theme that more recent commenters have attributed to the life and work of Walter White, as of Du Bois.

FREDERICK DOUGLASS

W. E. B. Du Bois was the archetypal African American whose embrace of racial multiplicity and ambiguity has not generally been recognized. Walter White chose to eschew phenotype and embrace monoracial Blackness. Jean Toomer was the sole individual among those examined here who allowed himself a sustained encounter with the fact of his mixedness. White and Du Bois worked politically, publicly, in a monoracial space. But all three lived in a racial space that had great fluidity, ambiguity, and mixedness. In a later age, when other people, operating from an uninterrogated monoracial framework, came to write the histories of Du Bois, White, and others, they saw only the public positioning and not the personal lives.

Gregory Stephens points to Frederick Douglass as an emblem of the ambiguity these people's life choices present. Although Douglass, unlike White, Toomer, and perhaps even Du Bois, probably could not have passed for White, he possessed multiracial ancestry and inhabited a multiracial social space. Indeed, even as he was the nineteenth century's most ardent and honored agitator for the rights of Black Americans in slavery and freedom, he worked and socialized with White people, married a White woman, and pointed toward a hoped-for future of the sort that Nelson Mandela would one day call a nonracial democracy. Stephens characterizes Douglass's racial stance thus: "In 1886, he told an audience: '[A man painting me insisted I show] my full face, for that is Ethiopian. Take my side face, said I, for that is Caucasian. But should you try my quarter face you would find it Indian. I don't know that any race can claim me, but being identified with slaves as I am, I think I know the meaning of the inquiry.' Douglass' public persona was that of a defender of the rights of Afro-Americans. But his private identity was multiethnic. . . . He believed

Frederick Douglass.
By Mathew Brady Studio.
Courtesy of
Ronald L. Harris.

that his multiethnic identity and community were not abnormal, but rather represented the future of America."[29]

Stephens presents Douglass as a meta-mulatto, a larger-than-life advocate of nonracial democracy and of an end to racial thinking. Stephens goes too far.[30] Whatever measure of multiplicity Douglass— or Du Bois, or White, or even Toomer—may have experienced in his private life, his embrace of a complex identity did little to undermine the social power of the Law of the Excluded Middle (see chapter 2). Du Bois, or White, and others like them embraced political Blackness and confraternity with monoracial African Americans and were tireless advocates of the cause of Black America, monoracially defined.[31] From sometime in the late nineteenth century until very late in the twentieth, multiracial people part of whose ancestry was Black almost always passed as unmixed African Americans. They constituted an anomaly in the binary racial system, not a challenge to it, and their multiraciality was covered over. Those few people like Jean Toomer who attempted to challenge the binary racial system were rendered irrelevant and invisible. In this period, the monoracial fact overwhelmed the multiracial fact. Such was the power of Blackness.

PAUL SPICKARD

NOTES

An earlier version of this chapter was presented to the Collegium for African American Research, Münster, Germany, March 20, 1999. Several people there made comments that improved this chapter. In addition, I am grateful for the patient suggestions of Patrick Miller, Reg Daniel, Puk Degnegaard, and Lori Pierce.

1. Other prominent members of the beigeoisie in those decades included P. B. S. Pinchback, Reconstruction-era acting governor and senator-elect from Louisiana; Adella Hunt Logan, fighter for women's suffrage and professor at Tuskegee Institute; Homer Plessy, challenger of Louisiana's Jim Crow railroad car law; Charles W. Chesnutt, the first major novelist in the African American literary pantheon; John Hope, president of Atlanta University; Archibald Grimké, political rival of Du Bois and Booker T. Washington; Mary Church Terrell, first president of the National Association of Colored Women; Mordecai Johnson, first African American president of Howard University; Charles Drew, surgeon and pioneer in blood plasma research and blood banking; and Adam Clayton Powell Jr., member of Congress from Harlem.

2. See also G. Reginald Daniel, "Passers and Pluralists: Subverting the Racial Divide," in *Racially Mixed People in America,* ed. Maria P. P. Root (Newbury Park, Calif.: Sage, 1992), 91–107. On multiracial people passing for White, see Adrian Piper, "Passing for White, Passing for Black," *Transition,* no. 58 (1992): 4–32; Paul R. Spickard, *Mixed Blood: Intermarriage and Ethnic Identity in Twentieth-Century America* (Madison: University of Wisconsin Press, 1989), 329–39; F. James Davis, *Who Is Black? One Nation's Definition* (University Park: Pennsylvania State University Press, 1991); Robert McG. Thomas Jr., "Thyra Johnston, 91, Symbol of Racial Distinctions, Dies," *New York Times,* November 29, 1995; Countee Cullen, "Two Who Crossed the Line," in *Color* (New York: Harper, 1925), 16–17; and almost every issue of *Ebony* during the 1950s.

Passing for Black is a phenomenon that has not been examined critically, although it is implied in works such as Kathy Russell, Midge Wilson, and Ronald Hall, *The Color Complex: The Politics of Skin Color among African Americans* (New York: Harcourt Brace Jovanovich, 1992); E. Franklin Frazier, *Black Bourgeoisie: The Rise of a New Middle Class* (New York: Free Press, 1957); Charles S. Johnson, "The Social Significance of Color in Negro Society," Charles Spurgeon Johnson Papers, Fisk University Archives, Nashville, Box 173, folder 35; Verna M. Keith and Cedric Herring, "Skin Tone and Stratification in the Black Community," *American Journal of Sociology* 97.3 (1991): 760–78. Even unmixed White people sometimes chose to pass for Black; see John Howard Griffin, *Black Like Me* (Boston: Houghton Mifflin, 1961); Grace Halsell, *Soul Sister* (New York: Fawcett, 1969).

3. Throughout this chapter I speak of the construction of race in terms of Black and White. It is essential to note that there have always been more than just African- and European-derived peoples on this continent and that the others are part of the equation of any racial construction, as other chapters in this volume make clear.

4. Winthrop D. Jordan, *White over Black* (Chapel Hill: University of North Carolina Press, 1968), 3–43, 136–78; Joel Williamson, *New People: Miscegenation and Mulattoes in the United States* (New York: Free Press, 1980), 5–59; Spickard, *Mixed Blood,* 235–52; Martha Hodes, *White Women, Black Men: Illicit Sex in the 19th-Century South* (New Haven: Yale University Press, 1997); Winthrop D. Jordan, "American Chiaroscuro: The Status and Definition of Mulattoes in the British Colonies," *William and Mary Quarterly,* 3d ser., 19 (1962): 183–200; Carter G. Woodson, "The Beginnings of Miscegenation of Whites and Blacks," *Journal of Negro History* 3 (1918): 335–53.

5. James Thomas Flexner, *The Young Hamilton* (Boston: Little, Brown, 1978), 8–26. So much of race making and the constraints placed on race choosing depends on context. The possibility of African ancestry in Hamilton's case was a certainty for Alexander Pushkin and Alexandre Dumas, larger-than-life figures in Russian and French letters a generation later. Yet though their ancestry was known, they were not marked by the dominant cultures of Russia and France as Black, and their artistic work did not take shape in ways that reflected a Black consciousness or identity.

6. Daniel, "Passers and Pluralists"; Davis, *Who Is Black?* 31–42; Williamson, *New People,* 5–59; Sybil Kein, ed., *Creole: The History and Legacy of Louisiana's Free People of Color* (Baton Rouge: Louisiana State University Press, 2000); Virginia R. Domínguez, *White by Definition: Social Classification in Creole Louisiana* (New Brunswick, N.J.: Rutgers University Press, 1986); Sister Frances Jerome Woods, *Marginality and Identity: A Colored Creole Family through Ten Generations* (Baton Rouge: Louisiana State University Press, 1972).

7. Williamson, *New People,* 61, 3, 109.

8. David Forcacs, ed., *An Antonio Gramsci Reader* (New York: Schocken, 1988), 189–221, 422–24; Bill Ashcroft, Gareth Griffiths, and Helen Tiffin, *Key Concepts in Post-Colonial Studies* (London: Routledge, 1998), 116–17.

9. W. E. B. Du Bois, "The Talented Tenth: Memorial Address," *Boulé Journal* 15 (October 1948): 3–13; reprinted in *W. E. B. Du Bois: A Reader,* ed. David Levering Lewis (New York: Henry Holt, 1995), 347–53; Willard B. Gatewood, *Aristocrats of Color: The Black Elite, 1880–1920* (Bloomington: Indiana University Press, 1990).

10. I am emphatically not arguing that it was their admixture of European ancestry that brought such people to prominence. In slavery, being the master's child may have brought some privilege, education, even manumission. In

freedom, White descent may have brought some social advantage. But there is no evidence, contrary to the opinions of both Du Bois and Edward Byron Reuter, that White ancestry brought greater ability. Contrast the interpretations of Du Bois, "Advance Guard"; Edward Byron Reuter, *The Mulatto in the United States* (New York: Negro Universities Press, 1969; orig. 1918), 183–215 passim. I write here about leaders simply because they left writings that give us clues to their thoughts on these issues. Lives of everyday people of multiracial ancestry and various identifications can be examined in Domínguez, *White by Definition;* Shirlee Taylor Haizlip, *The Sweeter the Juice: A Family Memoir in Black and White* (New York: Simon and Schuster, 1994); Kent Anderson Leslie, *Woman of Color, Daughter of Privilege* (Athens: University of Georgia Press, 1995); Victoria E. Bynum, "'White Negroes' in Segregated Mississippi: Miscegenation, Racial Identity, and the Law," *Journal of Southern History* 64.2 (1998): 247–76; Edward Ball, *Slaves in the Family* (New York: Ballantine, 1999).

11. W. E. Burghardt Du Bois, *Dusk of Dawn: An Essay toward an Autobiography of a Race Concept* (New Brunswick, N.J.: Transaction, 1984; orig. 1940), 18–19, 115.

12. W. E. B. Du Bois, *The Souls of Black Folk* (New York: Fawcett, 1961; orig. 1903), 16.

13. Du Bois, *Dusk of Dawn,* 25–49, 115.

14. David Levering Lewis, *W. E. B. Du Bois: Biography of a Race* (New York: Holt, 1993), 72–73.

15. Du Bois, *Souls of Black Folk,* 16–17.

16. Du Bois, *Dusk of Dawn,* 11–12, 104–13.

17. Ibid., 97–133.

18. Ibid., 116–17.

19. David Levering Lewis, *W. E. B. Du Bois: The Fight for Equality and the American Century, 1919–1963* (New York: Henry Holt, 2000), photo following p. 206; Lewis, *Biography of a Race,* cover and photo following p. 304. The book's darkness may well be the work of someone in marketing at Holt and not reflect Lewis's reading of Du Bois's racial identity.

20. Toomer biographies include Cynthia Earl Kerman and Richard Eldridge, *Lives of Jean Toomer* (Baton Rouge: Louisiana State University Press, 1987); Charles R. Larson, *Invisible Darkness: Jean Toomer and Nella Larsen* (Iowa City: University of Iowa Press, 1993); Charles Scruggs and Lee Vandemarr, *Jean Toomer and the Terrors of American History* (Philadelphia: University of Pennsylvania Press, 1998); Jon Woodson, *To Make a New Race: Gurdjieff, Toomer, and the Harlem Renaissance* (Jackson: University Press of Mississippi, 1999); H. William Rice, "Searching for Jean Toomer," *American Legacy* 3.3 (fall 1997): 16–22.

21. Jean Toomer, *Cane,* introd. Darwin T. Turner (New York: Liveright, 1975; orig. 1923).

22. Alice Walker, "The Divided Life of Jean Toomer," *New York Times,* July 13, 1980, reprinted in Alice Walker, *In Search of Our Mothers' Gardens* (New York: Harcourt Brace Jovanovich, 1983). It is worth noting that Langston Hughes owned his multiplicity even as he chose a mainly Black identity; see Hughes, *The Big Sea* (New York: Hill and Wang, 1940), esp. 50–51. It is important to understand that Toomer was emphatically not attacking African Americans after the fashion of the racially mixed Negrophobe William Hannibal Thomas; John David Smith, *Black Judas: William Hannibal Thomas and the American Negro* (Athens: University of Georgia Press, 2000).

23. Kerman and Eldridge, *Lives of Jean Toomer,* 341–42.

24. Walter White, *A Man Called White* (Athens: University of Georgia Press, 1995; orig. 1948), 3–4; Walter White, "Why I Remain a Negro," *Negro Digest* (February 1948): 12–19.

25. Ibid., 11–12.

26. Ibid., 134–38.

27. Poppy Cannon, *A Gentle Knight: My Husband, Walter White* (New York: Rinehart, 1952); idem, "How We Made Our Mixed Marriage Work," *Ebony* (June 1952): 24–40; idem, "How We Erased Two Color Lines," *Ebony* (July 1952): 47–59; idem, "Love That Never Died," *Ebony* (January 1957): 17–20.

28. White, *A Man Called White,* 366.

29. Gregory Stephens, "Douglass, Not Lincoln, Bolsters GOP," *Los Angeles Times,* December 31, 2000, M2–M3.

30. Gregory Stephens, *On Racial Frontiers: The New Culture of Frederick Douglass, Ralph Ellison, and Bob Marley* (Cambridge: Cambridge University Press, 1999). G. Reginald Daniel explores the concept of the meta-mulatto in "Machado de Assis and the Meta-Mulatto," in *Encruzilhadas: Symposium on Portuguese Traditions,* ed. Claude L. Hulet (Los Angeles: UCLA, 1995), 64–67.

31. For other leaders who blended multiracial social lives with monoracial political lives, see Adam Clayton Powell Jr., *Adam by Adam* (New York: Dial, 1971); Wil Haygood, *King of the Cats: The Life and Times of Adam Clayton Powell, Jr.* (Boston: Houghton Mifflin, 1993), 10–12, 18, 78 ff; 87, 104, 252, 265, 323–25; Mary Church Terrell, *A Colored Woman in a White World* (Salem, N.H.: Ayer, 1966; orig. 1940).

6

"THE WHITES HAVE CREATED MODERN HONOLULU"

Ethnicity, Racial Stratification, and the Discourse of Aloha

LORI PIERCE

On September 25, 1915, Liliʻuokalani returned to Iolani Palace for the first time in twenty-two years. Deposed in a bloodless coup d'état fomented by a small group of Haole[1] businessmen and politicians, the former ruling sovereign of the nation of Hawaiʻi had become resigned to her status as "ex-queen," as the local press referred to her. The Hawaiian nation had been supplanted, first by the hastily constituted Republic of Hawaiʻi and then by the United States, which annexed and transformed the islands into the territory of Hawaiʻi. Despite President Grover Cleveland's admission of the complicity of the United States in the illegal overthrow of the Hawaiian monarchy,[2] the election of William McKinley in 1896 left Liliʻuokalani without political allies powerful enough to reverse the course of events. Although she was dearly loved by the Hawaiian community, her presence at such a public occasion was merely nostalgic.

The occasion on which Liliʻuokalani returned to the palace was Balboa Day, a celebration contrived by Alexander Hume Ford, founder and secretary of the Pan Pacific Union. Ford had conceived of the event as a way to celebrate the discovery of the Pacific by Europeans but also as a way to promote Hawai'i as the crossroads of the Pacific. Ford, also editor of *Mid-Pacific Magazine* and founder of the Outrigger Canoe Club, had come to Hawai'i less than a decade earlier. He quickly found a niche as a civic booster and one of the earliest promoters of tourism to the islands. But he also had an idealistic vision. He was captivated by Hawai'i and fascinated by the seemingly harmonious nature of the relationships among ethnic groups. Fancying himself a social scientist, Ford declared that in all his years of travel, he had never come across a place where the many races of humankind lived together in such harmony. He settled in Hawai'i to study the phenomenon. "Here in Hawai'i," he said, ". . . the oldest and newest civilizations meet [and] can be studied side by side. In Hawai'i, the several races seemed as one. Here there was no noticeable racial prejudice."[3] Hawai'i was, for Ford, something of a paradise. The languid climate certainly qualified the islands for this status, but he also believed the lack of overt bigotry made them unique and worthy of celebration. The diversity of the ethnic groups and their ability to get along with one another qualified Hawai'i as a racial paradise.

To that end, Ford found ways to promote and celebrate Hawai'i's ethnic diversity. He organized a series of civic organizations, devoted to promoting scholarly civic dialogue in order to address the problems of Pacific nations.[4] Balboa Day was Ford's idea, and it was Ford who invited Lili'uokalani and Sanford Dole, former president of the Republic of Hawai'i and the first governor of the territory of Hawai'i, to be present at its inaugural celebration. The symbolism of the ceremony was all the more poignant because of the reconciliation of these enemies. Hawai'i was a place where petty differences, particularly those based on racial distinctions, could be overcome.

Lili'uokalani was featured in the celebration. Hundreds of schoolchildren, dressed in the costumes of their parents' native lands, carried flags, banners, and other symbols of their nationality. They sang, danced, and performed oratorical recitations. As each group paraded onto the grounds of Iolani Palace, the Royal Hawaiian Band played the national anthem of their country, and a single member of the delegation mounted the stairs to present a flag to Lili'uokalani. Included were organizations from China, Australia, Japan, the Philippines, Korea, and Canada. The definition of "Pacific nation" was stretched to include Oregon and California, and the concept was tortured further by including Portugal by virtue of the fact that it was the colonial ruler of Macao. John Bains, who reported on the event for *Paradise of the Pacific,* recalled that the Hawaiian delegation was the most impressive and was composed of "a bevy of young Hawaiian women, all garbed in white and followed by a detachment of Kamehameha cadets."[5]

Jean West Maury, writing for *Mid-Pacific Magazine,* reflected on the deeper significance of the celebration: "In Honolulu . . . race meets race on equal ground, and . . . the color of a man's skin and the slant of his eye has nothing at all to do with the color of his heart or the slant of his brain." Balboa Day "represents a democracy of interest hitherto unrealized, a depth of understanding that the entire civilized world sooner or later will have to accept, and a feeling of brotherly love that has been dreamed of since the birth of dreams." The display of ethnic harmony and racial tolerance exhibited at Balboa Day would "unite the interests of all the great nations of the world. And when the great powers are united in their interests, and recognize their union, the little scraps among the little fellows won't amount to much."[6]

Balboa Day was one of many civic celebrations in the early twentieth century that featured the ethnic diversity of Hawai'i. That heterogeneity, however, was not an accident. It was the deliberate policy on the part of Haole plantation owners to import a cheap, exploitable labor force, largely from Asia. Working on short-term contracts in nearly unbearable conditions, laborers from Korea, China, Japan, the Philippines, Portugal, and Puerto Rico supplemented native Hawaiians and helped to create one of the most profitable sugar industries in the world.[7] The result was that by 1900, 87,000 of the 154,000 residents of Hawai'i were of Asian ancestry.

That this non-White labor force constituted the majority of the population of Hawai'i represented a significant challenge to the Haole ruling class. When they organized and created unions, they repeatedly challenged the plantation owners by striking for higher wages and better working conditions.[8] And although Chinese and Japanese immigrants were not eligible for citizenship, their children who were born in the United States were rapidly coming of age. The Haole-dominated Republican Party secured the loyalty of native Hawaiians by doling out political patronage jobs. But the second-generation

Japanese, the Nisei, were rapidly becoming a factor in the political life of the territory. In 1920 they represented only 2.5 percent of registered voters; by 1926 they were 7.6 percent of potential voters; and by 1936, they represented 25 percent of voters.[9] The threat of Japanese voting as a bloc, and thereby displacing Whites, was a constant source of worry for Haole politicians and businessmen.[10]

Racial tensions lay just beneath the surface of daily life in Hawai'i, but race as a source of conflict or distress was rarely if ever discussed publicly. Instead, the Haole ruling class constantly depicted Hawai'i as a racial paradise, a place where the Hawaiians, Haole, Japanese, and Chinese lived cooperatively. Civic celebrations such as Balboa Day that featured all of the ethnic groups of Hawai'i were typical. These parades, pageants, and public celebrations were a way of depicting life in Hawai'i to tourists, residents, and mainland audiences, who read about them in *Paradise of the Pacific* and *Mid-Pacific Magazine*. The message being communicated was that ethnic diversity was not a threat to the Haole ruling class. In fact, Euro-Americans were firmly in control and turning Hawai'i into a thoroughly American territory.

I argue here that the ruling White minority attempted to present an image of Hawai'i that conformed to American expectations about ethnicity and race. During the early twentieth century, in other areas of the country, White European immigrants were being urged to assimilate and Americanize, to replace the language, values, and customs of their native lands with American substitutes. The process of Americanization was not uniformly executed, but it was clear that in the late nineteenth and early twentieth century native-born Americans responded to the intrusion of millions of immigrants from Europe by devising an image of American values and ideals that was articulated through schools, workplaces, and settlement houses.[11]

In Hawai'i Americanization campaigns raised the question of race and the ability of America to absorb non-White, non-European immigrants. It was unclear whether the White minority in Hawai'i was influential enough to assure the complete assimilation of Asian immigrants and native Hawaiians to American customs and values. Would so small a population of Euro-Americans be capable of building and maintaining American institutions? Could Asians be successfully Americanized? The passage of anti-Asian immigration laws in 1882, 1907, and 1924 suggested that the vast majority of Euro-Americans did not believe that Asians belonged or could belong in

America.[12] More problematic were Hawaiians, whose presence served as a constant reminder that the land that was now a territory had formerly been a sovereign kingdom. Hawaiians had actively resisted the annexation by petitioning the U.S. Congress and, sometimes, inciting rebellion.[13]

The history of Hawai'i as a sovereign kingdom, the presence of an Asian laboring class, and the influence of Euro-Americans in the political and social structure resulted in a complex set of cultural interactions. The White supremacy of the plantation structure was mediated by the perception of Hawai'i as a racial paradise. I contend that in Hawai'i contradictory attitudes about race and ethnicity were resolved by resorting to a discursive strategy that I call the "discourse of aloha," a way of speaking and writing about Hawai'i that celebrated ethnic diversity in such a way that it did not threaten Haole hegemony. The discourse of aloha was used on a daily basis to disavow racial tensions and to distract attention from the prevalence of institutional racism. It appropriated the Hawaiian values of love, generosity, and open-heartedness and promoted them as the central value of Hawaiian culture and island life. According to the discourse of aloha, because this central value was so essential to the local culture and because it promoted harmony, equanimity, and friendship, racial tensions, when they arose, were considered a violation of the aloha spirit. The discourse of aloha reinforced the image of Hawai'i as a racial paradise, an image that was especially important because of the potential for ethnic relationships to become unruly. Labor strikes, segregated housing on plantations and in urban Honolulu, and Hawaiian cultural resistance to assimilation all had the potential to reveal the degree to which political and social relationships in Hawai'i were structured by a racial hierarchy. In civic celebrations such as Balboa Day and the Mid-Pacific Carnival, I argue, we can see the discourse of aloha in action. Ethnic groups were invited to participate on an equal footing, representing themselves and their communities as one of the many cultures that made Hawai'i a unique territorial acquisition.

In these same venues, the presentation of Hawaiian ethnicity had to be divorced from any lingering sense of nationalism or political sovereignty associated with movements to resist annexation by native Hawaiians. Hawaiian culture was understood as central to the social and cultural life of Hawai'i but not in ways that were threatening to

Haole political control. White Americans in Hawai'i had a stake in helping to perpetuate an image of Hawaiian culture that did not challenge their right to rule. Hawaiian culture was represented as a unique feature of life in the islands *and* the same as the culture of other ethnic groups in the territory. At public civic celebrations where ethnicity was featured, Hawaiians—like Japanese, Chinese, and Koreans—were an ethnic group on the way to becoming American. These public demonstrations of ethnicity in Hawai'i reflected Euro-American culture and values.

Hawai'i's Race Problem: Assimilation and Social Control

The White community had long enjoyed social and political dominance in Hawai'i. The descendants of the earliest missionaries, who arrived in Hawai'i in 1820—prominent families such as the Castles, Judds, Thurstons, and Campbells—mingled with the descendants of those who made their fortunes in the maritime, agricultural, and financial industries. This elite Haole class formed their own segregated schools (Punahou), clubs (the Pacific Club, the Outrigger Canoe Club), and social fraternities (Masons, Elks, Oddfellows). These men ran businesses large and small, and their wives followed in the tradition of ladies of leisure by calling on one another for tea and evening socials. They were also engaged in public philanthropy and donated their time and money to social reform movements such as the Young Men's Christian Association, the Free Kindergarten Association, and the Outdoor Circle.[14]

The racial stratification of the political economy of Hawai'i is a well-established fact.[15] The plantation economy was built by a small number of European and American men, some of whom were the descendants of missionaries and traders who arrived in Hawai'i in the early nineteenth century. Many others came from abroad to make their homes and fortunes in Hawai'i. Once control of the land was secured by the institution of Western land tenure by the Mahele, or mass land distribution, of 1848,[16] White Europeans and Americans were able to build empires on land speculation and the cash crops of sugar and pineapple. Plantations were labor intensive and relied on contract workers obtained in Asia. Although attempts were made to encourage European and American immigration, it was generally concluded that White men could not stand the stoop labor and abhorrent conditions of field labor, especially at the wages plantation owners were willing to pay. As Gavan Daws writes, "Portuguese, Norwegians, Swedes, and Germans were welcome, but . . . they had Western views on matters such as wages, and this made them unacceptable to the planters."[17] Once a formula was settled on—White *luna* (foremen) supervising a predominantly Asian workforce—the only distinctions to be made were the wage differentials between the various Asian plantation laborers. On most plantations, foremen and skilled workers earned the highest wages. And on most plantations, foremen and skilled workers were White or Hawaiians. However, it was also the custom if not the policy of many plantations to base the wages of workers on their ethnicity.[18]

Although Hawaiians represented the majority of the electorate during the first two decades of the territorial period, Haole politicians rapidly gained control over the political life of Hawai'i. The first election in the territory in 1900, for example, sent the Hawaiian nationalist Robert Wilcox to Congress. In 1902 Wilcox was soundly defeated by Jonah Kuhio Kalanianaole, a Hawaiian candidate backed by the Haole-dominated Republican Party. After Wilcox's defeat and death, his Home Rule party disintegrated, giving White Republicans a virtual monopoly in the politics of Hawai'i. The amount of control Whites enjoyed over the majority population in Hawai'i is difficult to overestimate. The Haole elite owned the largest banks and other financial agencies, as well as the plantations and businesses that supported them, which were the foundation of Hawai'i's economy. According to Gary Okihiro, the legendary Big Five—American Factors, C. Brewer, Alexander and Baldwin, Castle and Cook, and Theo Davies—"controlled businesses associated with the sugar plantations, including banking, insurance, transportation, utilities, and wholesale and retail merchandising. Through interlocking directorate, intermarriages and social association, the haole elite managed to keep the wealth within a small circle of families."[19]

The Haole elite exercised a measure of social control that matched their political and economic dominance in the islands. As one notable citizen, William Castle, expressed it in *Hawai'i Past and Present*, "Hawaii is a land of law and order. Different as it may be in its outward aspects, one feels it to be essentially an outpost and a distant center of American civilization. [T]he missionaries saw to that."[20] From the viewpoint of the Haole ruling class, even before the overthrow of the monarchy and annexation, "Hawaii was already American in language and institutions."[21] American values and customs, Castle contended, had "an assimilative and uplifting power" in Hawai'i and would continue to do so.[22] The schools, Castle reminded his readers, were conducted in English and were compulsory. The teachers were largely American (meaning White), and the population enjoyed a high degree of literacy. The territorial government had also made improvements in public works designed to guarantee the health of the community. During the first two decades of the twentieth century, the territory of Hawai'i established a sewage system, weekly garbage pickups (twice weekly for the businesses and merchants of downtown), built a home for the insane, instituted a system of juvenile justice within the judiciary, and created homes for delinquent boys and wayward girls.[23]

Euro-Americans were socially, politically, and economically dominant but still a distinct minority in Hawai'i. Outnumbered by Asians and Hawaiians, they dealt with their minority status in the context of maintaining a measure of domination and control over the Americanization of the islands. The Haole ruling class approached the non-White majority with an attitude of liberal paternalism. Only rarely did they resort to bigotry or terrorism, but any threat to economic domination could and did bring to the surface overt expressions of racism. For example, in a speech before the Social Science Association on November 13, 1922, Walter F. Dillingham, a prominent member of the Haole elite, discussed the repercussions of the unsuccessful 1920 strike by Japanese workers. Dillingham expressed his misgivings about the presence of "certain elements" in the Japanese community: "Perhaps the most lasting impression left by the strike has been the feeling that our Japanese residents are not being Americanized, but are rather continuing as members of a distinct and separate community that can and does move as a unit among us, Japanese in thought, characteristics and actions." Dillingham's concerns were clear; the Japanese community must "Americanize"—speak English, convert to Christianity, and support American business interests—or the result would be strikes and other social unrest. If the Japanese community did not assimilate, did not "mingle freely with Americans in our clubs [and] Churches," the result would be a "Bronze America."

For Dillingham, a bronze America was a clear threat to the future of Hawai'i and the United States: "No matter how much we may admire the thrift, industry and ambition of the Japanese . . . is it safe for us to sit idly by and permit the situation to drift, by sheer force of numbers, to the point where these aliens in our midst threaten to assume control?"[24]

Whites' advocacy of assimilation was rarely consistent, however, and generally combined one of the three dominant models of assimilation common during the early twentieth century: Anglo-conformity, melting pot assimilation, and cultural pluralism. According to Milton Gordon, Anglo-conformity assumed "the desirability of maintaining English institutions[,] . . . the English language, and English-oriented cultural patterns as dominant and standard in American life."[25] In Hawai'i the assertion of Anglo-conformity was most often an issue in the political battles over the public schools and language. Proficiency in the English language was usually cited as the reason non-White locals did not (or could not) advance from working-class to middle-class status. Not only did the territory face the problem of Asian immigrants who wished to retain the use of their language and pass it along to their children, but children, especially those raised on the plantations, spoke pidgin, or Hawai'i Creole English. Whites dismissed Creole as gibberish and used the inability of non-Whites to speak pure or unaccented English as a way to maintain exclusive, White-only schools.[26] Facility in English was treated as an implicit racial characteristic that could be read by all as a way of securing White privilege and access to desirable jobs. For example, in an edition of the Honolulu City Directory, an advertisement for an employment agency, illustrated with a picture of a White woman, asked: "Do you need a stenographer with English ability?" The none-too-subtle suggestion was, of course, that securing the services of a White female secretary was the only way to guarantee "English ability."[27]

The melting pot ideal assumed that America would absorb all of its immigrants, in the process creating a new (and presumably better) nation. This idealism did not demand conformity to Anglo norms and values but assumed that in America the best of the world's cultures would somehow blend and mesh, making one American indistinguishable from the next. The melting pot ideal took on added significance in Hawai'i given its unusually high rate of interethnic marriage.[28] The acceptance of interethnic relationships and marriages in

Hawai'i has been ascribed to the warm and generous Hawaiians, who accepted the children of the liaisons between Hawaiians and White sailors because they had no inborn prejudices. This legend was passed down through scholarly and popular discourses about the supposed lack of racial antagonisms in Hawai'i. The image of Hawai'i as a place where the races mingled freely was cited as proof that the territory would eventually reflect the American melting pot.[29] The presence of American institutions and values, combined with the erasure of strong ethnocentrism and nationalism among the various immigrant groups, would lead to the emergence of a new American, a Hawaiian American. Sidney Gulick's *Mixing the Races in Hawai'i* is perhaps the best example of advocacy of the melting pot ethic as the solution to Hawai'i's race problem. In Hawai'i, Gulick argued, "a Hawaiian-Caucasian-Chinese-Japanese-Portuguese-Puerto-Rican-Korean-Filipino race of enthusiastic American is in the process of becoming. Hawai'i is in truth a gentle melting pot that is actually fusing into one of the most diverse of human bloods. A homogeneous people speaking a single language is coming into being under the most favorable conditions."[30] For Gulick, this mixing was not only metaphorical but also biological. The new Hawaiian American would be biologically distinct, combining the best characteristics of all the races into one new human type.[31] Gulick argued that the mixing of the races in Hawai'i would not lead to a degraded human being, as was the belief among some eugenicists at the time. Rather, he suggested that it was entirely possible that this mixing would improve the races involved and, possibly, the whole of humanity: "When it is noted that the civilization of a people is the work of a small group of superior individuals, it becomes at once apparent that in a highly mixed population like that of Hawaii, the possibility of geniuses is large, and the prospect for a rapidly developing civilization and culture is relatively high."[32] Gulick, however, betrayed the influence of eugenics on his thinking by suggesting that while race mixing might produce superior civilization, it must be done in combination with a program of discouraging breeding among those at the lower end of the scale—congenital imbeciles and the insane. He was optimistic about the chances of Hawai'i producing a superior civilization, not only because of the prevalence of race mixing, but also because the social conditions were especially beneficial. Its climate, educational and economic opportunities, and sound moral and religious life were all factors that worked in favor of Hawai'i becoming the literal melting pot of twentieth-century America.

The literary critic Randolph Bourne argued for cultural pluralism on the grounds that rampant Anglo-conformity would turn America into a "tasteless, colorless fluid of uniformity."[33] Mindless conformity, in Bourne's estimation, would lead to a citizenry of "men and women without a spiritual country, cultural outlaws, without taste, without standards but those of the mob. We sentence them to live on the most rudimentary planes of American life."[34] Immigrant communities made valuable contributions to American life and, in fact, were the basis of a common American culture. In Hawai'i the most persistent advocates of this pluralist vision of the future were members of the Department of Sociology at the University of Hawai'i. Led by Romanzo Adams, the department produced reams of scholarship that demonstrated that Asian immigrants were successfully making the transition to American life and making positive contributions to Hawai'i. Like their counterparts on the mainland, immigrants to Hawai'i made concessions to America but retained customs and habits of their home culture. Given enough time, they would eventually be fully assimilated into American life. Adams described immigrants to Hawai'i as compared to the immigrants to other parts of the United States:

> In Hawai'i the Chinese immigrants are sufficiently alert to adopt modern mechanical devices and business methods, but when a man dies his bones are sent back to his old home village. . . . The daughter of a Japanese man wears American style clothing on the street, but at her wedding she is dressed in a costume of old Japanese style. . . . The Hawaiian Portuguese in relation to business affairs are much like the Americans of New England ancestry, but when they worship, they go mainly to the church of the old Portuguese tradition.[35]

The persistence of these traditions and customs was not a threat to America but constituted a stage on the way to full assimilation.

The peaceful coexistence of ethnic groups was most often viewed as a unique feature of Hawai'i and became a selling point as tourism to the islands grew in the early twentieth century. Hawaiians and Hawaiian culture provided a colorful backdrop to the new American territory. Visitors disembarking from passenger liners were immediately enthralled by the sight of dozens of Hawaiian women and children selling *leis*. The literature that sold Hawaiʻi, both as a tourist destination and as an American territory, regularly featured the image of Hawaiians eating or pounding poi, throw-net fishing, or dancing the hula. Hawaiʻi was a modern, vibrant place that still retained features of its ancient past. Further, it was a place that welcomed foreign immigrants and readily assimilated them. William Atherton Du Puy described his encounter with the ethnic diversity of modern Honolulu:

> [O]ne in ten is conventional Anglo-Saxon pink, one in ten is of a darkness beyond that of the American Indian and with no yellow glow back of it. These are Hawaiians. There is a sprinkling of Latins—swarthy Portuguese from the Azores. But the mass of the population shows the yellow of the Orientals—Chinese, Japanese, Korean, Filipino—each with distinctive traits but each also postmarked, as it were, on that other fringe of the Pacific. All of these wear American clothes (there is not a pigtail in Honolulu) and disport themselves much as do natives of Vermont or Virginia, but their skins are yellow. And the young people are blends of these, emerging blithely from the melting pot and setting forth impudently to find what life under a western flag has to offer.[36]

The ethnic diversity of Hawaiʻi was always contextualized within an American assimilationist framework. Hawaiians, Chinese, and Japanese were regularly depicted as groups on their way to becoming fully American. Given their dominance, the Haole elite rarely felt the need to assert their control through bigotry or racial terrorism. Cultural diversity was rarely seen as a threat, so long as that diversity could be contained with a model of ethnicity that ensured the continuity of White supremacy through control of Hawaiʻi's political, economic, and social institutions. The White supremacy implicit in descriptions of ethnic diversity in Hawaiʻi was also represented in the way this diversity was displayed in public venues and celebrations.

In addition to the exertion of political and economic control over immigrant and native groups, Euro-Americans promoted Americanization through the careful celebration of ethnic diversity. Ethnic assimilation in Hawaiʻi primarily took on a positive or celebratory tone. Unable to ignore or hide large numbers of non-Whites in Honolulu, tour promoters and other Haole businesspeople took advantage of their presence and began to market Hawaiʻi as an exotic, almost foreign destination that was nevertheless safely under American control.

SYMBOLIZING ETHNICITY

Parades, pageants, and other civic celebrations provide insights into a society's social structures and cultural values.[37] Mary Ryan has described the institutionalization of the American parade as a civic celebration that gradually became an ethnic festival. Unlike Europeans, who marched to a specific point in order to enact a specific ritual, Americans seemed to parade for the sake of parading. In her study of the evolution of the American parade in the early nineteenth century, she contends that parades gradually became ritualized collective movement through the streets that served to unify a community around a common civic celebration. They acted as a kind of cultural performance that told a story about social identity. The American parade was invented during an era of rapid industrialization and expansion. Parades were urban spectacles that "allowed the many contending constituencies of the city to line up and move through the streets without ever encountering one another. [T]he parade was much like the social world in which it germinated—mobile, voluntaristic, laissez-faire, and open. Like a civic omnibus, the parade offered admission to almost any group with sufficient energy, determination, organizational ability, and internal coherence to board it."[38] Parades were originally organized into units made up of skilled artisans, trade guilds, and other labor groups, but Ryan argues, especially in New York City, Irish immigrants increasingly used civic parades as a way to assert their political rights and ethnic identity: "The parade evolved as a civic ceremony at a time when many groups resorted to processions in order to assert their civic rights. . . . Groups of immigrants, especially the Catholic Irish, marched through the streets to demand the full rights of citizenship in defiance of rampant nativism."[39] Parades, then, were a way for ethnic groups to assert their political presence in a safe public venue.

Public celebrations of ethnicity are complicated by the degree to which ethnic groups have control over their representation. Whereas public celebrations are obviously situated within larger institutions of social control, they also provide ethnic groups with the opportunity to define and control the consumption of their image. John Coggelshall has argued that ethnic groups use festival celebrations not just to display their cultural practices but also to hide certain aspects of their communal life from public consumption. In his study of Greek and German festivals, Coggelshall suggests that these festivals are a means by which ethnic groups both enhance and protect their cultural identity. By hiding some aspects of their community and overemphasizing others, Coggelshall contends, ethnic groups maintain a measure of control over their community life.

[G]roups offer a facade of cultural elements which they consciously choose to present to others as an expression of their own identity, and which others interpret contextually in a variety of ways. Equally important, however, are those symbols of identity which emically are considered definitive . . . but which are nevertheless kept hidden from the prying view of outsiders. The screen of ethnicity . . . represents a "safe" or "correct" view of a group's identity. The fact that the group considers some symbols too valuable to present in public also helps to define the group.[40]

Coggelshall also suggests that audiences bring different levels of sophistication and understanding to an ethnic festival that affect what is or is not being communicated: "[S]ymbols unveiled during these performances speak on several levels: some will be obvious to members and non-members; some will be apparent to insiders but not to outsiders; some will be understood by visitors but overlooked by locals."[41] For example, to the unsophisticated visitor, poi is a gelatinous mass of purplish material that sticks to the fingers and is of questionable palatability. Visitors to Hawai'i can participate in Hawaiian culture by sampling poi, or by watching native practitioners pound taro into poi, but they will never fully understand the significance of poi and taro to the native Hawaiian. To the Hawaiian, because poi is made from taro and because Hawaiians trace their genealogy to taro, poi symbolizes the organic relationship among Hawaiians, the land, and the gods.[42]

Coggelshall concludes that the emphasis on a certain aspect of ethnic identity rather than others in these public venues owes much to the creation of an acceptable presentation of American ethnicity:

"Why ethnic expressions such as food and dance are overtly presented (even emphasized), and others such as language or values are ignored or downplayed, perhaps demonstrates a general definition of hyphenated Euro-Americans in American culture. Thus, it may be possible to read ritualized Euro-American ethnic festivals as macro-symbols of 'ethnicity' in general American culture."[43] In other words, ethnic displays define as well as symbolize the common understanding not only of what it means to be a member of a specific ethnic group but also what it means to be an ethnic American.

It is this process of delimiting ethnicity that we see in the early territorial period in Hawai'i. Added to this is the process of racialization, or fitting these ethnic identities into the hierarchical structure of race that was operative in Hawai'i at the time. The interplay among internal ethnic identity, its public presentation, and how that representation was fitted into an overall racial hierarchy helped to define how ethnicity was conceived in the territory of Hawai'i.

PACIFIC PAGEANTS: BALBOA DAY AND
THE MID-PACIFIC CARNIVAL

Balboa Day was not an entirely original celebration, nor was it the first that showcased the ethnic diversity of Hawai'i. In an article examining the origins of similar celebrations in early-twentieth-century Hawai'i, Steven Friesen argues that Lei Day[44] "functioned as an arena for the display and discussion of some of Hawaii's most severe tensions: large immigrations of diverse people, building identity in multi-ethnic communities, the public role of disenfranchised native culture, and the appeal of native customs to settlers and tourists."[45] Lei Day, which was first celebrated in 1928, had several precedents—other floral parades and public pageants that involved large segments of the community. Friesen describes the participation of public and private school children in May Day pageants, which were instituted in Hawai'i because of White New Englanders' nostalgia for the traditional spring festival (see fig. 1). Eventually these celebrations evolved into elaborate productions, staged to celebrate "European heritage, rooted in Greek culture and mediated by America."[46] Parades at these May Day festivities often were object lessons, orchestrated to show children the march of civilization:

Figure 1. May Day pageant, 1912. Courtesy of the Hawaiʻi State Archives, Honolulu.

[T]he 1912 pageant represented all of world history as the progression of civilization through the following stages: tree and cave dwellers[;] . . . North American Indians; Classical Greece; Rome; the Middle Ages; the English May Day; Columbus's voyage to the America; colonial and revolutionary America; and finally a mythic scene in which Miss Columbia and Uncle Sam host a party where all the states and territories including Hawaiʻi were represented by students.[47]

Native Hawaiian customs were not a feature of these early May Day celebrations, but Friesen notes that on at least two occasions, the governor of the territory hosted large children's festivals on May Day, in which children and adults were invited to dress up in English garb, as queens, monks, or common villagers. The emphasis on English royalty led naturally to an invitation to the still-living Hawaiian queen to participate. Although Liliʻuokalani did not attend the celebration, Friesen argues that "by drawing the image of Hawaiian royalty into proximity with the traditions of May Day, the Hawaiian monarchy was revalued as a medieval custom that was, like May Day itself, transitional to the modern period."[48]

These May Day celebrations, which featured flowers, a nod to Hawaiian culture, and an educational imperative, coincided with celebration of the Mid-Pacific Carnival. First organized in 1904, it was conceived of as a parade to celebrate George Washington's birthday. In the next decade, it expanded from one day to one week in late February and included banquets, dances, parades, and pageants, that is, plays or dramatic reinterpretations of historical or mythological events. The organizers were keenly aware of their purpose. In the 1915 program guide Albert Taylor, one of the event promoters, stated the reason for the festival: "The primal ideal for the Washington's Birthday celebration was to institute in the minds of youth of the islands a visual lesson in patriotism."[49] Thus the parade featured a float depicting George Washington being confronted by his father after having chopped down the cherry tree. Carnival organizers soon realized that a celebration of this type could be sold to tourists as an attractive reason to come to or extend their stay in Hawai'i during the slow winter months. A 1917 account in *Paradise of the Pacific* described the carnival as world famous, "drawing tourists in large numbers from the mainland and attracting visitors from all over the earth." The best advertising for the carnival and for Hawai'i was "the satisfied tourists who come, and see, and go away and relate what they have enjoyed. . . . In the pageant are beheld the colorful variety of the garbs of nationalities, the specialties of wide-apart races on parade, the best that each people can exhibit in studied effort to present an excellent exhibition, and the fascinating cosmopolitanism of it all brought together in a great Mid-Pacific fiesta."[50]

The photographs of the Mid-Pacific Carnival reveal the nature of this cosmopolitanism and the degree to which these tropes of ethnicity were safely ensconced in an American celebration. The parade consisted of flower-bedecked automobiles and horse-drawn carts representing civic, commercial, and fraternal organizations, as well as regiments of marchers representing the various ethnic groups in the local community (fig. 2). Men, women, and children came attired in native costumes (fig. 3). Chinese shopkeepers promoted their businesses by sponsoring a traditional lion dance with firecrackers. In the 1909 parade the members of the Improved Order of Redmen (Hawaiian Tribe No. 1) were dressed in leather-fringed pants and shirts and wearing feathered headdresses and moccasins. A tepee tottered at the edge of the float. Some of the men grasp what appear to be spears, possibly guns. The group was pulled by a horse-drawn cart decked out in red, white, and blue bunting and an enormous American flag.[51]

Figure 2.   Mid-Pacific Carnival, early 1900s. Courtesy of the Hawaiʻi State Archives, Honolulu.

Figure 3.   Mid-Pacific Carnival, early 1900s. Courtesy of the Hawaiʻi State Archives, Honolulu.

Figure 4.   Mid-Pacific Carnival, early 1900s. Courtesy of the Hawai'i State
Archives, Honolulu.

Nearly every float, especially those sponsored by an ethnic community, used a series of symbols to represent their community. The
German float carried maidens in dirndls and men dressed as knights,
suggesting a link to Germany's medieval past. The Japanese floats
and marching groups featured geishas dressed in binding kimonos
and wearing elaborate headpieces and wigs, men dressed as samu-
rai, and children wearing traditional Japanese clothing and shoes,
miniature versions of the adults—nothing at all like what they would
have worn in their everyday lives working in the hot sugarcane and
pineapple fields. One float in the 1914 parade featured a display of
Japanese lanterns painted with American flags. Sometimes it seemed
not to matter who was doing the representing. In one parade, an un-
identified young man donned a kimono and wig and, accessorized
with a parasol, rode his decorated bicycle along the parade route
(fig. 4). In a photo captioned "Japanese Tea House Garden Fete,"
two clearly non-Japanese women wear kimonos and are surrounded
by Japanese lanterns and parasols.

In many parades, significant events from the history of Hawai'i
were represented, not just by Hawaiians, but by any and all segments
of the community. Hawaiian culture was to be shared by all locals.

For example, the Punahou Alumni showed "ancient dances." The Ad Club showcased a taro patch. The Boy Scouts showed how fire was first brought to Hawai'i. The Trail and Mountain Club showed ancient burden bearers. One large group representing the Kindergarten Association, the Civic Federation, and the Country Club sponsored floats demonstrating a luau and the preparation of tapa cloth.[52] In these public celebrations the audience is reminded that everyone from the Boy Scouts to the Ad Club had a stake in (and, perhaps, a right to) Hawaiian culture.

The muddle of ethnic images reinforced the ideal of American national life as the blending and melting of distinct ethnic groups. So a Euro-American dressed as a geisha or a Native American provided the opportunity for Americans to assert the literal melting pot, blending and mixing internal ethnic consciousness with external ethnic symbols. Ethnicity was represented by a free-floating set of signifiers not permanently attached to anything or anyone.

The pageants, a featured part of the Mid-Pacific Carnival, "told the story of Hawaii's olden customs and conditions, of her rapid development and her present circumstances."[53] Sometimes the pageants were specifically identified and heavily produced. The 1917 carnival pageant, which told the story of the romance of Iwakauikana, involved a cast of seventy Hawaiians.[54] Often, however, the story was more familiar; for example, the 1913 pageant depicted the landing of Kamehameha in Waikiki. A sequence of photographs in the 1913 commemorative album depicted the presentation of a royal court (one photo is captioned "Wives of the 'Napoleon of the Pacific,'" and another "Kamehameha's Amazonian Guard"). The court came ashore in an outrigger canoe accompanied by a group of Hawaiian men and women, carrying spears and dancing. The king wore a feathered cape and helmet gourd and others in the court carry *pololu* (wooden spears) and *kahili* (royal standards). The dancers were appropriately attired in *malo* (loincloths) and kukui nut *leis* (fig. 5).

Kamehameha was revered by both Hawaiians and Euro-Americans but for vastly different reasons. Unlike Lili'uokalani, the still-living deposed monarch, Kamehameha existed in a legendary past. As the monarch who united the islands, he was considered by Hawaiians a *mo'i* (leader) with tremendous mana. He was reputed to be absurdly brave in battle and a shrewd politician. For Euro-Americans, Kamehameha was an admirable figure because he used military might

LORI PIERCE

Figure 5. Pageant of the royal court of Kamehameha, 1913. Courtesy of the Hawai'i State Archives, Honolulu.

and political savvy to consolidate his power. What is more, he availed himself of European advisers and armaments to secure his power. For that he earned the moniker "Napoleon of the Pacific."[55] For Europeans and Americans, his memory was safe and nonthreatening because war and political manipulation were features of Hawaiian culture that they admired and respected. Kamehameha was a safe Hawaiian hero because he operated in a way that Westerners could understand.[56]

The erasure of the Hawaiian nation, legally and symbolically, was a necessary step in the creation of an American pattern of ethnicity and racial formation in Hawai'i. All non-Whites, but especially Hawaiians, were transformed from immigrants and natives into ethnic Americans. No longer loyal to their former homelands, they were being tutored in the knowledge of democratic institutions that would ultimately transform them into Americans.

The discourse of aloha asserted the equality of ethnic groups through assimilation. Every group in Hawai'i was equally welcome and had an equal claim on the right to be in Hawai'i. Hawaiians themselves were incorporated into this system of ethnic equality in order to undermine their prior claim to the right to control the political and social destiny of Hawai'i. Euro-Americans, newcomers, and *kama'aina* were welcome and perceived in this discourse the same as all other groups. The discourse of aloha distracts attention from the injustice done to Hawaiians and the control exercised by the Haole minority.

The discourse of aloha was apparent in attempts to objectively examine race relations in Hawai'i. Romanzo Adams's perceptions and theoretical outlook dominated studies of race and ethnicity well into the late twentieth century. Adams's presumption was that assimilation was the natural process of all immigrant groups. He did not question the propriety of Euro-American control over Hawai'i and therefore did not question the legitimacy of asking native Hawaiians to assimilate into a system that was foreign to them. The assimilationist model does not allow us to question this.[57]

The discourse of aloha as an explanation for the presumed racial harmony is problematic on a number of levels. The ideology of racial harmony loudly trumpeted and celebrated in a society that was so plainly racially stratified created a series of ironic juxtapositions and contradictory behavior on the part of all participants. The discourse of aloha was a public virtue that was appealed to on civic occasions and in community fora. But the appeal to aloha as a public virtue also had the effect of relegating ethnic and racial antagonism to the private sphere. And if ethnic antagonism existed only in the private sphere, talking about it in public violated the egalitarian code of conduct. If the mention of racial segregation and discrimination was a violation of an unspoken code of conduct, if it violated the symbolic representation of equality, then the issue simply disappeared from civic discourse. Hawai'i effectively became a racial paradise, not because the problems that accompanied a racialized political economy did not exist, but because it became taboo to acknowledge them.

The encounter between Native Hawaiians, Asian immigrants, and Euro-Americans in the early territorial period was fraught with tension but structured by an understanding of race and ethnicity that simultaneously promoted ethnic identity and encouraged assimilation. This understanding of ethnicity subsumed into White culture and supported by the discourse of aloha effectively maintained the rigidly racially stratified political economy of Hawai'i by appealing to the public value of egalitarian social customs and calm interethnic relations.

The dominance of the discourse of aloha predisposed residents and visitors to emphasize those elements of culture in Hawai'i that highlighted a sense of universal brotherhood. The image of Hawai'i that was disseminated throughout the world was of a place where congenial fellowship, based on the equality of all humans, was not only possible, but on the verge of being achieved.

In 1932, shortly after the infamous Massie-Kahahawai case,[58] Du Puy was dispatched to Hawai'i by Ray Lyman Wilbur, secretary of the interior. The Massie-Kahahawai case, involving the charge of the rape of a White woman at the hands of non-White men, received intense media coverage. Her accusation was not substantiated in court, and her husband took it upon himself to avenge her honor by arranging the murder of one of the defendants, Joseph Kahahawai. The case was fraught with racial tension and raised the question of whether Hawai'i was safe for White women and whether the territory was being properly administered by the Haole ruling class. Du Puy, a well-known newspaper reporter, was sent to Hawai'i "to observe the facts and report his findings" to the Department of the Interior. The department published the report, entitled *Hawai'i and Its Race Problem.*

Du Puy's report is a curious document and a faithful representation of the discourse of aloha. The case itself is not mentioned; instead, in introducing the report to the general public, Secretary Wilbur spoke indirectly of "events" in fall 1931 that suggested that "a delicate race situation existed in Hawaii."[59] Wilbur contended that given the unprecedented nature of the social relationships in Hawai'i, the situation required investigation into "how they get along, one with the other, and how they are fitting into that scheme of self government born to the blue-eyed peoples of the other side of the world."[60] The conclusion seems foregone, and Du Puy's report reiterated what was already known. Rather than discuss any race problem that Hawai'i might have had, Du Puy described the lack of a race problem. True to the discourse of aloha, he elided the issue of institutional racism implicit in the outcome of the Massie case in favor of reassuring his White audience that Hawai'i was being carefully managed by responsible citizens. Further, he reported, the non-White population of Hawai'i was under control. Du Puy said nothing that might explain why the local population of Hawai'i was outraged by the Massie case. Instead, he ignored the racial implications of this miscarriage of justice in favor of reinforcing the image of Hawaiʻi as a racial paradise.

The captions that describe the copiously illustrated report (seventy-nine photographs in 130 pages) convey the relevant message. Hawaiʻi is a place of uncommon and dramatic beauty: "a lava fountain on Mauna Loa"; "the glory of the night blooming Cereus." Hawaiʻi retains some elements of the ancient ways such as "riding the surf board," "lei making," and "throw net fishing." But Hawaiians are modern and participate in urban life, for example, "native girls working in the cannery." Even "the Hawaiian cowboy is quite thoroughly Americanized," and "the policeman is a Polynesian." The plantation laborers "are all descendants of coolies from somewhere," but "children born of Japanese coolie laborers are making their first step toward becoming Americans." In fact, because "institutions are built on the American model," "the White man's manner of life prevails." Even though "a bit of the old life survives," "the Whites have created modern Honolulu."[61]

Indeed.

NOTES

1. "Haole" is a Hawaiian term meaning "foreigner" but has come to be used to refer to White Euro-Americans. Therefore, I use these terms interchangeably.

2. In his December 18, 1893, message to Congress, Cleveland conceded that the report of his investigator, James Blount, made it impossible to conclude anything other than the fact that "Hawaiʻi was taken possession of by the United States forces without the consent or wish of the Government of the islands. . . . Therefore the military occupation of Hawaiʻi by the United States on the day mentioned was wholly without justification." See Grover Cleveland, "A Friendly State Being Robbed of Its Independence and Sovereignty," in *Hawaiʻi: Return to Nationhood,* ed. Ulla Hasager and Jonathan Friedman (Copenhagen: International Working Group on Indigenous Affairs, 1994), 129.

The 103d Congress, in 1993, acknowledged the facts of the overthrow in Joint Resolution 190, which "apologizes to Native Hawaiians on behalf of the people of the United States for the overthrow of the Kingdom of Hawaii on January 17, 1893 with the participation of agents and citizens of the United States, and the deprivation of the rights of Native Hawaiians to self-determination" (U.S. Public Law 103–150, 103d Congress, Joint Resolution 190, November 23, 1993).

3. Alexander Hume Ford, "The Genesis of the Pan-Pacific Union," *Mid-Pacific Magazine* (October 1925): 377.

4. The Pan Pacific Union was the most well known of Ford's groups. The union itself grew as an umbrella organization that contained many of Ford's enterprises. He began by organizing Hands-around-the-Pacific clubs in many Pacific nations. These clubs were akin to civic chambers of commerce dedicated to the promotion of international goodwill through tourism and related businesses. In Hawai'i the clubs organized luncheons and yearly banquets, most notably the 12-12-12 luncheons, which gathered 12 Euro-American, 12 Chinese, and 12 Japanese "prominent men" to have frank discussions about interracial problems in the community. These luncheons eventually became known as the Good Relations Clubs. The Pan Pacific Union developed to contain all these efforts and to promote and organize international conferences on science and education. The only biographical treatment of Alexander Hume Ford is Valerie Noble, *Hawaiian Prophet: Alexander Hume Ford, a Biography* (Smithtown, N.Y.: Exposition Press, 1980). Ford himself reminisced about his life and the development of the Pan Pacific Union in the pages of *Mid-Pacific Magazine.* He wrote a fifteen-part history of the union under the title "The Genesis of the Pan Pacific Union" which ran monthly from September 1925 to November 1926. See also Paul Hooper's history of internationalism in Hawai'i, *Elusive Destiny: The Internationalist Movement in Modern Hawai'i* (Honolulu: University of Hawai'i Press, 1988). Ford is also remembered in the history of the Outrigger Canoe Club: Harold Yost, *The Outrigger Canoe Club of Honolulu, Hawai'i* (Honolulu: Outrigger Canoe Club, 1971).

5. John W. Bains, "Pacific Peoples Flag Pageant," *Paradise of the Pacific* (December 1915): 65.

6. Jean West Maury, "Balboa Day in Hawai'i," *Mid-Pacific Magazine* (September 1919): 228.

7. Of the racialized nature of Hawai'i's labor force, Ed Beechert wrote: "The concept of racial superiority underlay the often brutal seizure of power over labor supplies and land. Important in this rationalization was the notion that the white race could not perform labor under the difficult conditions of tropical and subtropical plantations. Accompanying the forcible conversion of domestic labor was the racist conviction that the objects of this attention were thereby improved and brought to a higher degree of civilization through the acquisition of western values and work discipline." Edward D. Beechert, *Working in Hawai'i: A Labor History* (Honolulu: University of Hawai'i Press, 1985), 40. On this point, see also Ronald Takaki, *Pau Hana: Plantation Life and Labor in Hawai'i, 1835–1920* (Honolulu: University of Hawai'i Press, 1984); Gary Okihiro, *Cane Fires: The Anti-Japanese Movement in Hawai'i, 1865–1945* (Philadelphia: Temple University Press, 1991).

8. Plantation owners frequently took advantage of and instigated antagonisms between the various ethnic groups. Laborers lived and worked largely segregated from one another, and the foremen of work crews would pit ethnic groups against one another by requiring that they compete for bonuses. For many years, this prevented effective labor organizing. See Beechert, *Working in Hawai'i*, esp. chaps. 10, 11.

9. Dorothy Ochiai Hazama and Jane Okamoto Komeiji, *Okage Sama De: The Japanese in Hawai'i, 1885–1985* (Honolulu: Bess Press, 1986), 111.

10. Eileen Tamura does a thorough job of documenting the Haole response to Japanese demographic dominance in Hawai'i. See Eileen Tamura, *Americanization, Acculturation and Ethnic Identity: The Nisei Generation in Hawai'i* (Urbana: University of Illinois Press, 1991). See also Okihiro, *Cane Fires*.

11. The standard reference on Americanization is John Higham, *Strangers in the Land: Patterns of American Nativism* (New York: Atheneum, 1963). However, more recent scholarship expands on Higham's basic historical insights. See, for example, James R. Barrett, "Americanization from the Bottom Up: Immigration and the Remaking of the Working Class in the United States, 1880–1930," *Journal of American History* 79, no. 3 (December 1992): 996–1020. Barrett extends Higham's discussion by describing how immigrant communities appropriated, adopted, and advocated Americanization in their own communities.

12. The Chinese Exclusion Act, passed in 1882, was the culmination of decades of agitation in California against so-called coolie labor in mines and in the railroad industry. See Andrew Gyory, *Closing the Gate: Race, Politics and the Chinese Exclusion Act* (Durham, N.C.: University of North Carolina Press, 1998). In 1907 the Gentleman's Agreement between Japan and the United States headed off an international incident precipitated by the San Francisco School Board's move to educate Japanese children in segregated schools. As a result, the Japanese government agreed to stop issuing passports to laborers headed for the United States. The era of anti-Asian immigration legislation ended with the passage of the Immigration Act of 1924, which prohibited admission of aliens ineligible for citizenship, that is Asian immigrants. See Roger Daniels, *The Politics of Prejudice: The Anti-Japanese Movement in California and the Struggle for Japanese Exclusion* (New York: Atheneum, 1973).

13. See Noenoe Silva, "Ku'e! Hawaiian Women's Resistance to the Annexation," *Women in Hawai'i Sites, Identities, and Voices: Social Process in Hawai'i* 38 (1997): 2–15; Thomas Osbourne, *Annexation Hawai'i* (Waimanalo: Island Style Press, 1998).

14. There has not yet been a satisfactory study of the ruling elite Haole class in Hawai'i during these years. It could be argued that most of the social and political histories of Hawai'i focus unduly on this small caste. However,

in focusing on the political intrigue and the pattern of ethnic group mobility (as is the case with Daws's *Shoal of Time*) there is very little scholarship that explores the social dynamics that took place between the various segments of the Haole community or the intellectual and cultural influences that would provide the basis of comparison to a similar caste in the plantation culture of the Deep South or the upper strata of the elites in larger American cities. See Gavan Daws, *Shoal of Time: History of the Hawaiian Islands* (New York: Macmillan, 1968). On patterns of residential segregation in Hawai'i , see Youngmin Lee, *Ethnicity toward Multiculturalism: Socio-Spatial Relations of the Korean Community in Honolulu, 1903–1940* (Ph.D. dissertation, Louisiana State University, 1995).

15. Very little of the scholarship on Hawai'i fails to note the unique set of historical circumstances that resulted in the complex mix of ethnic groups in the islands. Race is a central feature of the two major social histories of Hawai'i: Lawrence Fuchs, *Hawai'i Pono: A Social History* (New York: Harcourt, Brace and World, 1961); and Daws, *Shoal of Time*. Asian American Studies in Hawai'i also presume the centrality of racism and discrimination in the social formation of local identity. Labor historians have certainly not neglected the racist paternalism of plantation owners. And, of course, a new generation of Hawaiian scholarship is revealing the depth of racial thinking and its influence on social and political interactions between Hawaiian and Haole. See Beechert, *Working in Hawai'i;* Takaki, *Pau Hana;* Okihiro, *Cane Fires;* Noel Kent, *Hawai'i: Islands under the Influence* (Honolulu: University of Hawai'i Press, 1983); Lilikala Kame'eleihiwa, *Native Land and Foreign Desires: Pahea la e pono ai* (Honolulu: Bishop Museum Press, 1992).

16. Euro-Americans who served in the cabinets of Hawaiian *ali'i* (royalty) pushed for a system of land tenure whereby property could be bought and sold. Some historians argue that Haole ministers had the best interests of Hawaiians at heart and created these legal structures to protect Hawaiians from unscrupulous land speculators and squatters. However, the ownership of land was a concept entirely anathema to Hawaiian sensibilities, which were grounded in the belief in reciprocal relations among the land, the people, the ali'i and the gods. The result was the near-complete disenfranchisement of Hawaiians from their land. See Jon Chinen, *The Great Mahele: Hawai'i's Land Division of 1848* (Honolulu: University of Hawai'i Press, 1958). For a reinterpretation of the Mahele from the viewpoint of native Hawaiians, see Kame'eleihiwa, *Native Land.*

17. Daws, *Shoal of Time*, 211.

18. See Beechert, *Working in Hawai'i;* Takaki, *Pau Hana.*

19. Okihiro, *Cane Fires,* 14. See also Daws, *Shoal of Time*, 312–14.

20. William R. Castle, *Hawai'i Past and Present* (New York: Dodd, Mead, 1917), 16.

21. Ibid., 55.

22. Ibid., 17.

23. See *Annual Report of the Governor of the Territory of Hawai'i to the Secretary of the Interior,* 1900–1906, 1907–28 (Washington, D.C.: U.S. Government Printing Office).

24. Walter F. Dillingham, "Hawai'i's Labor and Racial Problems," November 13, 1922, minutes of the Social Science Association of Honolulu, Hawai'i State Archives.

25. Milton Gordon, *Assimilation in American Life: The Role of Race, Religion, and National Origins* (New York: Oxford University Press, 1964), 88.

26. See Judith R. Hughes, "The Demise of the English Standard School System in Hawai'i," *Hawaiian Journal of History* 27 (1993): 65–89.

27. Honolulu City Directory, 1928, 201. Margaret Dietz's Commercial School advertised heavily in the City Directory, using various slogans, including, "Will Send You a Stenographer with English Ability" and "High Standard English."

28. See Romanzo Adams, *Interracial Marriage in Hawai'i: A Study of the Mutually Conditioned Process of Acculturation and Amalgamation* (New York: Macmillan, 1937). Perhaps the most comprehensive source on interethnic marriage is Paul R. Spickard, *Mixed Blood: Intermarriage and Ethnic Identity in Twentieth-Century America* (Madison: University of Wisconsin Press, 1989).

29. Hawai'i was possibly the only place in the United States at the time where interracial sex was perceived of as a desirable form of assimilation. However, it should be noted that interethnic marriages were not advocated for all groups. Japanese and Haole had relatively low rates of intermarriage before World War II. Interracial mixing is better ascribed to the fact that many Asian immigrants came to Hawai'i as groups of single men and that disease had nearly devastated the native Hawaiian community. Interracial liaisons may have been much more practical than is generally supposed.

30. Sidney Gulick, *Mixing the Races in Hawai'i* (Honolulu: Hawaiian Board Book Rooms, 1937), 1–2.

31. Gulick literally depicted this new race by including several pages of pictures of racial types. He borrowed photographs from the Kamehameha Schools and the University of Hawai'i, and instead of listing a name beneath each photograph, the subjects are identified by the mathematical formula of their racial type. One girl is $\frac{4}{8}$ Hawaiian, $\frac{1}{8}$ Chinese, and $\frac{3}{8}$ Caucasian. One boy is $\frac{1}{4}$ Hawaiian and $\frac{1}{4}$ Caucasian (no mention is made of the other half of his racial identity). Illustrating racial mixtures by this kind of literal depiction and tortured mathematical computation was not unusual and frequently featured young children or women. Interestingly, however, Adams's seminal work on

interracial marriage in Hawai'i also uses photographs of Hawaiian types, but he is careful to point out that he uses them to illustrate social rather than racial types (*Interracial Marriage in Hawai'i,* xvii).

32. Gulick, *Mixing the Races in Hawai'i,* 47.

33. Randolph Bourne, "Trans-National America," in *History of a Literary Radical and Other Essays,* ed. Van Wyck Brooks (New York: B. W. Huebsch, 1920), 278.

34. Ibid., 280.

35. Adams, *Interracial Marriage in Hawai'i,* 311–12.

36. William Atherton Du Puy, *Hawai'i and Its Race Problem* (Washington, D.C.: U.S. Department of the Interior, 1932), 19–20.

37. On parades and American ethnicity, see Simon Peter Newman, *Parades and the Politics of the Street: Festive Culture in the Early American Republic* (Philadelphia: Temple University Press, 1997); Susan Davis, *Parades and Power: Street Theatre in Nineteenth-Century Philadelphia* (Berkeley: University of California Press, 1986); April Schultz, *Ethnicity on Parade: Inventing the Norwegian-American through Celebration* (Amherst: University of Massachusetts Press, 1994). David Glassberg's *American Historical Pageantry: The Uses of Tradition in the Early Twentieth Century* (Chapel Hill: University of North Carolina Press, 1990) also provides an interesting context for understanding civic celebrations of this type. Glassberg argues that historical pageantry during the Progressive era promoted civic unity and the assimilation of immigrant communities. The ethnic pageants discussed here certainly can be interpreted in this light, but my analysis suggests that in Hawai'i these celebrations have a longer history and a genesis more organic to Hawai'i than the Progressive era celebrations he examines.

The other body of literature that is important here pertains to ethnographic display and the performance of ethnicity in these venues. The display of indigenous peoples has a long history, dating to Columbus, who returned to Spain with an Arawak man who died after two years of being exhibited. Hawaiians were among the many indigenous peoples who were displayed at world's fairs and international expositions beginning in the mid-nineteenth century. Robert Rydell's work is definitive: *All the World's a Fair: Visions of Empire at American International Expositions, 1876–1916* (Chicago: University of Chicago Press, 1984).

But the display of Hawaiians seemed to have less to do with their status as natives than with the romanticized, exoticized, and sexualized images that circulated in the media and American popular culture in order to sell Hawai'i as a tourist destination. There have been several institutions in which the performance of Hawaiian cultural practices has been used as a tourist attraction. Lalani Village, Ulumau Village, and the Polynesian Cultural Center might be interpreted in the light of the history of ethnographic display. On the Polynesian Cultural Center, see Verniece Wineera, "Selves and Others: A Reflexive Study of Negotiation, Compromise, and the Representation of Culture in Touristic Display at the Polynesian Cultural Center" (Ph.D. dissertation, University of Hawai'i, 2000).

38. Mary Ryan, "The American Parade: Representations of the Nineteenth-Century Social Order," in *The New Cultural History*, ed. Lynn Hunt (Berkeley: University of California Press, 1989), 137.

39. Ibid.

40. John Coggelshall, "Sauerkraut and Souvlaki: Ethnic Festivals as Performances of Identity," in *Celebrations of Identity: Multiple Voices in American Ritual Performance*, ed. Pamela R. Frese (Westport, Conn.: Bergin and Garvey, 1993), 37.

41. Ibid.

42. See Lilikala Kame'eleihiwa, *"Ua Mau Ke Ea O Ka Aina i Ka Pono:* The Concepts of Sovereignty and Religious Sanction of Correct Political Behavior," in Hasager and Friedman, eds., *Hawai'i: Return to Nationhood*, 34–43.

43. Coggelshall, "Sauerkraut," 44.

44. In Hawai'i, May Day is Lei Day, a semiofficial holiday during which schoolchildren stage pageants, usually including a Lei Day king and queen, hula, and other festivities. Lei Day is also an adult celebration and features a royal court, parade, and charity dances.

45. See Steven J. Friesen, "The Origins of Lei Day: Festivity and the Construction of Ethnicity in the Territory of Hawai'i," *History and Anthropology* 10, no. 1 (1996): 2.

46. Ibid., 8.

47. Ibid., 7.

48. Ibid., 10.

49. Albert Taylor, "Carnival Yesterday and Today," 1915 Mid-Pacific Carnival Program Guide, Hawaiian Collection, University of Hawai'i Library.

50. "Mid-Pacific Carnival," *Paradise of the Pacific*, March 1917, 1–3.

51. Philip Deloria argues that organizations such as the Improved Order of Redmen that appropriated Native American traditions afforded Euro-Americans the opportunity to identify with natives in both positive and negative ways. The literal co-opting of native identity as a weekend leisure activity in early twentieth-century-America when actual natives were being coerced out of their nativeness creates an ironic twist on ethnic American identity. See Philip Deloria, *Playing Indian* (New Haven: Yale University Press, 1998).

52. "Mid-Pacific Carnival," 2.

53. Ibid., 3.

54. "A 1917 Carnival Feature," *Paradise of the Pacific*, February 1917, 8.

55. The respect given to Kamehameha by Europeans and Americans is symbolized by the famous statue of him, located in downtown Honolulu across

from Iolani Palace and duplicated in Statuary Hall on Capitol Hill in Washington, D.C. Kamehameha is represented in much the same way that Julius Caesar is, with one arm outstretched. I am indebted to Stephen Morrillo, in the Department of History at Wabash College, for pointing this out to me.

56. The accumulation of *mana* was roughly equivalent to having wealth based on land, gold, jewels, or other European equivalents. Kamehameha was not the first to attempt to rule all the islands, but according to Lilikala Kameʻeleihiwa, the way was paved by Kahekili, whose love of war brought all the islands except Hawaiʻi under his influence. The influence of Western military technology was important but irrelevant if both sides in battle had access to it. So, according to Kameʻeleihiwa, the unification of the islands under Kamehameha had more to do with the powerful mana of Kahekili than it did with the implements of war and the advice given to Kamehameha by John Young and Isaac Davis, as is usually supposed. Lilikala Kameʻeleihiwa, e-mail correspondence with the author, November 16, 1999. See also Kameʻeleihiwa, *Native Lands, Foreign Desires*.

57. For an interesting critique of Romanzo Adams and early sociology in Hawaiʻi, see John Mei Liu, "Cultivating Cane: Asian Labor and the Hawaiian Sugar Plantation System within the Capitalist World Economy" (Ph.D. dissertation, University of California, Los Angeles, 1985).

58. On the Massie case, see Theon Wright, *Rape in Paradise* (New York: Hawthorn Books, 1966); Eric Takayama, "Error in 'Paradise': Race, Sex and the Massie-Kahahawai Affair of 1930's Hawaiʻi" (M.A. thesis, University of Hawaiʻi, 1997).

59. Du Puy, *Hawaiʻi and Its Race Problem,* ix.

60. Ibid., x.

61. Ibid., vii–viii.

PART 3

Monoracial Challenges to Racial Hierarchy

7

Looking Backward, Moving *Adelante*

A Critical Analysis of the African American and Chicana/o Civil Rights Movements

RALPH ARMBRUSTER-SANDOVAL

In the 1950s and 1960s, after years of resistance and struggle, the African American and Chicana/o[1] civil rights movements emerged.[2] Both movements challenged centuries of racial oppression and struggled for social change and equality. African American and Chicana/o activists in these movements marched, sang, and fasted for *la causa* and their freedom. Yet freedom, as the song goes, was a constant struggle. These activists encountered deeply held hostilities and fierce opposition. Some, for instance, lost their jobs and homes; others were arrested, beaten, even killed. They kept their eyes on the prize, however, and finally they, along with the organizations they were members of, succeeded in eliminating the most overt forms of racism in the United States.

The abolition of segregation marked a key turning point in American history. For hundreds of years, a suffocating system of racism, known as White supremacy, dominated and shaped—but did not determine—the everyday lives of people of color. Slavery, segregated public schools, lynchings, reservations, genocide, forced repatriation, and internment camps are some of the most obvious and blatant manifestations of White supremacy. The transformation of this racial order, along with the introduction of social reforms, such as affirmative action, created more opportunities and actually generated upward mobility for *some* people of color. Nonetheless, persistent problems, such as poverty, unemployment, sexism, and heterosexism, limited more widespread advances for women, gays and lesbians, and working-class people of color.

The African American and Chicana/o civil rights movements realized that the struggle against these forms of oppression was just as crucial as the fight against racism. Both movements, however, while ideologically and politically diverse, primarily concentrated on race and secondarily on class, but generally excluded issues of gender and sexuality. Some lesser-known organizations and activists in both movements overcame this tendency by recognizing the interlocking nature of oppression, as well as the multiple identities that exist in the African American and Chicana/o communities. These groups and activists claimed that more wide-ranging social change would come about only through a radical restructuring of class and power relations in American society. Yet even these organizations, which typically emphasized the relationship between race and class, were riddled with internal contradictions, such as the marginalization of women and gays and lesbians.

My objective here is to critically examine the general ("mainstream") ideological and political trajectory of the African American and Chicana/o civil rights movements and compare them to more unfamiliar groups within both that called for radical social change. I contend that although both mainstream and radical "tendencies" achieved some remarkable victories, they did not overcome exclusionary or essentialist practices that limited their achievement of even greater success. The key question, I believe, for social justice–minded scholars and activists today is, how do "we" create "new" social movements that simultaneously attack interlocking forms of oppression and generate meaningful and substantial social change? I argue that one of the first steps in moving *adelante* (forward), toward answering that question, is to look back and analyze the achievements and limitations of these two social movements.

Given these goals and objectives, I begin with an overview of some of the key organizations, activists, and events of the African American civil rights movement. This synopsis serves two functions: it illustrates the race, class, and gender dynamics of the movement; and it demonstrates the internal cleavages and conflicts that existed in it. I conclude this section with a brief analysis of three organizations, the Poor People's Campaign, the Black Panther Party, and the League of Revolutionary Black Workers, that challenged not only racial but class inequality as well. I then examine the organizational trajectory, key moments, and conflicts of the Chicana/o civil rights movement from a race, class, and gender perspective. I also examine a relatively unknown group within *el movimiento* (the movement), Centro de Acción Sociedad Autónoma (Center for Autonomous Social Action [CASA]), which adopted a Marxist framework and focused on the intersection of race and class. In concluding, I assess the strengths and weaknesses of both movements and examine race and the "global justice" movement.

The African American Civil Rights Movement

The Beginning, 1955–1965

The African American civil rights movement began rather simply. On December 1, 1955, in Montgomery, Alabama, Rosa Parks, a seamstress and the secretary of the local branch of the National Association for the Advancement of Colored People (NAACP), sat down in the "Black section" of the bus. Moments later, the bus driver noticed that the "White section" was full and that a White passenger was standing up. The driver demanded that Parks and three other Black passengers move so that the White person could sit. Parks refused. An altercation ensued, and she was arrested and jailed. Word of her arrest spread quickly through Montgomery's tight-knit Black community, and later that night Jo Ann Robinson, an English professor at Alabama State College, along with some of her students and members of the middle-class-based Women's Political Council (WPC), worked until dawn making informational leaflets. The leaflets called for a one-day boycott of the city's buses to protest Parks's arrest, as well as the beatings, shootings, and even deaths of other Black bus riders. Over the next two days, Robinson, Alabama State College students, and the WPC distributed the leaflets all over the city. On the day of the boycott the buses were virtually empty, and the protest was seen as an overwhelming success.[3]

Later that night, boycott organizers and local activists, such as E. D. Nixon, state president of the Brotherhood of Sleeping Car Porters, held a mass meeting at a local church. Several thousand people attended and pushed for a continuation of the boycott. After some debate, the boycott was extended, and a new organization, known as the Montgomery Improvement Association (MIA), was established. The MIA, whose first president was a young and relatively unknown minister named Martin Luther King Jr., coordinated the boycott. At this time, King, then the twenty-five-year-old pastor of Dexter Avenue Baptist Church in Montgomery, understood the intellectual and moral basis of nonviolence but had some reservations about it.[4] Nonetheless, after a series of conversations with Bayard Rustin, a longtime pacifist and civil rights activist who had been ousted from the Fellowship of Reconciliation (FOR) in 1953 after he was arrested on "morals charges" stemming from having sex with two men, King, the MIA, and other local residents and activists decided that they would continue the boycott in a nonviolent manner until their demands, which included desegregating the city's buses, were met.[5]

The boycott lasted a little over a year. During that period, a broad cross section of Montgomery's Black citizens—men and women, young and old, middle- and working-class—walked for miles or took "collective taxis" or carpools to work, to school, and to places they simply needed to go. These tactics were successful, and they enraged the city's White power structure, police force, and racist organizations, such as the Ku Klux Klan (KKK) and the White Citizens' Council. Working together, these groups launched an all-out attack to defeat the boycott. Local police officers, for example, ticketed, fined, and harassed carpool drivers, and the homes of Martin Luther King and E. D. Nixon were bombed. More than ninety MIA activists were arrested for violating a state antiboycott law. Local White youths also shouted racial epithets, threw eggs, and beat some of the boycotters.[6]

The city's Black community did not back down, however. MIA attorney Fred Gray filed a lawsuit, for instance, under the *Brown v. Board of Education* decision, challenging the constitutionality of Montgomery's bus seating laws.[7] A federal court of three judges backed the MIA's position, ruling that the city's bus segregation laws were unconstitutional. White city officials appealed the decision to the U.S. Supreme Court, and the boycott continued. Finally, in November 1956, the Supreme Court upheld the lower court's decision and ordered the city to integrate its buses. On December 21, 1956, for the first time in more than a year, Blacks boarded the city's buses and sat down wherever they pleased.

The Montgomery Bus Boycott helped to spark a militant ethos among African Americans all over the country. As Jack Bloom contends in *Class, Race, and the Civil Rights Movement*, decades of White racism and terror had created feelings of self-doubt, hatred, fear, and apathy among a large segment of the African American community in the South.[8] Social movement theorists, such as Doug McAdam and Alberto Melucci, have held that the construction of a collective identity and a shift in consciousness are crucial for the emergence of social movements.[9] Bloom argues that rising expectations, protests, years of pent-up frustration, and a series of legal victories, such as the *Brown* decision, after World War II indicated that new forms of consciousness, as well as a sense of hope and efficacy, were developing.[10]

This dynamic was clearly evident in Montgomery. When Rosa Parks was arrested, the city's Black community rallied around her and actively supported the boycott because they understood what she experienced and were no longer willing to take it. This common history of oppression united Black Montgomerians and gave them the feeling that despite their class and gender differences, they were members of a racially oppressed group that was struggling against a similar foe—racism—and that they were fighting for the same goal—their freedom. The bus boycott then facilitated the development of strong bonds of solidarity, a collective identity, and a new insurgent consciousness among many African Americans inside and outside the South.

These three factors provided the movement with the catalyst that got it off the ground. The fledging movement could not be sustained over time without the establishment of organizations that could mobilize people and resources, as well as enter into negotiations with elites and policy makers. One of the key and most well known organizations within the African American civil rights movement, which emerged shortly after the bus boycott, was the Southern Christian Leadership Conference (SCLC).[11] The SCLC's founding members were a group of relatively young ministers that included Martin Luther King, Ralph Abernathy, and Fred Shuttlesworth, as well as Ella Baker, a longtime civil rights activist. The SCLC primarily focused on voter registration and nonviolent direct action (e.g. boycotts, marches), and it clashed with older civil rights organizations, such as the NAACP, because the latter favored confronting segregation through class-action lawsuits and other legal remedies.

The SCLC was created during the same year that federal troops were sent into Little Rock, Arkansas. In 1957, after a lengthy delay, President Dwight D. Eisenhower finally ordered the deployment of army units because Arkansas Governor Orval Faubus had steadfastly refused to implement the *Brown* decision, and, three years after that decision, the state's public schools remained racially segregated. Faubus's intransigence, as well as that of other southern governors, was a crucial test for the movement because it could ill afford to lose the momentum it had gained after the Montgomery Bus Boycott. White segregationists regarded the battle with equal importance. As one White southerner said apocalyptically, "Little Rock is the last battle. If we win, integration is dead. If we lose, the Republic of the United States is gone forever."[12]

Both sides, then, viewed Little Rock as a major turning point in the struggle for civil rights. In September 1957, after a federal court ordered the city's school board to desegregate its schools, Faubus called out the National Guard to block the entrance of nine Black teenagers at Central High. The teenagers endured angry White mobs and chants of "nigger" as they walked and tried to enter the school, but the Guardsmen turned them back. The stand-off eventually became violent when a group of White demonstrators beat two Black reporters. They would have been killed, but the crowd shifted its attention to the teenagers, who quietly slipped through the back entrance of the school. They were eventually driven out, and the crisis, which generated widespread media and television coverage, continued.

Sensing the constitutional crisis and international embarrassment that the Little Rock conflict had created, President Eisenhower reluctantly acted and sent in federal troops to escort the teenagers into Central High. Because of fierce opposition, the troops stayed inside the school for the remainder of the year, but there would be no turning back. The walls were coming down; justice, as King said during one of his sermons, was beginning to roll like a "mighty stream," and it looked like segregation and Jim Crow were coming to an end.[13]

Brown, the Montgomery Bus Boycott, and the Little Rock victory gave African Americans a tremendous sense of hope that their long American nightmare, as Malcolm X later put it, was nearly over. White southerners saw these achievements, as well as sustained Black militancy, in more catastrophic terms, however. Many thought their "way of life and culture," as well as "American Civilization," were at risk. These concerns led a number of White southerners to create and revive White supremacist organizations such as the KKK and White Citizens' Councils that were committed to maintaining segregation by "any means necessary." They accomplished this goal by obtaining political offices and refusing to implement *Brown*, along with other desegregation statutes and decisions. The KKK and the White Citizens' Councils also resorted to terror, intimidation, and murder.[14]

From the perspective of many White southerners, "massive resistance," as it was known, was successful. It temporarily halted the momentum of the movement, and it virtually stopped public school segregation in the South. For example, Bloom notes that "[b]y June 1961, Alabama, Georgia, Mississippi, and South Carolina still had no blacks in desegregated schools. Florida, Louisiana, North Carolina, and Virginia had less than .1 percent of their pupils in desegregated schools. Arkansas and Tennessee had less than 1 percent and Texas had 1.2 percent in desegregated public schools."[15]

The slow pace of social change did not generate despair. "Massive resistance" actually created a sense of urgency and anger among a large segment of the African American community. These sentiments were perhaps most strongly felt among young Black college students. As Bloom argues, White resistance did not frighten them; they felt that they had the right to be treated equally.[16]

These feelings led the students to take action. On February 1, 1960, four Black college students sat down at a lunch counter in

Greensboro, North Carolina. They were refused service under the city's segregation laws, but they did not leave. They politely continued their protest until the store closed. They came back the next day, but again, they were refused service. Over the next several days, hundreds of protestors joined them, and sit-ins were held throughout the city. The sit-in movement then spread beyond Greensboro. For instance, over the next three months sit-ins occurred in seventy cities.[17]

The students who were active in these creative protests realized they needed to establish an organization to coordinate their efforts. Thus, in April 1960, under the guidance of Ella Baker and with financial assistance from the SCLC, a group of student activists that included Diane Nash, John Lewis, Bernard Layfette, and Marion Berry met at Shaw University in Raleigh, North Carolina, to create what later became known as one of the most fearless and militant organizations of the movement, the Student Nonviolent Coordinating Committee (SNCC).[18] At this initial meeting, Baker made the suggestion that SNCC should remain independent from the SCLC. She had been executive director of the SCLC for three years but resigned because she felt that it marginalized women and was based on a charismatic, top-down leadership structure. Baker candidly discussed the reasons for her departure:

I had known that there would never be any role for me in a leadership capacity [at the SCLC]. First, I'm a woman; I'm not a minister. And second, I'm a person who feels I have to maintain some degree of personal integrity, and [be guided] by my own barometer of what is important and what is not. I knew that my penchant for speaking honestly about what I considered [desirable] would not be tolerated. The combination of being a woman and an older woman presented problems. I was old enough to be the mother of the leadership. The basic attitude of men, especially ministers, as to what [should be] the role of a woman in their church setup [was] that of taking orders, not providing leadership. This would have never lent itself to my being a leader.

I even heard something to the effect that I hated Martin [Dr. King]. But I think that this stems from the fact that I did not have the kind of awe for the charismatic role that he gained, or was playing. Martin wasn't basically the kind of person—

certainly at the stage when I knew him the closest—[to] engage in dialogue that questioned the almost exclusive rightness of his position. And because I had no such awe, I would raise questions that I considered fundamental. . . . I've never felt it necessary for any one person to embody all that's needed in the leadership of a group or people. This comes back to my old cliché about a leadership-centered group [SCLC] as against a group-centered leadership [SNCC]. The group came first in my mind. The most important thing was to develop people to the point where they don't need the strong savior-type leader.[19]

The young student activists in SNCC welcomed Baker's suggestions and critiques and incorporated them, along with her notion of participatory democracy. For Baker, "participatory democracy" rested on three key tenets: the involvement of local, everyday people in the decisions that affect their lives; group-centered leadership; and direct action as a mechanism for overcoming fear and creating social change.[20] These guiding principles shaped the foundation of SNCC and the unique style of organizing and leadership that emerged within it.

SNCC activists believed that segregation and racial discrimination were immoral and that they should be immediately abolished through nonviolent direct action. After the Shaw University meeting, they began working with local communities throughout the South to achieve that goal. SNCC activists worked to nurture indigenous leadership and facilitate the development of sustainable, independent, community-based organizations that would focus on local issues and concerns. This was no easy task because Black southerners, especially those living in rural areas, had been terrorized for decades. Many were simply too scared to get involved in the movement. SNCC activists understood their fears and tried to overcome them by eating, sleeping, and talking with local residents. They carried out these activities on a daily basis, and over time, local people began trusting them and eventually became activists and leaders in the movement.[21]

This organizing model embodied SNCC's philosophy. SNCC, following Baker's maxim that strong people do not need strong leaders, felt that local people had the power to change their lives through organization and direct action.[22] This belief was firmly rooted in the growing sentiment that "great leaders" were not necessarily the "real agents" of change; rather, everyday people were. In the early 1960s many young activists adopted this position because they were frustrated with the slow pace of change. They grew impatient with Martin Luther King and NAACP executive director Roy Wilkins because they claimed that they made compromises with political elites that did not bring about meaningful social change. SNCC also criticized King and the SCLC for focusing national attention on a specific city and then leaving without creating stable community-based groups that could protect local residents and sustain the momentum that had been created. SNCC disagreed with the SCLC's decision-making process as well, because it generally excluded local leaders and organizations and primarily involved a small group of well-educated, middle-class ministers.[23]

SNCC, in contrast, made decisions in collaboration with local people based on consensus and internal democracy. SNCC activists worked carefully with local residents before launching any direct action or voter registration campaign, and its style of organizing and leadership sought to make them subjects, not objects, of social change. SNCC also shunned back-room deals with political elites, instead favoring sit-ins, marches, demonstrations, and even going to jail. SNCC activists took tremendous pride in their willingness to put their bodies on the line, and their fearlessness—their willingness to do anything and go anywhere despite the risks—gave others the courage to act and get involved in the movement.

These strategic differences between SNCC and the SCLC indicate that there were some serious internal cleavages in the African American civil rights movement in the early 1960s. The conflict between these two groups flared up during the Freedom Rides. In 1961 the northern-based Congress of Racial Equality (CORE) made plans for an interracial group of volunteers to ride buses from the North to the South to test whether the federal government would enforce a Supreme Court decision that banned segregated bus terminal facilities. At first, the buses encountered no resistance, but when they arrived in Montgomery, an angry crowd of White demonstrators burned one bus and seriously beat many of the passengers in the other one.[24]

These brutal attacks were captured on national television. The public became outraged, and the ensuing outcry led President John F. Kennedy to federalize the National Guard to protect the Freedom

Riders. CORE and SNCC (which later participated in the Freedom Rides) welcomed this move, but they were upset with Kennedy for waiting so long before taking action. The two organizations were also angry because King refused to participate in the rides, and they believed he favored the Kennedy administration's calls for voter registration, moderation, and compromise over direct action. Some activists also questioned King's moral authority after the Freedom Rides, while others challenged the strategic value of nonviolence.[25]

Despite these differences, the movement continued. In April 1963 the SCLC launched a comprehensive attack against segregation in Birmingham, Alabama. King and his advisers carefully selected the city because its police chief, Bull Connor, a die-hard segregationist and member of the White Citizens' Council, was likely to be provoked into a major confrontation with Blacks, which would create national outrage. They were right. After showing initial restraint, Connor arrested young children and turned dogs and water hoses on Black demonstrators. These images were broadcast all over the country and shocked many people, including President Kennedy, who introduced the Civil Rights Act banning segregation in all public facilities. Kennedy was assassinated before he could sign the bill, but President Lyndon B. Johnson enacted it one year later.[26]

Several months after Birmingham, in late August 1963, the March on Washington took place. Longtime labor leader A. Philip Randolph and Bayard Rustin, who King advised to resign from the SCLC in 1960 because of concerns about his sexuality, helped to plan and organize the protest.[27] King supported Rustin's involvement, but Wilkins and the NAACP did not, although after Strom Thurmond called Rustin a communist and a homosexual, Wilkins changed his mind.[28] The march brought together Black civil rights organizations from virtually all across the ideological spectrum, although SNCC's John Lewis was essentially forced to tone down his remarks (which criticized the Kennedy administration's gradual approach), and Malcolm X infamously called it the "farce on Washington."[29] Black female activists such as Dorothy Height, Pauli Murray, and Anna Arnold Hedgerman were also excluded from speaking during the march. Height recalled the discussions surrounding this issue:

> I went along with Anna Arnold Hedgerman, a woman with a long history of working for freedom and equality, to meet with

Bayard Rustin. We discussed the women's participation in the March. We were amazed to hear the response, "Women are included." Rustin asserted that, "Every group has women in it, labor, church," and so on. When we asked Rustin who was doing the planning, he referred to the heads of the National Council of Churches, NAACP, Urban League, several Jewish groups, and other organizations. There was an all-consuming focus on race. We women were expected to put all our energies into it. Clearly there was a low tolerance for anyone raising questions about women's participation, per se.

The men seemed to feel that women were digressing and pulling the discussion off the main track. But it wasn't just a male attitude. There were black women who felt that we needed to stick with the "real" issue of race. It was thought that we were making a lot of fuss about an insignificant issue, that we did not recognize that the March on Washington was about racism, not sexism. We all knew that. But, we made it clear that we wanted to hear at least one woman in the March dealing with jobs and freedom.[30]

Despite the limitations placed on some Black male and female activists, the March on Washington and the subsequent passage of the Civil Rights Act were major victories for the movement. Blacks throughout the South still did not have the right to vote, however, and in some states, like Mississippi, segregation was still the law of the land. SNCC understood that Mississippi was a "lawless state": churches were burned and people beaten and killed, while local law enforcement officials and the FBI did nothing. SNCC did not give up hope. In fact, it developed plans for a major voter registration drive that included sending White college students to Mississippi in summer 1964. SNCC's Robert Moses thought that the project, known as Freedom Summer, would provoke a violent confrontation. He believed that physical attacks against White students would inflame public opinion and force the federal government to intervene and enforce the Constitution.[31]

The anticipated showdown occurred shortly before Freedom Summer officially began. James Cheney, a Black college student, and Michael Schwerner and Andrew Goodman, White college students, were kidnapped, beaten, and killed by local police officers. The brutal murders sent shock waves across the country, but the federal government and the FBI neither seriously investigated them nor provided other Black and White volunteers with protection. Indeed, over the next three months, hundreds of activists were arrested, dozens of churches and houses were burned, and six more volunteers were killed.[32]

Voter registration was nearly impossible under these conditions. SNCC recognized this situation and shifted gears. It began registering Blacks in a new statewide party called the Mississippi Freedom Democratic Party (MFDP). The objective was to challenge the all-White state delegation at the Democratic National Convention in Atlantic City, New Jersey. Fannie Lou Hamer, co-chairperson of the MFDP, spoke on behalf of the party when she asked plaintively, "[I]s this America—the land of the free and the home of the brave?" Her question highlighted the contradiction between the American ideals of democracy and freedom and the reality of racial oppression that existed in her home state. After her stirring speech, the convention's credentials committee offered the MFDP a compromise—two at-large seats in exchange for assurances that the all-White party would adopt democratic selection procedures or be barred from subsequent conventions. King, Rustin, and other civil rights and labor union activists, Black and White, encouraged the MFDP to accept the deal, but Hamer defiantly stated, "[W]e didn't come all this way for no two lousy seats."[33]

The halfhearted measures and machinations of White liberals during Freedom Summer and the Atlantic City Democratic Convention caused bitterness and anger within SNCC. These feelings, combined with the growing popularity of Malcolm X and anticolonial movements sweeping Africa, sparked an internal debate in SNCC in 1964–65. One group, called the "nonstructure" faction, favored nonviolence, community empowerment, consensus-based decision making, and interracial organizing. The other group, the "structure" faction, emphasized hierarchy, centralization, and an incipient form of Black nationalism.[34]

Within this debate, a third position also emerged. Mary King and Casey Hayden, both White and longtime SNCC volunteers who identified with the nonstructure group, published two position papers that critiqued sexism inside and outside of SNCC and called for the development of a feminist consciousness and politics in SNCC and the larger civil rights movement.[35] Interestingly, Black women such as Diane Nash, Ruby Doris Smith, and Donna Richards Moses, who held leadership positions in SNCC, did not support this call from their White sisters.[36] They, like their male counterparts, increasingly favored Black nationalism and thus focused primarily on racism as the main focus of struggle, ignoring, for the time being, issues of gender and sexism. As Cynthia Washington, a Black SNCC activist stated, "I'm certain our single-minded focus on the issues of racial discrimination and the Black struggle for equality blinded us to other issues."[37] The Black nationalist position eventually prevailed in SNCC, and all non-Black volunteers, including the Chicana activist Elizabeth Sutherland Martínez, were asked to resign.[38]

The Emerging Black Power Movement: Racism as the Key Site of Struggle

The transformation of SNCC indicates that the movement was becoming more essentialist and exclusionary (i.e., narrowly focusing on one axis of oppression) in the mid-1960s. In its early days, SNCC and the SCLC, despite their strategic differences, believed that Blacks and Whites were equal and that segregation and racial discrimination were immoral and unjust. These beliefs were rooted in the conviction that an interracial and socially just society could be created through nonviolent direct action. This humanistic vision and ethos gave Black activists and local people strength and determination, and finally, after hundreds of years of oppression and exploitation, they obtained their freedom.

The Civil Rights and Voting Rights Acts of the mid-1960s brought about tremendous change and weakened certain forms of racial inequality, but they did not ameliorate inequality and oppression based on class, gender, and sexuality. Key organizations, as well as female and male activists (with the exception of Ella Baker, among others), during this phase of the movement generally overlooked these forms of inequality and concentrated on racism. The "humanistic thrust" of the civil rights movement at this time largely excluded the issues and concerns of Black women and working-class Blacks because it was based on the essentialist notion that all Blacks had the same interests and that they were united by racial oppression.

From this perspective, the "humanistic-based" civil rights movement and the newly emerging Black Power movement were very similar: both focused on racism and marginalized issues of class and gender. But these movements were very different. The linchpin of the humanistic or mainstream-oriented civil rights movement was that Black and White folks could work together and eliminate racism, whereas the Black Power movement claimed that *intraracial* solidarity and the development of Black economic and political power were necessary for achieving the same goal. The monoracial nature of the Black Power movement illustrated that it was perhaps even more essentialist and one-dimensional than the humanistic-oriented civil rights movement. Nonetheless, both movements overlooked the multiple identities and interlocking forms of oppression that existed in the African American community. This constituted a major weakness as the struggle for social and economic justice moved beyond the South in the mid-1960s.

Race and Class, 1965–1975

In August 1965 the largely African American community of Watts, California, exploded. A routine traffic stop of a young African American man brought out a large crowd of people, and angry words were soon exchanged between police officers and local residents. Bottles were thrown, tear gas was used, and a riot ensued. The uprising lasted six days, leaving thirty-five people dead. Residential segregation, overcrowding, unemployment, and police brutality were some of the key issues that precipitated the disturbances known as the Watts Riots.[39] Urban uprisings occurred in some twenty other cities over the next two years. In 1967, for example, rioting left forty-three people dead and $500 million in property damages in Detroit.[40]

These violent upheavals were somewhat paradoxical because they occurred outside the South. In Los Angeles and Detroit, Blacks did not face police dogs, water hoses, lynchings, or the KKK, but they did confront lead paint, run-down apartments with holes in the ceiling and broken toilets, high prices for basic consumer goods, and very few job opportunities. The grinding poverty and realization that local White elites dominated public and private institutions generated feelings of anger and hostility among northern Blacks. Malcolm X tapped into these sentiments with his fiery, street-savvy speeches that often rejected nonviolence and embraced social change, "by any means necessary." Malcolm's provocative rhetoric made him popular, especially with young urban Blacks who were dissatisfied with mainstream civil rights leaders like Martin Luther King, but he was assassinated shortly after he left the Nation of Islam and created the short-lived Organization of Afro-American Unity (OAAU).[41]

Malcolm's death did not stem the tide of Black insurgency. King understood this, and he realized that his vision of nonviolent social change was under attack and that unless he made some decisive moves, the Black Power movement would effectively cast him aside. Given these considerations, King went on the offensive, addressing the economic issues that provoked the urban uprisings. His first target was the Vietnam War. In 1967, in a controversial and sometimes overlooked speech, King came out strongly against the war, eloquently stating, "[E]very bomb that falls in Vietnam falls in our nation's cities, destroying the hopes and dreams for a decent America." He took this position because he believed that the war was immoral and diverted precious resources from antipoverty programs that provided economic opportunities not only for poor Blacks, but for all poor people. King later raised critical questions about the nature of capitalism and the unequal distribution of wealth in American society and began privately calling himself a "democratic socialist."[42]

These speeches and remarks infuriated FBI Director J. Edgar Hoover and President Johnson, as well as more moderate civil rights groups such as the Urban League and the NAACP. Hoover became so enraged that he ordered his agents to conduct a massive surveillance campaign of King and his associates.[43] These activities did not derail King. In late 1967 he, along with several of his closest advisers (including Rustin), held a series of meetings on what became known as the Poor People's Campaign (PPC).[44]

King envisioned the PPC as a vehicle for bringing together poor and working-class Whites, Blacks, Chicanas/os, and Native Americans in a unique interracial coalition that would culminate in a major nonviolent march in Washington, D.C. Rustin, becoming more cautious and conservative by the late 1960s, opposed the PPC, but King pressed on.[45] He hoped that the PPC would help to launch a new multiracial poor people's movement and that the federal government would respond with more jobs, housing, social programs, and other redistributive measures. King was assassinated before the campaign got off the ground, however. The PPC continued, but conflicts within the SCLC and FBI infiltration weakened the campaign and it soon fell apart.[46]

King's new short-lived strategy illustrated that he had developed a more nuanced understanding of racial inequality. He realized that the African American community, like other communities of color, experienced racial *and* class oppression, and he believed it was necessary to actively confront both forms of inequality. King's views upset his former allies, but they, along with even more radical critiques of the relationship between racism and capitalism, became more common in a number of organizations in the late 1960s.

The Black Panther Party (BPP), for example, criticized the mainstream-oriented civil rights movement and the "cultural nationalist" wing of the Black Power movement for focusing exclusively on racial inequality. The Panthers claimed that U.S. imperialism had colonized people of color both within and outside the United States. They believed, therefore, that racism and capitalism were inextricably linked and that an international revolution was necessary for overthrowing both. The party developed strategic alliances with revolutionary movements all over the world, as well as with radical organizations in the United States, based on this global perspective. Party members also concentrated on "local" issues such as police brutality, housing, and nutrition, and they advocated armed self-defense.[47]

The party's militancy and radical ideology shocked the ruling establishment on a far deeper level than did the PPC. The FBI asserted that the BPP was a "national security threat," and it worked with local police departments to create divisions within the organization. These law enforcement agencies also engaged in a series of violent confrontations with the party that left nearly thirty members dead over a two-year period.[48] These activities weakened the BPP, but it maintained, nevertheless, that race and class oppression (as well as sexism and heterosexism) were interlocking systems of oppression, and it continued organizing poor African Americans, as well as gang members and criminals, until its demise in the mid-1970s.[49]

The Black Panthers and the Poor People's Campaign were not the only organizations that challenged racial and class inequality in the late 1960s. In Detroit, a radical group of Black auto workers and intellectuals, who had studied Marxism, visited Cuba, and published an independent paper called the *Inner City Voice,* organized a wildcat strike in May 1968. The strike occurred at the Chrysler-Dodge Hamtramck factory. The speed of production, poor and dangerous working conditions, and institutional racism on the shop floor and inside the United Auto Workers (UAW), along with the union's close ties to Chrysler-Dodge management, ignited the walkout. The Dodge Revolutionary Union Movement emerged from the strike, and soon thereafter "revolutionary union movements" (RUMs) were established throughout the city in Ford and General Motors factories. These new militant working-class-based organizations came together and formed the League of Revolutionary Black Workers in 1969.[50]

The League coordinated the RUMs and recruited hundreds of new members in auto factories, primarily in California and New Jersey. It viewed itself as a revolutionary Black Marxist-Leninist organization and believed that racism and capitalism were responsible for Black inequality and that both systems of oppression should be dismantled. Black workers, the League reasoned, would be the "revolutionary vanguard" of the working class because they were more militant and class-conscious than White workers, who often supported racism and imperialism. The League initially gained popularity among Black workers but fell apart in less than two years because of repression and internal ideological disputes.[51]

Two Steps Forward and Two Not Taken: A Revolution without Women or Queers?

Although the League of Revolutionary Workers, the Black Panthers, and the Poor People's Campaign were all short-lived, they went beyond the narrow vision of the mainstream civil rights movement and the nationalist Black Power movement. Both of the latter movements achieved remarkable victories, but they focused almost exclusively on race and overlooked issues of class, gender, and sexuality. The organizations of the late 1960s and early 1970s, in contrast, claimed that Black inequality stemmed from racial *and* class oppression, and they actively challenged both. However, these groups did not confront sexism, and in the few cases in which Black women, such as the Black Panthers' Elaine Brown and Kathleen Cleaver, gained a "taste of power," they ended up leaving because some Black male party members resented them and even attacked them physically.[52] Furthermore, while Black Panther leader Huey Newton said, "[H]omosexuals might be the most oppressed group in society," Minister of Information Eldridge Cleaver remarked that "homosexuality was a sickness."[53]

These viewpoints and practices illustrate that the "radical" civil rights and Black Power organizations of the late 1960s and early 1970s had a complicated, contradictory, and inconsistent vision of social justice. On a rhetorical level, some groups (especially the BPP) challenged racism, capitalism, sexism, and heterosexism, but more often than not there were persistent and glaring gaps between theory and practice. Revolutionary discourse could not be easily transformed into revolutionary action, as many deeply committed and passionate activists themselves noted during that time. The inability to actively confront or "rage against" all four interlocking "machines"—racism, sexism, capitalism, and heterosexism—was a major weakness of these organizations, and it later proved a serious problem for the Chicana/o civil rights movement as well.

THE CHICANA/O CIVIL RIGHTS MOVEMENT

The United Farm Workers

The Chicana/o civil rights movement began in the grape fields of California. On Mexican Independence Day, September 16, 1965, Chicana/o and Mexicana/o farmworkers joined their Filipino sisters and brothers on the picket lines in Delano. Low wages, backbreaking labor, substandard housing, and poor and dangerous working conditions ignited the *huelga* (strike). The main forces behind the strike were the Agricultural Workers' Organizing Committee (AWOC) and the National Farm Workers Association (NFWA), and the key organizers among them were Larry Itliong from AWOC and César Chávez, Dolores Huerta, and Gilberto Padilla from the NFWA.[54]

The strike initially targeted the largest grape growers, such as Schenely Industries and the DiGiorgio Corporation, and it involved thousands of farmworkers. Picket lines were organized throughout the San Joaquin Valley, with strikers chanting, "Huelga, huelga," and blocking *esquiroles* (scabs) from working in the fields. These activities gained widespread publicity, transforming Chávez into the leader of the farmworkers' movement. The strike and the national attention it generated upset the grape growers, of course. They developed close ties with local sheriffs and law enforcement agencies and intimidated and harassed strikers through arrests and legal injunctions.

These measures did not stop Chávez or the two unions involved in the strike. Chávez read Gandhi, followed the African American civil rights movement, and became a disciple of nonviolence. Deeply religious, like many farmworkers, Chávez decided to organize a three-hundred-mile pilgrimage from Delano to Sacramento to dramatize the issues that sparked the grape strike. During the march, workers carried the union's red-and-black eagle strike flag and pictures of the Virgen de Guadalupe. Shortly after the march reached its final destination, Schenely made a stunning decision and negotiated a contract guaranteeing higher wages and better working conditions with the NFWA.[55]

This victory did not mean that the strike was over. The NFWA's next target was the DiGiorgio Corporation. DiGiorgio was the second-largest grape grower in the state, and it was deeply antiunion. The company, not surprisingly, opposed the union's organizing campaign, but it favored the pro-management and corrupt teamsters union that had won the right to represent its employees in a highly flawed election. The NFWA and AWOC pressured state labor officials to hold a new election, and this time the newly created United Farm Workers (UFW) union won and negotiated a contract with DiGiorgio.

These two contracts were important, but hundreds of workers were still on strike in Delano. The union turned its attention, therefore, to Guimarra Vineyards, the largest grape producer in the state. Guimarra resisted the union's call for contract negotiations and used legal injunctions and scabs to break the strike. The UFW responded with a nationwide consumer boycott of Guimarra grapes, but it initially had little impact because the company sold its products under the labels of different companies. Given this situation, the union called for a national boycott of *all* California table grapes. The UFW dispatched Dolores Huerta, Jessica Govea, Eliseo Medina, and dozens of other organizers and volunteers across the country and into Canada to carry out the infamous grape boycott. These organizers, along with Chicana/o students, passed out leaflets and urged consumers and supermarkets to stop buying grapes. The boycott gained tremendous publicity and sparked public sympathy for la causa. In July 1970, sensing defeat, the grape growers finally capitulated and negotiated contracts with the union that ended the five-year strike.[56]

The UFW's victory over the grape growers illustrated that it was a strong and vibrant *labor* organization. Chávez viewed the union through a much broader lens, however. For him, it was a *social movement* that was struggling on behalf of all farmworkers. He believed that all campesinos—White, Black, Brown, Filipino, and Middle Eastern—had basic rights that included decent wages, good working conditions, health care, housing, dignity, and respect. He viewed these rights as universal and fought for them using nonviolent strategies such as boycotts, marches, and hunger strikes.[57]

Chávez not only fought for economic justice; he also struggled for racial equality. He was painfully aware of how racism shaped the lives of Chicanas/os in the Southwest. Segregated and assimilationist-oriented public schools, employment and housing discrimination, and political disenfranchisement meant very few opportunities for social mobility for Chicanas/os.[58] Chávez, along with many other union activists, believed that these racial barriers should be eliminated.

The union, despite its remarkable achievements, did not seriously confront sexism, however. This does not mean that Chicanas were not active in the union. Dolores Huerta, Jessica Govea, Jessie de la Cruz, and Helen Chávez, César's wife, were heavily involved.[59] Huerta negotiated nearly all of the UFW's contracts with the grape growers. She was the exception, though. As Margaret Rose has demonstrated, union activism was divided along gender lines.[60] Chicanas handled domestic responsibilities (e.g., child rearing, cooking, and cleaning) and undertook gendered boycott activities such as picketing and answering phones. They typically did not make speeches or key decisions. From the outside, Chicanas were invisible, whereas Chicanos were highly visible activists. This division of labor reinforced sexism and traditional gender roles. Nonetheless, the boycott had one positive outcome for Chicanas: it mobilized them and gave them self-confidence, self-esteem, and the awareness that they were equal to men. This perspective indicates that the boycott may have indirectly laid the foundation for the growth of feminist consciousness among Chicanas and Mexicanas.[61]

The UFW's record, then, from a race, class, and gender perspective, was mixed. The union struggled against racial and class inequality but did not seriously challenge sexism. Despite this shortcoming, the UFW achieved major victories and inspired thousands of young Chicanas/os who formed a number of new organizations that became a key part of the Chicana/o civil rights movement.

Cultural Nationalism

The organizations that were established by young Chicanas/os were much different from the UFW. They were more radical, and they emerged from the barrios and public schools of Colorado, New Mexico, Texas, and southern California. Among these groups were the Alianza Federal, the Crusade for Justice, and the La Raza Unida Party, whose leaders included Reies López Tijerina, Rodolfo ("Corky") Gonzales, and José Angel Gutiérrez.

These groups gained strength in the mid- and late 1960s, a period when cultural nationalism dominated the movement. Cultural nationalism embodied a complex set of ideas, but it generally emphasized the notion that Chicanas/os were racially oppressed and colonized in the United States.[62] Internal colonization contained three key elements—racial, economic, and cultural exploitation—that made social mobility nearly impossible.[63] This system of oppression began when the United States conquered Aztlán (the U.S. Southwest), the mythical home of the Aztecs, in the mid-nineteenth century. Many Chicana/o activists believed that the conquest transformed the "Chicana/o community" into an oppressed "nation" within the borders of the United States and that the only way to bring about social change was to "reclaim Aztlán."[64]

This viewpoint gained widespread popularity within the broader movimiento. Activists found it compelling because it challenged popular as well as mainstream academic discourse that stated "cultural deviancy," rather than racism, was the cause of Chicana/o inequality.[65] The internal colony model also achieved acceptance because it documented the historical and cultural contributions of the Aztecs, along with Mexican revolutionaries, labor activists, and others who resisted racism and imperialism and fought for social justice. This emphasis made people like Moctezuma, Emiliano Zapata, Pancho Villa, and Joaquín Murietta icons within el movimiento, and they were celebrated in Corky Gonzales's epic poem, *Yo Soy Joaquín* (I Am Joaquín).

Yo Soy Joaquín created a sensation among young Chicanas and Chicanos because it gave them a sense of history and identity.[66] In *Joaquín*, Gonzales claimed that Chicanas/os were a "bronze people" fighting against racism and injustice. He also vividly illustrated the historical ties and connections between Chicana/o "outlaws," Mexican revolutionaries, and Aztec warriors. *Joaquín* became the "anthem of the movement" and thrust Gonzales and his Crusade for Justice into the national spotlight.[67]

In 1966, in Denver, Colorado, Gonzales established the Crusade after he was fired from a community-based youth program for being outspoken and clashing with Democratic Party officials whom he claimed did not represent the interests of the city's Chicana/o population.[68] The Crusade initially focused on police brutality and the establishment of independent police review boards. It later participated in the Poor People's Campaign, where Gonzales issued *El Plan de Barrio,* which called for bilingual education, land restitution, and the development of barrio-controlled businesses.[69] The Crusade subsequently organized the Chicano National Youth Liberation Conference in March 1969, where *El Plan Espiritual de Aztlán* was released. *El Plan Espiritual de Aztlán* was a seminal document that called for Chicana/o self-determination, freedom, and liberation. Its evocative and poetic language electrified the conference participants:

> In the spirit of a new people that is conscious not only of its proud historical heritage, but also the brutal "Gringo" invasion of our territories, We, the Chicano inhabitants and civilizers of the northern land of Aztlán whence came our forefathers, re-clai[m] the land of their birth and consecrat[e] the determination of our people of the sun. . . . Aztlán belongs to those that plant the seeds, water the fields, and gather the crops, and not the foreign Europeans. . . . With our heart in our hands and our hands in the soil, We Declare the Independence of our Mestizo Nation. We are a Bronze People with a Bronze Culture. Before the world, before all of North America, before all our brothers in the Bronze Continent, We are a Nation, We are a Union of free Pueblos, We are Aztlán.[70]

El Plan de Barrio and *El Plan Espiritual de Aztlán* were based on cultural nationalism and the broad notion of reclaiming Aztlán. The term "Aztlán" was ambiguous, but some activists took it literally, in a territorial and spatial sense, stating that Chicanas/os should separate themselves from White society and establish their own nation within the United States.[71] Gonzales rejected this perspective, realizing it was too impractical. Yet he supported local forms of separatism. He believed that "reclaiming Aztlán" meant taking control of local school boards, businesses, city councils, health clinics, and other community-based institutions, for instance. Barrio control and locally based separatism were among his solutions for combating racism and bringing about social change.[72]

Gonzales's ideas were popular, but, as Juan Gómez-Quiñones notes, they had one fundamental weakness: Gonzales assumed that "Chicanas/os" were a unified, homogeneous group that was bound together by racism and internal colonialism.[73] He believed that racism was the key site of struggle and that if Chicanas/os could somehow reclaim Aztlán at the local level, then the problems facing the "Chicana/o community" would magically disappear.

The "Chicana/o community" is not a monolithic, essentialist entity, however. It includes women, working-class people, and queers. These groups have different sets of interests because they confront multiple, interlocking forms of oppression. Gonzales's plan for gaining control of Aztlán did not include struggling for the liberation of Chicanas or working-class Chicanas/os. He focused on race and, to a lesser extent, class and marginalized gender and sexuality.[74] At the Chicano National Youth Liberation Conference, some Chicanas challenged Gonzales for concentrating exclusively on racism, and they criticized the sexism that existed within the movement. But, in a controversial move, the Chicana Crusade for Justice activists claimed, on behalf of all Chicanas at the conference, that "it was the consensus of the group that the Chicana woman does not want to be liberated."[75]

This statement indicated disenchantment with the (White) women's liberation movement, which identified sexism and patriarchy as the main axis of oppression. Chicana feminist activists such as Ana Nieto-Gómez rejected this logic as well as the criticism from some Chicanas and Chicanos that she was a *vendida* (sellout). She viewed "sexist racism" as the "enemy."[76] This more complex perspective, emphasizing the interlocking nature of racial and gender oppression (sometimes called the "double burden"), became more popular in the writings of Chicanas and other women of color in the 1970s, 1980s, and 1990s.

The National Youth Liberation Conference marked the high point of popularity for the Crusade, Gonzales, and the politics of cultural nationalism, which was embraced by many organizations including the Alianza Federal and La Raza Unida party. The Alianza was one

of the most influential and militant organizations of the Chicana/o
civil rights movement. Its leader, a former Pentecostal minister named
Reies Lopez Tijerina, and its members established the Alianza in 1963
with the objective of taking back millions of acres that were illegally
acquired after the 1846–48 U.S.-Mexico war. The Alianza claimed
that those lands were the property of native New Mexicanos (*hispanos*) under the provisions of the Treaty of Guadalupe Hidalgo.
Tijerina was not a native New Mexicano, but he understood that the
loss of these lands impoverished local hispanos and stripped them of
their culture and collective way of life. His fiery speeches tapped into
the anger they felt, and his charismatic personality made him into a
leader of the New Mexico land grant movement.[77]

The Alianza's initial activities were based on nonviolence. Organization members, for instance, held a peaceful, fifty-mile march
to the state capitol in Santa Fe, where they talked with Governor John
Campbell. Campbell's aides stated that the *aliancistas* did not have
the right to claim these lands. This decision temporarily took the
steam out of the Alianza, but it regrouped in October 1966, taking
over a land grant called San Joaquín del Río de Chama, which was
located on U.S. National Forest Service property. During the week-
long occupation, Alianza activists created the so-called Republic of
San Joaquín del Río de Chama, thereby openly questioning the sovereignty of the federal government. The state government, in turn,
responded and arrested (and later released) Tijerina, along with five
other Alianza activists.[78]

Neither Tijerina nor the Alianza was discouraged. In fact, after
a new slightly pro-Alianza governor was elected, the organization
made plans for occupying San Joaquín del Río Chama once again.
Before these plans could be carried out, Tierra Amarillo County Attorney Alfonso Sánchez ordered the state police to break up a meeting of the Alianza. The officers followed Sánchez's orders and arrested
eight activists. This move infuriated Tijerina. He and several other
activists decided they would go into the county courthouse, arrest
Sánchez, and release their fellow aliancistas. On June 5, 1967, they
raided the courthouse. A shoot-out ensued, and two officers were
wounded.[79]

Tijerina escaped after the confrontation, but he was eventually
captured and thrown into jail on charges unrelated to the raid. After
serving his one-month sentence, he took part in the Poor People's

Campaign with Corky Gonzales and leaders of the American Indian Movement. On arriving back in New Mexico, Patsy Tijerina burned several National Forest park signs and her husband, Reies, tried to arrest a top-ranking National Forest Service official. This escapade landed him in jail again, this time for five years. The Alianza faltered in his absence, and by the time he got out in 1974, it had fallen apart.[80]

While the Alianza was active it inspired and motivated many young Chicanas and Chicanos and made Tijerina into a leader of the Chicana/o civil rights movement. Tijerina's position was that White settlers had stolen lands that rightfully belonged to hispanos. He blamed White society and racial discrimination for creating the problems that hispanos faced and believed that, by reclaiming these lands, they could achieve social change. This strategy overlooked the fact that Chicana/o inequality stemmed not just from racism but from capitalism, sexism, and heterosexism as well. The Achilles' heel of Tijerina, like Gonzales and other cultural nationalists of el movimiento, was his concentration on only one axis of the matrix of domination—race.

This incomplete vision of social change also affected La Raza Unida Party (LRUP). The LRUP emerged out of the Mexican-American Youth Organization (MAYO), a student group based in South Texas. José Angel Gutiérrez was a key leader of MAYO and later became an influential force in the LRUP. MAYO focused on educational reform (e.g., introducing Chicana/o Studies courses, hiring more Chicana/o teachers and administrators), community economic development, and police brutality. It organized boycotts, or "blow-outs," of local schools and used confrontational rhetoric to expose "Anglo oppression" and racial discrimination. MAYO embraced cultural nationalism and viewed society through a racialized "gringo versus Mexicano" lens, which made racism the key site of struggle.[81]

MAYO's tactics were largely successful, but the group realized that more far-reaching change could be achieved through obtaining political power. In 1970 MAYO activists, therefore, established the LRUP, which ran candidates for city council in Crystal City, Texas. The new party won two council seats and over the next two years gained strength and participated in statewide elections. Meanwhile, LRUP branches were formed in Colorado and California in the early 1970s. In 1972 these three statewide LRUPs held a national convention in El Paso, Texas. At the convention, the national La Raza Unida

Party was created, and after a bitter internal conflict, Gutiérrez was elected party chairperson over Gonzales.[82]

The national party was extremely divided, limiting its ability to obtain a mass support base. The personality disputes between Gutiérrez and Gonzales further weakened its effectiveness and the party never really functioned on a national basis. Nonetheless, state-level LRUPs continued to organize, and some, like the Texas party, ran candidates for office until 1978. These organizations espoused a nationalist-oriented politics and did not seriously address class, gender, or sexuality. Some Chicanas, such as María Elena Martínez, Texas LRUP chairperson in the mid-1970s, were active, but by and large Chicanos controlled the parties, and they failed to challenge sexism within them or in the broader Chicana/o community.[83]

The LRUP, the Crusade for Justice, and the Alianza dominated the cultural nationalist phase of the Chicana/o civil rights movement between the late 1960s and the mid-1970s. They generated a sense of pride, identity, and militancy among Raza, and they achieved social, political, educational, and economic change throughout Aztlán. These organizations were essentialist, however, and basically ignored the multiple forms of oppression that exist in the Chicana/o community. One of the few groups, with the exception of the UFW, that recognized the internal complexity of the Chicana/o community was Centro de Acción Sociedad Autónoma–Hermandad General de Trabajadores (Center for Autonomous Social Action–General Brotherhood of Workers [CASA-HGT, or CASA]).

The Chicana/o Civil Rights Movement and the Left

CASA was established in 1968 as a "resource center" that provided social services to undocumented residents. CASA's organizational base of strength was in Los Angeles, and its key activists were relatively young Raza who were dissatisfied with the nationalist thrust of the movement. In the early 1970s these activists adopted a Marxist perspective and claimed that the struggle against racism and capitalism was crucial for Chicana/o liberation and self-determination. They also developed the concept of *sin fronteras* (without borders), by claiming that Chicanas/os, Mexicanas/os (those who lived in Mexico), and undocumented residents all constituted the working class and therefore shared similar interests.[84]

CASA's Marxist orientation and concern for undocumented workers led its activists to get involved in various labor organizing campaigns. CASA activists such as Magdalena Mora helped to organize undocumented workers and challenged labor unions to do the same. CASA also formed ties with the Mexican Communist Party and the Puerto Rican Socialist Party, and it played a key role in several immigration conferences in the late 1970s.[85]

CASA remained active until 1978. Internal conflicts and conflicts with other leftist groups, such as the Socialist Workers Party and the August Twenty-Ninth Movement, were some of the factors that contributed to its demise.[86] CASA, unlike the nationalist wing of the movimiento, recognized, however, that Chicanas/os faced racial *and* class oppression, and it fought both. This was a positive step forward, but in praxis, CASA primarily emphasized class and, like all other organizations of the movement, ignored gender and sexuality. As the Chicana historian Vicki Ruiz explains, "Chicanas had to fight for leadership positions within CASA and even the choice of dating partners was not an individual decision. Chicanas were also expected to bear the brunt of women's work in planning fund-raisers, selling tickets, and preparing food."[87]

The failure of the movimiento to interrogate and challenge race, class, gender, and sexuality in a holistic and consistent manner constituted one of its major weaknesses. This assessment came from Chicana and Chicano activists themselves. I mention it here because it raises the big question, is it possible to struggle against capitalism, racism, sexism, and heterosexism at the same time without privileging or marginalizing one form of oppression or the other? This question is explored below.

MOVING ADELANTE: WHERE DO WE GO FROM HERE?

There can be little doubt that the African American and Chicana/o civil rights movements had a far-reaching impact on American society. The African American civil rights movement eliminated segregation and gave African Americans the right to vote, to sit down wherever they wished in movie theaters and restaurants, and, through affirmative action, the opportunity to obtain jobs once reserved for Whites only. The Chicana/o Civil rights movement brought about similar outcomes: higher wages and better working conditions for farmworkers, the establishment of Chicana/o Studies courses, programs, and departments, and higher college enrollment figures. Beyond these accomplishments, both movements had a cultural impact. They provided African Americans and Chicanas/os with a sense of collective identity, self-awareness, and a historical and political consciousness through music, art, theater, and literature that made them proud to be Black or Brown.

We should not overlook their weaknesses, however. The primary limitation of both movements, I believe, was also their greatest strength. What I am suggesting here is that while both movements were certainly different, they were similar in two respects. First, they mobilized around issues of racial inequality, and second, they assumed that the African American and Chicana/o communities were homogeneous entities and that all Blacks and Chicanas/os had the same interests because they were united by their common experiences with racial oppression. This "strategically essentialist"[88] practice was positive in the sense that it gave these movements a clear sense of purpose: racism was harmful, unjust, and immoral; therefore, it had to be eliminated through direct action. This perspective influenced thousands of African Americans and Chicanas/os, women and men, straight and queer, working-class and middle-class, young and old, to get involved in these movements for social change.

On the other hand, the strategic essentialism that informed these two movements overlooked one basic fact: not all African Americans and Chicanas/os are the same. They do not just face racism; they encounter a complicated matrix of domination that involves class, gender, sexuality, and racially based forms of oppression. The African American and Chicans/o civil rights movements assumed that "Black" and "Brown" people had one underlying identity based on race and that they consequently faced only one form of inequality. This racial essentialism led both movements to marginalize the issues of poverty, gender-based discrimination, and equal rights for gays and lesbians. While some organizations, such as the UFW, CASA, the Black Panther Party, the League of Revolutionary Workers, and the Poor People's Campaign, challenged racial and class inequality, they did not take on sexism and heterosexism. In fact, some activists reinforced the latter two systems of inequality.

Given this assessment, my overall conclusion is that the discourses and practices of both movements were incomplete. This viewpoint, based on hindsight, may sound rather harsh. Is it fair to criticize these movements, organizations, and activists forty or fifty years after the fact? Was the lack of focus on gender and sexuality an unfortunate, although understandable by-product of that era? These are complex questions that defy simplistic responses. I think we can highlight the contradictions, limitations, and inconsistencies of these movements because activists during and before this period did so. James Baldwin criticized Martin Luther King, for instance, for not supporting Bayard Rustin after Adam Clayton Powell attacked his sexuality. After W. E. B. Du Bois fired his close associate, Augustus Granville Dill, who was arrested for having gay sex in a subway toilet, in 1928, he worried about this decision for the rest of his life.[89] This is remarkable given that mainstream as well as academic discourse on homosexuality did not change until the 1970s, after the gay and lesbian movement emerged.

Social movements are fragile and complex. They involve a wide variety of actors and organizations that operate in a fluid, although time-bound context. The African American and Chicana/o civil rights movements took place in a highly charged and chaotic national and global environment. What they achieved was truly remarkable. What they left unfinished was not entirely their fault. My aim here is not to point fingers but to point out shortcomings, weaknesses, and limitations so as to move adelante.

There were many activists and organizations that followed a circuitous journey. Bayard Rustin's life is illustrative. He briefly joined the Communist Party in the late 1930s, resisted the draft and was jailed during World War II, and became a leading member of the pacifist Fellowship of Reconciliation in the late 1940s. He was ousted from the FOR in 1953, played a key role in the 1955–56 Montgomery Bus Boycott, and dropped out of the SCLC in 1960. Rustin came back and helped to organize the March on Washington in 1963, although he played a key role in excluding women from speaking at it, despite his own experiences of being dismissed from the FOR and the SCLC. He later came full circle, supporting the Vietnam War as well as the AFL-CIO's role in toppling leftist regimes in Latin America, Asia, and Africa.[90]

How does one evaluate his life or that of Huey P. Newton, Eldridge Cleaver, Malcolm X, Martin Luther King Jr., Fannie Lou Hamer, Jo Ann Robinson, Rosa Parks, Mary King, Casey Hayden,

Diane Nash, Ruby Doris Smith, Angela Davis, Stokely Carmichael, John Lewis, Roy Wilkins, Elizabeth ("Betita") Martínez, María Varela, Dolores Huerta, Jessie de la Cruz, Magdalena Mora, Corky Gonzales, Reies López Tijerina, José Angel Gutiérrez, Ana Nieto-Gómez, or César Chávez? How does one assess the organizational trajectory of the Women's Political Council, CORE, SNCC, the SCLC, the Black Panthers, the League of Revolutionary Black Workers, the United Farm Workers, the Crusade for Justice, La Raza Unida Party, Alianza Federal, or CASA? There are no saints or sinners among these individuals and organizations. All of them were heroic, yet flawed.

Having said all this, African Americans and Chicanas/os still face institutional racism, class inequality, sexism, and heterosexism *today*. How do we attack these problems, as well as globalization, the prison-industrial complex, police brutality, AIDS, global warming, the widening gap between the rich and poor, and the threat of the never-ending and ever-expanding "war on terrorism"? The key question now is, as Martin Luther King Jr. put it thirty-five years ago, "Where do we go from here?"

This question lies beyond the scope of this chapter, but let me say this. I disagree with those scholars who contend that social movements cannot be created that cut across multiple subject-positions (race, class, gender, sexuality), as well as with the traditional Marxist notion that class will somehow unite all these folks into one grand coalition. This kind of reasoning seems either too gloomy or too sanguine.

The large demonstrations against the World Trade Organization in Seattle in 1999 and the protests that followed raised expectations all over the world that a new global justice movement had emerged. As activists debated nonviolence versus violence, anarchism versus socialism, the "true" nature of the "enemy," and the movement's "revolutionary potential," the Chicana activist Elizabeth Martínez pointedly asked, "[W]here was the color in Seattle?"[91] Her widely circulated piece raised a crucial rhetorical question, how can this new social movement have a global and revolutionary thrust without the involvement of people of color in the United States?

The current makeup (mostly young, White, middle-class) of the global justice movement in the United States illustrates some of its contradictions and limitations. It is important to point out, however, that around the world, indigenous, working-class people of color, especially women, are leading this movement. They may not have been in Seattle, Washington, D.C., Prague, Quebec City, or Genoa, but they are resisting corporate-led globalization, just as people of color, each in their own way, are doing in the United States.

The task ahead—creating and sustaining a more cohesive global people's movement for social and economic justice—will be difficult. In this post–September 11th environment, in which political debate has been considerably narrowed, this objective may seem improbable. I recognize this larger reality but hope that this unwieldy and still unfolding social movement will be just as successful as the African American and Chicana/o civil rights movements were. We must not forget Martin Luther King's words, "[T]he arc of the moral universe is long, but it bends towards justice." It is up to us to make that happen. *Sí se puede.*

NOTES

1. Like all racial categories, "Chicano" is a social construction. It typically refers to people of Mexican descent born in the United States, although this is not a universally accepted definition. Some scholars suggest that "Chicano" is gender neutral. Over the past twenty years, Chicana scholarship and activism have eclipsed this perspective. The terms "Chicana and Chicano," "Chicana/o," and "Chican@" are most widely used today. To avoid any possible confusion, I use "Chicana/o" in this chapter as the "Chicano" civil rights movement included both women and men. I feel that this fact has not been properly acknowledged in the literature on the *movimiento*.

2. Of course, African Americans and Chicanas/os had been struggling for social justice long before the 1950s and 1960s. For more on the rich historical legacy of resistance in both communities, see John Egerton, *Speak Now against the Day: The Generation before the Civil Rights Movement in the South* (Chapel Hill: University of North Carolina Press, 1995); Rudolfo Acuña, *Occupied America* (San Francisco: Canfield Press, 1972).

3. For more information on the boycott, see Mary Fair Burks, "Women in the Montgomery Bus Boycott," in *Women in the Civil Rights Movement: Trailblazers and Torchbearers, 1941–1965*, ed. Vicki L. Crawford, Jacqueline Anne Rouse, and Barbara Woods (Bloomington: Indiana University Press, 1990), 71–83; Willy S. Leventhal, ed., *The Children Coming On: A Retrospective of the Montgomery Bus Boycott* (Montgomery: Black Belt Press, 1998); Jo Ann Robin-

son, *The Montgomery Bus Boycott and the Women Who Started It* (Knoxville: University of Tennessee Press, 1987). It should be pointed out here that the WPC originally planned the boycott in March 1955—some nine months before Parks's arrest. The arrest of fifteen-year-old Claudette Colvin brought local Black organizations together, but after word leaked out that she was pregnant, support for protest activities declined. See Robinson, *The Montgomery Bus Boycott*, 16.

4. Jervis Anderson, *Bayard Rustin: The Troubles That I've Seen* (Berkeley: University of California Press, 1997), 185–86.

5. For more on Rustin's arrest, see Anderson, *The Troubles That I've Seen*, 153–65. For Rustin's conversations with King on nonviolence as well as his sometimes rocky relationship with local ministers in the MIA, see Anderson, *The Troubles That I've Seen*, 183–96. Also see Robinson, *The Montgomery Bus Boycott*, chaps. 2–4, for more details on the strategy discussions behind continuing the boycott. It is crucial to mention here that the Fellowship of Reconciliation (FOR), led by A. J. Muste, helped to establish the Congress of Racial Equality (CORE) in 1942. Later, in 1947, CORE organized, under the leadership of Rustin and James Farmer, an integrated, interstate bus protest, known as the Fellowship of Reconciliation, to enforce a U.S. Supreme Court decision banning segregated interstate commerce. The nonviolent action ended without fulfilling its larger purpose, but it planted the seeds for the Montgomery Bus Boycott and the Freedom Rides in 1961.

6. Robinson, *The Montgomery Bus Boycott*, chaps. 5–6.

7. For more information on Fred Gray and the legal issues surrounding the bus boycott, see Fred Gray, *Bus Ride to Justice* (Montgomery: Black Belt Press, 1995).

8. Jack Bloom, *Race, Class, and the Civil Rights Movement* (Bloomington: Indiana University Press, 1987), chap. 5.

9. Doug McAdam, *Political Process and the Development of Black Insurgency, 1930–1970* (Chicago: University of Chicago Press, 1982); Alberto Melucci, *Nomads of the Present* (Philadelphia: Temple University Press, 1989). The theoretical literature on social movements is vast. For a good overview, see Doug McAdam, John McCarthy, and Mayer Zald, eds., *Comparative Social Movements: Political Opportunities, Mobilizing Structures, and Cultural Framings* (Cambridge, Mass.: Harvard University Press, 1996).

10. Bloom, *Race, Class, and the Civil Rights Movement*, chap. 5.

11. David Garrow, *Bearing the Cross: Martin Luther King Jr. and the Southern Christian Leadership Conference* (New York: William Morrow, 1986).

12. Bloom, *Race, Class and the Civil Rights Movement*, 111.

13. For an overview of the Little Rock crisis, see Melba Pattillo Bates, *Warriors Don't Cry: A Searing Memoir of the Battle to Integrate Little Rock's Central High* (New York: Washington Square Books, 1994).

14. For a fuller analysis of White resistance in the late 1950s, see Numan Bartley, *The Rise of Massive Resistance* (Baton Rouge: Louisiana State University Press, 1969); Bloom, *Race, Class, and the Civil Rights Movement*, chap. 4.

15. Bloom, *Race, Class, and the Civil Rights Movement*, 152.

16. Ibid., 122–54.

17. For more on the sit-in movement, see David Halberstam, *The Children* (New York: Random House, 1998); Aldon Morris, *The Origins of the Civil Rights Movement* (New York: Free Press, 1984); Clayborne Carson, *In Struggle: SNCC and the Black Awakening* (Cambridge, Mass.: Harvard University Press, 1981).

18. For more on SNCC, see Carson, *In Struggle;* Halberstam, *The Children;* James Forman, *The Making of Black Revolutionaries* (Seattle: University of Washington Press, 1997); Mary King, *Freedom Song: A Personal Story of the 1960s Civil Rights Movement* (New York: William Morrow, 1987); Cleveland Sellers, *The River of No Return: The Autobiography of a Black Militant and the Life and Death of SNCC* (Jackson: University of Mississippi Press, 1990); Howard Zinn, *SNCC: The New Abolitionists* (New York: Beacon Press, 1964). For an assessment twenty-five years after SNCC was established, see Cheryl Lynn Greenberg, ed., *A Circle of Trust: Remembering SNCC* (New Brunswick, N.J.: Rutgers University Press, 1998).

19. Anderson, *The Troubles That I've Seen*, 199–200. For more on Baker's life as well as her clashes with King, see Joanne Grant, *Ella Baker: Freedom Bound* (New York: Wiley, 1998); Carol Muller, "Ella Baker and the Origins of Participatory Democracy," in Crawford, Rouse, and Woods, eds., *Women in the Civil Rights Movement*, 51–70; Barbara Ransby, "Behind the Scenes View of a Behind the Scenes Organizer: The Roots of Ella Baker's Political Passions," in *Sisters in the Struggle: African American Women in the Civil Rights–Black Power Movement*, ed. Bettye Collier-Thomas and V. P. Franklin (New York: New York University Press, 2001), 42–57.

20. Muller, "Ella Baker and the Origins," 51–52.

21. Carson, *In Struggle;* John Ditmer, *Local People: The Struggle for Civil Rights in Mississippi* (Urbana: University of Illinois Press, 1994); Zinn, *SNCC: New Abolitionists.*

22. Muller, "Ella Baker and the Origins," 51.

23. Carson, *In Struggle;* Zinn, *New Abolitionists.*

24. For more on CORE and the Freedom Rides, see James Farmer, *Lay Bare the Heart* (New York: Arbor House, 1985); Halberstam, *The Children;* John Lewis, *Walking with the Wind: A Memoir of the Movement* (New York: Harcourt Brace, 1998).

25. For a fuller discussion of these issues, see Bloom, *Race, Class, and the Civil Rights Movement;* Taylor Branch, *Parting the Waters: America in the King Years, 1954–63* (New York: Simon and Schuster, 1988); Carson, *In Struggle.*

26. For more on Birmingham and the subsequent passage of the Civil Rights Act, see Branch, *Parting the Waters;* Halberstam, *The Children.*

27. Randolph had originally made plans for a march on Washington in 1941 to protest racial discrimination in the defense industries. After President Franklin D. Roosevelt signed Executive Order 8802 banning that practice, the march was called off. A much younger and more militant (and former communist) Rustin opposed Randolph's decision. After many years, Rustin and Randolph reconciled, with the former ironically carrying out the latter's lifetime dream. King, incidentally, did not back Rustin after New York congressional representative Adam Clayton Powell erroneously claimed in 1960 that the two men had a sexual relationship. Rustin could have publicly defended himself against these slanderous accusations, but he resigned, sparing the SCLC and King more negative publicity. The Black gay novelist James Baldwin criticized King for not supporting Rustin. For more on these issues, see Anderson, *The Troubles That I've Seen*; Devon Carbado, Dwight McBride, and Donald Weise, eds., *Black Like Us: A Century of Lesbian, Gay, and Bisexual African American Fiction* (San Francisco: Cleis Press), 110.

28. Carbado, McBride, and Weise, *Black Like Us,* 111.

29. Anderson, *The Troubles That I've Seen,* 239–64.

30. Dorothy Height, "We Wanted the Voice of a Woman to Be Heard: Black Women and the 1963 March on Washington," in Collier-Thomas and Franklin, eds., *Sisters in the Struggle,* 83–94.

31. For more on Freedom Summer and Robert Moses, see Sally Belfrage, *Freedom Summer* (Charlottesville: University of Virginia Press, 1990); Eric R. Burner, *And Gently He Shall Lead Them: Robert Moses and Civil Rights in Mississippi* (New York: State University of New York Press, 1994); Doug McAdam, *Freedom Summer* (New York: Oxford, 1988).

32. For more on these events, see Bloom, *Race, Class, and the Civil Rights Movement,* 181; Seth Cagin and Philip Dray, *We Are Not Afraid: The Story of Goodman, Schwerner, and Cheney and the Civil Rights Campaign in Mississippi* (New York: Macmillan, 1988).

33. For more on Fannie Lou Hamer and the MFDP, see Chana Kai Lee, *For Freedom's Sake: The Life of Fannie Lou Hamer* (Urbana: University of Illinois Press, 1999); Kay Mills, *This Little Light of Mine* (New York: Plume, 1993).

34. Kristin Anderson-Bricker, "Triple Jeopardy: Black Women and the Growth of Feminist Consciousness within SNCC, 1964–1975," in *Still Lifting, Still Climbing: African-American Women's Contemporary Activism,* ed. Kimberly Springer (New York: New York University Press, 1999).

35. For an excellent overview of these issues, see Anderson-Bricker, "Triple Jeopardy"; King, *Freedom Song;* Paula Giddings, *When and Where I Enter: The Impact of Black Women on Race and Sex in America* (New York: Bantam, 1984); Lynne Olson, *Freedom's Daughters: The Unsung Heroines of the Civil Rights*

Movement from 1830 to 1970 (New York: Scribner, 2001); Deborah White, *Too Heavy a Load: Black Women in Defense of Themselves, 1894–1994* (New York: Norton, 1999). See Greenberg, *A Circle of Trust,* 127–51, for King's and Hayden's, as well as black female SNCC activists', reflections on these issues twenty-five years later.

36. Giddings, *When and Where I Enter,* 302.

37. Ibid.

38. Anderson-Bricker, "Triple Jeopardy"; King, *Freedom Song;* Elizabeth Sutherland Martínez, "Neither Black nor White in a Black-White World," unpublished manuscript on file with author.

39. Gerald Horne, *The Fire This Time: The Watts Uprising and the 1960s* (Charlottesville: University Press of Virginia, 1995).

40. Bloom, *Race, Class, and the Civil Rights Movement,* 199–200.

41. For more on the OAAU, see William Sales, *From Civil Rights to Black Liberation: Malcolm X and the Organization of Afro-American Unity* (Boston: South End, 1994).

42. For King's turn toward democratic socialism and his stand on the Vietnam War, see Michael Eric Dyson, *I May Not Get There with You: The True Martin Luther King* (New York: Free Press, 2000).

43. David Garrow, *The FBI and Martin Luther King Jr.* (New York: Norton, 1981).

44. For more on the Poor People's Campaign, see Garrow, *Bearing the Cross;* Gerald McKnight, *The Last Crusade: Martin Luther King, the FBI, and the Poor People's Campaign* (Boulder, Colo.: Westview, 1998).

45. Anderson, *The Troubles That I've Seen,* 305–7.

46. McKnight, *The Last Crusade.*

47. For more on the Panthers, see Elaine Brown, *A Taste of Power: A Black Woman's Story* (New York: Pantheon, 1992); Rod Bush, *We Are Not What We Seem: Black Nationalism and Class Struggle in the American Century* (New York: New York University Press, 1999); David Hilliard and Lewis Cole, *This Side of Glory: The Story of David Hilliard and the Black Panther Party* (Boston: Little, Brown, 1993); Tracye A. Matthews, "No One Ever Asks What a Man's Role in the Revolution Is," in Collier-Thomas and Franklin, eds., *Sisters in the Struggle,* 230–56; Huey P. Newton, *To Die for the People* (New York: Random House, 1972).

48. For a devastating overview of these activities, see Ward Churchill and Jim Vander Wall, *Agents of Repression: The FBI's Secret Wars against the Black Panther Party and the American Indian Movement* (Boston: South End, 1988).

49. Huey P. Newton claimed in a 1970 essay, "[W]hatever your personal opinions and insecurities about homosexuals and various liberation movements among homosexuals and women (and I speak of homosexuals and women as

oppressed groups), we should try to unite with them in a revolutionary manner." He also said, "[H]omosexuals might be the most oppressed group in society." *To Die for the People*, 152–53.

50. The two "best" sources on the League are James Geschwender, *Class,
Race, and Worker Insurgency: The League of Revolutionary Black Workers* (London: Cambridge University Press, 1977); and Dan Georgakas and Marvin Sur-
kin, *Detroit, I Do Mind Dying* (Boston: South End, 1998).

51. Geschwender, *Class, Race, and Worker Insurgency.*

52. Elaine Brown, *A Taste of Power.* Black women's activism within the
BPP has been the subject of much debate and discussion. Matthews's piece,
"No One Ever Asks," takes a nuanced view, citing interviews with Black female
activists who said they "ran the organization on a daily basis" (in a perhaps
overly "masculine" manner) while acknowledging its sexist practices. Matthews's essential argument is that the BPP encouraged Black female (and even
queer) activism on a rhetorical and sometimes tangible level, but there were
major and consistent gaps between theory and practice. For another view of
Black female revolutionary activism in the late 1960s and early 1970s, see Joy
James, *Shadowboxing: Representations of Black Feminist Politics* (New York:
St. Martin's Press, 1999).

53. Carbado, McBride, and Weise, *Black Like Us*, 113–14.

54. The literature on the grape strike and the UFW is vast. Two relatively recent sources are Susan Farriss and Ricardo Sandoval, *The Fight in
the Fields: César Chávez and the Farmworkers Movement* (New York: Harcourt Brace, 1997); and Richard Griswold del Castillo and Richard A. García,
César Chávez: A Triumph of the Spirit (Norman: University of Oklahoma
Press, 1995).

55. Farriss and Sandoval, *Fight in the Fields*, chap. 4.

56. Ibid.

57. Griswold del Castillo and García, *César Chávez.*

58. Ibid.

59. There still does not exist a single book-length volume of the life of
Dolores Huerta. This is rather startling given her crucial role in the UFW. One
of the few works that examines a female UFW activist is Gary Soto's *Jessie de
la Cruz: A Profile of a United Farm Worker* (New York: Persea, 2000).

60. Margaret Rose, "Women in the United Farm Workers" (Ph.D. dissertation, University of California, Los Angeles, 1988).

61. Ibid., chap. 4.

62. For more on cultural nationalism and the ideological underpinnings
of the movement, see Carlos Muñoz Jr., *Youth, Identity, and Power* (London:
Verso, 1989); Ignacio García, *Chicanismo: The Forging of a Militant Ethos
among Mexican Americans* (Tucson: University of Arizona Press, 1997).

63. For more on the internal colony model, see Mario Barrera, Carlos Muñoz, and Charles Ornelas, "The Barrio as Internal Colony," *Urban Affairs Annual Research Review* 6 (1972): 465–98; Robert Blauner, *Racial Oppression in America* (New York: Harper and Row, 1972).

64. García, *Chicanismo,* 43–67.

65. Ibid; Alfredo Mirandé, *The Chicano Experience: An Alternative Perspective* (Notre Dame: University of Notre Dame Press, 1985).

66. Rodolfo Gonzales, *I Am Joaquín/Yo Soy Joaquín* (New York: Bantam Books, 1972).

67. F. Arturo Rosales, *Chicano! The History of the Mexican American Civil Rights Movement* (Houston: Arte Público, 1996), 180.

68. Ernesto Vigil, *The Crusade for Justice: Chicano Militancy and the Government's War on Dissent* (Madison: University of Wisconsin Press, 1999), 24–27.

69. Rosales, *Chicano!* 180; Vigil, *Crusade for Justice,* 26–63. The latter work points out that the Crusade often formed strategic alliances with African Americans over issues such as racial discrimination, jobs, police brutality, and the Vietnam War.

70. Vigil, *The Crusade for Justice,* 97–98.

71. For more on the philosophical, political, ideological, and literary underpinnings of Aztlán, see Rudolfo Anaya and Francisco Lomelí, eds., *Aztlán: Essays on the Chicano Homeland* (Albuquerque: Academia/El Norte Publications, 1989); Cherríe Moraga, "Queer Aztlán: The Re-Formation of the Chicano Tribe," in *Last Generation* (Boston: South End, 1993), 145–74; Rafael Pérez-Torres, "Refiguring Aztlán," *Aztlán* 22.2 (fall 1997): 15–42.

72. Vigil, *Crusade for Justice.*

73. Juan Gómez-Quiñones, *Chicano Politics: Reality and Promise, 1940–1990* (Albuquerque: University of New Mexico Press, 1990), 141–42.

74. Vigil, *Crusade for Justice,* 27–28.

75. For more on sexism and the National Chicano Youth Conference, see Enriqueta Longeaux y Vásquez, "The Mexican-American Woman," in *Sisterhood Is Powerful: An Anthology of Writings from the Women's Liberation Movement,* ed. Robin Morgan (New York: Vintage, 1970), 379–84; and episode 1 ("The Quest for a Homeland") of the four-part video series, *Chicano!* (Galan Productions and the National Latino Communications Center, 1996). See also Rosales, *Chicano!* 182–83.

76. Ana Nieto-Gómez, "La Femenista," *Encuentro Femenil* (1973): 34–47. For more on the debates surrounding racism, sexism, and the Chicana/o movement, see Alma García, *Chicana Feminist Thought: The Basic Historical Writings* (New York: Routledge, 1997); Marcie Miranda-Arrizon, "Building Herman(a)dad: Chicana Feminism and Comisión Femenil Mexicana Nacional" (M.A. thesis, University of California, Santa Barbara, 1998); Beatriz M. Pesquera and Denise A. Segura, "There Is No Going Back: Chicanas and Femi-

nism," in *Chicana Critical Issues,* ed. Mujeres Activas en Letras y Cambio Social (MALCS) (Berkeley: Third Woman Press), 95–117; Benita Roth, "On Their Own and for Their Own: African-American, Chicana, and White Feminist Movements in the 1960s and 1970s" (Ph.D. dissertation, University of California, Los Angeles, 1998); Vicki Ruiz, *From Out of the Shadows: Mexican Women in Twentieth-Century America* (Oxford: Oxford University Press, 1998); Ada Sosa-Riddell, "Chicanas and El Movimiento," *Aztlán* 5 (spring–fall 1974): 155–65.

77. There are very few sources on the Alianza and Tijerina. See Rudy Val Busto, "Like a Mighty Rushing Wind: The Religious Impulse in the Life and Writing of Reies Lopez Tijerina" (Ph.D. dissertation, University of California, Berkeley, 1991); Peter Nabokov, *Tijerina and the Courthouse Raid* (Albuquerque: University of New Mexico Press, 1969); Reies López Tijerina, *They Called Me "King Tiger": My Struggle for the Land and Our Rights* (Houston: Arte Público, 2000); Rosales, *Chicano!*

78. Rosales, *Chicano!* 159–61.

79. See Nabokov, *Tijerina and the Courthouse Raid,* for more on these events.

80. Rosales, *Chicano!* 168–70.

81. Armando Navarro, *Mexican-American Youth Organization* (Austin: University of Texas Press, 1995).

82. Ignacio García, *United We Win: The Rise and Fall of La Raza Unida Party* (Tucson: University of Arizona Press, 1989).

83. García, *Chicanismo,* 108.

84. For more on CASA, see David Gutiérrez, *Walls and Mirrors: Mexican Americans, Mexican Immigrants, and the Politics of Identity* (Berkeley: University of California Press, 1995); and Arturo Santamaría Gómez, *La izquierda norteamericana y los trabajadores undocumentados* (Mexico City: Ediciones Cultural Popular, 1988).

85. Santamaría Gómez, *La izquierda,* 141–94.

86. Gutiérrez, *Walls and Mirrors;* Santamaría Gómez, *La izquierda.*

87. Ruiz, *From Out of the Shadows,* 118.

88. For more on the concept of strategic essentialism, see Donald Landry and Gerald MacLean, eds., *The Spivak Reader: Selected Works of Gayatri Chakravorty Spivak* (New York: Routledge, 1995).

89. Carbado, McBride, and Weise, *Black Like Us,* 9–10.

90. Paul Buhle, *Taking Care of Business: Samuel Gompers, George Meany, Lane Kirkland, and the Tragedy of American Labor* (New York: Monthly Review Press, 1999).

91. Elizabeth Martínez, "Where Was the Color in Seattle?" in *Globalize This! The Battle against the WTO and Corporate Rule,* ed. Kevin Danaher and Roger Burbach (Monroe, Maine: Common Courage Press, 2000).

8

THE ASIAN AMERICAN MOVEMENT
A Quest for Racial Equality, Social Justice, and Political Empowerment

WILLIAM WEI

"I walk tall, and look at all things in a different way. I knew there was something different about me today. . . . And I feel us growing stronger, building something new." These lyrics, sung by troubadours Nobuko Miyamoto, Chris Iijima, and "Charlie" Chin in 1970, captured the sentiments of a generation of political activists in the Asian American movement. The "Movement," as it was called by many of its early participants, was essentially a struggle for racial equality, social justice, and political empowerment in a culturally pluralist America. The struggle was carried out through an inter-Asian coalition that embraced the entire spectrum of Asian ethnic groups,[1] acknowledging their common experiences in American society and calling for a higher level of solidarity. It was the last of the "ethnic consciousness" movements to emerge in the 1960s.[2] Yet it is virtually unknown.

The Movement's lack of visibility stems from its lack of national leaders and specific aims and the comparatively small number of participants. Perhaps more important, its invisibility stems from the persistent perception that race relations in the United States are a matter of Blacks and Whites. It is little wonder that the struggles of other "third world" people tend to be ignored. As I show in this history of the Asian American movement, the challenge to racial hierarchy in America is more than simply Blacks versus Whites.

ETHNIC CONSCIOUSNESS

The genesis of Asian American activism can be traced to individual Asian Americans who participated in the civil rights, New Left, and other social movements organized during the 1960s to advance the interests of the country's historically marginalized citizens. Asian American political activism emerged spontaneously in different places, at different times, and with different perspectives; it was not simply a product of the Third World Strike at San Francisco State, as is popularly believed. On the West Coast, it began when community activists focused attention on the deteriorating social circumstances of San Francisco's Chinatown ghetto and campus activists protested the absence of their historical experiences in college and university curricula. On the East Coast, in New York City, Nisei (second-generation Japanese American) women began organizing in response to the absence of an ethnic community and the steady erosion of a Japanese American identity among their children. In the Midwest, Asian American activism began when Asian American college students came together for mutual support and collective action to oppose the Vietnam War.

Across the nation, Asian Americans began to experience an ethnic awakening. They began to learn their history and culture, to become aware of such injustices as the Chinese Exclusion Act (1882) and the incarceration of 110,000 Japanese Americans in concentration camps during World War II. As Asian Americans became increasingly conscious of their common oppression, they began to realize that the goals of equality, justice, and empowerment could only be achieved through an inter-Asian coalition based on a pan-Asian identity.

WAR IN VIETNAM

The Movement coalesced around opposition to the war in Vietnam (1965–75). The antiwar movement reached its apex in the late 1960s just as a statistically and socially significant number of Asian Americans began to attend college. Before this period, there were few Asian American youth, as exclusion laws effectively limited the ability of most Asian immigrants to establish families in the United States. Those that were able to do so found it difficult to provide their children with an adequate education, since they were forced to place them in inferior, segregated schools or in private schools. But the eventual elimination of these discriminatory laws and the baby boom of Asian Americans during the immediate post–World War II period resulted in a significant number of college-aged Asian Americans in the 1960s. In 1970, 107,366 of them were enrolled in colleges and universities.[3] Of that group, 83 percent were Chinese and Japanese Americans. Except for a few young people from the working-class community, these college students made up the majority of the Asian American antiwar protesters. For many of them, it was the first engagement in any sort of political protest. And they found it an exhilarating and exhausting experience.

Asian American antiwar activists were particularly concerned about the reawakening of the sociomilitary phenomenon known as "gookism," which made no distinction between the Vietnamese, Laotians, and Cambodians (and other Asians) encountered overseas, on the one hand, and Asian Americans at home, on the other. "Gooks," a racial epithet that implied Asians were something other than human, was used during the Vietnam War to prepare soldiers psychologically to maim and kill Southeast Asians. As one veteran explained, "You are trained 'gook, gook, gook' and once the military has the idea planted in you that these people are not humans . . . it makes it a bit easier to kill 'em."[4] As a result of their dehumanization by the military and their brutalization by the war, American soldiers committed numerous atrocities. The most infamous was the My Lai Massacre (March 1968), when, without provocation, a platoon of soldiers led by Lt. William L. Calley murdered in cold blood almost all the villagers of My Lai.

Unfortunately, the phenomenon of "gookism" persists to the present. Sen. John McCain, a former POW, repeatedly used the term "gook" to refer to his North Vietnamese captors while campaigning for the Republican Party presidential nomination in 2000.[5] After it was finally reported in the press, McCain belatedly apologized for using the racial slur. Asian Americans noted that the incident received little media coverage,[6] in marked contrast to the earlier attention paid to the use of the word *niggardly* by a city councilman's aide. Although, unlike "gook," "niggardly" lacks any negative racial connotations, its use led to the aide's resignation and a national debate over political correctness and racial sensitivity. Together, the incidents raise questions about the nation's sensitivity to racial issues beyond Black and White.

Asian American antiwar activists, therefore, opposed the Vietnam War as unjust *and* racist. They believed that racial hatred was the underlying reason for the numerous "war crimes" committed overseas. Evoking memories of the Holocaust, they argued that American soldiers were waging a genocidal war against Asian people considered biologically and culturally inferior, an assumption that was traceable historically to nineteenth-century imperialism in Asia. Making the connection to racist polices at home, they accused Euro-Americans of having carried out genocidal policies against Asian Americans through exclusion laws that were designed to extinguish their presence. They perceived such laws as a legalized form of "ethnic cleansing."

In retrospect, Asian American antiwar activists engaged in hyperbole, reflecting the emotions of the period but failing to make the case for genocide against their people.[7] While the Vietnam War resulted in widespread death and destruction and the laws aimed at the exclusion of an entire people, they were not on the same massive scale as Hitler's final solution. Moreover, they lacked the specific intent of Hitler's policy of ridding the world of so-called inferior peoples, that is, Jews, Gypsies, and the mentally handicapped.

Asian American antiwar activists emphasized the racial underpinnings of the Vietnam War because other antiwar activists were ignoring that crucial facet. For slogans like "Give peace a chance" and "Bring the G.I.'s home," Asian American activists substituted "Stop killing our Asian brothers and sisters" and "Asian lives are not cheap and Asians must say so now!" When they tried to publicize this perspective on the war, however, they were roundly rebuffed by fellow antiwar dissidents intent on ending the war without addressing the divisive and distracting issue of race. Consequently, Asian Americans became increasingly disillusioned with the White-dominated antiwar movement, just as feminists became dissatisfied with the movement's refusal to recognize that American soldiers were raping Asian women.

Asian Americans continued to support the antiwar movement, but they did so on their own terms. In the beginning, that often meant forming separate groups in the major demonstrations that were erupting across the country. For example, in the November 1969 antiwar demonstration in San Francisco, several hundred Asian Americans (80 percent of whom were students and youths, equally divided between Chinese and Japanese) chose to march as a separate contingent. Similarly, when the coordinating committee of the April 1971 antiwar demonstration in Washington, D.C., declined to adopt a statement against racism, Asian Americans decided to march apart from the main body of protesters. Sometimes Asian Americans' resolve to protest the war on their own terms led to provocative actions. To "read a statement supporting the Vietnamese peoples struggle against U.S. aggression, and denouncing [antiwar organizers'] disregard for Asian people,"[8] for instance, a group of Asian American activists felt compelled to seize the speakers' platform at an April 1971 antiwar rally at San Francisco's Golden Gate Park. To make their presence felt in the broader antiwar movement, Asian American activists also organized their own antiwar coalitions, including the Bay Area Asian Coalition Against the War, Los Angeles Asian Coalition, Sacramento Asian Coalition Against the War, East Coast Ad Hoc Committee of Asians Against the War, and Asian-American Veterans Against the War. In bringing Asian American activists together to participate in a common cause that transcended the college campuses and Asian ethnic communities, the antiwar movement helped to transform previously isolated instances of political activism into a social movement that was national in scope—the Asian American movement.

The origins of the Asian American movement, then, can be traced to the convergence of two historical developments—the emergence of a generation of college-age Asian Americans and the coalescing of public protests around the Vietnam War during the late 1960s. Indeed, the antiwar movement helped to unify Asian Americans politically and was the first of many national issues that brought together inter-Asian coalitions. As antiwar activists, they overcame ethnic differences and geographic limitations in a common struggle to stop the war. In the process of traveling to other parts of the country to work against the war, they met other Asian Americans with whom they shared similar concerns and perspectives. Participation in the antiwar movement (as well as other social movements) convinced many campus and community activists that if they were ever to have a voice in this country, they would have to work together as Asian Americans.

IDENTITY AND CULTURE

The underlying psychological basis for the Movement has been the search for identity and the creation of a new culture. Unlike Euro-Americans, who could easily incorporate their personal identities into their sense of being American, Asian Americans had to create an entirely new identity—that of the Asian American. Although this identity is still in the process of formation, it is at least clear that Asian Americans have transcended the communal and cultural limits of specific Asian ethnic groups to identify with the past experiences, present circumstances, and future aspirations of all Asians in America. By appealing to Asian Americans' shared ethnicity and experience in America, a pan-Asian consciousness has evolved. By developing an integrated identity and a coherent culture, they have begun to build the psychological and intellectual foundations for a pan-Asian solidarity that will enable them to approach mainstream society on a more equal footing and participate more effectively in a culturally pluralist society.

Defining their identity as Asian Americans involved, among other things, challenging directly the distorted images, from Fu Manchu to Charlie Chan, that have diminished Asian Americans as individuals and degraded them as a group. The protest over Abercrombie & Fitch's sale of racist T-shirts is the most recent example of this.[9] In a misguided attempt to attract Asian American consumers, the clothier marketed four graphic T-shirts featuring derogatory portrayals of Asian Americans wearing conical hats and carrying logos such as "Two Wongs Can Make It White." Across the nation, Asian American students and young professionals picketed Abercrombie & Fitch stores to express their outrage, demanding the recall of the offensive shirts and advocating a boycott of the store. Asian American groups such as the Organization of Chinese Americans and the 80-20 Initiative, a national organization seeking political empowerment for Asian Americans, contacted Abercrombie & Fitch officials to register their disapproval. Within days, the retailer began removing the shirts from its 311 stores in fifty states in response to the criticism.

In addition to protesting derogatory images, Asian Americans have sought to replace them with accurate images based on historical knowledge. This has been part and parcel of the ongoing effort to create a pan-Asian counterculture that reflects their values and experiences. In so doing, Asian Americans have instilled pride and self-esteem among themselves and given birth to their own forms of expression, enriching the multicultural mosaic that is America. Through revisionist history, literature, art, and film, they recovered old traditions, customs, and values and at the same time developed new sensibilities, perspectives, and connections to serve as the basis for a new cultural synthesis that gives definition and depth to their ethnic identity. Activists consciously wrote literary works such as the provocative plays by Frank Chin, "Chickencoop Chinamen" and "The Year of the Dragon," dealing with the angst and alienation of being Asian American, and in doing so, they attracted a loyal following in Movement cultural circles. Others, like Maxine Hong Kingston, author of the popular work, *The Woman Warrior: A Memoir of a Girlhood among Ghosts,* have generated controversy within the Movement but attracted public acclaim from mainstream society. While Kingston writes about the Asian American experience, her perspective is decidedly feminist. Without necessarily intending it, Asian Americans have thus contributed significantly to the broadening of American culture.

Social Change

From the beginning of the Movement, pan-Asian identity and unity have produced significant achievements. Asian American activists have participated in inter-Asian coalitions at the local, regional, and national levels to work for bilingual-bicultural education, civil rights, the enactment of nondiscriminatory immigration laws, justice for victims of anti-Asian violence, and other significant social issues. By employing a combination of radical politics and conventional politics, Asian Americans have been able to achieve a measure of social change. Though often initiated by a specific Asian ethnic group to address a single issue, these actions attracted broader support because of their implications for the racial equality and political empowerment of all Asian Americans. One of the earliest was *Lau* v. *Nichols,* a 1974 landmark case involving non-English-speaking Chinese students whose parents filed a successful suit against the San Francisco Board of Education for failing to provide equal educational opportunities for students like them. As a result, bilingual-bicultural education for Asian as well as Latino children was introduced into the school system. Another victory was the Japanese American redress and reparations movement. After many years of persistent effort, on August 10, 1988, President Ronald Reagan signed the Civil Liberties Act, authorizing $1.25 billion in reparations payments to an estimated seventy thousand Japanese Americans who were survivors of America's concentration camps during World War II. These campaigns have proven the political effectiveness of Asian Americans and their ability to overcome their diversity as a community and to set a common agenda.

In the 1970s, as women activists grappled with the problem of racial inequality in American society, they became acutely aware of the problem of gender inequality within the Movement. Almost from the beginning, they became conscious that Asian American women suffered from dual forms of oppression. Like the Movement, the Asian American women's movement began with small informal groups for personal support and political study and evolved into large formal organizations that addressed the status and concerns of Asian American women throughout the nation. This development has benefited the Movement in important ways: by actuating the potential of women activists, it has widened their participation in the Movement; and by politicizing formerly inactive women, it has moved them to participate in the common struggle for equality and empowerment. Even more significantly, it has empowered women to face inequalities in their lives and communities and to develop skills to challenge them.

Since the 1980s Asian Americans have begun participating in increasing numbers in electoral politics and defending the earlier gains made in civil rights, which were eroded during the Reagan and first Bush administrations through the weakening of the U.S. Civil Rights Commission and the dilution of affirmative action programs. Asian Americans were, for example, active members of Jesse Jackson's Rainbow Coalition, supporting his bid for the presidency in 1984 and 1988 and his quintessentially American ideal of the dignity and equality of all human beings. They have also run for political office, participated in partisan politics, and succeeded in gaining appointments to government boards and commissions.[10] By the beginning of the twenty-first century, the Rainbow Coalition had faded into history but not the need for political empowerment. In spring 2002, in an effort to transcend the rivalry for resources and recognition, members of the Congressional Black, Hispanic, and Asian Pacific Caucuses gathered together for a tricaucus retreat to discuss a common agenda on education, economics, health care, and immigration, thereby embarking on a new era of coalition politics.[11] Through these mainstream activities, Asian Americans have exercised their political rights and civic responsibilities, expressing their commitment to democracy in no uncertain terms. However, not every activist initially shared this strategy for political change.

REFORMERS AND REVOLUTIONARIES

From the beginning of the Movement, Asian American activists have been divided into two groups, reformers and revolutionaries, with markedly different perspectives on what is best for the community.

Asian American Studies

On college and university campuses, Asian American reformers established Asian American Studies (AAS), a new field of inquiry in higher education that has been consciously counterhegemonic. During the late 1960s, the struggle for Asian American Studies began at San Francisco State College (now San Francisco State University) and at the University of California, Berkeley. Asian American student activists participated in the Third World Liberation Fronts on both campuses to protest the absence of their story from the college curriculum and to demand its inclusion.

In addition, Asian Americans wanted to show their solidarity with other students of color. Indeed, Asian American Studies defines the racial identity of Asian Americans as a people of color rather than simply as another immigrant group and seeks to participate in the development of a pan-Asian culture that is part and parcel of a culturally pluralist America. Throughout the country AAS has introduced students to the Asian American experience, emphasizing a history of racial oppression and resistance, and has produced scholarship that offers a radical interpretation of that experience by challenging the glaring omissions and misrepresentations in existing texts and curricula. Among Asian American students, it has instilled the self-confidence and self-esteem that are essential for personal achievement and social activism. Finally, AAS has served as a vehicle for mobilizing students to challenge the existing power structure and work for social change.

In the mid-1990s the struggle to include Asian American Studies courses and programs in college curricula reached a high level of intensity. In spring 1995, at Princeton University, Asian American students held a thirty-five-hour sit-in at the president's office, and at Northwestern University, they held a twenty-three-day hunger strike to demand the establishment of Asian American Studies programs on their campuses. Black and Latino students joined Asian American students in a show of ethnic solidarity.

There has been a campaign also to incorporate ethnic studies into the K–12 curriculum. For example, in spring 2000 students from the Asian Youth Promoting Advocacy and Leadership worked for curriculum reform in the Oakland Unified School District, California's sixth largest, so that they could learn about their history and culture and not just the interaction of their people with those of Europe. They believed that ethnic studies course would serve as a "system of mediation in Oakland schools, which are fragmented by racial tension."[12] In July 2001 the Asian Pacific American Educators' Summit in Seattle initiated an effort to develop a strategy for promoting a national curriculum to combat ignorance of Asian American history and culture and insensitivity to Asian American communities.[13]

The struggle for the establishment of Asian American Studies is part of the larger culture war being waged on college campuses throughout the nation to diversify higher education, allowing once-marginalized people to tell their stories. It is part of the difficult re-visioning of America from a monocultural to a multicultural society, that is, a common culture resulting from the interactions of its subsidiary cultures, of which the Asian American culture is one. As such, multiculturalism is a repudiation of the old melting pot perspective that advocated the end of ethnicity and expected the emergence of a homogeneous dominant Euro-American culture. It argues that ethnicity has always been an integral part of America's identity and is rooted in its democratic tradition. In other words, it is what makes America, America. What will emerge from multiculturalism is nothing less than a redefinition of who is an American, one that will include people of color, who are no longer willing to be treated as second-class citizens, or, in the case of Asian Americans, as perpetual foreigners in their own country.

WILLIAM WEI

Community-based Organizations

In the Asian ethnic enclaves of America, Asian American reformers have tried to make the existing social order more equitable by establishing two types of community-based organizations: social service organizations that provide services and resources to mainly working-class Asian immigrants and refugees and alternative grassroots organizations that address such significant issues as discrimination in the workplace and in the classroom. Of the two, the social service organizations, such as the Chinese-American Planning Council, Inc. (also called the Chinatown Planning Council) in New York and Self-Help for the Elderly in San Francisco, both of which were founded in the 1960s, have been more adaptable to the existing social system. This has enabled them to become institutionalized in the community and serve their constituents over a longer period.

Both types of organizations, however, have contributed significantly to the social stability of the Asian American community by providing counseling services, welfare assistance, recreational facilities, and employment opportunities. They have mitigated the deprivations of the ghetto, helping individuals to survive, families to remain intact, and communities to thrive. In doing so, they have eclipsed the traditional Asian ethnic organizations such as the Chinese Consolidated Benevolent Association (also called the Chinese Six Companies in San Francisco) that have failed to carry out their responsibility to provide for the welfare of the community. Furthermore, they have become a political force in their own right, challenging the control of these conservative organizations and democratizing the community. And they have assumed the role of intermediaries to the dominant society as traditional leaders and their organizations have become increasingly irrelevant in the community. Perhaps most important, these community-based organizations have contributed to the Asian American community's cohesion, a necessary condition for collective action and advancement in a democratic pluralist society.

The Fate of the Revolution

In contrast to the reformers, Asian American revolutionaries belonging to such Maoist-oriented groups as the Red Guards in San Francisco and the I Wor Kuen in New York City considered the existing social, economic, and political order corrupt. In their view the "system" was irredeemable and should be replaced by a new order, presumably under their direction. Consequently, they believed that the new campus and community institutions would have little lasting value and would eventually engender widespread frustration. Yet they sought to exploit these same institutions to obtain resources and influence in the Asian American community, as they prepared for the social revolution that was always looming on the political horizon. That revolution has not materialized—in part because the existing social order has been open and flexible enough to adapt to the needs of Asian Americans and other people of color.

Moreover, the Asian American community tired of the revolutionaries' sectarian wars and found their ideologies irrelevant and poor guides to political action. A case in point was the failure of Maoist sects to work on the Asian admissions issue, which focused on the lower college admissions rates of Asian Americans compared to that of Euro-Americans and the underenrollment of Asian American students even though the number of their applications had increased. Officials at such prestigious schools as the University of California, Berkeley, Brown, Harvard, Princeton, and Stanford were accused of establishing tacit quotas to limit the enrollment of Asian American students. The Maoist sects found the issue "too bourgeois" and never really organized around it, viewing it as unrelated to their community work that emphasized the working class.

The Maoist sects were also overtaken by larger external events. In China, Maoism was repudiated and the country moved toward a capitalist economy based on market forces. Equally important was the Tiananmen Square Massacre on June 4, 1989, when the People's Liberation Army killed Chinese youth who had gone on hunger strikes and held mass demonstrations for democratic reform. Also that year, much to the surprise of everyone, the United States won the cold war by default when the Soviet Union and the eastern European bloc nations began to disintegrate as a result of bankrupt economies and corrupt governments. With their ideology discredited, disillusioned Asian American Maoists forsook their revolutionary past to work for progressive change through community-based organizations or electoral politics. Still, revolutionaries brought a progressive political agenda to the Movement and helped to politicize the community by raising important issues. And as experienced and disciplined cadres, they provided leadership and channeled resources to various social and political struggles.

In the final analysis, the significance of the Asian American revolutionaries lies in their having eroded the power of the conservative Asian American elite and having served as a lightning rod for its malevolence. The chief beneficiaries were the reformers, whom the elite perceived as the lesser of two evils. Reformers were able to thread their way between the revolutionaries and conservatives to effect social change in the community.

After the War

When the Vietnam War ended in 1975, a major mainstay of the Asian American movement disappeared. However, the antiwar movement had created a generation of Asian American activists who are aware, astute, and willing to act for the collective benefit of the Asian American community.

Anti-Asian Violence

Since the mid-1970s Asian American activists have continued to organize inter-Asian coalitions with a pan-Asian ideology to work on Asian American concerns and issues. With the increased harassment of and violence against Asian Americans, anti-Asian violence has been one of the issues that has generated widespread support among Asian Americans on campuses and in the community. Since the brutal killing of Vincent Chin in 1982 by two unemployed Detroit auto workers who mistook him for a Japanese, Asian Americans have been aware of the problem of anti-Asian violence and the inability of the judicial system to punish its perpetrators. They realized that the murder of Vincent Chin was more than simply an isolated case; it was symptomatic of widespread anti-Asian sentiment that often expressed itself in violence. As "perpetual" foreigners in their own country, they have been used historically as convenient scapegoats for the dominant society's ills. Chin's murderers, Ronald Ebens and Michael Nitz, were brought to trial, but they were allowed to plead guilty to the lesser charge of manslaughter, given four years' probation, and fined about $3,000 each. Needless to say, the Asian American community was outraged by the light sentences and demanded justice. While justice for Vincent Chin was never attained, the campaign served to politicize Asian Americans.

Since the Vincent Chin tragedy, there have been numerous cases of individuals who have been harassed, beaten, and murdered for no other reason than they were Asian Americans. Among these acts of anti-Asian violence, none was more senseless than the one committed by Patrick Purdy, an insane young man with a hatred of Southeast Asians. On January 17, 1989, Purdy, armed with an assault rifle, opened fire in a schoolyard in Stockton, California, killing five Indochinese children. Of the thirty-one wounded, twenty-two were of Southeast Asian descent. Among recent victims of anti-Asian violence are Won-Joon Yoon, a Korean student, killed on July 4, 1999, by the White supremacist Benjamin Nathaniel Smith, and Joseph Ileto, a Filipino American postman, killed on August 10, 1999, by the White supremacist Buford Furrow.[14] In the wake of the terrorist attacks on the World Trade Center and the Pentagon on September 11, 2001, there has been a backlash against Asian Indian Americans and Arab Americans. As a result of the egregious error committed against the Japanese Americans during World War II, government officials have been careful to distinguish between Arab Americans and Arabs and to oppose violence against people of Middle Eastern ancestry. Still, there have been personal attacks and religious persecution, the worst being the murder of a Sikh American gas station owner after being mistaken for a Muslim because he wore a turban.

Asian Americans have sought to combat incidents of anti-Asian violence by calling on the media to recognize them as racist crimes and by demanding that the police investigate them as such and that the judicial system punish the perpetrators. Realizing that the perpetrators of such crimes are a greater threat to society because they target a large group rather than a specific individual, they have worked for the passage of hate crime laws, which provide for stiffer sentences against those who seek to harm people because of their race, religion, ethnicity, and sexual orientation.

Interethnic Strife

Anti-Asian violence has emerged from an unexpected quarter—other people of color. There have been recurring incidents of interethnic strife, indicating that the solidarity that existed among so-called third world people during the late 1960s and in Jesse Jackson's Rainbow Coalition during the 1980s has all but disappeared. Until the 1992 riots in Los Angeles, during which the Korean American community was singled out for looting and burning, most of the attention had been focused on the conflicts between African Americans and Latinos over increasingly scarce resources. Usually, these conflicts were depicted as erupting between two "have-not" groups competing for a piece of the American Dream.[15] The underlying cause for these racial tensions and violent outbreaks has been the growing economic injustices and social disintegration in urban ghettos and the failure of American society to deal with inequality among the races.

In the Asian American community, this interethnic conflict has been mainly between Korean Americans and African Americans. The best-known example is the 1992 Los Angeles Riots that destroyed over 1,800 Korean-owned businesses in Koreatown and South Central Los Angeles.[16] As is well known, the Los Angeles Riots were precipitated by the unexpected acquittal of four White policemen for the brutal beating of Rodney King, an African American. During the riots, African Americans and Latinos targeted Korean Americans for "ethnic cleansing." An additional aspect of the tragedy in Los Angeles was the feeling of betrayal that Korean Americans felt when the police ignored their pleas for protection, which forced them to use firearms to protect themselves, their families, and their businesses from rioters. The irony, of course, was that African Americans and Latinos displayed the sort of race-driven hatred that has been visited on them all too frequently in American history.

The underlying cause was scapegoatism. Mainly African Americans, who have become increasingly frustrated by rising unemployment and police brutality, singled out Korean Americans as economic scapegoats. Like other immigrant groups before them, notably Jews fleeing anti-Semitism in Europe, Korean American families have opened marginal businesses (the proverbial mom-and-pop store) in poor and dangerous neighborhoods, where they put in long hours for small profits. They do so because this is one way that Korean immigrants with poor language skills and little capital (usually accumulated through relatives and friends) can make a living. Unfortunately, they have been mistakenly perceived by an African American community that has been experiencing declining public assistance as a privileged group receiving government support. An erroneous corollary is the complaint that the government is unwilling to do the same for African Americans, which presumably explains why there are so few Black-owned businesses in the local area.

After the Los Angeles Riots, tensions between African Americans and Asian Americans continued to flare. Following the historical pattern—most Americans still cannot distinguish one Asian group from another—the anti–Korean American sentiment has also resulted in violence against other Asian Americans. In New York City, for example, an African American youth gang attacked three Vietnamese, mistaking them for Korean Americans.

The Wen Ho Lee Case

The latest example of scapegoatism is the strange case of Wen Ho Lee, a Taiwan-born physicist suspected of being a Chinese spy. Although he was not charged with a crime per se, Lee was indicted on fifty-nine counts of violating the Atomic Energy Act and Foreign Espionage Act. If found guilty, Lee faced possible life imprisonment. Federal agents interrogated him harshly and threatened him with the same fate as the Rosenbergs, who were executed in 1953. They even lied to him, saying that he had failed a polygraph test on whether he was a Chinese spy, to make him confess. He was summarily thrown into solitary confinement for 278 days. Understandably, while languishing in jail, Lee concluded, "No matter how smart you are, no matter how hard you work, a Chinese person, an Asian person like me, will never be accepted. We always will be foreigners."[17] Lee was also denied bail because he was considered a "flight risk." Thus, he supposedly represented a "clear and present danger" to the nation. It was the sort of treatment usually associated with victims of America's erstwhile cold war enemies.

Lee's travails began as early as 1996, when the United States concluded that recent Chinese advances in nuclear weaponry could have been accomplished only through espionage. Consequently, the federal government took steps to prevent further Chinese espionage, including the enhancement of security at the nation's nuclear weapons laboratories. In the course of these actions, suspicion fell on Lee as an individual who might have provided the People's Republic of China with the information necessary to replicate the W-88, America's most advanced miniature warhead. Now it is known that no one at Los Alamos National Laboratory, where Lee worked, had the plans that might have been acquired by China for its nuclear missile development.

While the investigation into the possible theft of nuclear weapons secrets was in process, there were premature disclosures to the press. According to an internal memo, John J. Dion, chief of the Justice Department's internal security section, said that the government may have "intentionally revealed facts about the investigation to the news media in order to pressure Lee to confess, or out of vindictiveness toward Lee for not confessing."[18] On the basis of information leaked from the Cox Report, a seven-hundred-page congressional committee report on U.S. military and commercial dealing with China, the media began to stereotype Chinese Americans as potential spies and Lee as the spy that had been found out. In other words, the media engaged in the character assassination of the entire Chinese American community and found Lee guilty in the court of public opinion. More than any other newspaper, the *New York Times* was responsible for the public bashing of the Asian American community. In its March 6, 1999, story, "China Stole Nuclear Secrets from Los Alamos, U.S. Officials Say," the *New York Times* revealed information about the Lee investigation, though not identifying him by name.[19] It is highly likely that the story led to the termination of his job at the Los Alamos laboratory two days later.

Under normal circumstances, Lee's violations—downloading data to his home computer—would have been characterized as minor and considered commonplace among the scientists working at Los Alamos, and certainly no worse than those committed by top government officials. For example, John M. Deutch, former head of the CIA, had acknowledged that he too had downloaded data. However, in Deutch's case, the punishment was a loss of security clearance rather than a loss of liberty. It is clear that at the very least Lee is the victim of a double standard.

In response to these allegations and actions, Lee sought to defend himself on the CBS newsmagazine *60 Minutes*. On national television, he proclaimed his innocence and expressed his bewilderment at what was happening to him and his family. When asked why he was targeted for investigation, Lee implied that the authorities needed a scapegoat and that as an ethnic Chinese he fit their needs perfectly. But as Ling-chi Wang has pointed out, "Lee . . . fell short of saying that he was singled out on account of his race."[20] Robert S. Vrooman, former head of counterintelligence at Los Alamos National Laboratory, confirmed this, saying that Lee was "unfairly singled out for Federal investigation because of his ethnicity."[21] Moreover, Vrooman noted that federal investigators had "not one shred of evidence" that linked Lee to espionage.[22]

Indeed, the absence of any evidence of espionage eventually resulted in his freedom. As part of a plea bargain, Federal Judge James Parker released Lee, saying, "I apologize to you, Dr. Lee, for the unfair manner you were held in custody by the executive branch," and scolded the Justice and Energy Department officials for overstating the evidence against him and embarrassing the nation.[23] To attain his freedom, Lee pleaded guilty to one felony count of misusing classified information when he downloaded nuclear weapons data onto portable tapes and then stored them in his unsecured personal computer. Since then Lee has written a book, *My Country versus Me*, describing his ordeal and is pursuing a lawsuit against the FBI and the Justice and Energy Departments for engaging in a campaign of news leaks that violated his privacy and wrongfully portrayed him as a spy. Meanwhile, what Wen Ho Lee would like is a pardon from his president and an apology from his government.

The Asian American community rallied around Wen Ho Lee. It set up a defense fund to help defray his legal costs, held rallies on his behalf, signed petitions demanding that he be treated fairly, and donated money to his defense fund. The Committee of 100, a group of prominent Chinese Americans, the Asian American Legal Defense and Education Fund, the Asian Pacific American Legal Center, the Asian Law Caucus, and other Asian American groups have offered their support. According to Cecilia Chang, chair of the defense fund, "This is probably the equivalent of the Rodney King case in the African American community!"[24]

Asian Americans realize that Lee's case has significant implications for the entire community. In the post–cold war era when Asia in general and China in particular have been seen as economic rivals and potential military threats, they realize that the continued inability of mainstream Americans to distinguish Asians from Asian Americans make them vulnerable to accusations of being the enemy. Indeed, in a country where people mistakenly equate ethnicity with loyalty, Asian Americans have every reason to be concerned that they will be perceived as disloyal. As Frank Wu notes, "Every news account about Lee describes him as a 'Chinese spy.' That ambiguous characterization suggests not only that he is a spy for China, but also a spy of Chinese ethnicity."[25] It was just this sort of phenomenon that led to the mass imprisonment of Japanese Americans in concentration camps during World War II on the basis of the spurious excuse of "military necessity."

Unfortunately, the Lee case has intensified the problem of the racial profiling of Asian Americans. In the wake of the Lee case, the Department of Energy's effort to improve security and institute counterintelligence procedures resulted in making their Asian American employees feel that they were suspected of disloyalty. Among other things, it used insensitive and inappropriate training materials such as the one that showed "a consultant asking why there were so many Chinese restaurants in Los Alamos, answering his own question by suggesting, 'for spying, of course.'"[26] Its ad hoc committee against racial profiling has made many recommendations to improve the situation. Bill Richardson, secretary of the Department of Energy at the time of the incident, pledged "zero tolerance" of discrimination against Asian Americans. Meanwhile, tired of the constant insults and slurs they have had to endure over the years, Asian American workers at the Lawrence Livermore Laboratories have filed a joint complaint against the University of California, which oversees the government laboratories at Livermore and Los Alamos, alleging racial discrimination and bias.

The Yamanaka Affair

While the struggle against anti-Asian violence and support for Dr. Wen Ho Lee has brought Asian Americans together, contributing to pan-Asian solidarity, other issues have divided them. Ironically, Asian American Studies has become a source of division and its professional association a site of contention, revealing the dark side of identity politics. The Yamanaka affair is a case in point.

The affair centers on allegations of racism in Lois-Ann Yamanaka's novel, *Blu's Hanging*. Her work is a complex narrative about the racial, ethnic, sexual, and class conflicts experienced by the Ogata family, a dysfunctional working-class Japanese American family in Molokai, Hawaii. In the course of the story, they interact with a number of minor characters, such as the Reyes family, who live next door. The young Reyes sisters are depicted as sexually promiscuous and their uncle Paulo as a sexual predator who engages in incest with them and abuses adolescents, including the title character, Blu Ogata. In a book filled with decidedly disturbing figures, the members of the Reyes family are admittedly the most detestable.

Instead of treating *Blu's Hanging* as simply a story reflecting a brutal reality refracted through the prism of Yamanaka's imagination, critics have taken it to task as a cultural construct that perpetuates negative stereotypes about Filipino Americans. They argue that these negative representations damage Filipino Americans emotionally and reinforce "entrenched stereotypes of sexually predatory Filipino men and women in a way that exacerbates already existing discriminatory conditions Filipinos in Hawaii face."[27] Using a purely political criterion rather than an aesthetic one, they consider Yamanaka's novel politically incorrect and condemn her as a racist.

Criticism notwithstanding, the AAAS Fiction Award Committee judged *Blu's Hanging* the best work among the more than fifteen Asian American literary works it considered for the honor. They were impressed by its "powerful, original, and unflinching depiction of local cultural politics and the vagaries of Japanese American childhood" and its "deployment of 'nonstandard' pidgin as a visceral language of stunning beauty and pain."[28] Realizing that their choice was controversial, the committee called for an open debate about the literary merits of the book rather than allow the book to suffer censorship or suppression, actions that threatened to "undermine the coalitional foundation of the Association"[29]—but to no avail.

Rather than engage in a public debate over the literary merits of *Blu's Hanging,* the Filipino American Caucus and the Anti-Racism Coalition worked assiduously to strip Yamanaka of the 1998 literature award, an action that is reserved in other professional academic organizations for plagiarism. They appealed directly to the AAAS membership to do so, circumventing the organization's book award policy and overturning the Fiction Award Committee's decision. To demonstrate solidarity with the Filipino American community, the majority of the AAAS members approved the resolution to revoke Yamanaka's award. Those who supported Yamanaka felt that the Filipino American Caucus and Anti-Racism Coalition had essentially "hijacked the conference and imposed mob-rule."[30]

It should be noted that this was not an isolated incident. Indeed, Yamanaka's artistic works have been at the center of controversy for several years. In 1994, when her work of poetry, *Saturday Night at the Pahala Theatre,* was given the AAAS literature award, the Filipino American Caucus complained about the characterization of Filipino Americans in the first poem in the volume, "Kala Gave Me Anykine Advice Especially about Filipinos When I Moved to Pahala." In an act of sheer vindictiveness, the caucus opposed her receiving the 1997 literature award for her novel, *Wild Meat and the Bully Burgers,* even though it was not in itself considered particularly offensive. By a narrow majority, the executive board voted not to give a literature award that year as a way to avoid controversy. Its decision was for naught, since it led to the Literature Committee resigning in protest. The committee realized that the board's decision was undermining its "autonomy, integrity, and expertise, as well as the beginnings of Association-sanctioned censorship,"[31] which, lamentably, proved to be true the following year at the 1998 AAAS meeting in Hawaii.

The Yamanaka affair exposed to the public several problems within Asian American Studies. Perhaps the most obvious is that Filipino Americans feel marginalized within the AAS community. Indeed, one can interpret their opposition to Yamanaka's work as "acting out" their resentment at having been disempowered by the more powerful Chinese Americans and Japanese Americans. Undoubtedly one of the salutary outcomes will be an effort to increase their representation, as well as that of other underrepresented groups such as Southeast Asian Americans, Asian Indian Americans, and Pacific Islander Americans. In addition to an increase in their participation in decision-making bodies in AAAS, one can expect that studies on them and by them will also be encouraged.

What may be at stake is the future of AAAS and, by extension, the field of Asian American Studies. For some critics, giving Yamanaka the award was unconscionable because it violated one of the founding purposes of the organization, namely, to foster closer ties among Asian American groups and to advocate and represent their interests. Yamanaka's work did neither. As far as they were concerned, this represented the latest chapter in the betrayal of the origins of AAAS. Instead of meeting the need of the Asian American community for positive representations of Asian Americans in literature, members of the AAAS Fiction Award Committee were adhering to irrelevant "professional" standards. That is why one of the outcomes of the Yamanaka affair may well be a move to take back the AAAS from the "professionals" and return it to the "grassroots activists," an action that could only further erode the organization's credibility as an academic body.

SIGNIFICANCE OF THE MOVEMENT

The Asian American movement is an implicit challenge to America's racial hierarchy. Embodying the spirit of dissent that gave birth to this country, it opposes the relegation of Asian Americans to second-class status and strives for racial equality, social justice, and political empowerment. In doing so, it has validated ethnic pluralism. Instead of increasing social fragmentation and racial tribalism as some pundits feared, the Movement has contributed to greater cohesion and inclusivity by serving as an effective means for Asian Americans to assert, on their own terms, their right to belong in U.S. society and to be treated as respected and responsible members of it. The Movement is therefore a necessary intermediate step to becoming members of the national community and part of the ongoing process of redefining the national identity, which, it is hoped, in the twenty-first century will no longer be equated with only Euro-American traditions, values, and institutions.

Though American cultural pluralism has hardly met its ideal specifications, it remains a viable concept and certainly one worth pursuing. For that reason, a new generation of Asian American student activists has emerged to participate in the multicultural education movement, revitalizing the Movement at the beginning of the twenty-first century. Multiculturalism traces its lineage to ethnic studies and is based on the belief that the country's common culture is the result of the interaction of its subsidiary cultures. In other words, America's common culture is itself multicultural. Multiculturalism repudiates the melting pot perspective and instead favors the pluralistic perspective, which accepts and affirms ethnic pluralism as a positive phenomenon. In a milieu where ethnic diversity is valued as a good—in itself or in its results—Asian Americans have done their share to oppose racial subordination, protest against social injustices, and participate in the political process, helping to build a stronger and more perfect union.

Notes

This chapter is based on William Wei, *The Asian American Movement* (Philadelphia: Temple University Press, 1993) and "Forward Movement," *Asian-Week,* December 15, 1995, 13–15.

1. In addition to Chinese, Japanese, Korean, and Asian Indian Americans (the four oldest Asian American groups), the term "Asian Americans" includes Pacific Islanders such as Filipino Americans and Hawaiian Americans and, since the end of the Vietnam War, the various Southeast Asian Americans. In an effort to be more inclusive, the term "Asian Pacific Americans" is often used and is synonymous with "Asian Americans."

2. See Ralph Armbruster-Sandoval, "Looking Backward, Moving *Adelante:* A Critical Analysis of the African American and Chicana/o Civil Rights Movements," chapter 7 in this volume, for a discussion of Black and Chicana/o ethnic consciousness movements.

3. According to U.S. Department of Commerce, Bureau of the Census, Subject Reports: Japanese, Chinese, and Filipinos in the United States (1970), there were 51,256 Chinese Americans, 38,329 Japanese Americans, and 5,043 Korean Americans enrolled in college.

4. Vietnam Veterans Against the War, *The Winter Soldier Investigation: An Inquiry into American War Crimes* (Boston: Beacon Press, 1972), 44–45.

5. Frank Bruni and Alison Mitchell, "Sharply Diverging Paths as Vote Nears in South Carolina," *New York Times on the Web,* February 18, 2000, C (March 11, 2000).

6. Editorial, "A Second-Class Slur?" *AsianWeek,* February 24, 2000, 4, and "McCain's Ethnic Slur: Gone, but Not Quite Forgotten," *New York Times,* March 5, 2000, 7.

7. According to the United Nations Geneva Genocide Convention, genocide is an act, such as murder and torture, that is carried out with a specific

intent to destroy, in whole or in substantial part, a national, ethnic, racial or religious group. In 1988 the U.S. Senate ratified the convention; later, it was incorporated into the U.S. Criminal Code.

8. "Bay Area Asian Coalition against the War," *New Dawn* (June 1972).

9. Ian Dapianoen, "Furor over 'Offensive' T-Shirts," *International Examiner: Asian American Journal,* May 1, 2002, 1, 5; Andrew Chow, "APAs to Abercrombie: 'It's Not Over Yet,'" *AsianWeek,* April 25, 2002, 10.

10. For the latest developments on Asian American electoral politics, see Pei-te Lien, *The Making of Asian America through Political Participation* (Philadelphia: Temple University Press, 2001); Gordon H. Chang, ed., *Asian Americans and Politics* (Stanford: Stanford University Press, 2001).

11. Lynette Clemetson, "Minority Caucuses Seek Capitol Hill Bond," *New York Times,* May 19, 2002, 1, 22.

12. Joyce Nishoka, "High Schoolers Push for Ethnic Studies," *AsianWeek,* April 15, 2000, 12.

13. Erik Derr, "National APA Curriculum Initiative Suffers Start-up Challenges," *AsianWeek,* May 9, 2002, 14A.

14. For a summary of hate crimes against Asian Americans, see "The Bloody Legacy of Hate Crimes: From Vincent Chin to Joseph Ileto, the Killing Continues," *AsianWeek,* August 19, 1999, 13–15.

15. Jack Miles, "Blacks vs. Browns," *Atlantic Monthly* (October 1992): 41–68.

16. Sam Chu Lin, "Moving Past the Fires," *AsianWeek,* April 25, 2002, looks at the legacy of the Los Angeles Riots ten years later.

17. Michael Isikoff, "Wen Ho Lee: A Scientist's Secrets," *Newsweek,* January 21, 2002, 37.

18. Ibid., 36.

19. James Risen and Jeff Gerth, "China Stole Nuclear Secrets from Los Alamos, U.S. Officials Say," *New York Times on the Web,* March 6, 1999, http://www.nytimes.com/library/world/asia/030699china-nuke.html (March 4, 2000).

20. Ling-chi Wang, "Spy Hysteria," *AsianWeek,* March 25, 1999, 5.

21. William J. Broad, "Official Asserts Spy Case Suspect Was a Bias Victim," *New York Times on the Web,* August 18, 1999, http://www.nytimes.com/library/world/asia/081899china-nuke.html (28 February 2000).

22. Ibid.

23. Isikoff, "Wen Ho Lee," 37.

24. "Wen Ho Lee Denied Bail," *AsianWeek,* December 16, 1999, 8.

25. Frank H. Wu, "China: The New Scapegoat," *AsianWeek,* May 6, 1999, 9.

26. Frank Wu, "Task Force Reports Findings, *AsianWeek,* January 27, 2000, 11–13.

27. Candance L. Fujikane to aaascommunity@uclink4.berkeley.edu, "AAAS Community: AAASPosts: Blu's Hanging," April 21, 1998.

28. Caroline Chung Simpson et al. (1997 Fiction Award Committee) to Yen Le Espiritu, *AAAS Newsletter* (May 1998): 6.

29. Ibid., 7.

30. Jamie James, "This Hawaii Is Not for Tourists," *Atlantic Monthly* (February 1999): 94.

31. Yen Le Espiritu (AAAS president) to AAAS members, *AAAS Newsletter* (May 1998): 5.

9

BLACK ESSENTIALISM AND THE AFROCENTRIC IDEA

The Demise of Eurocentrism or Eurocentrism in a New Guise?

G. REGINALD DANIEL

EUROCENTRISM: THE ORIGIN OF THE MASTER RACIAL PROJECT

The Dialectical Setting

The Eurocentric paradigm, and its companion pieces White racism and White supremacy, have had egregious implications for the non-Western Other, especially for individuals of African descent. Throughout the history of the United States, Eurocentrism served to justify African enslavement and, moreover, became the basis for the rule of hypodescent, or one-drop rule, whereby individuals were identified as either Black or White.

By drawing boundaries that solidified subordinated racial identity and excluded African Americans from interacting with European Americans as equals, the rule of hypodescent has paradoxically had the unintended consequence of legitimating and forging group identity accordingly.[1] Its use for cultural and political mobilization is most obvious in currents of Afrocentric discourse and in other racial projects that rely on the notion of a primordial African "race" and nation. It has been viewed as a form of what Gayatri Spivak calls "strategic essentialism," a necessary if originally oppressive means not only of maintaining a distinct but equal African American racial and cultural plurality but also, and more important, mobilizing Blacks in the continuing struggle against White privilege.[2]

But the effectiveness of any organizing principle as the basis for essentialized collectives (viewed as if they were "natural," static, and eternal units) is inherently fraught with irreconcilable contradictions. Some of the discourses and practices of radical Afrocentrists are not merely pro-Black but also anti-White, if not actually "racist" in the strict sociological meaning of the concept. Before the late 1960s sociological definitions of racism relied heavily on notions of individual psychological biases and discriminatory attitudes. Since that time racism has been viewed as more than simple antipathy to and discrimination against individuals based on a person's racial prejudice. It is now defined as an overarching and more systematic implementation of discrimination based on the desire and power of dominant groups to maintain advantages for themselves at the expense of racialized Others. According to this view, racially subordinate groups—which by definition lack structural power—are not capable of "racism."[3]

This is not to suggest that it is desirable to dismiss Afrocentric concerns with identity politics. Something on the order of Afrocentrism in the form of Garveyism, Negritude, Black Power, or pan-Africanism has long had adherents, given the pervasiveness of White supremacy that has sought to prevent the formation of radical African diasporic subjectivity or plurality. Accordingly, the strengths of this perspective and analysis are undeniable—the fostering of group pride, solidarity, and self-respect among African-descent individuals and an interrogation of the ideology of inegalitarian integration (assimilation) and the perpetuation of differences in the manner of inegalitarian pluralism (apartheid).[4]

Figure 1 presents a diagram of pluralistic and integrationist dynamics. The assimilationist dynamic is captured in column b. The linking of the circles indicates the integrative relationship, which is hierarchical (inegalitarian) and therefore premised not only on the dominance of the white circle but also on the conformity of the gray

Figure 1. Pluralist and Integrationist Dynamics

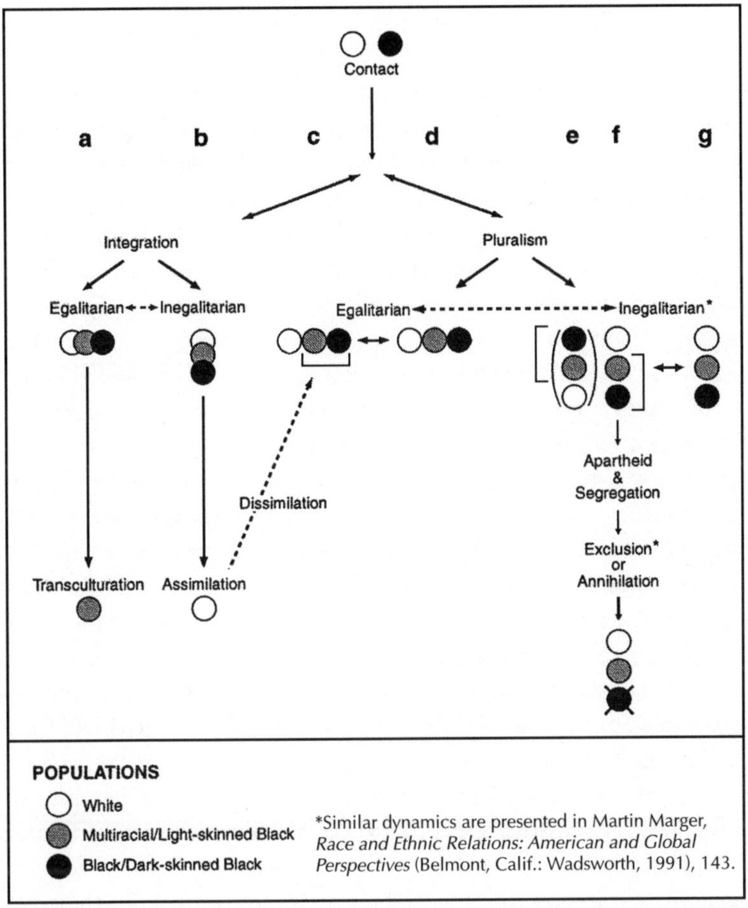

*Similar dynamics are presented in Martin Marger, *Race and Ethnic Relations: American and Global Perspectives* (Belmont, Calif.: Wadsworth, 1991), 143.

and black circles to the beliefs, ideals, values, meanings, and goals of the white circle. The apartheid dynamic is captured in column f. There the circles are separated, indicating the pluralistic relationship. The relationship is not only vertical (inegalitarian) and thus hierarchical, but, more important, the gray and black circles are bracketed into one category. This results in the exclusion of both, despite the somewhat higher positioning of the gray circle in relation to the black one.

The contradictions and weaknesses of radical Afrocentrism, however, are also readily apparent. Its exponents often criticize the validity of the concept of race while reinscribing essentialist notions of

Black identity.[5] They thus rearticulate the notion of purity that under-pinned the scientific racism associated with the Eurocentric paradigm. This line of reasoning has used race (or geno-phenotypical characteristics) generally to define historical progress or regression in terms of the degree to which individuals respectively approximate or diverge from European definitions of intellectual sophistication premised on the sensate mode of thinking (or materialist rationalism).

Quite apart from the longer-standing "color prejudice" that had existed in some form since antiquity, scientific racism—which rested on genetic arguments supporting notions of inherent intellectual as well as somatic inferiority and superiority—had its roots in the biological thinking of the eighteenth century. However, it was not until well into the nineteenth century that this system of thought came to full fruition and emerged for the first time as a central current in Western consciousness. The theorists of the period argued that racial "purity" was a necessary prerequisite for a civilization to be creative. This shift in consciousness made it increasingly unacceptable that Greece, the designated birthplace of the modern West, could have been the result of the blending of indigenous Europeans, African Egyptians, and Semitic Phoenicians, whether in the form of colonization or mere cultural (and racial) exchange resulting from contact through trade, war, and so on (see chap. 1). However, once the forces of an emergent capitalism were propelled into full drive, Eurocentric theories served as the justification for the enslavement of Africans. These dynamics shaped the subsequent historiography and anthropology of Africa's relation to the Mediterranean world during the Classical Age. Accordingly, Africans were necessarily excluded from any discussion that focused on their contribution to the development of the West.[6]

The "Whitening out" of African participation in the formation of the West is one of many injustices that have been inflicted on individuals of African descent, as well as on the whole of human civilization. It is imperative, therefore, to deconstruct the Eurocentric rendering of history.[7] Nevertheless, few scholars contest the notion that ancient Egyptian civilization was a specialized, refined variant of Nile Valley culture—as well as a variant of a broader continental African type—that contained a largely blended population with a strong if not predominant Africoid geno-phenotypical, ancestral, and cultural component. In addition, there is general acceptance of the fact that Egyptian civilization significantly antedated and "influenced" Greek civilization and thus ultimately influenced what Eurocentrists have designated as the early formation of the West. Furthermore, Afrocentrists are on solid ground in pointing out that even this comparatively more modest version of the African presence in Egyptian civilization, and the African influence on the fountainhead of western Europe, has not been the traditionally transmitted version of either Egypt, Greece, or the evolution of the West.

Also, there now seems to be fairly unanimous agreement on the central African origins of the human species. Although the evidence is inconclusive, it is reasonable to assume that this early human population may have resembled modern sub-Saharan Africans in terms of some anatomical features, particularly pigmentation. The findings suggest, however, that the phenotypic traits we have come to associate with modern Asian, European, and African populations all appear to have been later developments from an earlier, less diversified type originating on the African continent, which did not display the same cluster of phenotypic traits—pigmentation in conjunction with facial physiognomy and especially hair morphology—commonly found among modern populations indigenous to Africa south of the Sahara. Furthermore, it is important to acknowledge, for example, the African ancestry of prominent figures such as Alexandre Dumas and Alexander Pushkin, who were unquestionably of partial African descent (Ludwig von Beethoven's African ancestry is somewhat contested).[8]

Eurocentrism in a New Guise?

Many radical Afrocentrists have responded to the legacy of Eurocentric distortions by applying the term "Black" to anyone and anything of African ancestry—no matter how remote in space or time. This ignores the complex ancestral, genetic, and cultural diversity and blending that has taken place over the eons, which is a fact that radical Afrocentrists, much as Eurocentrists, generally have failed to grasp in their support of racial essentialism and search for racial "purity."[9] Indeed, the more racially essentialist and radical varieties of Afrocentrism rarely explore, and sometimes openly dismiss, the profound dynamics of racial and cultural blending and multiple identities found throughout the African diaspora.[10]

Accordingly, radical Afrocentrists incorporate the Egyptian history of thousands of years ago into contemporary issues and thus run the risk of positing a transhistorical "Black" essence. Even if the Egyptians were "Black," the meaning of Blackness could hardly be the same then as it is in the modern era. The incorporation of the Egyptian history of thousands of years ago into contemporary racial politics is thus as full of pitfalls as of potential.[11] Furthermore, Afrocentric claims that Greek philosophers "stole" Egyptian knowledge—that is, appropriated it without giving credit to its Egyptian source—and notions of Egyptian "colonization" of Greece have not held up well under recent scrutiny.[12]

The more nuanced analyses provided by moderate variants of Afrocentrism are frequently absent from those offered by more radical tendencies. The latter delineate the contours of Blackness and the African diasporic experience from a photographic negative of Whiteness.[13] At best, they perpetuate a gross oversimplification of prehistory and contemporary history, and at worst, a new distortion. The legitimacy of the Afrocentric desire to give voice to the shared global disillusionment and alienation embedded in the African diasporic experience is not in question. Yet the end result of some strains of Afrocentric revisionism—particularly its more radical variants—is very similar to the oppressive mechanism of the one-drop rule. This social device originated in the "either/or" paradigm that has served as the underpinning of Eurocentric consciousness. Consequently, radical Afrocentrists actually promote the collective historical amnesia they seek to cure.

If, therefore, Afrocentric discourse is to dismantle Eurocentrism, it must also deconstruct the either/or paradigm that has served as the latter's foundation. Essentially, this requires radical Afrocentrists to shift to a mentation that in current academic parlance is often referred to as postmodernism, which is more emblematic of moderate variants of Afrocentric thought. Postmodernism inscribes an elusive, not to mention contradictory, sense of presence that defies any consensual definition. Yet it has made itself felt in a variety of disparate, yet ultimately related, trends, which reject not only modernity's, and thus Eurocentrism's, dichotomization of differences into mutually exclusive and antithetical categories of experience but also its hierarchical ranking of differences, that is to say, disassociation, or differentiation in the manner of inegalitarian pluralism (fig. 1[f]).[14]

In addition, postmodernism jettisons modernity's totalizing universalism that was actually inegalitarian integration (or assimilation in disguise) and came to dominate large segments of the globe through western European colonialism and imperialism (fig. 1[b]). Postmodernism seeks to replace the inegalitarian modalities of both pluralism and integration with a nondichotomous and nonhierarchical "transmodern" dynamic in which egalitarian pluralism (fig. 1[d]) becomes a prelude and counterpart to a new higher dedifferentiation in the manner of egalitarian integration (fig. 1[a]). These phenomena display a horizontal (egalitarian) dynamic in which no circle dominates. In figure 1(d), the relationship is pluralistic such that mutual respect is accorded to the uniqueness of each circle; in figure 1(a), a fusion emerges out of the three circles such that mutual value is attached to the contribution each makes to the resulting blend. This composite is a melding of the three circles and similar to the intermediate gray circle but is not in fact the result of its dominance. The relationship in figure 1(d) is horizontal (egalitarian) and, therefore, differs significantly from the dynamics in column f, which is hierarchical and inegalitarian. The goal is to establish a horizontal (as opposed to hierarchical) and thus egalitarian relationship that valorizes the white, gray, and black circles. This would be a necessary prerequisite to achieving the egalitarian integrationist dynamics in column a, as well as guarding against the inegalitarian dynamics in columns b and f.

Radical or extreme deconstructivist postmodernists more frequently espouse the pluralistic trend, whereas the integrative trend is more common among more moderate, affirmative, and constructivist postmodernists.[15] Yet both trends are part of a more generalized assault on the polarization of things into either Black or White. Accordingly, phenomena are seen as relative and complementary rather than hierarchical and absolutely antithetical categories of experiences on a continuum of grays.

In addition, postmodernism involves a critique of the conception of a linear connection of subjects to an objective world in which reality is made transparent from a uniquely privileged vantage point through the application of rationality and empirical disciplines. The postmodernist deconstruction of the notion that the truth can be found in any absolutely impartial and objective sense has been instrumental in pointing out that all categories, racial and otherwise, are largely sociocultural constructs, which are grounded in history rather than fixed and inalterable essences.[16] This is a fact that both radical Afrocentrists and Eurocentrists generally have failed to grasp in their search for "purity." History is based on interaction rather than on isolation in any absolute sense. Replacing Eurocentric half-truths with new radical Afrocentric ones is like injecting poison into medicine. If anything, the goal should be to move beyond both modes of thinking in order to embrace a postmodern paradigm based on "both/ neither," which would come closer to the actual truth.[17]

The new multiracial identity that gained momentum in the United States during the 1990s moves beyond the either/or thinking that underpins both Eurocentrism and radical Afrocentrism and supports instead the both/neither paradigm. Individuals who display this identity maintain ties with European Americans but seek to do this without diminishing their affinity to the experience of African Americans.[18] Nevertheless, many Afrocentrists find the new multiracial identity problematic. This opposition to the perpetuation of a multiracial identity, or rather, to acknowledging the potentially legitimate differences between the experiences and identities of Black and multiracial-identified individuals, is in part premised on the belief that these differences are automatically and inherently invidious distinctions. They believe that a multiracial identity maintains the hierarchical valuation of Whiteness over Blackness. These dynamics are reflected in columns g and b of figure 1, both of which disconnect the bracketing between the two subdominant circles in column f. The difference is that in column b the gray circle is linked to the white circle. In column g no such linkage occurs, but the goal is to maintain the somewhat more privileged position of the gray circle as compared to the black. In both cases, however, the hierarchy remains intact. The desire to embrace a White racial background is considered a means of avoiding racial social stigma and seeking to gain White racial privilege that comes with European ancestry. A multiracial identification is therefore considered inimical to the goal of forging African Americans into a cohesive political force (fig. 1[c]).[19]

In fact, many radical Afrocentrists would argue it is no accident that the concept of a multiracial identity and the postmodern agenda and their problematization of Black identity have emerged at precisely the moment when African-descent individuals are not only acting as subjects, rather than simply objects, of history but also have become a major challenge to Eurocentrism's universalist imperative in public, intellectual, and cultural life.[20] In this sense, they view a multiracial identity as merely one of the latest in a series of recent attacks on the integrity of the African American community that are inspired, however indirectly, by Eurocentric thinking, if not exactly operating in the service of Eurocentric thought. Rather than indicate the demise of Eurocentrism, a multiracial identification is, therefore, tantamount to Eurocentrism in a new guise.

Radical Afrocentrism and Ontological Blackness

This criticism, nevertheless, obscures the potential that a multiracial identification may hold for challenging from within and from without the imposition of what Victor Anderson calls a myopic and constricting "ontological Blackness"—and in extreme cases, a concomitant lack of desire or willingness to engage in a critical discourse with individuals of European-descent at any level. By focusing primarily on forging a singular egalitarian African American plurality (fig. 1[c]) Afrocentrists have overlooked, or outright rejected, the possibility of an egalitarian multiracial identity that emphasizes a nondichotomous and nonhierarchical mentation (fig. 1[d]). This bias, in turn, precludes the exploration of new possibilities not only for the construction of self and community but also for critiquing the pathologies of racism that have been sustained by the U.S. binary racial project.

The new multiracial identity as a racial project is not, however, synonymous with this social structural pathology. Rather, this identity is indicative of an egalitarian dynamic that seeks to resist both the dichotomization and hierarchical valuation of African American and European American cultural and racial differences. This new identity recognizes the commonalities among Blacks and Whites in the manner of egalitarian integration (fig. 1[a]) and at the same time appreciates the differences in the manner of egalitarian pluralism (fig. 1[d]). More important, it is posited on an egalitarian blending of pluralism and integration—integrative pluralism or pluralistic integration—in which Blacks and Whites are seen as relative, rather than absolute, extremes on a continuum of grays.

In figure 1, a and d, the relationship is horizontal (egalitarian) such that no circle dominates. In column d the relationship is pluralistic so that mutual respect is accorded to the uniqueness of each circle; in a, a fusion emerges out of the three circles in which mutual value is attached to the contribution each makes to the resulting blend. This composite is a melding of the three circles and similar to the intermediate gray circle but is not in fact the result of its dominance. Both c and d have the advantage of being egalitarian. In c, however, the black and gray circles are bracketed by virtue of their shared dissimilarities to the white circle. Yet considering the affinity that the gray circle has with both the black and the white circle, it could just as legitimately be bracketed with the white circle without actually changing the power dynamics between the three circles. Consequently, these dynamics do not really affirm the uniqueness of each of the three circles as is the case with d.

Moreover, the new multiracial identity is actually compatible with the Afrocentric paradigm.[21] One factor that divides Afrocentrism from the new multiracial identity is that the former means different things to different people, and this has obscured its deeper significance. The most common perception is that Afrocentrism seeks to expose individuals—particularly through the education system—to the historical accomplishments and contributions of individuals of African descent in the manner of egalitarian pluralism (fig. 1[c]). Another prevailing view is that Afrocentrism is a new form of Black Nationalism that exposes White racism and promotes racial separatism (or inegalitarian pluralism). In extreme cases, the goal has been to replace White superiority with a new hierarchy premised on the superiority of Blackness (fig. 1[e]). This type of Afrocentrism is said to have emerged because of the African American disenchantment with the post–civil rights era, that is, with the perceived failure of civil rights legislation and philosophy to ameliorate the economic, political, social, and psychological oppression that continues to plague African Americans.[22] The contrast between these two types of pluralism is captured in e and f of figure 1. The pluralistic relationship is indicated by the fact that the circles are separated, as opposed to linked, as they are in the integrationist half of the chart. Yet the relationship in figure 1(e) is not only vertical (inegalitarian) and thus hierarchical, but the positions of the previously subdominant black and dominant white circles in figure 1(f) are reversed.

Although Afrocentrism is significantly related to African history and originated in Black Nationalist thought, it is more appropriately described as a paradigm that places African-descent individuals at the center of their analyses. In addition, Afrocentrism is predicated on traditional African philosophical assumptions. It assumes that all elements of the universe have a metaphysical base, that is, are created from a similar universal substance, and are functionally interconnected. In addition, the Afrocentric perspective makes no absolute demarcation between the spiritual or metaphysical (ideational) and the physical (sensate).[23] This rejection of clearly delineated boundaries extends to morality, temporality, and the very meaning of reality. Afrocentrism values knowledge gained through intuition and feelings as much as that gained through the senses and intellect. The Afrocentric paradigm fosters a human-centered orientation that values interpersonal connections more highly than material objects. In sum, Afrocentrism rejects the dichotomization and hierarchical valuation of differences typified by Eurocentric thinking, which divides things into mutually exclusive and unequal categories of value, privilege, and experience.[24]

More important, Afrocentrism also rejects the hierarchical ranking of racial difference that has been perpetuated by the Eurocentric paradigm. Whereas Eurocentrism places Europe at the center of everything and dislocates African contributions, Afrocentrism relocates or recenters Africa to its rightful place in human history in terms of human origins and the origins of civilization. It achieves this without ethnocentrism and without making Africa the center of attention. Rather, it posits a cosmovision that happened to originate in Africa, and is centered in an African worldview, simply because Africa is the birthplace of humanity. It acknowledges a common cultural inheritance that all humans share as descendants of the first diaspora out of Africa. If Afrocentrism has a special meaning for people of the African diaspora, it also provides a mode through which all individuals can liberate themselves from the restrictive dichotomization and hierarchical concepts that are the basis of the Eurocentric model.

More moderate (or postmodern) variants of Afrocentrism *and* the new multiracial identity challenge essentialist and reductionist constructions of racial identities in a manner that makes it possible to point out how racial categories are altered by lived experience and are compatible with the new multiracial identity.[25] Both display a nonhierarchical and nondichotomous configuration that is part of a larger postmodern trend that is engaged in a critique of the pathologies of Eurocentrism, modernity, and the sensate-dominated worldview, which gained ascendancy in western Europe in the period from the Renaissance to the Enlightenment. They challenge the limitations of both Eurocentrism and radical Afrocentrism, as well as call into question notions of authentic and essentialist identity in individual consciousness and in mass culture. Consequently, both have the potential to open up new possibilities for the construction of self and community. The more inclusive "postmodern Blackness" that would emanate from this shift in consciousness not only would allow African-descent Americans to acknowledge the way in which the collective African American experience has been altered by sex or gender, class, and a host of other categories of experience but also would take into consideration the empirical conditions of individual lives.[26]

By ignoring diversity and variations on an African-derived theme—which acknowledges pluralism within a larger integrated Black plurality—it is all too easy to view African-descent individuals as falling into two mutually exclusive categories, pluralist or integrationist, Black-identified or White-identified, and so on.[27] Molefi Asante states that Afrocentrism is based on "pluralism without hierarchy," or "parallel frames of reference," in the manner of egalitarian pluralism (see fig. 1[d]). The goal is to gain respect for truth based on the specificity of cultural experience.[28] Jerome Schiele and other scholars, as well as Asante himself, emphasize that Afrocentrism also views the structure of phenomena from the perspective of interdependency, integration, and holism. Accordingly, integration without hierarchy in the manner of egalitarian integration (see fig. 1[a]) is one of Afrocentrism's simultaneous goals as well.[29]

The struggle for a radical African American collective subjectivity that furthers Black liberation must be rooted in part in a process of decolonization that continually challenges and goes beyond the perpetuation of racial essentialism and the reinscription of notions of authentic identity. Yet the reluctance of many African-descent Americans to critique the essentialist underpinnings of radical Afrocentrism—and their concomitant rejection of the postmodern paradigm and the new multiracial identity—is rooted in the legitimate fear that this would cause individuals to lose sight of the experience of the African diaspora and the unique sensibilities and culture that have arisen from it. bell hooks proposes that we can criticize essentialism while emphasizing the significance of the authority of experience. She argues that there is a significant difference between the repudiation of the idea of an African-derived essence and the recognition that African-derived identity has been forged through the experience of exile and struggle.[30] The goal should be to recognize and embrace the multiple experiences of African-descent identity, which are the lived and empirical conditions that make diverse identities and cultural productions possible.[31]

This should include the search for ways of constructing self and community that oppose any reification of the blackness that whiteness created in the manner of the one-drop rule. Accordingly, the new multiracial identity is quintessentially Afrocentric in the deepest meaning of the word. Rather than implode African American identity, this new identity has the potential to forge more inclusive constructions of Blackness (and Whiteness) and provide the basis for new and varied forms of bonding and integration. This process, which George Lipsitz calls "strategic antiessentialism,"[32] would accommodate the varieties of African-derived subjectivity without at the same time negating a larger African-derived plurality, or maintaining that plurality as a dichotomous space, which is a photographic negative and the complete antithesis of Whiteness.[33] Furthermore, it would challenge Eurocentric notions of African-derived identity that represent Blackness and Whiteness in one-dimensional ways in order to reinforce and sustain White domination and Black subordination.[34]

POSTCOLONIAL DISCOURSE: DECENTERING EUROPE AND DECONSTRUCTING THE WEST

Colonialism and Its Aftermath

The dismantling of European overseas colonial empires has been one of the most historically significant developments of the twentieth century. It raised the hopes of the newly independent countries for the emergence of a truly postcolonial era. Such optimism proved short-lived, however. It became apparent that, although it had given up colonialism as its primary mechanism of control, the West had not in fact relinquished control. Rather, structures of control based on colonial domination and exploitation increasingly have been replaced by neocolonial structures. This neocolonial trend—which is characterized by what the Italian political theorist and activist Antonio

Gramsci describes as "hegemony"—allows dominant groups effectively to maintain control and hierarchy but create the illusion of equality by selectively including its subjects and incorporating its opposition.[35]

"Neocolonial" implies a passage into something "new" but emphasizes repetition with difference, a regeneration or prolongation of colonialism through other means. The persistence of neocolonialist structures and practices in the contemporary world is very obvious, as compared to the less immediately perceptible—but more far-reaching in its effects and implications—continued globalizing spread of imperialism, that is, the globalization of the capitalist mode of production and mass culture. Originating in the sixteenth century, capitalism has now spread outward from its European heartland such that it constitutes a truly global economy.[36]

This continuing Western influence is maintained through a flexible yet complex interweaving of economic, political, military, ideological, and cultural dynamics and power relations, including interventionist politics in the postindependence era.[37] For example, formal "creole" political independence in Latin America during the nineteenth century has not prevented Monroe Doctrine–style military or "free trade" economic interventions. Similarly, Egypt's formal political independence in 1923 did not prevent British control, which provoked the 1952 revolution.[38] The hegemonic processes that underpin these neocolonial dynamics thus subtly downplay and mask contemporary forms of exploitation and control of subordinated Others.[39]

"While both 'colonialism' and 'neocolonialism' imply oppression and the possibility of resistance, 'postcolonialism' neither posits clear domination nor calls for clear opposition."[40] Consequently, the term "postcolonial" obscures the traces of colonialism that still exist in the present. The colonial structures and conceptual frameworks generated over the past five hundred years cannot be easily vaporized with the prefix *post*. By suggesting that colonialism has come to an end, the term "postcolonial" lacks a political analysis of contemporary power relations, for example, of recent U.S. militaristic involvements in Grenada, Panama, Kuwait, Iraq, and Yugoslavia, or of the symbiotic links forged between U.S. political and economic interests and those of local elites.[41]

Largely emanating from the academy in the United States during the late 1980s in the form of discursive analyses inflected by poststructuralism, the prefix *post* aligns "postcolonialism" with "post-modernism" and, more important, "poststructuralism." Each of these phenomena shares the notion of "movement beyond" obsolescent discourses. Yet "postmodernism" and "poststructuralism" refer to moving beyond archaic philosophical, aesthetic, and political paradigms. "Postcolonial" implies going beyond not only colonialism but also anticolonial nationalist theory—which sought and led to the dismantling of formal political colonial domination—as well as a movement beyond a specific point in history. Postcolonial thought therefore stresses deterritorialization, the constructed nature of national borders and nationalism, and the obsolescence of anticolonialist discourse.[42]

Since "*post*colonial" on one level suggests a stage "after" the demise of colonialism, it is imbued, quite apart from its users' intentions, with a spatial and temporal ambiguity. "Postcolonial" tends to be associated with "third world" countries that gained independence after World War II. Yet it can also refer to the "third world" diasporic presence in "first world" metropolises. "Postcolonial" also collapses diverse chronologies such that the term could be expanded exponentially. It can include processes of liberation originating in all societies affected by colonialism, including areas in North and South America that gained political independence during the late eighteenth and early nineteenth century. However, the majority of countries in Africa and Asia achieved independence during the twentieth century; "some in the 1930s (Iraq), others in the 1940s (India, Lebanon), and still others in the 1960s (Algeria, Senegal, the Congo) and the 1970s (Angola, Mozambique)."[43] The term's globalizing tendency tends to ignore "multiplicities of location, as well as the discursive and political linkages between postcolonial theories and contemporary anticolonial (or anti-neocolonial) struggles and discourses in Central America, in the Middle East, in Southern Africa, and the Philippines."[44] These phenomena cannot be dismissed as a mere rearticulation of obsolescent discourses.

Hybridity, Hierarchy, and Hegemony

Ambiguities and contradictions notwithstanding, the term "post-colonial" may be applied to a broader process that involves the dismantling of Eurocentrism.[45] For example, the concept of hybridity, that is, racial and cultural blending, in postcolonial discourse calls attention to the complex and multilayered identities generated by geographic displacements. It also interrogates Eurocentric notions of purity, racial and otherwise. Although racial and cultural hybridity have existed from time immemorial, European colonial expansion beginning in the sixteenth century accelerated and actively shaped a new world of practices and ideologies of racial and cultural blending. This is particularly the case in the Americas, which have been the site of unprecedented combinations of indigenous peoples, Africans, Europeans, and, later, immigratory diasporas from all over the world.[46] In addition, the themes of hybridity—"syncretism," "creolization," and "mestizaje"—were invoked during the late nineteenth and early twentieth century by diverse cultural and intellectual programs in Latin America, which commonly come under the rubric "modernism."[47]

On one level, the celebration of hybridity, including the new multiracial identity, counters the colonialist obsession with racial "purity," which viewed different racial groups as different species created at different times that were therefore forbidden to "interbreed." The hostility to miscegenation—particularly in Anglo–North America—was encapsulated in such pejorative terms as "mongrelization" and "mulattoes" (seen as necessarily infertile). Yet, while rejecting the colonialist obsession with purity, postcolonial hybridity also counterposes itself against the rigid essentialism that underpins third world discourse, including radical Afrocentrism and much Black Nationalist thought.

In addition, the concepts of racial and cultural hybridity in postcolonial theory are admirably honed to deal with the complexities and contradictions "generated by the global circulation of peoples and cultural goods in a mediated and interconnected world."[48] The hybrid globalized human subject is confronted with the challenge of moving among the diverse modalities of sharply contrasting cultural and ideological worlds. Consequently, hybrid identities are not reducible to a fixed formula; rather, they form a changing repertory of cultural modalities.[49]

However, the impulses behind and implications of the celebration of hybridity and multiracial identity are themselves "mixed."[50] The deconstruction of dichotomous notions of purity should not obscure the potentially problematic agency of postcolonial racial and cultural hybridity. A celebration of racial and cultural hybridity per se, if not articulated by simultaneously taking into consideration questions of hegemony, risks downplaying contemporary forms of neocolonialism that effectively maintain racial hierarchy but create the illusion of equality by means of token gestures of inclusion without those in power actually giving up control. For example, national racial and cultural identities in Latin America have often been officially articulated as hybrid, multiracial, and egalitarian (see fig. 1[a]). Yet they have been hypocritically integrationist, that is, assimilationist, ideologies, seeking Whitening through racial and cultural blending and deliberately obscuring subtle hegemonies that reproduce racial hierarchies in a new guise (see fig. 1[b]).

From Center to Periphery

Despite these caveats, postcolonial notions of racial and cultural hybridity are part of a broader process instrumental to demystifying or deconstructing Europe and acknowledging the specificity of its development by reading its history through multiple racial and cultural lenses. A closer analysis of the celebrated markers in the historical formation of Europe—Greece, Rome, Christianity, the Renaissance, the Enlightenment—indicates that each is a moment of hybridity and integration: Greece, strongly influenced by, if not an actual colony or outpost of, Egyptian, Phoenician, and Asian civilization; Rome, "strongly indebted" to Greece, Egypt, and Carthage; Christianity, originally a religion of Asian origin, whose link with Byzantium, the Nestorians, and Gnostics at times "loomed larger" than its relationship with European, that is, Latin, Christendom; the Renaissance, "a recovery of Hellenic civilization passed on through Arabic civilization and deeply engaged with non-European cultures"; the Enlightenment, "another period wide open to non-European influences, from China to Egypt."[51]

Some scholars have interrogated what at times appears to be the postcolonial, and, by extension, Afrocentric obsession with claiming in part for Africans and other non-Europeans the achievements of western European civilization, particularly those in science and technology. This phenomenon supposedly reflects an attempt to enhance, for example, Egypt's, and therefore Africa's, reputation and prestige by linking Africans with the impressive accomplishments of Greece originating in the sensate sociocultural mode and thus to point out their role in the formation of the West. That said, this linking of the Afro-Asian world with the formation of western Europe in post-colonial (and Afrocentric) discourse should come as no surprise given that the scientific and technological achievements of western Europe have been the benchmark by which Other civilizations have been ranked as inferior and superior. The participation of Africans and other non-Europeans in the evolution of Western civilization—and the process of civilization generally—has been dismissed, if not excluded, by virtue of their supposed divergence from the European norm.

The impetus for the current postcolonial and Afrocentrist revisions of Eurocentric history is not necessarily the desire to enhance the role of Africa and individuals of African descent, or the non-Western world, by linking them with the much-vaunted achievements of western Europe. Rather, their goal is to point out that many of the philosophies, political principles, and forms of knowledge in physics, chemistry, technology, medicine, metallurgy, and art that have been attributed singularly to western Europe by virtue of its supposedly inherent superiority are to a considerable extent multicultural and multiracial, that is, plural, in origin (fig. 1[d]) and transcultural and transracial (or egalitarian integrative) in composition (fig. 1[a]). Indeed, syncretism has always pervaded the arts. In architectural terms, for example, the great mosque at Cordoba hybridizes the diverse cultures that passed through Spain: Carthaginian, Greek, Roman, Byzantine, Arab-Moorish.[52]

The actual borders between the West and the larger non-Western world have been, rather, blurred and porous frontiers.[53] The transculturalization and transracialization of Europe—particularly Mediterranean Europe—with the African and Asian worlds is the corollary to its structurally "middle minority" position in global commerce and social intercourse over many centuries.[54] José Piedras's description of the Mediterranean as "the dark child of Europe and the light child of Africa" is not an exaggeration.[55] Indeed, Napoleon himself argued that Africa begins in the Pyrenees.[56] Western European domination and imposition in the manner of inegalitarian pluralism (apartheid) and the inegalitarian integration (assimilation) of others constitutes merely one, albeit important, side of the historical narrative. The positive valuation of racial and cultural difference in the manner of egalitarian pluralism, as well as hybridization originating in the absorption, blending, and adaptation of a multiplicity of sources in the form of egalitarian cultural and, not infrequently, racial integration, is the other side.

European civilization thus becomes more transparent if we look at Europe as part of Eurasia and southern Europe as part of a larger Mediterranean continuity encompassing North African as well as West African influences. The West was historically both multiracial and multicultural (fig. 1[d]) and transracial and transcultural (fig. 1[a]) long before it became demographically so in the twentieth century with the arrival of third world immigrants from previous colonial possessions and elsewhere.

Accordingly, the notion of a singular Europe has been an obstacle to understanding not just European but world history as well. To a considerable extent what is referred to as European civilization "is actually a universal human heritage that for historical, political, and geographical reasons" has been bequeathed to the modern world "in the guise of a European or Western synthesis."[57] It is significant that the synthesis and the stamp are uniquely European. Yet the fact that the sources are plural and intercontinental is equally meaningful.[58] This is particularly so if we consider that the racial and cultural narcissism that buttressed Eurocentrism and European colonialism and imperialism has deliberately obscured these connections. This was done to maintain the purity and thus "superiority" of European identity while furthering the image of Others as people without history.[59]

In response to this historical amnesia, postcolonial thought is dedicated to redressing outcasts of all sorts, both ideas and individuals. It thus celebrates Otherness in almost every guise.[60] Yet this cultural relativism may also mask a romanticization of the Other and an appropriation of the experience of Otherness to enhance the discourse on difference, or to be radically chic. Accordingly, this may do Others an injustice by not contextualizing the historical relationship between the politics of multiculturalism, that is, difference in the manner of egalitarian pluralism (fig. 1[d]), and the politics of racism, that is, difference in the manner of inegalitarian pluralism (fig. 1[f]).[61]

Interrogating the Concept of Race

In its general assault on Eurocentrism, postcolonial discourse not only challenges any notion of racial purity but also necessarily interrogates the notion that race is an objective reality absolutely fixed in biological datum. Given that modern science has been unable to produce empirical data that confirm the existence of clearly delineated biophysical racial boundaries, many "deconstructive" postcolonial thinkers recommend that the concept be dispensed with altogether. They tend to present race as a problem, a legacy of the past, and a misconception that should be transcended. Many argue that any kind of racial identification—multiracial or otherwise—is fraught with irreconcilable contradictions. Any notion of transcending race by reifying it through a multiracial identification is thus hopelessly naive if not downright regressive.[62]

Note, however, that this opposition to a multiracial identity does not simply originate in a belief in the falseness of the concept of race. It often originates in the misinterpretation of the discourse on multiracial identity as grounded in biological rather than ancestral notions of race. Biological notions of race and those based on ancestry may overlap, but they are not synonymous. The former is based on one's genetic inheritance irrespective of ancestral background. The latter is grounded in one's lineage or genealogy, irrespective of genetic concerns, and is the basis of the new multiracial identity. Exposure to these backgrounds enhances and unequivocally helps to concretize a feeling of kinship. Simple awareness of those backgrounds, however, can catalyze this sentiment, and lack of contact does not preclude its presence.

Critics also dismiss claims that the new multiracial identity is "new" at all, because everyone is in fact "multiracial." Although it is true that a multiracial lineage or background is normative among humans, most individuals have monoracial identities despite the many backgrounds that may make up their genealogies. The new multiracial identity belongs to individuals who feel kinship with more than one racial community by recognizing the multiple racial backgrounds in their genealogies. Those who question the legitimacy of a multiracial identity on the grounds laid out above would probably challenge multiethnic identity on similar grounds. Such a deconstructivist perspective reflects the underlying belief that all categories and identities—racial and otherwise—are sociocultural constructs, mere fictions with no basis in reality.

Other postcolonial thinkers challenge the notion that race is something we can or should move beyond. Many of these "constructive" postcolonial thinkers agree that the concept of race invokes biologically based human characteristics in the form of "racial traits" but do not view racial categories and boundaries as being absolutely fixed in biological fact. From their perspective, the racialization process divides human bodies into presumed exclusive units and imposes on them attributes and features that conform to ideological and social values. Racial categories in turn signify and symbolize social conflicts and interests and represent principles by which society allocates rewards and status. In addition, they argue that the selection of these particular human features for purposes of racial signification has changed over time and is always and necessarily a historical process.

Racial categories and identities are understood as unstable and decentered complexes of sociocultural meanings that are constantly being created, inhabited, contested, transformed, and destroyed by political struggle. This constructive postcolonial discourse views racial formation as a major mode of social differentiation grounded in historical consciousness and in the very structure of social institutions. Consequently, a multiracial identity may be thought of not only as an element of social structure but also as a dimension of human cultural representation and signification—rather than an illusion.[63]

In sum, postcolonial thinkers signal the formation of a new master racial project. Deconstructive postcolonial discourse interrogates, seeks to transcend, and, ultimately, seeks to discard the concept altogether in pursuit of a universal humanism. From the standpoint of constructivist postcolonial thinkers, evoking such as a goal dangerously denies continuing racial inequalities. Any notion of "transcending race"—even if it were a possibility—would be unthinkable until the struggle to achieve equality of racial difference has been won. Instead, constructive postcolonial discourse posits "racial transcendence" by acknowledging a more inclusive identity based on a multiplicity of ancestral backgrounds.

The new multiracial identity is part of this broader postcolonial social transformation and consciousness, although it does not dismiss the concept of race. It does, however, interrogate essentialist and reductionist notions of race and decenters racial categories by pointing out the ambiguity and multiplicity of identities that exist in each of us. This makes it possible to acknowledge the way in which those categories are altered by lived experience. The new multiracial identity, along with Afrocentrism, is part of a larger oppositional framework that variously interrogates colonial discourse and seeks to bring about the demise of the dominant Eurocentric paradigm. Consequently, this identity may be viewed as part of a spectrum of tactics engaged in continuing and completing the struggle for Black liberation and independence.[64]

NOTES

1. G. Reginald Daniel, "Beyond Black and White," in *Racially Mixed People in America*, ed. Maria P. P. Root (Thousand Oaks, Calif.: Sage, 1992), 333–41; Rhett S. Jones, "The End of Africanity? The Bi-Racial Assault on Blackness," *Western Journal of Black Studies* 18, no. 4 (1994): 201–10.

2. Daniel, "Beyond Black and White"; Jones, "The End of Africanity?"; Gayatri Spivak, "Strategies of Vigilance: An Interview with Gayatri Chakravorty," *Block* 10 (1985): 8.

3. Others make a distinction between individual racism, which is defined as everyday individual antipathy based on race, and institutional racism, which has larger social structural implications in terms of the distribution of wealth, power, privilege, and prestige. Molefi Asante, *Kemet, Afrocentricity, and Knowledge* (Trenton, N.J.: Africa World Press, 1990), 17–22; Werner Sollors, "The Idea of Ethnicity," in *The Truth about the Truth: De-Confusing and De-Constructing the Postmodern World*, ed. Walter Truett Anderson (New York: Putnam, 1995), 58–65; Ali Rattansi, "'Western' Racisms, Ethnicities and Identities in a 'Postmodern' Frame," in *Racism, Modernity and Identity: On the Western Front*, ed. Ali Rattansi and Sallie Westwood (Cambridge, Mass.: Polity Press, 1994), 57; Christie Farnham Pope, "The Challenge Posed by Radical Afrocentrism: When a White Professor Teaches Black History," *Chronicle of Higher Education*, March 30, 1994, B1; Gerald Early, "Understanding Afrocentrism: Why Blacks Dream of a World without Whites," *Civilization* 2 (July–August 1995): 31–39.

4. bell hooks, "Postmodern Blackness," in *Yearning: Race, Gender, and Cultural Politics* (Boston: South End, 1995), 23–31; Manning Marable, *Beyond Black and White: Transforming African American Politics* (New York: Verso, 1995), 121–22; Jerome H. Schiele, "Afrocentricity for All," *Black Issues in Higher Education* 8.18 (September 26, 1991): 27; Kwame Nantambu, "Pan-Africanism versus Pan-African Nationalism: An Afrocentric Analysis," *Journal of Black Studies* 28.5 (May 1998): 561–74.

5. Marable, *Beyond Black and White*, 122; Rattansi, "'Western' Racisms, Ethnicities and Identities," 57; Molefi Asante, *Afrocentricity: The Theory of Social Change* (Buffalo: Amulefi, 1980), 105–8; Asante, *Kemet, Afrocentricity, and Knowledge*, 17–22.

6. Mahgan Keita, "Deconstructing the Classical Age: Africa and the Unity of the Mediterranean World," *Journal of Negro History,* 79.2 (spring 1994): 146–66.

7. Mary Lefkowitz, *Not Out of Africa: How Afrocentrism Became an Excuse to Teach Myth as History* (New York: Basic Books, 1996), 161; Molly Myerowitz Levine, "Review Article, The Use and Abuse of *Black Athena,"* *American Historical Review* 97 (April 1992): 440–64; George Will, "Intellectual Segregation: Afrocentrism's Many Myths Constitute Condescension toward African-Americans," *Newsweek,* February 19, 1996, 78.

8. Joel Augustus Rogers, *World's Great Men of Color,* vol. 2 (New York: Macmillan, [1947] 1986, 79–88, 109–22; Joel Augustus Rogers, *Sex and Race,* vol. 3 (New York: Helga M. Rogers, 1944), 306–9; Allison Blakely, *Russia and the Negro: Blacks in Russian History and Thought* (Washington, D.C.: Howard University Press, 1986), 50–56; G. Reginald Daniel, "Eurocentrism, Afrocentrism, or Holocentrism?" *Interrace Magazine* 3.2 (1992): 33.

9. Daniel, "Eurocentrism, Afrocentrism, or Holocentrism?" 33; Cornel West, *Beyond Eurocentrism and Multiculturalism,* vol. 1 (Monroe, Maine: Common Courage Press, 1993), 1–30.

10. Marable, *Beyond Black and White,* 117–24.

11. Robert Young, "Egypt in America," in Rattansi and Westwood, eds., *Racism, Modernity and Identity,* 158; Daniel, "Eurocentrism, Afrocentrism, or Holocentrism?" 33.

12. Lefkowitz, *Not Out of Africa,* 161; Levine, "The Use and Abuse of *Black Athena*"; Will, "Intellectual Segregation."

13. Marable, *Beyond Black and White,* 122; Rattansi, "'Western' Racisms, Ethnicities and Identities," 57; Asante, *Afrocentricity,* 105–8; Asante, *Kemet, Afrocentricity, and Knowledge,* 17–22.

14. Joseph Natoli and Linda Hutcheon, Introduction to *A Postmodern Reader,* ed. Joseph Natoli and Linda Hutcheon (Albany: State University of New York Press, 1993), ix–xiv; Richard Lowy, "Development Theory, Globalism, and the New World Order: The Need for a Postmodern, Antiracist, and Multicultural Critique," *Journal of Black Studies* 28.5 (May 1998): 594–615.

15. Ken Wilber, *A Brief History of Everything* (Boston: Shambhala, 1996), 166, 187–92, 261–72. The former trend is more frequently espoused among radical or extreme postmodernists and the latter among more moderate and affirmative postmodernists. Nevertheless, both trends are part of a more generalized assault on the polarization of things into either Black or White. Rattansi, "'Western' Racisms, Ethnicities and Identities," 30; Steven Seidman, ed., *The Postmodern Turn: New Perspectives on Social Theory* (New York: Cambridge University Press, 1994), 8–9; Pauline Marie Rosenau, *Postmodernism and the Social Sciences: Insights, Inroads, and Intrusions* (Princeton: Princeton University Press, 1992), 5–7.

16. Robert Hollinger, *Postmodernism and the Social Sciences: A Thematic Approach* (Thousand Oaks, Calif.: Sage, 1994), 1–19; Rattansi, "'Western' Racisms, Ethnicities, and Identities," 28; Rosenau, *Postmodernism and the Social Sciences,* 128–33; Steven Seidman, "Introduction," in Seidman, ed., *The Postmodern Turn,* 1–21; David Slater, "Exploring Other Zones of the Postmodern: Problems of Ethnocentrism and Difference across the North-South Divide," in Rattansi and Westwood, eds., *Racism, Modernity and Identity,* 87–90.

17. Daniel, "Eurocentrism, Afrocentrism, or Holocentrism?" 33; West, *Beyond Eurocentrism and Multiculturalism,* 1–30.

18. The complexities of multiracial identity are not limited to the experience of individuals of partial African descent but include those with a wide variety of backgrounds. Indeed, there are more Asian American–European American, Native American–European American, and European American–Latina/o than African American–European American intermarriages and offspring. Nevertheless, the rule of hypodescent presents unique challenges to all multiracial-identified individuals of partial African descent, particularly those of Black-White backgrounds. hooks, "Postmodern Blackness"; Patricia Hill Collins, "Setting Our Own Agenda," *Black Scholar* 23.3–4 (1993): 52–55; Victor Anderson, *Beyond Ontological Blackness: An Essay on African American Religious Criticism* (New York: Continuum, 1995,) 11–19.

19. Charles Lemert, *Sociology after the Crisis* (Boulder, Colo.: Westview Press, 1996), 86; Rosenau, *Postmodernism and the Social Sciences,* 52; John Michael Spencer, "Trends of Opposition to Multiculturalism," *Black Scholar* 23.3–4 (1993): 2–5.

20. Ibid.

21. Schiele, "Afrocentricity for All," 27. The configuration of and impetus for the new multiracial identity is not, therefore, synonymous with this phenomenon or with previous multiracial identity projects (e.g. "passing," blue-vein societies, Louisiana Creoles of color, and triracial isolate communities). Generated by racist pressure that has rewarded Whiteness and punished Blackness, those phenomena themselves were inegalitarian. They were less a reaction to the forced denial of European ancestry than to the denial of privileges that such ancestry implied. They merely challenged the dichotomization of Blackness and Whiteness while leaving intact the racial hierarchy that maintains White privilege. These projects perpetuated a divisive and pernicious "colorism" among African-descent Americans.

Although the new multiracial identity project differs significantly from this social structural pathology, it is not inherently immune to the lingering effects of previous, persistent racial ideologies that privilege Whiteness and stigmatize Blackness. The desire to embrace a European ancestral background as a means of affirming a more egalitarian identity could be co-opted by these larger social structural forces. Accordingly, multiracial individuals could be granted the status of new "insiders" who are rewarded with greater opportunities to achieve wealth, power, and privilege. In this scenario the majority of African Americans would be pushed farther to the periphery of society. This type of politics of "racial inclusion" of multiracial people would undermine the very gains in civil rights that today make possible the recognition of a multiracial identity. These dynamics would also further the illusion of power sharing without European Americans actually giving up structural control. Thus the new multiracial identity should not be viewed as a solution, in and of itself, to racism and racial inequality. In addition, it remains to be seen how many individuals will actually live out this promise of identity and help to create a more egalitarian racial order in the United States. We must emphasize that there is no single multiracial voice but many different voices, including those of reactionaries and radical visionaries. Some individuals will undoubtedly reinscribe racial hierarchies, but not all will do this. G. Reginald Daniel, *More than Black? Multiracial Identity and the New Racial Order* (Philadelphia: Temple University Press, 2001).

22. Schiele, "Afrocentricity for All," 27.

23. Ibid.; Molefi Asante, *The Afrocentric Idea* (Philadelphia: Temple University Press, 1987), 3–18; Linda James Myers, "The Deep Structure of Culture: Relevance of Traditional African Culture in Contemporary Life," in *Afrocentric Visions: Studies in Culture and Communication,* ed. Janice D. Hamlet (Thousand Oaks, Calif.: Sage, 1998), 1–14; Norman Harris, "A Philosophical Basis for an Afrocentric Orientation," in Hamlet, ed., *Afrocentric Visions,* 15–26; Terry Kershaw, "Afrocentrism and the Afrocentric Method," in Hamlet, ed., *Afrocentric Visions,* 27–44.

24. Jennifer L. Hochschild, *Facing Up to the American Dream: Race, Class, and the Soul of the Nation* (Princeton: Princeton University Press, 1995), 137–38; Asante, *Afrocentric Idea,* 3–18; Jerome H. Schiele, "Rethinking Organizations from an Afrocentric Viewpoint," in Hamlet, ed., *Afrocentric Visions,* 73–88; Linda James Myers, *Understanding an Afrocentric World View: Introduction to an Optimal Psychology* (Dubuque, Iowa: Kendall/Hunt Publishing, 1988), 1–28.

25. Rattansi, "'Western' Racisms, Ethnicities and Identities," 30; Seidman, "Introduction," 8–9; Roseneau, *Postmodernism and the Social Sciences,* 5–7.

26. hooks, "Postmodern Blackness"; Schiele, "Afrocentricity for All," 27; Asante, *Kemet, Afrocentricity, and Knowledge,* 5, 26, 28, 39.

27. Sollors, "The Idea of Ethnicity," 63.

28. Asante, *Kemet, Afrocentricity, and Knowledge,* v, 7, 12.

29. Schiele, "Afrocentricity for All," 27; Asante, *Kemet, Afrocentricity, and Knowledge,* 5, 26, 28, 39.

30. hooks, "Postmodern Blackness."

31. Ibid.; Anderson, *Beyond Ontological Blackness,* 9–11; Paul Connolly, "Racism and Postmodernism: Towards a Theory of Practice," in *Sociology after*

Postmodernism, ed. David Owen (Thousand Oaks, Calif.: Sage, 1997), 65–80; Rattansi, "'Western' Racisms, Ethnicities and Identities," 30; Seidman, "Introduction," 8–9; Rosenau, *Postmodernism and the Social Sciences,* 5–7.

32. George Lipsitz, "Noise in the Blood: Culture, Conflict, and Mixed Race Identities," Keynote Address at Crossing Lines: Race and Mixed Race across the Geohistorical Divide, a Graduate and Undergraduate Student Conference, April 13, 2002.

33. hooks, "Postmodern Blackness."

34. Ibid.

35. Michael Omi and Howard Winant, *Racial Formation in the United States from the 1960s to the 1990s,* 2d ed. (New York: Routledge, 1994), 66–69, 84, 115, 148.

36. Ella Shohat and Robert Stam, *Unthinking Eurocentrism: Multiculturalism and the Media* (New York: Routledge, 1994), 1–54; Patrick Williams and Laura Chrisman, "Colonial Discourse and Post-Colonial Theory: An Introduction," in *Colonial Discourse and Post-Colonial Theory: A Reader,* ed. Patrick Williams and Laura Chrisman (New York: Columbia University Press, 1994), 1–19; Helen Tiffin, "Introduction," in *Past the Last Post: Theorizing Post-Colonialism and Post-Modernism,* ed. Ian Adam and Helen Tiffin (Calgary, Alberta: University of Calgary Press, 1990), vii–xvi.

37. Shohat and Stam, *Unthinking Eurocentrism,* 1–54.

38. Ibid.

39. Ibid.

40. Ibid., 39.

41. Ibid.

42. Ibid., 38–44; Albert J. Paolini, *Navigating Modernity: Postcolonialism, Identity, and International Relations,* ed. Anthony Elliot and Anthony Moran (Boulder, Colo.: Lynne Rienner, 1999), 49–62; Tiffin, "Introduction."

43. Shohat and Stam, *Unthinking Eurocentrism,* 39.

44. Ibid.

45. Ibid.

46. Ibid.

47. Ibid.

48. Ibid., 42.

49. Ibid.; Williams and Chrisman, "Colonial Discourse and Post-Colonial Theory," 17; Paolini, *Navigating Modernity,* 91–128; Chris Bongie, *Islands and Exiles: The Creole Identities of Post/Colonial Literature* (Stanford: Stanford University Press, 1998), 3–24; Tiffin, "Introduction."

50. Shohat and Stam, *Unthinking Eurocentrism,* 41.

51. Jan Nederveen Pieterse, "Unpacking the West: How European Is Europe?" in Rattansi and Westwood, eds., *Racism, Modernity and Identity,* 130–46; Shohat and Stam, *Unthinking Eurocentrism,* 1–54.

52. Shohat and Stam, *Unthinking Eurocentrism*, 1–54.

53. Ibid.; Nederveen Pieterse, "Unpacking the West."

54. Keita, "Deconstructing the Classical Age," 160.

55. José Piedras, "Literary Whiteness and the Afro-Hispanic Difference," in *The Bounds of Race: Perspectives on Hegemony and Resistance*, ed. Dominick LaCapra (Ithaca: Cornell University Press, 1991), 280.

56. Ivan Van Sertima, "The Moor in Africa and Europe: Origins and Definitions," 2; Edward Scobie, "The Moors and Portugal's Global Expansion," 337, both in *Journal of African Civilizations*, special issue, *The Golden Age of the Moor*, ed. Ivan Van Sertima, 2 (fall 1991).

57. Pieterse, "Unpacking the West," 144.

58. Ibid.

59. Eric Wolfe, *Europe and the People without History* (Berkeley: University of California Press, 1982), x.

60. Hollinger, *Postmodernism and the Social Sciences*, 126–27; Steven Connor, *Postmodern Culture: An Introduction to Theories of the Contemporary* (Oxford: Blackwell, 1989), 224–37; Seidman, *The Postmodern Turn*, 7; Huston Smith, *Beyond the Post-Modern Mind*, rev. ed. (Wheaton, Ill.: Theosophical Publishing House, 1989), 238–39.

61. hooks, "Postmodern Blackness"; Paolini, *Navigating Modernity*, 63–90.

62. Williams and Chrisman, "Colonial Discourse and Post-Colonial Theory"; Rainier Spencer, *Spurious Issues: Race and Multiracial Identity Politics in the United States* (Boulder, Colo.: Westview Press, 1999), 1–48, 189–97; Naomi Zack, *Race and Mixed Race* (Philadelphia: Temple University Press, 1994), xi–xiv; Naomi Zack, "Introduction," in *American Mixed Race*, ed. Naomi Zack (Lanham, Md.: Rowman and Littlefield, 1995), xv–xviii; Omi and Winant, *Racial Formation*, 55–61; John M. Murphy, "The Importance of Social Imagery for Race Relations," in *Postmodernism and Race*, ed. Eric Mark Kramer (Westport, Conn.: Praeger, 1997), 17–31; Jund Min Joi, "Racist Ontology, Inferiorization, and Assimilation," in Kramer, ed., *Postmodernism and Race*, 117–27; George Wilson and Jomills Braddock, "Analyzing Racial Ideology: Post-1980 America," in Kramer, ed., *Postmodernism and Race*, 129–43; Kwame Anthony Appiah, *In My Father's House: Africa in the Philosophy of Culture* (New York: Oxford University Press, 1992), 28–46, 137–57; Smedley, *Race in North America: Origin and Evolution of a Worldview*, 2d ed. (Boulder, Colo.: Westview Press, 1998), 331–32; Yehudi Webster, *The Racialization of America* (New York: Saint Martin's Press, 1992), 1–23; Yehudi Webster, *Against the Multicultural Agenda: A Critical Thinking Alternative* (Westport, Conn.: Praeger, 1997), 1–11, 80–81, 122–27.

63. Omi and Winant, *Racial Formation*, 55–61.

64. Marable, *Beyond Black and White*, 121.

10

WHAT'S CRITICAL ABOUT
WHITE STUDIES

PAUL SPICKARD

In spring 1966 many Black and some White and Asian students at
Seattle's inner-city Garfield High School went on strike, asking the
school board to devote more resources to educating minority chil-
dren, hire more minority teachers, and install an antiracist curricu-
lum. One of the speakers at a rally and workshop at Mt. Zion Baptist
Church was James Bevel, an organizer for the Southern Christian
Leadership Conference and intimate of Dr. Martin Luther King Jr.
One of the White participants asked Bevel, "What is the place of
White people in the Negro revolution?" (This was 1966. The terminological turn to Black Power would not hit the streets of African
American neighborhoods for another year.) He apparently considered himself a member of the liberal vanguard. He was excited about
attending this revolutionary gathering and wanted specific direction
on how to be helpful. He may also have wanted to be told what a fine
thing it was for him, a White person, to support Blacks.

So it was with some dismay that he received Bevel's reply: "There
is no place for White people in the Negro revolution. We are trying
to organize ourselves to take control of our lives. White people are
the problem. You need to go back to White people and teach them

not to be racists." It was not what he wanted to hear, for he was looking for a way to be at the center of the action, where Black people were making a social revolution. Instead, he was being told to go home and attend to a less glamorous chore—the subtle and difficult task of addressing White racism from within the White community. To his credit, he did just that and spent much of the next decade talking to White people about racism.

The sentiment in Bevel's injunction to go back to White people and teach them not to be racists seems at the base of the recent vogue in White studies. There has been an extraordinary outpouring of literature examining Whiteness. If one typed the word "Whiteness" into a library catalog in 1995, one might find a half-dozen references. Typing the same word in 2003 yields hundreds. This chapter surveys that literature, its premises, preoccupations, and themes. Further, it attempts to sort out what parts of the White studies literature are helpful for challenging the racial hierarchy that governs American social relations and what parts tend toward other effects—to determine, in short, what is critical about White studies.

Jonathan Rutherford, a British critic, writes about his motivation for studying Whiteness:

> I was prompted to start thinking about my own ethnic identity by the contemporary generation of black and Asian English intellectuals—Paul Gilroy, Stuart Hall, Kobena Mercer, Isaac Julien, Lola Young, Pratibha Parmar—who were thinking reflexively and historically about race, gender and ethnicity. My involvement in radical politics on the left had taught me to disavow the racial exclusivity of white ethnicity, but never to analyse or try and understand it. Being white was a vague, amorphous concept to get hold of; it wasn't a colour, it was invisible. And who wanted the risible, sometimes ugly, baggage of Englishness? Everything which signified Englishness—the embarrassing legacy of racial supremacy and empire, the union jack waving crowds, the royalty, the rhetoric about Britain's standing in the world— suggested a conservative deference to nostalgia. The problem with intellectually disowning white English ethnicity was that the left never got around to working out what it was, and what our own emotional connections to it were.[1]

Noel Ignatiev and John Garvey pride themselves on being "race traitors." Like Rutherford, they are White but would disavow Whiteness. They begin with an insight with which this writer would not disagree: "[T]he key to fundamental social change in the U.S. is the challenge to the system of race privilege that embraces all whites." Their definition of Whiteness is perhaps a bit idiosyncratic: "The white race consists of those who partake of the privileges of white skin. . . . [P]eople were not favored socially because they were white; rather they were defined as 'white' because they were favored." Then, invoking the memory of John Brown, they issue a call to "focus on whiteness and the struggle to abolish the white race from within," by disavowing the privileges of White skin.[2]

This, they say, is the "key to solving the social problems of our age." "[T]he majority of so-called whites in this country are neither deeply nor consciously committed to white supremacy; like most human beings in most times and places, they would do the right thing if it were convenient. . . . By engaging these dissidents in a journey of discovery into whiteness and its discontents, we hope to take part . . . in the process of defining a new human community." They conclude: "The existence of the white race depends on the willingness of those assigned to it to place their racial interests above class, gender, or any other interests they hold. The defection of enough of its members to make it unreliable as a determinant of behavior will set off tremors that will lead to its collapse." What is not clear in this formulation is just how that "defection" from the White race is to be accomplished, nor is it clear how one can disavow one's Whiteness and make it stick.[3]

OLDER TRADITIONS IN WHITE STUDIES

Garvey, Ignatiev, and Rutherford would study Whiteness in order to dethrone it. This is a different business from most earlier studies of White people, although, as we shall see, there are some points of similarity.[4] Earlier Whiteness studies took several perspectives. First were the rantings of early-twentieth-century pseudoscientific racialists. Their name was legion, but among the most memorable were Madison Grant and Lothrop Stoddard. Grant's masterwork was *The*

Passing of the Great Race, or The Racial Basis of European History (1916), in which he divided all of humankind into "races" on supposedly scientific principles and told why it was that vigor and virtue emerged out of competition among races as the distinctive qualities of Nordic peoples who drew their origins from Aryan ancestors. Grant argued that "conservation of [the White] race" was "the true spirit of Americanism." Hitler apparently read Grant and thought it the true spirit of the Third Reich as well. Stoddard followed shortly with *The Rising Tide of Color against White World-Supremacy* (1920), which made dire predictions that White people in Europe and North America would be outbred and eventually overrun by fecund hordes of "inferior stocks"—Asians, Africans, and Latin Americans. Stoddard's writing and Grant's played a part in the racially inflected quotas and exclusions that distinguished the Immigration Act of 1924.[5]

Grant and Stoddard were crude White supremacist race-baiters. Yet their racial assumptions have found marginally more genteel echoes in our own time, covered by a thin veneer of pseudoscience and policy concern. None is more prominent than Richard Herrnstein and Charles Murray's *The Bell Curve* (1994), an attack on affirmative action hidden in a welter of bad science and bogus statistics. Almost as widely read and no less pernicious was Peter Brimelow's *Alien Nation* (1996). Here, an Anglo-Saxon immigrant attempted to pull up the ladder behind him, charging that Brown and Yellow immigrants were "making America . . . a freak among the world's nations because of the unprecedented demographic mutation it is inflicting on itself." These were relatively explicit celebrations of what the authors regarded as White superiority, a kind of literary Klanism.[6]

There has also been a less overtly malevolent but still insidious literature—studies that focused on the experiences of White ethnic groups in such a way as to ignore the fundamental differences between the experiences of White people and those of people of color in the United States. Books like Thomas Sowell's *Ethnic America* (1981), Nathan Glazer's *Ethnic Dilemmas* (1983), and Michael Novak's *The Rise of the Unmeltable Ethnics* (1973) all treat African Americans and other peoples of color as if they were ethnic groups just like Greeks and Swedes. The tendency of such works is to focus on the hardships faced by some White immigrant groups, to bare their grievances, and to shade into justification of White privilege by denying its distinctive existence.[7]

Quite a large number of studies of White immigrant groups lacked the racist political agenda of the books described above, among them, John Bodnar's *The Transplanted* (1985), Bernard Bailyn's *Voyagers to the West* (1986), David Hackett Fischer's *Albion's Seed* (1989), and Richard D. Alba's *Ethnic Identity* (1990).[8] These works focused on White people and tried to understand and represent their experiences without a racist edge to their interpretations.

Finally, there were studies of White attitudes about race. Again, the list includes many distinguished books, such as Gordon W. Allport's *The Nature of Prejudice* (1954), Winthrop D. Jordan's *White over Black* (1968), George M. Fredrickson's *The Black Image in the White Mind* (1971), Edmund S. Morgan's *American Slavery—American Freedom* (1975), and Robert Berkhofer's *The White Man's Indian* (1978).[9] These were varieties of Whiteness studies, too. They focused on the historical contexts in which and the social and psychological processes by which White people constructed the American racial system in slavery and colonialism and the outworkings of that system in White minds in later years.

This brief tour of early studies of Whiteness is not intended to assert direct lines of descent from, say, Madison Grant or Edmund Morgan to the Whiteness studies boom at the turn of the millennium. They were writers of different times, operating with different tools and insights and from different motives. I do intend to suggest, however, that the range of Whiteness studies in earlier eras—from studies of White racism to works on specific White groups to books that fail to recognize their racism and finally to those that openly express it—is echoed in the new. The New Whiteness studies, too, have produced substantial and important works that contribute vital insights to our understanding of race and racism; there are also books, alas, that shade over into White-centeredness and finally into racist abuse.

New Whiteness Studies

Among the older strands of Whiteness studies, the ones I have marked as racist (Stoddard, Herrnstein, et al.) had origins on the political right. The studies of White immigrant groups and White racial thinking before the 1990s hewed rather to the middle of the road. The new

Whiteness studies of the 1990s and the twenty-first century stem from the political left.

The founders of this latter movement are Alexander Saxton, David Roediger, and Toni Morrison. Saxton's book, *The Rise and Fall of the White Republic*, started the trend in 1990. It is an analysis of the role of racial thinking in the shifting class bases of political parties in the United States over the course of the nineteenth century. Saxton begins with the assumption that racial ideas began in North America as an attempt by Europeans to justify enslavement of Africans and expropriation and expulsion of Native Americans.[10] He then traces changes in racial thinking by various groups of Americans, as the vehicle to explain the changing alignments of White class groupings in the major political parties. In short, Saxton treats "the generation and regeneration of white racism 'as part of the process of class conflict and compromise.'"[11]

Saxton, then, sees racial thinking primarily as a tool created and used by White people to pursue class-based political alliances among White people. This is not quite crude Marxism—race as mere false consciousness, a gloss on class. It nonetheless amounts to an admittedly sophisticated and informed attempt to reduce racial oppression to an expression of class conflict.[12] *The Rise and Fall of the White Republic* is a serious attempt to understand the ways in which racial ideas and racial marking on the part of Whites shaped U.S. politics in the nineteenth century.

Roediger's acclaimed *Wages of Whiteness* (1991) is a book about class formation among Whites, too. It argues that White workers in the mid-nineteenth century gathered themselves into a self-conscious, activist working class, not only on the basis of class interests, but also on the basis of a racist intention to distance themselves from that other great part of the working class, Black workers. Roediger starts from an elaboration of W. E. B. Du Bois's notion of a psychic wage that accrued to Whites from their very Whiteness: "[T]he pleasures of whiteness could function as a 'wage' for white workers. That is, status and privileges conferred by race could be used to make up for alienating and exploitative class relationships, North and South. White workers could, and did, define and accept their class positions by fashioning identities as 'not slaves' and as 'not Blacks.'" Thus, "working class formation and the systematic development of a sense of whiteness went hand in hand for the U.S. white working class."[13]

The power of Roediger's book is enhanced by the subtlety of his argument and the variety of his methods and areas of inquiry. He examines political speech, crowd behavior, folklore, humor, and audience responses to minstrel shows, among other things. His argument is, in the end, equal parts psychological and class analysis: "[W]hiteness was a way in which workers responded to a fear of dependency on wage labor and to the necessities of capitalist work discipline. As the U.S. working class matured, principally in the North, within a slaveholding republic, the heritage of the Revolution made independence a powerful masculine personal ideal. But slave labor and 'hireling' wage labor proliferated in the new nation. One way to make peace with the latter was to differentiate it sharply from the former. . . . [T]he white working class, disciplined and made anxious by fear of dependency, began during its formation to construct an image of the Black population as 'other'—as embodying the preindustrial, erotic, careless style of life the white worker hated and longed for."[14]

Roediger starts from the conviction, adopted from Coco Fusco, that "[t]o ignore white ethnicity is to redouble its hegemony by naturalizing it."[15] This conviction stands at the ideological base of Whiteness studies. Yet if there is a criticism to be made of *The Wages of Whiteness*, it is that in it Roediger, like most of the Whiteness studies writers, expresses a rhetoric of normative Whiteness. "Workers" are assumed to be White unless they are racially marked as "Blacks," and the most important thing about Black workers is their Blackness, not their participation in the working class.[16] Roediger recognized the dangers in this posture and attempted to undercut it in two later works. A volume of essays, *Towards the Abolition of Whiteness* (1994), took up several themes tangential to *The Wages of Whiteness*. More consistently than in the first book, he treated Blacks and other people of color as actors, not merely as foils for White workers. In *Black on White* (1998), Roediger reproduced the writings of four dozen African American writers, from Anna Julia Cooper to Lewis Gordon. Here is a book about Whiteness, but it is not fixed on the ideas of White people. Rather, it seeks to dethrone White privilege by putting the analysis of Whiteness in the hands of Blacks.[17]

Toni Morrison completed the foundation of the White studies movement in 1992 with *Playing in the Dark: Whiteness and the Literary Imagination*. Whereas Roediger and Saxton are interested in the White working class and its relationship to racial identity politics,

Morrison's interest is American literature. Not only, Morrison said, has American literature been dominated by White male authors and White male critics, but the values of literary criticism, the decisions about what is important and excellent and true, have been appropriated by White men in hegemonic ways that have denied that appropriation. Valuing the universal (read "White") over the particular (read "Black"), they have virtually erased Black characters, Black authors, Black themes, and Black issues from the center of American literature. But just as Saxton and Roediger find White workers defining their identities against Black workers, so, too, Morrison finds that the White writers of the canon (Hemingway, Faulkner, etc.) define the major issues, indeed the national character, in relation to Blackness. She argues that "the metaphorical and metaphysical uses of race occupy definitive places in American literature, in the 'national' character, and ought to be a major concern of the literary scholarship that tries to know it."[18]

The Wages of Whiteness, Playing in the Dark, and *The Rise and Fall of the White Republic,* then, are foundational examples of what is substantive and distinctive about Whiteness studies. Morrison, Roediger, and, less explicitly Saxton, analyze Whiteness in order, one might say, to decenter it, to make it less hegemonic, to reduce its power. Other useful examples of White studies abound.

Theodore Allen joined the discussion with his two-volume work, *The Invention of the White Race* (1994, 1997). Instead of the nineteenth century as the critical time for White racial formation, Allen looks to America in the seventeenth and eighteenth centuries. He posits a time before the categories "White" and "Black" had social meaning, when national labels such as "English" and "Irish" were the modes of identity. He argues with polemical ferocity that the White race was invented no later than the mid-eighteenth century by the planter elite of the Chesapeake colonies, as a deliberate measure of social control. The laboring classes were divided, White and free on one side, Black and slave on the other.[19]

Tomás Almaguer expanded the discussion beyond the Black/ White dichotomy in *Racial Fault Lines* (1994). Roediger had made some mention of White workers defining themselves against Chinese workers in the West, but otherwise all the authors described up to this point saw race as a relationship between Black and White. Looking at the construction and uses of Whiteness in California in the second half of the nineteenth century, Almaguer paints a more complicated picture. Here there were not just White and Black people but Asians, Mexicans, and Native Americans as well.[20] Like Lori Pierce in chapter 6 of this volume, Almaguer found White people coming to the West with preexisting convictions about White racial superiority and then creating a new racial hierarchy out of local materials.

For Almaguer, as for Saxton, Allen, and Roediger, race making is critically intertwined with class making. But unlike them, Almaguer argues for "the primacy of race." "Beginning in 1870 and intensifying dramatically in the 1880s, an economy based on wage labor eclipsed that based on the unfree labor system of the Mexican period. Once unleashed, this proletarianization absorbed both the indigenous Mexican population and the numerous white and nonwhite immigrant groups that settled in the area." "Racial status" played a "central role" in co-creating the new class structure:

> Far from being merely an ideological construct or an anachronistic status designation, race became the key organizing principle structuring white supremacist economic, as well as political, institutions that were introduced in California. White male immigrants became farmers, proprietors, professionals, and white-collar employees, while the Mexican, Japanese, Chinese, and Indian male populations were securely ensconced at the bottom end of the class structure as unskilled manual workers.[21]

The multiple sides of Almaguer's analysis may tempt some to conclude that *Racial Fault Lines* is something other than Whiteness studies. But though he is sensitive to the existence and issues of other groups, the actors in his story are White people, and the story is about the ways in which they drew lines between themselves and various peoples of color—the ways in which they defined and used Whiteness.

Neil Foley echoed Almaguer's description of a multiple-sided racial encounter in *The White Scourge* (1997). Set in the cotton country of central Texas, mainly in the first decades of the twentieth century, this work examines the relationships among Blacks, Mexicans, and poor Whites. Whereas Almaguer focused on Whites making racial distinctions, Foley treats all three of the groups under study as actors and attends to the ways in which they negotiated their identities and class positions. For Foley, as for Almaguer, the critical item under negotiation was Whiteness. As cotton farming grew into agribusiness at the dawn of the century, former sharecroppers and tenant farmers became proletarian field-workers. Foley finds that for a time poor Whites lost some of their racial privilege relative to Black and especially Mexican agricultural workers. Conversely, for a brief period Mexicans were able to negotiate a place for themselves partway between Black and White, taking on, Foley says, a measure of Whiteness.[22]

George Lipsitz turned a harsh lens on White privilege in an influential essay and book, both titled *The Possessive Investment in Whiteness* (1995, 1998).[23] Lipsitz offers a brilliant tour of American racial history, showing how, in each era from Jamestown up to the present and in various sectors of the economy and polity, powerful Whites have chosen to establish structures that favored European-derived Americans over peoples of color and then masked those decisions with the language of individualism. "From the start," says Lipsitz, "European settlers in North America established structures encouraging possessive investment in Whiteness. The colonial and early-national legal systems authorized attacks on Native Americans and encouraged the appropriation of their lands. They legitimated racialized chattel slavery, restricted naturalized citizenship to 'white' immigrants, and provided pretexts for exploiting labor, seizing property, and denying the franchise to Asian Americans, Mexican Americans, Native Americans, and African Americans."[24]

This drawing of a line between Whites and people of color, and favoring the former over the latter, did not end with slavery, however. Lipsitz offers example after example of this practice, from the racist quality of the American seizure of the Philippines to the Bakke decision against affirmative action to the policies of the Federal Housing Administration that helped to create all-White suburbs. Nonetheless, he concludes, almost hopefully: "The problem with white people is not our whiteness, but our possessive investment in it. Created by politics, culture, and consciousness, our possessive investment in whiteness can be altered by those same processes, but only if we face the hard facts openly. . . . How can we account for the ways in which white people refuse to acknowledge their possessive investment in whiteness even as they work to increase its value every day? We can't blame the color of our skin. It must be the content of our character."[25]

One of the most sophisticated examples of the merits of White studies is Matthew Frye Jacobson's *Whiteness of a Different Color* (1998).[26] Jacobson attempts to chart the entire history of the European immigrant peoples of the United States and to examine the relationships among them. He divides American racial history into three periods. The first, 1790–1840, was when "free white persons" as designated in the first naturalization law was an amorphous category that had some element of hierarchy but did not sharply delineate among varieties of European-descended peoples. For Jacobson, the crucial tool that made these peoples a common White race was republican ideology—an estimate of their fitness for self-government. In the second period, 1840–1924, Jacobson finds the White race broken up into some groups that are White and some that are less so—perhaps even some that are not White (he is not consistent on that point)—under the force of more varied immigration, the rise of industry, and pseudoscientific racial theorizing. That hierarchy among Whitenesses explains the Anglocentric quota system at the heart of the 1924 Immigration Act. In the third period, 1924–65, White people were lumped together again into an amorphous group called Caucasians.[27]

The strength of *Whiteness of a Different Color* is that it takes seriously the hierarchies that existed among White people and tries to account for them. There are some problems near the book's core, however. For one thing, although on nearly every page Jacobson speaks of the "racial" character of this or that distinction, nowhere does he define what "racial" means for him.[28] So when he says that the differences among Anglo-Americans, Irish, and Jews were racial, we are not quite sure what he means. He seems to want to set up various European immigrant peoples as racially separate from the dominant group of Whites, especially in his middle period. Surely, there was hierarchy among Whites (and surely, by his own evidence but contrary to his schema, it existed in all three periods). But this does not mean that the disabilities suffered by Irish or Italians or Jews in the United States were at the same scale as those suffered by peoples of color. Some people may have used race language in the middle period to describe what they called "ethnic" differences in another period, but this may only mean that the language fashion changed.

Jacobson very seldom even mentions African or Native or Mexican or Asian Americans, but on the few occasions he does, it is clear that the disabilities suffered by subordinate White "races" pale by comparison. He writes:

> Reconstruction collapsed in the South, raising new questions about the relations among whites and blacks in an era of black Emancipation and the reintegration of the South into national political life. In the aftermath of Custer's demise . . . the Great Sioux Wars ended with the defeat of the Minneconjou Sioux; Sitting Bull escaped to Canada, and Crazy Horse surrendered to federal troops. A vocal and often violent anti-Chinese movement coalesced in the West, particularly in California, where white workers decried the labor competition of "Mongolians" and insisted upon a "white man's republic." The East and Midwest, meanwhile, were wracked by labor unrest which *raised questions* in some quarters about the white immigrant working class itself.[29]

"Raised questions" versus killed, enslaved, imprisoned on reservations, and excluded from the country. To be sure, there were groups of Whites who were set off from the dominant group, and they had less privilege, but they were not racially separate from dominant-group Whites, nor did their disadvantage come close to that experienced by peoples of color. They could vote, they were eligible for naturalization, and no one was killing them on account of their ethnicity. Theirs was, as the title suggests, not non-Whiteness but "Whiteness of a different color." Yet Jacobson's book is premised in part on their being more separate and disadvantaged than that, and the evidence just does not support this claim.

Despite its shortcomings, *Whiteness of a Different Color*, like *The White Scourge, The Wages of Whiteness*, and similar books, is a significant help to our understanding of the ways that race has been constructed and used. The best White studies are like these, historically grounded studies of how the White group was formed and how power has been employed to enhance and maintain it.[30]

There is a related movement—critical race theory—that is worth mentioning as an adjunct to Whiteness studies. Critical race theory is an intellectual movement primarily in legal scholarship circles. Some progressive legal scholars saw the modest gains experienced by people of color during the civil rights movement disappearing in the

1970s. They grew impatient with the standard liberal approaches to racial justice. Turning to neo-Marxist and postmodern ideas, they fashioned a new approach to the legal interpretation of racial issues.[31] Critical race theory intersects with Whiteness studies through one of its offshoots, critical White studies. The branching began with an article by Cheryl Harris in the *Harvard Law Review,* "Whiteness as Property" (1993). There, she made from a legal point of view much the same argument that Lipsitz would later make in terms more broadly cultural and political. In *White by Law* (1996), Ian Haney López broadened Harris's analysis to show how Whites used the law to draw lines around their Whiteness and reinforce their privilege. Richard Delgado and Jean Stefancic (1997) widened the discussion of critical White studies in a massive compendium of writings by legal scholars and others on the ways that White people have created and maintained White privilege.[32]

WE ARE OTHER TOO: THE PROBLEM WITH WHITENESS STUDIES

If there are many strengths and important achievements in Whiteness studies, are there weaknesses too? Alas, there are. The problems stem from what seem to be the motivations driving much of the White studies movement. One factor seems to be embarrassment on the part of some White people who regard themselves as sensitive to racial issues—embarrassment that they are White. Jonathan Rutherford, in the passage quoted early in this chapter, used that word to describe the root of his desire to study Whiteness.[33] No one wants to be part of the problem. People of sensitivity and goodwill want to be part of the solution. However, that desire may shade into a longing to be at the center of action, racially speaking. Like the young man whose story opened this chapter, Whiteness studies people want to be on the side of progressive social change in racial matters.

Embarrassment and a desire to be at the center of action lead some people to want to flee their Whiteness. Rutherford writes of a longing to "disown . . . white English ethnicity," and Ignatiev and Garvey call on progressive Whites to "defect" from, in fact to "abolish," the White race.[34] That would neatly solve the embarrassment problem and perhaps put one at the center of the action, but how can one do that? The Black theologian James Cone put a positive spin on the dilemma in 1970, long before the White studies movement: "There will be no peace in America until whites begin to hate their whiteness, asking from the depths of their being: 'How can we become black?' "[35]

One way, perhaps, to lessen the tension is to suggest that one is not an oppressor because one is not quite so White as the bad Whites who are the main oppressors. This leads to the We Are Other Too fallacy that is a significant subtheme in the Whiteness studies movement. Some White people, in desiring to flee or disavow their Whiteness, retreat into the comforting assertion that they (or some other Whites with whom they identify) are not, or were not always, quite so White as the main White oppressors.

They begin with the accurate observation that there has long been a hierarchy among White Americans along lines of ancestral nationality, and that it has sometimes assumed a racial tone (i.e., the language people have used to describe it has sometimes referred to supposedly innate characteristics and phenotype). This hierarchical ranking of Whiteness can be illustrated by the following exercise. More than one hundred audiences in the last two-plus decades—students, church groups, and the audiences at public lectures—have been asked to rank ten American ethnic groups "according to how closely they approximate the core of what it means to be an American." In every case, the audience, on average, gave a ranking that looked about like this:[36]

1. English
2. Swedish
3. Irish
4. Polish
5. Jewish
6. Black
7. American Indian
8. Japanese
9. Mexican
10. Arab

Something very like this hierarchy was coded into the Immigration Act of 1924, which set strict quotas on eastern and southern European immigrants and banned Asians outright. Such a hierarchy was assumed by Florence Ewing, a kind White woman from Missouri, who early in the twentieth century wrote the names of all her high school friends next to their pictures in her scrapbook. The ethnicity of her Anglo-American, German, and Scandinavian Protestant and Irish Catholic friends went unmarked, but she felt compelled to write "Jewish" next to the names of those to whom that appellation might be applied. It did not mean she was not equally their friend, only that their Jewish identity made them something less than other Whites.[37]

Starting from the observation of such a hierarchy among White people, some students of Whiteness take it a step further and assert that Jews or Irish or Italians or some other group of White people once were not White. Thus we now see books and articles about how whomever became White. The unspoken assertion is, We have race, too, the same as people of color. We are not part of the problem because we are Other, too.

The standard-bearer in this trend is Noel Ignatiev, in an influential book with the provocative title, *How the Irish Became White* (1995). Intrinsic to Ignatiev's argument is an idiosyncratic definition of Whiteness. He begins with the observations that race is not biological in origin but rather that people are assigned to races and that there is an intimate "connection . . . between concepts of race and acts of oppression." One is not White in one's person, and a group of people are not a White group in their being. Rather, they are White insofar as they participate in oppressing others who are defined as the racial target for subordination. For Ignatiev, "the white race consists of those who partake of the privileges of white skin." This provides him with the conceptual foundation from which to argue that for Irish Americans in the nineteenth century, "[t]o enter the white race was a strategy to secure an advantage in a competitive society."[38] That is, through the quirks of Ignatiev's definitions, the Irish were once not White, and then they worked to become White, by drawing a distinction between themselves and people who were not White and actively oppressing those people.

Ignatiev argues there was a time in Ireland when Irish people were oppressed in something like racial terms. English people colonized Ireland, took away people's lands and livelihoods, and created an ideology of Irish innate, quasi-biological inferiority—not quite Black, but not quite English either. Irish people came to America and were slotted into low-class positions—though not as low as slaves or free Blacks. Here, according to Ignatiev, instead of establishing class solidarity with Blacks, the Irish chose to be White—that is, to be oppressive—in order to distance themselves from Blacks and improve their social and economic possibilities. Through the Catholic Church, labor unions, and the Democratic Party they claimed a place in what was becoming the White Republic.

The important contributions of Ignatiev's polemic are his insistence on examining relations between White and Black members of the working class and his conclusion that adopting anti-Black attitudes and activities was essential to Irish Americans making a place for themselves above the bottom rung in the United States. His broader contention highlighted in the title, that the Irish were once not White and then chose to become White, is intelligible—but only if one recognizes and accepts his idiosyncratic definition of Whiteness not as biology or group identity but as a choice to act oppressively toward African Americans.

Yet the impact of the title and the argument is quite different. Very few people comprehend Ignatiev's definition of Whiteness, and fewer still accept it as normative. This writer has heard dozens of times since Ignatiev's book was published, from White laypeople and scholars alike, some version of the following statement: "You know, the Irish weren't always White. Once they were not White, and then they became White." The implication is that the kind of mobility that Irish Americans are said to have experienced is readily available to people of color in the United States. It is an easy step from there to the racist conclusion that Blacks or Latinos or Indians or Asians have chosen not to become White out of sheer perversity. Like the Irish, they could have become White and escaped the disabilities that are their lot.

Ignatiev would not own that interpretation. In *Race Traitor* and in *How the Irish Became White* he shows how vehemently he opposes White privilege and oppressiveness. That is why he wants to disown Whiteness. It is a noble urge but ultimately a misguided one. Ignatiev and other Whites (including this author) cannot effectively disown our Whiteness, much as we might like to do so. We necessarily carry White privilege whether we want to or not. To illustrate: Try as I may, I cannot change the fact that I can get a cab easily in midtown Manhattan, while a middle-aged Black man wearing similar clothing cannot. More consequentially, we will be seen differently when applying for a loan, seeking a job, or confronting a police officer. Whites as a group have better life chances than do African Americans or other people of color. We can hate White privilege, we can denounce it, but until race is irrelevant in America—a distant day indeed—we cannot be not privileged. We can fight against racial hierarchy and oppression daily, but we cannot abolish the White race. We still enjoy the fruits of Whiteness, whether we want them or not.

The We Are Other Too trend is carried further by Karen Brodkin in *How Jews Became White Folks and What That Says about Race in America*.[39] One hesitates to cast aspersions on a book as good as this one. Brodkin began the study as an attempt to understand how race, class, and gender interpenetrate in American society. Gradually, however, it turned into an exploration of changes in the nature of Jewishness and then into a kind of family history of racial identity. *How Jews Became White Folks* in fact does a superb job of illuminating how gender and class work together with race in the formation of identities and hierarchies in the American economic and political systems.

But in the more expansive theme that gives the book its title, Brodkin loses her way. Her central contention is that there was a time in American history when Jews were non-Whites. When she hews closer to her evidence, she describes Jews as being "not-quite white" or having "a whiteness of our own."[40] Here she refers to the fact that Jews have long held a lower position in the American ethnoracial hierarchy than White Gentiles (although that position has improved in recent generations and although it was never so low as any of the nation's peoples of color). But more frequently than such nuanced phrasings, Brodkin boldly asserts, again and again, and without any supporting evidence, that Jews were in fact non-White.

This is an example of Whiteness studies run amok. If this trend continues, one can expect to see books before long on how the Italians became White, how the Swedes became White, perhaps even how the English became White. It is pretty silly, and disrespectful of the genuine disabilities faced by people of color in America's racial system.[41]

The ultimate absurdity on the We Are Other Too theme is John Gennari's 1996 article, "Passing for Italian." The title appears on the cover of the trendy cultural studies journal *Transition* across a picture of Denny Mendez, Miss Italia 1996—an apparently Black woman. One might expect Gennari's article to be a meditation on the complexities of Italian identity in an age when immigrants (including the

Dominican-born Mendez) are remaking the ethnic map of places that are frequently thought to be racially homogeneous. That would be a worthy subject. Instead, we are treated to a self-indulgent essay whose central contention is that there is "a distinct tradition of inter-ethnic identification[,] . . . the black/Italian crossover fantasy," which Gennari calls "'goombah blackness'—an affective alliance between Italian and African Americans based on mutual desires and pleasures, and grounded particularly in a tradition of boisterous male assertiveness."[42] Blacks and Italians, says Gennari, are natural pals.

Gennari's evidence? He has almost none, beyond assertions that Marvin Gaye admired Frank Sinatra, that Sinatra admired Billie Holiday, that Sinatra hung out with Sammy Davis Jr., and that Sinatra and some gangsta rappers had similar attitudes toward women. The suspicion lingers that Gennari is just a White guy attempting to appropriate Blackness in order to make himself look more hip. It does not work. Sinatra's attitudes may have been similar to those of some hip-hop artists, and there surely have been times and places where Blacks and Italians (and others) have interacted. But I know of no Black neighborhood in the 1940s and 1950s where more than a tiny handful of people even listened to Frank Sinatra, much less thought him one of their own. There is no evidence at all of a special affinity between the Black and Italian American populations at large. "Passing for Italian" is pernicious silliness.

Thus many White studies authors assert, without adequate foundation, a parallel between racial divisions and the situations of White ethnic groups. And almost none ask the comparative questions that would be needed to prove their assumptions. For example, precisely how *are* the disabilities suffered by Jews or Italians like—and how are they unlike—those suffered by Blacks and Indians? Do those disabilities stem from the same causes? Are they equally susceptible to remediation? These and questions like them are worth asking, but one will not find them asked in Whiteness studies.

There is another theme in some studies of Whiteness by White feminists, and it borders on the We Are Other Too assertion. It is the implication that femaleness Blackens, that because a White person or group is female, that person or group does not partake of White privilege to the same degree as do White males. I take that to be a nearly spoken subtext in the interchange between Catharine A. MacKinnon and Martha R. Mahoney in the *Yale Journal of Law and*

Feminism.[43] I do not wish to contest or discount the very real disabilities faced by White women in a sexist society—quite the contrary. In fact, I offer this observation with the utmost tentativeness, as I am a White man and so am of the oppressing class on both counts. Nonetheless, there is something pernicious about adopting, even by subtle implication, the oppression of members of a group to which one does not belong. Salient refutations of such an assertion of common otherness are made by a number of feminists of color, among them, bell hooks, Hazel V. Carby, Haunani-Kay Trask, and Donna Awatere.[44]

Finally, the We Are Other Too vector in Whiteness studies extends to skinhead chic. The taking-off point here is a smart, funny, subversive collection of essays called *White Trash* (1997), edited by Matt Wray and Annalee Newitz. The editors describe their project thus: "Poor or marginal whites occupy an uncharted space in recent identity studies, particularly because they do not easily fit the model of whiteness-as-power proposed by many multiculturalist or minority discourses. Associated in mainstream culture with 'trashy' kitsch or dangerous pathologies rather than with the material realities of economic life, poor whites are treated as degraded caricatures rather than as real people living in conditions of poverty and disempowerment."[45] Thandeka, in a *Tikkun* essay entitled "The Cost of Whiteness" (1999), echoed that analysis: "I am not denying 'white privilege.' All whites . . . benefit from their wage of whiteness. Such talk of privilege, however, is incomplete unless we also speak of its penalty. For poorer wage earners without power, money or influence, their wage of whiteness functions as a kind of workers' . . . 'consolation prize' to persons, who, although not wealthy, do not have to consider themselves losers because they are, at least, white. . . . These workers are, in effect, exploited twice: first as workers and then as 'whites.' . . . Whiteness functions as a distraction from the pervasive class problem."[46] This is a convoluted way of saying that Thandeka wants the real problem to be class, not race. But it is also a serious attempt to address the disabilities faced by poor people who are White.

Where are the lines between (1) exploring Whiteness, (2) rescuing White working-class culture from abuse by outsiders, (3) celebrating Whiteness as a positive identity, and (4) embracing White supremacist racism? It is not always clear. A recent tour of who-bought-what-else from Amazon.com led from excellent Whiteness studies books by Roediger and Jacobson to White trash books like

Wray and Newitz's. Then the trail went on to Jim Goad's *Redneck Manifesto* (1998). Finally, it landed in the heart of Aryan Nation: *They Were White and They Were Slaves* (1993) by Michael Hoffman and *The South Was Right!* (1994) by James Ronald Kennedy.[47] Where exactly was it that the antiracist intent of Whiteness studies shaded into advocacy of White racism? It is not clear, but that is the path it took.

Brodkin, Ignatiev, and nearly all the authors of the We Are Other Too school express a desire to undermine White privilege. These authors, as much as Lipsitz, Roediger, and the other more successful writers on the theme, seem to be trying conscientiously to do what James Bevel instructed the young White man to do in 1966: go back and teach White people about their bigotry. The best examples of Whiteness studies achieve that goal. Still, even the best authors in this field spend nearly all their time talking about White people. And there are so many authors, writing so much about Whiteness these days.[48] Each of them surely makes a contribution to the understanding of Whiteness. And White studies has opened up space for some very creative and insightful riffing on activities surrounding race.[49] But they place White people at the center of investigation, saying by implication that it is White people who are the important ones.[50]

The sheer volume of Whiteness studies overwhelms the senses. Even in the study of race, all the attention these days seems to be going to White people. Not long ago I was standing on a street corner talking with a Filipino scholar about Whiteness studies. He asked, "Don't you White guys have enough already? You are the subject matter of almost all the departments on campus. Now you want ethnic studies too?" His observation was not far off the mark. How sad that some of the makers of White studies should, in attempting to dethrone Whiteness, end up examining it obsessively and placing it at the center yet again.

Notes

Patrick Miller, Lori Pierce, Nick Spreitzer, Puk Degnegaard, Stephen Cornell, Laurie Mengel, Reg Daniel, David Torres-Rouff, Ingrid Page, Lynda Dumais, Ivana Lauro, and Jonathan Glickstein have been generous in contributing to my thinking about White studies; none should be held responsible for the final shape of this chapter.

PAUL SPICKARD

As material in this chapter was being finalized, *International Labor and Working-Class History* featured an article by Eric Arnesen entitled "Whiteness and the Historians' Imagination" (60 [fall 2001]: 3–32), together with responses from several scholars (1–2, 33–92). Arnesen also published a review essay on the same subject, "A Paler Shade of White," *New Republic,* June 24, 2002, 33–38. I am grateful for copies provided by Arnesen. My take on the strengths and shortcomings of the Whiteness studies movement is different from Arnesen's, as my analysis proceeds from different principles and focuses on different issues. Arnesen takes David Roediger and other scholars of Whiteness to task for being less than careful about definitions and less than thorough in their research, in a jot-and-tittle analysis of their argument and evidence. I argue more broadly about themes, motives, and potential social impact. Despite our differences in approach, I find Arnesen's arguments and evidence generally convincing.

1. Jonathan Rutherford, *Forever England: Reflections on Masculinity and Empire* (London: Lawrence and Wishart, 1997), 5.

2. Noel Ignatiev and John Garvey, eds., *Race Traitor* (New York: Routledge, 1996), 1, 9, 10, 11.

3. Ibid., 12, 14.

4. Of course, one might point out that for many decades most studies of U.S. history and culture were studies of White people. In this chapter I focus on works that explicitly addressed the White race and its standing in the world.

5. Madison Grant, *The Passing of the Great Race, or The Racial Basis of European History* (New York: Scribner's, 1916; several later editions), ix; Lothrop Stoddard, *The Rising Tide of Color against White World-Supremacy* (New York: Scribner's, 1920; several later editions). See also Homer Lea, *The Valor of Ignorance* (New York: Harper, 1909) and *The Day of the Saxon* (New York: Harper, 1912); F. G. Crookshank, *The Mongol in Our Midst* (New York: Dutton, 1924). For analyses, see Elazar Barkan, *The Retreat from Scientific Racism* (New York: Cambridge University Press, 1992); Ivan Hannaford, *Race: The History of an Idea in the West* (Baltimore: Johns Hopkins University Press, 1996).

6. Richard J. Herrnstein and Charles Murray, *The Bell Curve: Intelligence and Class Structure in American Life* (New York: Free Press, 1994); Peter Brimelow, *Alien Nation: Common Sense about America's Immigration Disaster* (New York: Harper, 1996), xxi. See also J. Philippe Rushton, *Race, Evolution, and Behavior* (New Brunswick, N.J.: Transaction, 1997); Dinesh D'Souza, *The End of Racism: Principles for a Multiracial Society* (New York: Free Press, 1995); Jon Entine, *Taboo: Why Black Athletes Dominate Sports and Why We're Afraid to Talk about It* (New York: Public Affairs, 2000). For correctives, see Steven Fraser, ed., *The Bell Curve Wars: Race, Intelligence, and the Future of America* (New York: Basic Books, 1995); Stephen Jay Gould, *The Mismeasure of Man,* rev. ed. (New York: Norton, 1996); William H. Tucker, *The Science and*

Politics of Racial Research (Urbana: University of Illinois Press, 1994); Patrick B. Miller, "The Anatomy of Scientific Racism: Racialist Responses to Black Athletic Achievement," in *We Are a People: Narrative and Multiplicity in Constructing Ethnic Identity,* ed. Paul Spickard and W. Jeffrey Burroughs (Philadelphia: Temple University Press, 2000), 124–41; Jonathan Marks, *Human Biodiversity: Genes, Race, and History* (New York: Aldine de Gruyter, 1995).

7. Thomas Sowell, *Ethnic America* (New York: Basic Books, 1981); Nathan Glazer, *Ethnic Dilemmas* (Cambridge, Mass.: Harvard University Press, 1983), esp. "Blacks and Ethnic Groups: The Difference and the Political Difference It Makes," 70–93; Michael Novak, *The Rise of the Unmeltable Ethnics* (New York: Macmillan, 1973).

8. John Bodnar, *The Transplanted: A History of Immigrants in Urban America* (Bloomington: Indiana University Press, 1985); Bernard Bailyn, *Voyagers to the West: A Passage in the Peopling of America on the Eve of the Revolution* (New York: Knopf, 1986); David Hackett Fischer, *Albion's Seed: Four British Folkways in America* (New York: Oxford University Press, 1989); Richard D. Alba, *Ethnic Identity: The Transformation of White America* (New Haven: Yale University Press, 1990). One might even call a book like Langston Hughes's *The Ways of White Folks* (New York: Knopf, 1934) an example of Whiteness studies.

9. Gordon W. Allport, *The Nature of Prejudice* (Cambridge, Mass.: Addison-Wesley, 1954); Winthrop D. Jordan, *White over Black: American Attitudes toward the Negro, 1550–1812* (Chapel Hill: University of North Carolina Press, 1968); George M. Fredrickson, *The Black Image in the White Mind* (New York: Harper and Row, 1971); Edmund S. Morgan, *American Slavery— American Freedom: The Ordeal of Colonial Virginia* (New York: Norton, 1975); Robert Berkhofer, *The White Man's Indian* (New York: Random House, 1978).

10. His ideas here are essentially those of Edmund Morgan in *American Slavery—American Freedom.* For a different view, see Jordan, *White over Black.*

11. Alexander Saxton, *The Rise and Fall of the White Republic: Class Politics and Mass Culture in Nineteenth-Century America* (London: Verso, 1990), 1–18, 387, passim.

12. Perhaps the preeminent attempt to free Marxist interpreters from the assumption that class trumps, in fact is formative of, race, is Robert Miles, *Racism after "Race Relations"* (New York: Routledge, 1993). See also Michael Omi and Howard Winant, *Racial Formation in the United States from the 1960s to the 1990s,* 2d ed. (New York: Routledge, 1994).

13. David Roediger, *The Wages of Whiteness: Race and the Making of the American Working Class* (London: Verso, 1991), 13, 8. Roediger acknowledges his debt to Du Bois. It is not clear whether he intends to invoke the biblical contention that the wages of sin is death.

14. Ibid., 13–14.

15. Ibid., 6.

16. Ibid., 173 passim. Roediger later apologized for what he regarded as a mistake in the subtitle—adopting the rhetorical position that Whites (and in his reading of his own book, men) were the only members of the working class. *The Wages of Whiteness: Race and the Making of the American Working Class,* rev. ed. (London: Verso, 1991), 188–89.

17. David Roediger, *Towards the Abolition of Whiteness: Essays on Race, Politics, and Working Class History* (London: Verso, 1994); David R. Roediger, ed., *Black on White: Black Writers on What It Means to Be White* (New York: Schocken, 1998). Roediger's latest collection of essays on the theme is *Colored White: Transcending the Racial Past* (Berkeley: University of California Press, 2002). See also James R. Barrett and David Roediger, "Inbetween Peoples: Race, Nationality and the 'New Immigrant' Working Class," *Journal of American Ethnic History* 16.3 (spring 1997): 3–44.

18. Toni Morrison, *Playing in the Dark: Whiteness and the Literary Imagination* (Cambridge, Mass.: Harvard University Press, 1994), 63.

19. Theodore W. Allen, *The Invention of the White Race,* vol. 1, *Racial Oppression and Social Control* (London: Verso, 1994); vol. 2, *The Origin of Racial Oppression in Anglo-America* (London: Verso, 1997). Allen takes issue at length with the interpretations advanced by Jordan in *White over Black.* I find Jordan's arguments more persuasive, as they are based on a careful reading of the historical sources and advanced with little polemic aforethought. For a nuanced account of the other side of the coin—the making of African American identity—in a similar period, see Michael A. Gomez, *Exchanging Our Country Marks: The Transformation of African Identities in the Colonial and Antebellum South* (Chapel Hill: University of North Carolina Press, 1998).

20. Truth be told, there were not just White and Black people in the places Saxton, Roediger, Allen, and Morrison examined, but they tended not to see Native Americans and others.

21. Tomás Almaguer, *Racial Fault Lines: The Historical Origins of White Supremacy in California* (Berkeley: University of California Press, 1994), 209, 104.

22. Neil Foley, *The White Scourge: Mexicans, Blacks, and Poor Whites in Texas Cotton Culture* (Berkeley: University of California Press, 1997).

23. George Lipsitz, "The Possessive Investment in Whiteness: Racialized Social Democracy and the 'White' Problem in American Studies," *American Quarterly* 47.3 (1995): 369–87; George Lipsitz, *The Possessive Investment in Whiteness: How White People Profit from Identity Politics* (Philadelphia: Temple University Press, 1998).

24. Lipsitz, "Possessive Investment," 371.

25. Lipsitz, *Possessive Investment,* 233.

26. Matthew Frye Jacobson, *Whiteness of a Different Color: European Immigrants and the Alchemy of Race* (Cambridge, Mass.: Harvard University Press, 1998). The analysis and some of the language used here are drawn from my review of this book for *Social History* 26.1 (2001).

27. The periods were not that simple, of course; in fact, the processes were so complex that it takes Jacobson every bit of 135 pages just to describe them. Part of his problem is that his evidence does not fit his periodization; he is continually forced to explain why key developments happened outside the periods to which they belong thematically. The schema has a simple beauty at its most abstract level, but when Jacobson gets down to the details it does not hold together.

28. To be fair, neither does this chapter define race. For my take on the meaning of race, see Paul Spickard and W. Jeffrey Burroughs, "We Are a People," in *We Are a People: Narrative and Multiplicity in Constructing Ethnic Identity*, ed. Spickard and Burroughs (Philadelphia: Temple University Press, 2000), esp. 2–7. See also chapter 1 in this volume.

29. Jacobson, *Whiteness of a Different Color*, 140; emphasis added.

30. Other examples of excellence in Whiteness studies are Philip J. Deloria, *Playing Indian* (New Haven: Yale University Press, 1998); Grace Elizabeth Hale, *Making Whiteness: The Culture of Segregation in the South, 1890–1940* (New York: Vintage, 1998); and Robert G. Lee, *Orientals: Asian Americans in Popular Culture* (Philadelphia: Temple University Press, 1999).

31. Kimberlé Crenshaw, Neil Gotanda, Gary Pellar, and Kendall Thomas, eds., *Critical Race Theory* (New York: New Press, 1995); Richard Delgado, ed., *Critical Race Theory* (Philadelphia: Temple University Press, 1995).

32. Cheryl Harris, "Whiteness as Property," *Harvard Law Review* 106 (1993), abstracted in Crenshaw et al., *Critical Race Theory*, 276–91; Ian F. Haney López, *White by Law: The Legal Construction of Race* (New York: New York University Press, 1996); Richard Delgado and Jean Stefancic, eds., *Critical White Studies: Looking behind the Mirror* (Philadelphia: Temple University Press, 1997). Harris drew on a number of earlier legal studies of race, including A. Leon Higginbotham, *In the Matter of Color: Race and the American Legal Process* (New York: Oxford University Press, 1978). The title of this chapter is a play on the name of this movement. Looking beyond merely legal studies, it seeks to determine just what is critical (and what may not be) about White studies.

33. Rutherford, *Forever England*, 5.

34. Ibid.; Ignatiev and Garvey, *Race Traitor*, 10.

35. James H. Cone, *A Black Theology of Liberation*, 2d ed. (Maryknoll, N.Y.: Orbis, 1986), vii.

36. I have reported on this exercise in more detail in "Who Is an American? Teaching About Racial and Ethnic Hierarchy," *Immigration and Ethnic History Society Newsletter* 31.1 (May 1999): 1, 8–9.

37. Scrapbook in the possession of the author.

38. Noel Ignatiev, *How the Irish Became White* (New York: Routledge, 1995), 1–2.

39. Karen Brodkin, *How Jews Became White Folks and What That Says about Race in America* (New Brunswick, N.J.: Rutgers University Press, 1998). The analysis and some of the language used here are drawn from my review of this book in *Social History* 26.1 (2001).

40. Brodkin, *How Jews Became White Folks,* 22, 138.

41. This is not to assert that White groups did not suffer terribly in other settings. The Irish in Ireland suffered bitter oppression, as did Jews in Germany, Mennonites in Russia, and Armenians in Turkey. It is, however, to insist that there has been a qualitative difference between the disabilities suffered *in the United States* by lower-status Whites and those endured by people of color.

42. John Gennari, "Passing for Italian: Crooners and Gangsters in Crossover Culture," *Transition,* no. 72 (1996): 36–48, quote on p. 39.

43. Catharine A. MacKinnon, "From Practice to Theory, or What Is a White Woman Anyway?" *Yale Journal of Law and Feminism* 4 (1991): 13–33; Martha R. Mahoney, "Whiteness and Women, in Practice and Theory: A Reply to Catharine MacKinnon," *Yale Journal of Law and Feminism* 5 (1993): 217–51. For related themes, see also Abby L. Ferber, *White Man Falling: Race, Gender, and White Supremacy* (Lanham, Md.: Rowman and Littlefield, 1998); Ruth Frankenberg, *White Women, Race Matters: The Social Construction of Whiteness* (Minneapolis: University of Minnesota Press, 1993); Hauraki Greenland, "Maori Ethnicity as Ideology," in *Nga Take: Ethnic Relations and Racism in Aotearoa/ New Zealand,* ed. Paul Spoonley, David Pearson, and Cluny Macpherson (Palmerston North, N.Z.: Dunmore, 1991), 90–107; Jane Lazarre, *Beyond the Whiteness of Whiteness: Memoir of a White Mother of Black Sons* (Durham, N.C.: Duke University Press, 1996); Maureen T. Reddy, *Crossing the Color Line: Race, Parenting, and Culture* (New Brunswick, N.J.: Rutgers University Press, 1994). Lewis Gordon makes a reflexive assertion that Blacks constitute a race gendered female in "Sex, Race, and Matrices of Desire in an Antiblack World," in *Her Majesty's Other Children: Sketches of Racism from a Neocolonial Age* (Lanham, Md.: Rowman and Littlefield, 1997), 73–88.

44. bell hooks, *Ain't I a Woman: Black Women and Feminism* (Boston: South End Press, 1981); bell hooks, *Talking Back: Thinking Feminist, Thinking Black* (Boston: South End Press, 1989); Hazel V. Carby, "White Woman Listen! Black Feminism and the Boundaries of Sisterhood," in *The Empire Strikes Back: Race and Racism in 70s Britain* (London: Hutchinson, 1982); Haunani-Kay Trask, "Pacific Island Women and White Feminism," in *From a Native Daughter: Colonialism and Sovereignty in Hawai'i* (Monroe, Maine: Common Courage Press, 1993), 263–77; Donna Awatere, *Maori Sovereignty* (Auckland, N.Z.: Bradsheet, 1984), 42 and passim.

45. Matt Wray and Annalee Newitz, eds., *White Trash: Race and Class in America* (New York: Routledge, 1997), back cover.

46. Thandeka, "The Cost of Whiteness," *Tikkun* 14.3 (May–June 1999): 33–38. See also Thandeka, *Learning to Be White: Money, Race, and God in America* (New York: Continuum, 1999).

47. I made this investigation of www.amazon.com connections on July 29, 2000. Jim Goad, *The Redneck Manifesto: How Hillbillies, Hicks, and White Trash Became America's Scapegoats* (New York: Touchstone, 1998); Michael A. Hoffman, *They Were White and They Were Slaves: The Untold Story of the Enslavement of Whites in Early America* (New York: Wiswell House, 1992); James Ronald Kennedy, *The South Was Right!* (New York: Pelican, 1994). Cf. Jeffrey Kaplan, ed., *Encyclopedia of White Power: A Sourcebook on the Radical Racist Right* (Walnut Creek, Calif.: Alta Mira Press, 2000).

48. See, for example, Walter Benn Michaels, "Race into Culture: A Critical Genealogy of Cultural Identity," *Critical Inquiry* 18 (1992): 655–85; Avery Gordon and Christopher Newfield, "Critical Response: White Philosophy," *Critical Inquiry* 20 (1994), 737–57; Walter Benn Michaels, "Critical Response: The No-Drop Rule," *Critical Inquiry* 20 (1994): 758–69; Barbara J. Flagg, " 'Was Blind, But Now I See': White Race Consciousness and the Requirement of Discriminatory Intent," *Michigan Law Review* 91 (1993): 953–1017; Micaela di Leonardo, "White Ethnicities, Identity Politics, and Baby Bear's Chair," *Social Text*, no. 41 (winter 1994): 174–91; Shelly Fisher Fishkin, "Interrogating 'Whiteness,' Complicating 'Blackness': Remapping American Culture," *American Quarterly* 47.3 (1995): 428–66; Walter Benn Michaels, *Our America: Nativism, Modernism, and Pluralism* (Durham, N.C.: Duke University Press, 1995); Liam Kennedy, "Alien Nation: White Male Paranoia and Imperial Culture in the United States," *Journal of American Studies* 30 (1996): 87–100; Mike Hill, ed., *Whiteness: A Critical Reader* (New York: New York University Press, 1997); Michelle Fine et al., eds., *Off White: Readings on Race, Power, and Society* (New York: Routledge, 1997); Henry A. Giroux, "Rewriting the Discourse of Racial Identity: Towards a Pedagogy and Politics of Whiteness," *Harvard Educational Review* 67.2 (1997): 285–320; Howard Winant, "Behind Blue Eyes: Whiteness and Contemporary U.S. Racial Politics," *New Left Review*, no. 225 (September–October, 1997): 73–88; Jonathan W. Warren and France Winddance Twine, "White Americans, the New Minority? Non-Blacks and the Ever-Expanding Boundaries of Whiteness," *Journal of Black Studies* 28.2 (1997): 200–218; Ruth Frankenberg, *Displacing Whiteness: Essays in Social and Cultural Criticism* (Durham, N.C.: Duke University Press, 1997); Richard Dyer, *White* (London: Routledge, 1997); Joe Kincheloe, Shirley R. Steinberg, Nelson M. Rodriguez, and Ronald E. Chennault, eds., *White Reign: Deploying Whiteness in America* (New York: St. Martin's Press, 1998); Dona D. Nelson, *National Manhood: Capitalist Citizenship and the Imagined Fraternity*

of White Men (Durham, N.C.: Duke University Press, 1998); John Gabriel, *Whitewash: Racialized Politics and the Media* (New York: Routledge, 1998); Valerie Babb, *Whiteness Visible: The Meaning of Whiteness in American Literature and Culture* (New York: New York University Press, 1998); Thomas K. Nakayama and Judith N. Martin, eds., *Whiteness: The Communication of Social Identity* (Thousand Oaks, Calif.: Sage, 1999); Maurice Berger, *White Lies: Race and the Myths of Whiteness* (New York: Farrar, Straus and Giroux, 1999); Christine Clark and James O'Donnell, eds., *Becoming and Unbecoming White: Owning and Disowning a Racial Identity* (Westport, Conn.: Bergin and Garvey, 1999); Timothy B. Powell, ed., *Beyond the Binary: Reconstructing Cultural Identity in a Multicultural Context* (New Brunswick, N.J.: Rutgers University Press, 1999); Chris Weedon, *Feminism, Theory, and the Politics of Difference* (Oxford: Blackwell, 1999); Sarah Barnet-Weiser, *The Most Beautiful Girl in the World: Beauty Pageants and National Identity* (Berkeley: University of California Press, 1999); Patricia McKee, *Producing American Races: Henry James, William Faulkner, Toni Morrison* (Durham, N.C.: Duke University Press, 1999); John Hartigan, *Racial Situations: Class Predicaments of Whiteness in Detroit* (Princeton: Princeton University Press, 1999); Chris J. Cuomo and Kim Q. Hall, eds., *Whiteness: Feminist Philosophical Reflections* (Lanham, Md.: Rowman and Littlefield, 1999); Renee R. Curry, *White Women Writing White: H. D., Elizabeth Bishop, Sylvia Plath* (New York: Greenwood, 2000); Aime M. Carrillo Rowe, "Locating Feminism's Subject: The Paradox of White Feminity and the Struggle to Forge Feminist Alliances," *Communication Theory* 10.1 (2000): 64–80; Barbara A. Miller, "'Anchoring' White Community: White Women Activists and the Politics of Public Schools," *Identities* 6.4 (2000): 481–512; John Tehranian, "Performing Whiteness: Naturalization Litigation and the Construct of Racial Identity in America," *Yale Law Journal* 109.4 (2000): 817 ff.; Kalpana Seshari Crooks, *Desiring Whiteness: A Lacanian Analysis of Race* (New York: Routledge, 2000); Nelson M. Rodriguez and Leila E. Villaverde, eds., *Dismantling White Privilege: Pedagogy, Politics, and Whiteness* (New York: Peter Lang, 2000); Walter Bronwen, *Outsiders Inside: Whiteness, Place and Irish Women* (New York: Routledge, 2001).

49. See, for example, *The White Issue*, no. 73 of *Transition* (1996).

50. Richard Delgado makes essentially the same point, expressing amazement at "how white people, even ones of good will, twist discussions concerning race so that the conversation becomes about themselves." Delgado, *Critical Race Theory*, xiii.

PART 4

Multiracial Challenges to the Racial Binary

II

BLACK NO MORE OR MORE THAN BLACK?

Multiracial Identity Politics and the Multiracial Movement

G. REGINALD DANIEL

MULTIRACIAL IDENTITY AS A RACIAL PROJECT

The One-Drop Rule

The one-drop rule has had unintended consequences. Although its purpose was to draw boundaries that solidified racial subordination, it legitimated and forged African American identity. This formed the basis for the mass mobilization that ultimately led to the dismantling of Jim Crow segregation—including the removal of the last legal prohibitions against intermarriage in 1967—and the implementation of civil rights legislation. This in turn has resulted in increased intermarriage. Many interracial couples have challenged the one-drop rule by seeking to bring both Black and White backgrounds to the identity of their offspring. By the 1990s this growing population of interracial couples and offspring began lobbying for and successfully brought about changes in official racial classification that would make possible a "multiracial" identification. This multiracial phenomenon, combined with the post–Civil Rights Acts eradication of formal expressions of racism, has significant implications for racial formation in the United States, particularly considering the specificity of the place of Blackness in U.S. jurisprudence and the fact that African Americans have historically been the largest designated racial "minority" in the United States.

The Multiracial Experience

The dismantling of Jim Crow segregation and the implementation of civil rights legislation over the past thirty years dissolved formal barriers to equality. Although approximately 94 percent to 98 percent of Blacks and Whites still marry within their respective communities, comparatively more fluid social relations have led to increased intermarriage. The number of interracial couples continued steadily to increase such that by the 1990s there were approximately 1.5 million interracial unions, of which 883,000 were White-other unions and 246,000 were Black-White unions.[1]

Although statistical surveys do not make it possible to tabulate reliable data on the number of offspring from Black-White marriages, it is believed that there are from 600,000 to several million, ranging in age from infancy to young adulthood.[2] By the 1990s large numbers of Black-White couples and the growing population born to these unions had become part of a multiracial consciousness. This consciousness now encompasses a wide range of national advocacy groups and forums representing the interests of its actual and potential adherents, including individuals from a variety of racial backgrounds.

Yet the movement has attracted a disproportionate number of Black-White interracial couples and their first-generation (or "biracial") offspring because of the unique challenges presented by the one-drop rule. It has attracted a smaller number of "multigenerational" individuals who have backgrounds that have been blended for several generations and have been socially designated as members of the various traditional U.S. racial groups (e.g., European American, African American, Native American, Latina/o American). However, these individuals have resisted identifying solely with those socially assigned communities.

This multiracial consciousness has taken the form of micro-level racial projects in which single actors are the agents of resistance. It has also been manifest in collective action in the form of a full-scale social movement. On the one hand, multiracial consciousness is necessarily a discursive or cultural initiative, an interpretation, representation, or explanation of racial dynamics by means of multiracial identity politics, that is, racial signification and identity formation. What binds multiracial-identified individuals together most powerfully is the shared experience of racial liminality based on simultaneous identification with two (or more) different parent racial reference groups or backgrounds.[3]

Despite myriad differences in backgrounds, experiences, and identities and the fact that the experience of multiraciality, like other racial identities, is refracted through the lenses of sex and gender, class, and a host of other social categories, the common denominator among multiracial-identified individuals is the shared experience of liminality resulting directly from an identity that embraces multiple backgrounds.[4] Most multiracial individuals will never know each other. Yet in the minds of many lives the image of their communion (or imagined community), which provides connections across social and geographic space as well as across time.[5]

On the other hand, multiracial consciousness is a political initiative, which not only seeks to explain racial dynamics and reorganize the social structure along particular racial lines but also calls on the state to play a significant role in bringing this about. This political initiative has been most visible in the context of the decennial census— particularly the 1990 and 2000 censuses—and is all the more logical and critical if one considers the fact that the state is composed of institutions, policies, conditions, and rules that support and justify it and the social relations in which they are embedded.[6] More important, the racial state has historically exercised power not only in the politics of racial exclusion (and inclusion) but also, and especially, in enforcing racial definition and classification originating in the one-drop rule.

Any changes in official racial classification allowing for a multiracial identification would have consequences in the distribution of resources, in the enforcement and support of civil rights legislation and claims aimed at tracking historical and contemporary patterns of discrimination, and in achieving social and economic equity. Yet the mobilization of interracial couples and multiracial-identified individuals into a multiracial consciousness movement is not specifically aimed at achieving gains or advancement. Rather, the new multiracial identity politics has been aimed at rescuing multiracial identities from their distortion and erasure by the larger society's continued enforcement of the one-drop rule. This has involved the task of creating new identities, new collective subjectivities, and new meanings in hitherto unrecognized ways as these relate to pluralism and integration. It also recombines preexisting ideas and values about racial egalitarianism, which demand that both dominant and subordinate groups make major and more complex if subtle changes in terms of definitions of self and community, difference and hierarchy, and go well beyond any questions of gaining increased advantages in the political economy.

The Culture of Racial Resistance: From "War of Maneuver" to "War of Position"

The Civil Rights Movement and the Loving Decision

In the past, interracial couples and multiracial individuals have variously counterpoised their forms of organization and identity to the dehumanizing and enforced invisibility imposed by the dictatorial and comprehensively dominant White power structure. However, this racially defined opposition has historically been forced both outward, to the margins of society, and inward, to the relative safety of their own communities in what Antonio Gramsci has defined as a "war of maneuver."[7] This can be attributed to the lack of an officially defined larger collective subjectivity based on a multiracial identification and to the fact that interracial couples and multiracial-identified individuals historically have been anathematized and have lacked social standing. Consequently, they have lacked a significant power base on which to mount opposition that would achieve strategic incursions into the mainstream political process.

By virtue of this combination of factors, the new multiracial consciousness does not display historical continuity with previous multiracial identity projects, as has been the case, for example, with the long and continuous history of African American resistance and the struggle for civil rights. There is a historical parallel between the tri-racial isolate[8] and multiracial consciousness movement appeals for changes in official racial classification. Yet the motivation for the appeals differs significantly: the former originated in the desire to escape the social stigma of Blackness, whereas the latter originates in the desire to embrace an identity that reflects the various back-grounds in one's genealogy.

In addition, the Chicago-based Biracial Family Network (founded in 1980) and its predecessor in that city, the Manasseh Society (founded in the 1890s), seem to be directly related to similar historical cir-cumstances in turn-of-the-century Chicago that led to an opening up of opportunities for increased interracial marriage but also to iso-lation from the overwhelmingly hostile racial climate in the larger society during that period. However, most other similar organiza-tions that arose during the 1940s and 1950s in Los Angeles, Wash-ington, D.C., and Detroit were not in response to any national or local trend of increasing interracial marriages per se.[9] Rather, they were specifically organized by interracial military families returning to the United States after World War II from abroad, particularly Europe, where many had experienced comparatively greater accep-tance by the larger society. For the most part, the founders of con-temporary support groups have not, therefore, drawn inspiration from previous groups when inaugurating their own organizations and have generally been unaware of the existence of such groups.[10]

Thus the multiracial consciousness movement cannot be viewed as part of a continuous collective tradition of resistance to the one-drop rule, despite its natural affinity with some previous multiracial identity projects. The emergence of the movement is more directly related to and is one of the many fruits of the efforts and gains of the African American–led civil rights movement that dismantled Jim Crow segregation. Beginning after World War II, African Americans and other subordinated racial groups were able to make sustained strategic incursions into the mainstream political process. Indeed, the racial upsurges of the 1950s and 1960s were among the most tem-pestuous events in postwar U.S. history.[11]

Prepared in large measure by tactics that were employed under conditions of the war of maneuver, the struggles for voting rights, the sit-ins and boycotts to desegregate public facilities, the urban rebellions of the mid-1960s, and the political mobilizations of

Latinas/os, Native Americans, Asian Americans, Pacific Islanders, and so on, dramatically transformed the political and cultural landscape of the United States. More important, new conceptions of racial identity and its meaning, new modes of political organization and confrontation, and new definitions of the state's role in promoting and achieving "equality" were explored, debated, and contested on the battlegrounds of politics. These racial "minority" movements achieved comparatively limited but very real reforms. And these gains would provide a foundation for other oppositional political projects that eventually could confront the racial state in what Gramsci calls a "war of position."[12]

It could be argued that the continued existence of restrictions against interracial marriage was a direct affront to the achievement of full equality in the primary sphere. Yet the war of maneuver mounted by the African American–led civil rights movement, which ended legalized segregation in the public sphere, neither specifically attacked the restrictions against interracial marriage nor called into question the one-drop rule. Even with the removal of legal restrictions of interracial marriages, the one-drop rule continued to operate as a nearly "natural" phenomenon and a matter of "common sense" that remained unquestioned. Indeed, the one-drop rule is the linchpin of the U.S. binary racial project. It has become what Pierre Bourdieu calls *doxa,* a sacred, sacrosanct, and unquestioned social concept or dogma.[13]

Robert E. T. Roberts's interviews with individuals in Chicago would seem to confirm this and indicate the national trend. His data reveal that from the 1930s through the 1960s the majority of offspring of interracial marriages identified themselves as African American, although by the 1950s about one-third insisted on being identified as both Black and White.[14] In addition, data indicate that the June 12, 1967, *Loving* decision—which removed the last legal prohibitions against racial intermarriage—was not accompanied by an organized challenge, even by interracial couples themselves, to social forces that precluded multiracial identification through the enforcement of the one-drop rule. The 1970 census—the first to allow self-identification—and the 1980 and 1990 censuses indicate continuing high levels of parents' designation of their multiracial offspring as Black.[15]

Since the only alternative was the "other" box, it is possible that many couples selected "Black" in the tradition of the one-drop rule but were actually raising their children as biracial. Also, these data say more about the parents' than the children's choice of identities. Whatever the case may be, most Black-White interracial couples continued to identify their offspring as Black. In addition, these individuals were considered as such by the larger society. The one-drop rule, if originally oppressive, has not only been a means of mobilizing Blacks in the struggle against White privilege but also the site of unorthodoxy and resistance to commonsense notions of Black identity based on that rule, which paradoxically sowed the seeds of its own demise. With the exception of I-Pride (Interracial/Intercultural Pride), formed in February 1979, which petitioned the Berkeley Public schools to make it possible for their offspring to be identified as "interracial" on school forms, there was no organized collective mobilization against enforcement of the one-drop rule.

Yet gains achieved by interracial couples through the *Loving* decision provided the diverse institutional and cultural terrain on which other oppositional projects in the manner of a war of position could be mounted and on which the racial state could be confronted to bring about changes in official racial classification. Indeed, the new multiracial consciousness movement, like other racial movements, is inconceivable without the racial state, which provides a focus for political demands and structures the racial order, particularly regarding racial classification. By 1988 a critical mass of interracial couples and multiracial-identified individuals began lobbying for, and in the 1990s successfully brought about, changes in official racial classification that would make possible a "multiracial" identification.

From Civil Rights to Black Power

The African American–led civil rights movement that began in the 1950s was initially organized with the goal of integration. That perspective provided an analytic framework by which to assess the situation of African Americans and shaped the movement's political agenda. The early movement leaders were racial moderates who sought to end "race-thinking" and assure egalitarian integration of each individual under the tenets of the American creed. The movement initially focused its energies on the South, where the integration paradigm remained a challenging ideology to the racist logic of segregation in the manner of inegalitarian pluralism.[16]

At the same time, the problem of racial injustice and inequality was generally understood in a more limited fashion, as a matter of prejudiced attitudes or bigotry. In the liberal tradition of Gunnar Myrdal, the solution to the "American dilemma" was to be found in ending discriminatory practices—which would involve the overcoming of such attitudes and the achievement of tolerance, specifically among European Americans—and passing laws that prohibited discrimination with respect to access to public accommodations, jobs, education, and so on. The early civil rights movement explicitly reflected these views. In its litigation activities and agitation for civil rights legislation it sought to challenge discriminatory practices. In its espousal of integration and its quest for a "beloved community" it sought to overcome racial prejudice by appealing to the moral conscience of the nation.[17]

Later, when demands for racial reforms attained national scope and expanded beyond the African American movement to other racially defined minorities, the limited explanatory abilities and programmatic usefulness of the integration paradigm were revealed. The emergence of the slogan "Black power" (and soon after, of "Brown power," "Red power," and "Yellow power"), along with the wave of uprisings that swept through the central cities between 1964 and 1968 and the founding of radical movement organizations of a nationalist and Marxist orientation, coincided with the recognition that racial inequality and injustice were not simply the products of prejudice, nor was discrimination only a matter of intentionally informed action in the manner of inegalitarian pluralism. Rather, prejudice had much deeper roots and was an almost unavoidable outcome of patterns of socialization that were "bred in the bone," affecting not only Whites but racial "minorities" themselves.[18]

Far from manifesting itself only (or even principally) through individual actions or conscious policies, discrimination was the product of centuries of systematic exclusion, exploitation, and disregard of racially defined minorities. The combination of prejudice, discrimination, and institutional inequality defined the concept of racism at the end of the 1960s. Although the term had surfaced occasionally in the past, it did not become part of the lexicon of racial "common sense" until the 1960s.[19]

By the late 1960s the ambiguous triumph of the civil rights movement, therefore, not only led to a redefinition of the basis and meaning of racial inequality but also a sharp break with the integrationist vision on the part of many individuals seeking to achieve a racially egalitarian society. To some extent this opposition to integration occurred because the term had become closely identified with the problematic concept of the melting pot and thus synonymous with assimilation, that is, inegalitarian integration. The melting pot ideology, which called for conformity to Anglo-Protestant ideals, was established to incorporate European-descent Americans but effectively excluded Americans of color. It was thus viewed as the convergence of two inegalitarian paradigms—assimilation for European-descent individuals and apartheid for groups perceived as ethnoracially different. Furthermore, assimilation was considered a patronizing inegalitarian integration that created the illusion of power sharing without Anglo-Protestant Americans actually giving up control.

Any discussion of egalitarian integration seemed to deny the extreme power differences that existed between European Americans and Americans of color. If egalitarian integration were in fact to become a reality—albeit in the very distant future—it could not be achieved until the long and arduous struggle to achieve equality of difference had been won. Many activists felt that the best way to achieve these goals was to recover their own sense of themselves and become more effective as a collective in the world by building a power base in the manner of egalitarian group pluralism. What they envisioned, therefore, was a process of dissimilation that would give rise to a type of intergroup accommodation: a mosaic of mutually respectful separate, if not completely autonomous, racial and ethnic pluralities with de jure and de facto equal status.[20]

In the new scenario envisioned by the racial movements of the 1960s and 1970s, pluralism would be voluntary rather than mandated and enforced by European Americans, as had been the case with the apartheid paradigm. More important, if and when people of color chose to integrate, they would do so with the bargaining power of equals. The prevailing belief was that the rights and privileges of individuals as equal pluralities were premised not simply on the extension of equality by the removal of racial barriers. They also rested on the status of equality achieved by the group as a collective plurality, which would necessarily be facilitated in part through compensatory programs such as affirmative action. Both affirmative action and the racial creed have relied on color consciousness, that is, taking racial differences into account in the pursuit of their goals. Yet the goal of the racial creed was to exclude individuals on the basis of racial group membership, which prevented them from being able to integrate as equal individual pluralities into mainstream U.S. society according to the tenets of the American creed. Affirmative action, therefore, was a response to these previous and continuing color conscious attitudes and policies, and its goal was to achieve the equality of difference in the manner of egalitarian pluralism.

Accordingly, egalitarian group pluralism was seen as a necessary prerequisite to right a previous wrong in which difference had been the vehicle for perpetuating inequality, for depriving individuals of color of their rights as equally valued pluralities based on merit and excellence according to the color-blind tenets of the American creed (though standards for judging "merit" and "excellence" were not necessarily considered unambiguous or unproblematic). In sum, the affirmative action debate started with a simple, straightforward, and incontestable proposition: in a truly egalitarian integrated United States, there would be no need even to raise the question of affirmative action. If, in fact, this American creed based on individual equal rights had been the overriding philosophy by which the United States was to operate, inegalitarian group pluralism in the manner of apartheid precluded its fulfillment.[21]

Integrationists, in contradistinction to pluralists, sought to redefine (or reaffirm) their vision of race relations based on the premises of a universal humanism supporting the democratic principles of individual free association. They also sought to acknowledge the legacy of racism, without at the same time perpetuating the Manichean distinction between "White guilt" and "people of color victimization." Nevertheless, some integrationists predicated their vision on a myopic understanding of egalitarian pluralism. They believed that merely focusing on epidermal differences reinforced a divisive us/them dynamic that undermined the basic liberal democratic principles of individual free association but also framed these goals in a manner that failed to distinguish inegalitarian (or assimilationist) integration from egalitarian integration.

Consequently, they frequently misunderstood much of the admittedly abrasive and often chauvinistic rhetoric of many radical pluralists. They interpreted what was actually a defensive pro–people of color stance aimed at forging an oppositional egalitarian plurality as a means of mobilizing people of color against racial oppression as an offensive anti-White stance seeking to replace European American domination with a new domination by people of color.[22]

Some integrationists also began to believe that the official discrediting and repudiation of the ideology of White supremacy, and the elimination of de jure impediments to racial equality, had led to a decline in the significance of race if not de facto eradication of racism. Consequently, many were coming to view government intervention in enforcing affirmative action and racial discrimination regulations as no longer necessary and in fact detrimental to the project of eliminating the socioeconomic inequality that admittedly continued to plague African Americans. Some even argued that these entitlement programs were contrary to the American creed and had in fact gone too far in balancing the scales of racial justice such that they had now become a form of reverse discrimination against Whites.[23]

From Civil Rights to Multiracial Consciousness

By the 1970s the racial movements had lost their vitality and coherence as the result of repression, co-optation, and fragmentation. The ensuing economic, political, and cultural crises of the period led to erosion in the clarity of the term "racism," or "racial discrimination." By the 1980s even the moderate gains in racial equality also came under attack from a backlash composed of an alliance of right-wing and conservative forces. Despite these setbacks, racially based movements of the 1950s and 1960s—particularly the Black civil rights and consciousness movements—created what has sometimes been referred to as "the great transformation" of racial awareness and racial subjectivity. Race came to be understood not only as a matter of politics, economics, or culture but also as a matter of all three lived simultaneously. The racial movements of the period, therefore, were the first new social movements, that is, the first to expand the concerns of politics to the terrain of everyday life. Accordingly, race was considered a preeminently social phenomenon, something that not only penetrates state institutions and market relationships but also suffuses each individual identity, each family and community. These forces irreversibly expanded the terrain of political contest and set the stage for the general reorganization of U.S. politics.[24]

Taken together, the eclipse of the assimilationist integration paradigm and the emergence of new social movement politics premised on egalitarian group pluralism constitute an alternative or oppositional framework by which to assess the racial politics of the 1960s. This process gradually took shape within the civil rights movement as the challenge it had launched against segregation in the U.S. South was transformed into a national movement against racism. With the weakening of the assimilation paradigm and the growth of perspectives within the pluralistic paradigm of race, a vacuum was left in racial theory and politics. This created the political space for the resurgence of the assimilation paradigm in the 1980s.

Yet even as previous gains were rolled back beginning in the 1970s and most organizations proved unable to rally a mass constituency in communities of color, the racial meanings and new racial identities that developed during the 1960s persisted and continue to shape politics. They stand out as the single truly formidable obstacle to the consolidation of a new oppressive racial order, even in the period of reaction that began in the 1970s and 1980s. Apparently, the movements themselves could disintegrate, the policies for which they fought could be reversed, and their leaders could be co-opted or destroyed, but the racial subjectivity and self-awareness they developed had taken permanent hold and could not be reversed by any amount of repression or co-optation. The forging of new collective racial identities or subjectivities during that period has been the enduring legacy of the racial movements and suggests that racial identity, the racial state, and the very nature of racial politics as a whole were radically transformed.[25]

The new social movement politics would later prove contagious, leading to the mobilization of other groups—students, feminists, gays, and so on—that have drawn on the African American struggle "as a central organizational fact or as a defining political metaphor and inspiration." In the late 1970s, with the formation of I-Pride, this contagion spread to interracial couples and multiracial-identified individuals. In fact, many of the interracial couples as well as multiracial-identified adults in the vanguard of the multiracial movement came of age in the 1960s and were actively involved in the civil rights movement.[26] By the 1990s what had begun a decade earlier as a somewhat marginalized racial project organized by and largely limited to the membership of I-Pride expanded to include the growing number of similar support groups and educational organizations. Their constituents, along with other supporters, took their demands to the state, the site of official racial classification. This not only escalated and expanded the resistance to the informal maintenance of the one-drop rule but also led to the formation of a full-scale social movement organized to formally dismantle this device at the municipal, state, and national levels.

The carriers of the new multiracial identity—benefiting, as have other individuals of African descent, from the comparatively more fluid intergroup relations and from socioeconomic gains resulting from the first steps toward civil rights, particularly as evidenced in affirmative action programs—are not, therefore, seeking special privileges that would be precluded by identifying as Black. This identity represents, rather, the next logical step in the progression of civil rights, the expansion of our notion of affirmative action to include strategies not only for achieving socioeconomic equity but also for affirming a nondichotomous and nonhierarchical identity that embraces a holocentric racial self.

This new identity recognizes the commonalities among Blacks and Whites in the manner of egalitarian integration and, at the same time, appreciates the differences in the manner of egalitarian pluralism. More important, it is posited on an egalitarian blending of pluralism and integration in which Blacks and Whites are seen as relative, rather than absolute, extremes on a continuum of grays. Accordingly, this identity builds on the egalitarian pluralist tenets of the racial movements of the late 1960s, which sought to achieve the equality of difference, but resuscitates the integrationist goals of the late 1950s and early 1960s, which were rejected because of their assimilationist undercurrent, by simultaneously seeking to replace this hierarchical integration with a more egalitarian dynamic.

THE 1990 CENSUS: ENCOUNTERING THE RACIAL STATE

Challenging the Unstable Racial Equilibrium

When interracial couples in Berkeley, California, founded I-Pride in 1979 to provide support for interracial families, its specific goal was to get the Berkeley Public Schools to accurately reflect the identity of their offspring by including a multiracial designator on school forms. During 1979–80, the Berkeley Public Schools added the category "interracial" to its school forms, the first such designator in modern U.S. history. However, the national firestorm over the statistical implications of multiracial identity was not ignited until ten years later with the appearance of a January 20, 1988, *Federal Register* notice published by the Office of Management and Budget (OMB), the branch of the government responsible for implementing changes in federal statistical surveys. The notice solicited public comment on potential revisions in Directive No. 15, which was issued and implemented in May 1977 as the federal standard for collecting and presenting data on race and ethnicity.[27] The revisions would permit individuals to identify themselves as "other," if they believed they did not fall into one of the four basic official racial categories — Black, White, Asian/Pacific Islander, American Indian or Alaska Native—or into the so-called "ethnic" category—Hispanic or not of Hispanic origin.[28] Heretofore, the OMB advised that where there was uncertainty the category that most reflected the individual's recognition in his or her community should be used. (Although an "Other" category has not been used on all statistical surveys, it has been provided on each census since 1910 to increase the response rate to the race question. Write-in responses in the "Other" category are necessarily reassigned to one of the traditional racial categories.)

Many interracial couples and multiracial-identified individuals requested that a multiracial or biracial identifier, instead of "Other," be added to the five categories. (On the 1970 census multiracial offspring were classified in terms of the father's racial identity; in 1980 the Census Bureau shifted to a formula relying on the identity of the mother. Many multiracial children who have European American mothers thus have been designated as "White." In neither case, however, have they been designated as "multiracial" or "biracial.")[29]

The OMB received overwhelmingly negative responses from the public to the proposed changes in Directive No. 15, particularly the addition of a multiracial identifier. Among those who responded negatively were federal agencies such as the Civil Rights Division of the Department of Justice, the Department of Health and Human Services, the Equal Employment Opportunity Commission, the Office of Personnel Management, and several large corporations. Opposition was based in part on logistical and financial concerns about the increased burden of data collection, paperwork, changes in the format of forms and computer programs for data analysis, and the data burden on respondents.[30]

Various African American leaders and organizations also opposed the change. They argued that most if not all African Americans have some European or Native American ancestry (although most identify solely with the Black community) and that many individuals would designate themselves as "multiracial," rather than Black, to escape the continuing social stigma associated with African Americans. Similar concerns were expressed by individuals and organizations representing other traditional communities of color.

In addition, opponents argued that the one-drop rule, while originally oppressive, has been a means of mobilizing communities of color in the struggle against White racial privilege. More important, this mechanism has prevented a reduction in the number of individuals who would be counted as members of the traditional communities of color. These numbers are needed to enforce and support civil rights legislation and claims aimed at tracking historical and contemporary patterns of discrimination. They were particularly important in arriving at goals for achieving social and economic equity in the manner of affirmative action.

Conflict, Crisis, and Insulation

On November 12, 1988, the Association of Multiethnic Americans (AMEA) was formed in Berkeley. It would serve as an umbrella organization for a national network of more than fifty support groups pressuring for the addition of a multiracial identifier on the decennial census. These organizations included groups such as Multiracial Americans of Southern California (MASC) in Los Angeles, the Biracial Family Network (BFN) in Chicago, the Interracial Family Alliance (IFA) in Atlanta, and the Interracial Family Circle (IFC) in Washington, D.C. This coalition also included A Place for Us/National, a national nondenominational religious support network for interracial families. The AMEA's overall goal was to promote healthy images of interracial couples and multiracial individuals. Its specific purpose was to increase public awareness about the importance of adding a multiracial identifier on the decennial census. A flurry of telephone calls and correspondence between officials at the OMB and the Census Bureau and various individual groups affiliated with the AMEA ultimately resulted in some consensus about how multiracial individuals might be accommodated on the 1990 census.

Before the founding of the AMEA, there was no national agent to coordinate strategies for getting official recognition of multiracial-identified individuals. More important, from the racial state's standpoint before that time, multiracial identity politics was effectively a marginalized political project located outside the normal terrain of state activity that coexisted with the unstable racial equilibrium. However, the disparity, or conflict, between the preexisting racial order, organized and enforced by the state, and the growing oppositional ideology whose subjects were the real and potential adherents of a movement composed of intermarried couples and multiracial-identified individuals would eventually lead to what racial formation theory defines as a crisis phase.

Ultimately, the movement's efforts led to a minor but not insignificant reform in official policy that was enacted in part to meet opposition demands. In response, state institutions (the OMB and the Census Bureau) realized that the demand for recognition of multiracial-identified individuals was a greater irritant (or potential threat) to the racial order before these demands were met than after they were adopted in suitably moderate form. Accordingly, the state adopted a protracted policy of insulation, which confined the demand for the official recognition of multiracial-identified individuals to a terrain that was, if not entirely symbolic, at least not absolutely crucial to the operation of the racial order.[31]

Census officials quietly passed the word on to support groups that they would accept "biracial," "multiracial," or some other designation clearly indicating a blended identity as write-in responses in the "Other" category. Furthermore, these write-ins would be coded so that the actual number of people who identify in this manner could be counted. This would give the OMB a clearer indication of what, if any, changes should be made to include a multiracial identifier on the 2000 census.

This change in policy in the 1990 census is a radical departure from previous censuses. At no point previously had multiracial individuals been enumerated separately from an overarching African American statistical aggregate. On previous censuses, the enumeration of African Americans as Black and multiracial (mulatto, quadroon, octoroon, etc.) has been more a semantic distinction with few real social implications. Yet in neither case have individuals actually officially been designated as multiracial. Furthermore, these data do not make it possible to determine either how many individuals have an African component in their multiracial identity (except those who identified with terms more clearly associated with African ancestry, e.g., Creole, mulatto) or the various multiple backgrounds that constitute the larger multiracial-identified population. Therefore, none of the approximately 253,000 multiracial responses in the "Other" category could be used as a accurate estimate of the actual number of individuals who identify as multiracial, not to mention the vast numbers of individuals who followed the tradition of circling one box because they were unaware of any other alternative.

THE 2000 CENSUS: REFORMING THE RACIAL STATE

From Insulation to Rearticulation

Efforts to get the U.S. Census Bureau to add the term "multiracial" to the 1990 census were unsuccessful. Nevertheless, Project RACE (Reclassify All Children Equally)—an activist, informational, and educational organization founded in 1991—explicitly sought to politicize racial identities further through "normal politics" (state legislation, potential legal action, the Petri "Tiger Woods" Bill, etc.).[32] Project RACE made significant progress in gaining support at the state and municipal levels using the stand-alone multiracial identifier format (with the option in several states to break out the numbers in the multiracial category into the minimum single racial categories to the extent that administrative needs make this necessary). Because of the efforts of Project RACE, forms for the Operation Desert Shield/Storm Deployment Survey included a multiracial designator for the offspring of returning intermarried veterans and several states included "multiracial" as an acceptable official means of self-identification. A 1994 survey of eight hundred public school districts, conducted by the Education Office for Civil Rights, found that approximately 30 percent of the school districts use a special separate category. Some districts simply use the mother's racial designation; others use the father's.

The American College Testing Program (ACT), which is the alternative to the Scholastic Aptitude Test (SAT) college entrance exam, included "multiracial" as an acceptable means of identification. Most universities were resistant to any changes in the collection of racial data. However, Williams College in Williamston, Massachusetts, included a multiracial identifier on its official forms. Beginning in 1989, reports prepared by the Center for Assessment and Demographic Studies at Gallaudet University in Washington, D.C., counted individuals who indicated identification with a multiracial background. Nevertheless, these data were necessarily reassigned at the federal level to one of the four official racial categories (and the "Hispanic" identifier, when it is given as an option) or to the figures for *each* of the single-race groups with which multiracial individuals identify. This would be especially important when totaling the numbers for the historically underrepresented groups of color for the purposes of affirmative action.

Project RACE's successes helped to lay the foundation for a series of potential conflicts within and among state agencies (the standalone multiracial identifier at the state and municipal levels and the demand for single-race identifiers at the federal level). Correspondingly, particular demands were confronted and the terms of the state response were debated (concessions made to the "Other" category as compared to a stand-alone multiracial identifier, a check-more-than-one format, or a combined format that uses a multiracial identifier along with a check-more-than-one format). Strategic unity, therefore, became more necessary for the governing forces in order to guarantee the relative unity of the racial state by reducing the stakes of intrastate or interinstitutional conflict. This not only posed formidable obstacles to the fomenting of oppositional political projects but also minimized the government's need to strategize. More important, it helped to guarantee the likelihood of the automatic rearticulation of the prevailing order, obviously an optimum situation from the standpoint of the dominant racial groups.

Agency and constituent groups began exploring the range of potential accommodations, the possibilities for reconsidering the racial order, and their possible roles in a racial ideology "rearticulated" in light of oppositional themes.[33] Some agencies at the state and municipal levels (particularly public schools) had moved toward accommodation to challenging forces, whereas others (the OMB and the

Census Bureau) had remained entrenched in a protracted struggle to delay if not prevent changes at the federal level. Nevertheless, beginning in June 1993, officials in the nation's capital had begun a comprehensive review process to determine what changes could be made in this direction for the 2000 census. In March 1994 the OMB established and held the first meeting of the Interagency Committee for the Review of the Racial and Ethnic Standards. Given the range of suggestions and criticisms concerning Directive No. 15, the OMB sought in constituting the committee to have all agency stakeholders participate in this comprehensive review of the standards.

From Rearticulation to Incorporation

When the social changes set in motion by the multiracial consciousness movement, along with the persistence of its leadership, further threatened to disrupt the racial equilibrium, institutional competition and conflict within the state was augmented, and the establishment or restoration of conditions of a new unstable equilibrium became paramount. Reform policies of absorption (incorporation) were initiated and deemed potentially effective for achieving this goal.

On July 9, 1997, after extensive cognitive research and field testing of sample households, the OMB announced its findings and recommendations in a 150-page report prepared by the Interagency Task Force, which consisted of some thirty governmental agencies charged with the task of exploring possible changes in the collection of data on race and ethnicity. The report recommended that federal data collection forms be changed so that individuals could check one or more racial identifications. (The key findings based on the comprehensive review were that between 1.0 and 1.5 percent of the public would select a multiracial identifier when offered the opportunity to do so.) It unequivocally rejected a stand-alone multiracial identifier as well as the combined format, because, among other things, they would require too many changes in forms, would be too difficult for respondents, would be potentially divisive, and would undermine the historical continuity of data.[34]

On October 30, 1997, the OMB finally approved the recommended changes. Most activists had hoped for a combined format. The OMB proposed a format that reads: "What is this person's race? Mark [X] one or more races to indicate what this person considers herself/himself to be." This format was chosen in part in response to the unanimous support it received from the various federal agencies that require data on race and ethnicity. These agencies argued that the "mark one or more" alternative—unlike the combined format—would require fewer changes in formatting on existing forms and allow for data continuity. More important, the data could be tabulated in each of the existing official single-race categories with which multiracial individuals identified, including the historically "underrepresented" racial components in their background. This would be especially important for the purposes of the continued enforcement of civil rights legislation and in meeting affirmative action guidelines.

The "mark one or more" format also received strong support from traditional civil rights organizations such as the National Association for the Advancement of Colored People (NAACP), the Urban League, the Congressional Black Caucus, and the Mexican American Legal Defense Fund (MALDEF). They argued that a stand-alone multiracial identifier would lead to a loss of numbers. (It should be pointed out, however, that the combined format would also have prevented this loss. In addition, that format would have had the advantage of making it possible to count the data in each of the single-race groups with which multiracial individuals identify and would acknowledge the identity of multiracial individuals.) Furthermore, the traditional communities of color expressed concerns about the potential divisiveness of even the appearance of a multiracial box, whether as a stand-alone identifier or in combination with multiple boxes. These concerns were influential in prompting the OMB officials to choose the "mark one or more" format.

On February 17, 1999, the OMB issued its recommendations for the tabulation of racial and ethnic data in compliance with the new standards. According to a 215-page report entitled "Draft Provisional Guidance on the Implementation of the 1997 Standards for Federal Data on Race and Ethnicity," there are sixty-three potential single- and multiple-race categories, including six for those who marked exactly one race and fifty-seven categories for those who marked two or more races. The sixty-three mutually exclusive and exhaustive categories of race may be collapsed to seven mutually exclusive and exhaustive categories by combining the fifty-seven categories of two or more races. These seven categories are White alone, Black or African

American alone, American Indian and Alaskan Native alone, Asian alone, Native Hawaiian and Other Pacific Islander alone, some other race alone, and two or more races.[35]

In addition, officials decided that individuals reporting more than one race should not be listed as "multiracial" but as "persons reporting two races," "three races," "four races," "five races," "six races," and so on.[36] The traditional civil rights community and various members of the Census Advisory Committee not only opposed these proposals but also resisted using the term "multiracial" even if a separate tabulation of "multiple racial responses" was allowed. They contended that any attempt to keep a separate tally of individuals who use the term "multiracial" and check more than one box would prove that the whole reform was nothing more than an attempt to undermine affirmative action and other race-based government initiatives.[37]

Under the new regulations, data in the "one race" category and the "two or more races" category can be presented, but data in the latter category can also be broken down into various subcategories.[38] In each case, data on "Hispanic origin" or "not of Hispanic origin" can be reported along with the data on race. However, individuals who identify as both "Hispanic origin" and "not of Hispanic origin" (one Hispanic parent and one non-Hispanic parent) were not permitted to check both of these boxes on the ethnicity question, at least not on the 2000 census.

One method of tabulation would be to provide separate totals for those reporting the most common racial combinations and to collapse the data for less frequently reported combinations. The specifics of the collapsed distributions would have to await the results of particular data collections. In such cases individuals who checked more than one box could be assigned equally to each of the groups with which they identified. To avoid compromising the accuracy of data by an overcount of more than 100 percent per person, individuals would not be counted as whole numbers in those groups. Rather, their numbers would be tabulated as part of each group's total percentage of the general population. Another option would be to assign them to the largest or smallest non-White group they marked. These could be ascertained from the racial composition of the population for the relevant geography.[39] Using this method, no change would be needed in the statistical methods currently used by agencies, and, for a few years, those agencies that began collecting data under the new standards would use this allocation method to report new racial data for individuals who select more than one race. This would provide agencies with a measure of the changing racial characteristics in the population and would indicate when the final alternative should be implemented. In other words, this method could be an interim solution used until full implementation of the new standards. Following careful evaluation of 2000 data, decisions could be made that phase in the new standards in an analytically appropriate manner.[40]

Another method would be to report the total, selecting each particular race, whether alone or in combination with other races. Thus when data were reported it would be possible to determine two counts for each racial group. The lower count, or lower boundary, would include individuals who identify with one race only. The larger count, or upper boundary, adds to the lower boundary individuals who identify with the given racial category and one or more other racial categories. Thus the upper boundary Black count would include everyone who marked Black, either alone or in combination with one or more other racial categories. The remainder of the population would consist of those individuals who did not identify as Black.

Data from some geographic regions are expected to reflect larger numbers and percentages of respondents reporting themselves as belonging to more than one racial group. In most regions, however, few adults are expected to do this. Consequently, the upper and lower boundaries will not be substantially different, at least not initially. The key findings of the comprehensive review favoring the adoption of a method for reporting more than one race were that in self-administered and interviewer-administered surveys—including the 1990 census—only .5 percent of respondents selected more than one race when asked to select only one race. A slightly larger number— between 1.0 and 1.5 percent—selected a multiracial category when offered an opportunity to do so.

Another approach specifically for Equal Employment Opportunity (EEO) purposes would be to ask respondents to provide a micro-data file containing one record (without identifiers) for each employee. The micro-record would include the employee's race or races, ethnicity, gender, and occupational category. This approach might be simpler for employers and would provide agencies with the maximum amount of flexibility in using the information. Implementation of this approach appears to be a longer-term solution. The EEO agencies would need to work with respondents to design and implement the reporting format and method, and they would need to acquire the relevant software and hardware to process the information.[41] If this type of information became available from all employers, the EEO agencies could use any of the tests, depending on their needs, or they would be able to make the transition to applying the EEO methodology to any groups that become large enough to monitor for EEO, including those that involve more than one race. In some cases, this latter method could be used to compare data collected under the old and new standards. The total number reporting more than one race must be made available, if confidentiality and data quality requirements can be met, to ensure that any changes in response patterns resulting from the new standards can be monitored over time. It is also important that users with the same or closely related responsibilities adopt the same tabulation method. In addition, the methods for tabulating data on race and ethnicity must be carefully developed and coordinated among the statistical agencies and other federal data users.[42]

The OMB announced on March 9, 2000, that agencies were still in the process of reviewing the alternative approaches for tabulating data because of the complexities of collecting and using the data reported under the new standards for civil rights enforcement purposes. Indeed, the federal civil rights enforcement agencies agreed that they should adopt common database definitions for the racial and ethnic categories used to enforce civil rights legislation and other race-based initiatives and regulations. Clearly, agencies needed to consider the complex issues related to implementing the new standards, bridging to enforcement conducted using data collected under the old standard, and continuing to conduct the important business of ensuring equal employment opportunity during the transition years.[43]

That said, data for the 2000 census were tabulated and published in two broad categories: the "race alone" or "one race" population and the "two or more races" population, although a more detailed breakdown of the latter was provided according to "two races," "three races," "four races," "five races," "six races," and so on. The tabulations indicate that of the total U.S. population of 281.4 million, the number of individuals who reported more than one race totaled 6.8 million individuals, or 2.4 percent of the population. (Latinos/ Hispanics who reported more than one race were also included in the "two or more races" population.)[44] The OMB recommended, however, that individuals who check more than one racial group should be reassigned to one racial category for the purpose of monitoring discrimination and enforcing civil rights laws. Those who designated themselves as White and a "minority" background will be counted as members of the minority background when government officials analyze patterns of discrimination in enforcing the Voting Rights Act, job bias laws, and other civil rights aims and claims. Employers, schools, and others must report the four expected largest multiple-race categories: American Indian and White, Asian and White, Black and White, and American Indian and Black. Employers also must report any multiracial combination that claims more than 1 percent of the population, as well as include a category for any multiracial individuals not counted in any other group.

The New U.S. Racial Order: Beyond the One-Drop Rule

Reestablishing the New Unstable Racial Equilibrium

Change in the racial order, as well as the social meaning and political role played by race, had been achieved now that the state had initiated reforms and begun the process of generating new policies in response to the multiracial movement's demands. Correspondingly, the movement was capable of achieving these reforms only when there was significant decay in the capacities of preexisting state policies to organize and enforce extant racial ideology and classification. Once the general contours of state reformism are clear, a movement's internal divisions are generally intensified. In terms of the multiracial consciousness movement, this was reflected, for example, in divergent strategies for determining the format used in collecting data on multiracial-identified individuals.

One segment of the movement, the AMEA and its affiliates and supporters, along with its demands, was incorporated into the state. The remaining active segment, Project RACE and its affiliates and

supporters, became at least more persistent, if not actually more radi-
calized, in pursuing its goals. More recently, some representatives of
this contingent have begun a campaign to abolish official racial-ethnic
designators and to dispense altogether with the tracking of data based
on ethnicity and race.[45] However, as long as public policy deems it
necessary to collect data on race-ethnicity, particularly as a means of
tracking the nation's progress in achieving equity in the area of race-
ethnic relations, any change allowing for the inclusion of a multiracial-
identifier, no matter what the format, would provide a more accurate
picture of contemporary demographics and also help to alleviate the
psychological oppression embedded in current methods of data collection. Consequently, it would be another logical step in the progression of civil rights—as well as human rights—by changing the
societal attitudes reinforced by these methods, which force multiracial-identified individuals to make an inauthentic choice.

In addition, this change would help to deconstruct the notion of
racial "purity," as well as mutually exclusive racial categories, which
are the very means by which racist ideology and racial privilege are
perpetuated in the United States.[46] Correspondingly, this may encourage more individuals to question the taken-for-grantedness of
their racial and ethnic identities and, ultimately, open up a long over-
due national conversation about the shared lineages that have been
obscured if not erased by several hundred years of racism buttressed
by the one-drop rule.

Black No More

If it is true, as many have argued, that the denial of the legitimate
right to identify with the fullness of one's racial background is a constant reminder to multiracial individuals that they do not fit in or do
not exist—a situation that certainly does not support the development of a healthy sense of identity in children—the African American community's continued and tenacious maintenance of the one-
drop rule, along with its resistance to the formal recognition or even
informal validation of a multiracial identity, also alerts us to the fact
that any discussion of the topic must necessarily take into consideration its wide-ranging and long-term consequences. Given the lingering effects of largely insidious yet resilient assimilationist toxins
in the racial ecology that have reemerged since the 1980s, the new

multiracial identity is not therefore immune to larger social forces. These could potentially subvert the desire to embrace a European ancestral-cultural background as a means of affirming a more egalitarian identity and use it instead as a means of granting multiracial individuals the status of new "insiders." This would disguise the fact that the status accorded to race essentially remains unchanged—although the relationship between race and opportunity would be modified—by furthering the illusion of power sharing without European Americans actually giving up structural control.[47]

Indeed, this dynamic would be of strategic value considering that the currently defined "White" or European American population in the United States will lose its numerical majority status in the next century. As compared to previous efforts to limit the parameters of Whiteness through the one-drop rule, the dismantling of this device now makes it possible for the United States to expand the criteria for dominant group status through racial assimilation of select African-descent Americans, along with select previously racialized Others, who approximate the dominant psychosomatic norm image. This would have the advantage of not only bolstering the numbers of individuals with "insider" status but also maintaining the United States as an ostensibly "White" nation.[48]

The new multiracial identity originates in and is therefore juxtaposed to these comparatively more integrative albeit assimilationist dynamics originating in the official repudiation and discrediting of the ideology of White supremacy, the dismantling of Jim Crow segregation, and the implementation of civil rights legislation. Accordingly, both phenomena problematize "monoracial" and essentialized constructions of Blackness based on the one-drop rule. Yet the trend toward more inclusive definitions of Whiteness—"Black No More"—originates in an inegalitarian dynamic. It reflects the backlash and resurgence of the assimilationist paradigm that since the 1980s has been redefining conservative political, social, and cultural agendas and undermining the integrity of the African American community. However, the new multiracial identity seeks to expand definitions of Blackness as well as Whiteness—"More Than Black"—to include more multidimensional configurations. It is indicative of an egalitarian dynamic that seeks to resist both the Eurocentric dichotomization and the hierarchical valuation of African American and European American cultural and racial differences.

There should be special alertness to any halfhearted attack on the one-drop rule that merely attenuates the Eurocentric dichotomization of Blackness and Whiteness while leaving intact the hierarchical relationship between these two categories of experience that maintains White privilege. Otherwise, this would undermine the very gains in civil rights that now make the recognition of a multiracial identity a possibility. Being multiracial, in a hierarchical system, be it pluralist or integrationist, or both, may simply mean being just a little less Black and thus a little less subdominant but does not assure equality with Whites. The critical challenge is, therefore, to completely dismantle the Eurocentric underpinnings of U.S. race relations by deconstructing both the dichotomous and the hierarchical relationship between Blackness and Whiteness and make a genuine societal commitment to affirming the equality of differences in the manner of egalitarian pluralism while at the same time nurturing the equality of commonalities in the manner of egalitarian integration.

NOTES

1. Lise Funderburg, *Black, White, Other: Biracial Americans Speak about Race and Identity* (New York: William Morrow, 1994), 26; Jewelle Taylor-Gibbs, "Biracial Adolescents," in *Children of Color: Psychological Interventions with Minority Youth*, ed. Jewelle Taylor-Gibbs (San Francisco: Jossey-Bass, 1989), 323; Claudia Mitchell-Kernan and M. Belinda Tucker, "New Trends in Black American Interracial Marriage: The Social Structural Context," *Journal of Marriage and the Family* 52 (February 1990): 209–19; Sylvestre Monroe, "Love in Black and White: The Last Racial Taboo," *Los Angeles Times Magazine*, December 9, 1990, 14.

2. Funderburg, *Black, White, Other*, 11–12; Jewelle Gibbs and Alice Hines, "Negotiating Ethnic Identity," in *Racially Mixed People in America*, ed. Maria P. P. Root (Thousand Oaks, Calif.: Sage, 1992), 223–38; Maria P. P. Root, "The Multiracial Experience: Racial Borders as a Significant Frontier," in *The Multiracial Experience: Racial Borders as the New Frontier*, ed. Maria P. P. Root (Newbury Park, Calif.: Sage, 1996), xiii–xvii.

3. Observation of students at the University of California, Los Angeles, Santa Barbara, and Santa Cruz, and public behavior at local support group meetings, as well as regional and national conferences on the topic of multiracial identity and interracial marriage; G. Reginald Daniel, "Black and White Identity in the New Millennium: Unsevering the Ties That Bind," in Root, ed., *The Multiracial Experience*, 121–39.

4. Daniel, "Black and White Identity," 87.

5. Stephen Cornell and Douglas Hartmann, *Ethnicity and Race: Making Identities in a Changing World* (Thousand Oaks, Calif.: Pine Forge Press, 1998), 98.

6. William Petersen, *Ethnicity Counts* (New Brunswick, N.J.: Transaction, 1997), 51–72; Anthony W. Marx, "Contested Citizenship: The Dynamics of Racial Identity and Social Movements," *International Review of Social History* 40, suppl. 3 (1995): 159–83.

7. Michael Omi and Howard Winant, *Racial Formation in the United States from the 1960s to the 1990s,* 2d ed. (New York: Routledge, 1994), 80–81; Howard Winant, "Dualism at Century's End," in *The House That Race Built: Black Americans, U.S. Terrain,* ed. Wahneema Lubiano (New York: Pantheon Books, 1997), 91–93.

8. There are some two hundred communities of varying combinations of European American, Native American, and African American descent, scattered throughout the eastern United States, especially the Southeast. Although these communities have much in common and have been collectively designated by social scientists as triracial isolates, many vehemently reject the label. Commonalities among these communities have less to do with actual cultural bonds than with similarities in experience and in living conditions that unite them in their refusal to accept the U.S. binary racial project in which individuals suspected of having any African ancestry are necessarily considered Black.

By 1980 the Lumbee in North Carolina, the Nanticoke in Delaware, the Houma in western Louisiana, and the Poospatuck in Long Island, New York, had succeeded in officially changing their earlier classification as mulattoes to nontreaty Native Americans. Although this status excludes them from government benefits, it places them squarely on the aboriginal side of the racial divide. Groups such as the Jackson Whites and the Issues have succeeded in negotiating alternative identities as "other non-Whites." Groups such as the Brass Ankles and the Melungeons have persistently fought for legal status as White and have met with success in their local communities if not actually with the government.

9. Paul R. Spickard, *Mixed Blood: Intermarriage and Ethnic Identity in Twentieth-Century America* (Madison: University of Wisconsin Press, 1989), 276–77.

10. Observation of public behavior at local support group meetings, as well as regional and national conferences on the topic of multiracial identity and interracial marriage.

11. Omi and Winant, *Racial Formation,* 95–98.

12. Ibid.

13. Pierre Bourdieu, *Outline of a Theory of Practice,* trans. Richard Nice (New York: Cambridge University Press, 1977), 159.

14. Spickard, *Mixed Blood,* 333.

15. Mary Waters, "Multiple Ethnicities and Identity Choices: Some Implications for Race and Ethnic Relations in the United States," in *We Are a People: Narrative and Multiplicity in Ethnic Identity,* ed. Paul R. Spickard and Jeffrey Burroughs (Philadelphia: Temple University Press, 2000), 23–40.

16. Omi and Winant, *Racial Formation,* 96–97.

17. Ibid., 69.

18. Ibid.

19. Ibid.

20. Ibid., 101–4.

21. Ibid., 96.

22. Ibid., 97.

23. Observation of public behavior between 1989 and 1998 at local support group meetings and at regional and national conferences on the topic of multiracial identity and interracial marriage.

24. Omi and Winant, *Racial Formation,* 88–91, 95–97.

25. Ibid.

26. Ibid.

27. Ira S. Lowry, "The Science and Politics of Ethnic Enumeration," paper presented at the annual meeting of the American Association for the Advancement of Science, San Francisco, California, January 3–8, 1980, 15; Carlos A. Fernández, "Testimony of the Association of Multiethnic Americans before the Subcommittee on Census, Statistics, and Postal Personnel of the U.S. House of Representatives," in *American Mixed Race: The Culture of Microdiversity,* ed. Naomi Zack (New York: Rowman and Littlefield, 1995), 191–210; Carlos A. Fernández, "Government Classification of Multiracial/Multiethnic People," in Root, ed., *The Multiracial Experience,* 15–36; Office of Management and Budget, *Federal Register,* July 9, 1997, 62:36877.

28. OMB, *Federal Register,* October 30, 1997, 62:58782–58788.

29. Fernández, "Testimony of the Association of Multiethnic Americans," 5; Sharon Lee, "Racial Classification in the U.S. Census: 1890–1990," *Ethnic and Racial Studies* 16.1 (1993): 83.

30. OMB, "OMB's Proposed Guidelines for Federal Statistical Activities: A Summary of the Current Guidelines, Proposed Guidelines, and the Public Response to the Possible Changes," 1988, 18–20, 40–50; Office of Management and Budget, *Federal Register,* 1997, 62:36880.

31. Office of Management and Budget, *Federal Register,* 1997, 62:36880.

32. The Petri Bill, H.R. 830, was a piece of federal legislation that had been drawn up in 1996 and was pending congressional approval and supported a stand-alone identifier. The bill was introduced by Rep. Thomas E. Petri (R-Wisc.) in the U.S. House of Representatives just before the congressional session's closing but was reintroduced on February 25, 1997, and could be used

as a last resort if the OMB did not follow through in making changes on its own. The legislation, often referred to as the "Tiger Woods Bill," was named in honor of the golfer Tiger Woods, whose father is Black, Chinese, European American, and Native American and whose mother is Thai. Woods was the first multiracial-identified winner of the Masters Golf Tournament in Augusta, Georgia, on April 13, 1997. It appears that some activists viewed H.R. 830 as a last resort that could be used as heavy artillery if OMB officials were unwilling to support changes through the current and more traditional channels. The bill could serve as a means of prodding officials into supporting administratively the more moderate combined format so as to avoid the more heated and lengthy debate that would surround the implementation of a stand-alone multiracial identifier through legislative means. Charles Byrd, "Update on HR 830, OMB and the Newtmeister," *Interracial Voice*, June 16, 1997; "Letter from Paul D. Trampe, Legislative Assistant for Representative Tom Petri to Charles Byrd," *Interracial Voice*, March 10, 1997; Charles Byrd, "Wisconsin Congressman Introduces Multiracial Legislation in House of Representatives," *Interracial Voice*, March 10, 1997; Charles Michael Byrd, "IV Interviews Congressman Thomas Petri," *Interracial Voice*, April 23, 1997; G. Reginald Daniel, "Multiracial Identity in Brazil and the United States," in Spickard and Burroughs, eds., *We Are a People*, 153–78; G. Reginald Daniel, "Beyond Black and White: The New Multiracial Consciousness," in Root, ed., *Racially Mixed People in America*, 333–41.

33. G. Reginald Daniel, "Testimony for Hearings on Racial Census Categories," *Federal Measures of Race and Ethnicity and the Implications for the 2000 Census. Hearings before the Subcommittee on Government Management, Information, and Technology,* Committee on Government Reform and Oversight U.S. House of Representatives; 105th Congress, April 23, May 22, and July 25, 1997 (Washington, D.C.: U.S. Government Printing Office, 1998), 395–96, 575–76.

34. OMB, *Federal Register,* July 9, 1997, 62:36906. Preliminary 2000 census data released beginning in March 2001 indicated that about 2 percent of the nation's population of approximately 281.4 million identified with more than one race. This figure is somewhat higher than what was expected based on the findings of the comprehensive review. However, the numbers of individuals who identified with more than one racial group are still minuscule compared to those of individuals who identified with only one racial group (U.S. Census Bureau).

35. OMB, Tabulation Working Group Interagency Committee for the Review of Standards for Data on Race and Ethnicity, "Draft Provisional Guidance on the Implementation of the 1997 Standards for Federal Data on Race and Ethnicity," 41–51.

36. Ibid.

37. Ramona Douglass, president of Association of Multiethnic Americans, personal communication, June 19, 1997.

38. OMB, Tabulation Working Group Interagency Committee for the Review of Standards for Data on Race and Ethnicity, "Draft Provisional Guidance on the Implementation of the 1997 Standards for Federal Data on Race and Ethnicity," 41–51.

39. Ibid.

40. Ibid.

41. OMB, Tabulation Working Group Interagency Committee for the Review of Standards for Data on Race and Ethnicity, "Draft Provisional Guidance on the Implementation of the 1997 Standards for Federal Data on Race and Ethnicity," 41–51.

42. Ibid.

43. Ibid.

44. Nicholas A. Jones and Amy Symens Smith, "The Two or More Races Population: 2000—Census 2000 Brief," U.S. Department of Commerce. Economic and Statistics Administration. U.S. Census Bureau, November 2001, 1–10.

45. Among the individuals present at this meeting were Charles Byrd of *Interracial Voice;* James Landrith of the *Multiracial Activist;* Ward Connerly, University of California regent and founder of the American Civil Rights Institute; and Steve and Ruth White of A Place for Us. Charles Michael Byrd, "From the Editor, The Political Realignment: A *Jihad* against 'Race'-Consciousness," *Interracial Voice,* September–October 2000; Guest Editorial, Ward Connerly, "Loving America," *Interracial Voice,* September–October 2000; Herbert A. Sample, "Connerly Joins Foes of 'Silly' Queries on Census Forms: He Weighs Ballot Drive to Limit Race Data," *Bee Washington Bureau,* April 1, 2000.

46. Paul R. Spickard, Rowena Fong, and Patricia L. Ewalt, Undermining the Very Basis of Racism—Its Categories," *Social Work* 4.5 (1995): 581–84.

47. G. Reginald Daniel, *More than Black? Multiracial Identity and the New Racial Order* (Philadelphia: Temple University Press, 2001), 155–71.

48. Ibid.

12

RACE AND MULTIRACIALITY
Multiracial Challenges to Monoracialism

MICHAEL C. THORNTON

MCT is a child of the fifties and early sixties, when racial boundaries were clear and interracial marriages rare and often illegal. As the product of several racial-ethnic (Black, White, Native American, and Asian) and nationality (American and Japanese) groups, he was precariously situated betwixt and between social boundaries and did not fit easily into the convention of claiming only one racial heritage. Nonetheless, there were plenty who "knew" where he fit. Clearly, the uniform message was that he was not to claim as significant his ties to the racial majority (i.e., Whites). He could say that he was of Japanese heritage, but this was permitted only in private and was not a matter for public discussion, for his Black heritage was his exclusive public identity. That he was also Native American appeared to be of no social significance (to others or to himself).

In searching for his own identity during adolescence, MCT based many of his decisions about his ethnic identity on how others perceived his racial markers and how far he could realistically distance himself from being "recognized" as a Black person. Much of this effort revolved around trying to pass as some other ("mixed") racial group, such as Puerto Rican, or ostensibly bonding with biracials, an attempt on his part not to deny but to downplay his Blackness.

In this convoluted journey through racial boundaries and racial group membership, MCT struggled with formulating an ethnic identity well into his graduate school days. For most of this journey, how he looked and where he could acquire social value and fit into the social hierarchy was his raison d'être; ethnic identity based primarily on race was everything. It was only after graduate school and through examining families much like his own (Black, Japanese, and American) that he resolved the dilemma about where he fit into the world. Because what he was offered was unsatisfactory, he was forced to choose for himself. Now identifying with several groups and feeling comfortable doing so, MCT's ethnicity is no longer a pressing issue. Nonetheless, he has not yet arrived, for antiquated socialization remains when dealing with his feelings about what groups he feels closest to.

I am MCT. The weightiness of sitting on the margins of racial divides has become less prominent as I age. Despite the lack of official recognition, I retain my self-created, three-dimensional ethnic identity (Black, Japanese, and American).[1] I feel validated without an official government category. I do not claim a separate identity as a multiethnic person that does not have at its base a link with people of color generally and Blacks and Asian Americans particularly. If I feel an affinity with multiethnic people, it is with those who, like me, are of mixed Asian-Black ancestry, for in my experience that connection speaks to unique trials and tribulations not encountered by other so-called multiracial people. This chapter is my take on the issue of multiracial categories on government forms.

I explore here the movement to have multiracial heritage officially recognized in government documents, especially the census. While this is my general focus, I am most interested in the rationale offered by a segment of the movement that aims to have multiracials treated as a separate category, distinct from other so-called monoracial populations.[2] This move is spearheaded by people who have a personal stake in its success: members of mixed racial communities, often the monoracial parents of multiracial offspring. I understand their desire for validation, but I argue that a separate category will not serve their goal of legitimacy, makes little political sense given present-day realities of race and racial hierarchies, and is predicated on anachronistic notions of racial identity politics.

GOVERNMENT DESIGNATION OF RACE, OR
THE SOCIAL CONSTRUCTION OF RACE

Although the current rationale for including a multiracial category on census forms may be unique, the category itself is not. As a social construction, the definition and measurement of racial categories have changed over time, almost every decade, shaped by contemporary political and social agendas. These changes are shown in table 1. Censuses from 1790 to 1920 reflect the growing presence of Asians in the United States but also a concern with Black-White miscegenation. The ostensible artifacts of the latter trend disappeared after 1920, when the census ceased collecting information on proportions of Blackness. At that time there was a growing appreciation that most Blacks were of mixed heritage and that "pure" Blacks would soon be extinct.[3]

TABLE 1. Categories Used in the Census to Designate Race, 1790–2000

1790–1810		
Free Whites	Slaves	
All other Free persons (*except Indians not taxed*)		

1820–1840		
Free Whites	Free Colored	
Foreigners (*not naturalized*)	Slaves	

1850–1860		
White		
Black (*includes Mulatto: "perceptible trace of African blood"*)		

1870–1880		
White	Indian	Mulatto
Black	Chinese	

1890–1900		
White	Octoroon	Quadroon
Black	Chinese	Japanese
Mulatto	Indian	

1910–1920

White	Octoroon	Quadroon
Black	Chinese	Japanese
Mulatto	Indian	Other

1930

| White | Chinese | Japanese |
| Negro | Mexican | Indian |

1940

| White *(includes Mexican)* | Chinese | Indian |
| Negro | Japanese | |

1950

White	Japanese	Other
Negro	Chinese	
American Indian	Filipino	

1960

White *(includes Puerto Rican,*	Chinese	Negro
Mexican, and others	Other *(includes*	Japanese
of "Latin" descent)	*American Indian)*	Filipino
Hindu		

1970

White *(includes Chicano, Mexican*	Filipino	Hawaiian
American, Moslem, and Brown)	Japanese	Chinese
Negro or Black	Indian *(American)*	Korean
Other		

1980

White	Filipino	Guamian
Negro or Black	Hawaiian	Samoan
Indian *(American)*	Korean	Eskimo
Japanese	Asian Indian	Aleut
Chinese	Vietnamese	Other

1990

White	Asian or Pacific Islander *(includes*
Black or Negro	*Chinese, Filipino, Hawaiian, Korean*
Indian (American)	*Vietnamese, Japanese, Asian Indian,*
Eskimo	*Samoan, Guamian)*
Aleut	Other

2000

White	Korean
Black/African American/Negro	Native Hawaiian
American Indian/Alaska Native	Guamian or Chamorro
Asian Indian	Samoan
Chinese	Other Pacific Islander
Filipino	Other Asian
Japanese	Some other race

Source: U.S. Bureau of the Census, *200 Years of U.S. Census Taking: Population Housing Questions, 1790–1990* (Washington, D.C.: U.S. Government Printing Office, 1998). For 2000 data, www.census.gov/population/www/cen2000/briefs.html (1. Overview of Race and Hispanic Origin, C2KBR/01-1; accessed November 20, 2003).

The only consistent pattern across censuses is not shown by the data—the definition of "Black." In the United States, one drop of Black blood in one's known ancestry, the one-drop rule, has always been the defining quality of Blackness. As suggested by Thomas Sawyer, chair of the House Subcommittee on Census, Statistics and Postal Personnel, which examined racial and ethnic categories in the census in 1993, "We are unique in this country in the way we describe and define race and ascribe to it characteristics that other cultures view differently."[4] Historically, this definition has been a mixed blessing, for although it was intended to deny Blacks access to many of the fruits of life, without it Black American life would not have the contributions of many who played an integral role in the community and who are among the most celebrated individuals in American history: Crispus Attucks, Frederick Douglass, Booker T. Washington, W. E. B. Du Bois, Martin Luther King Jr. All these individuals had White ancestry but were defined as Black Americans.

"Black" has been defined consistently through most of U.S. history. However, racial types have not been assigned systematically. Initially, census takers discerned the respondent's race by sight (did they look Black or White?) or from his or her reputation in the community. Starting in 1964, however, with the erection of the framework of civil rights law, the government required highly detailed information about minority participation that could be gathered only by decennial censuses, the nation's supreme method for compiling demographic statistics. Race data were to become essential to monitoring and enforcing desegregation and legal equality.

The sloppiness and diversity of racial and ethnic categories rendered them all but meaningless for statistical purposes. With racial heritage to become the foundation of many policies, it was important to clarify what "race" meant. In 1973 Secretary of Health, Education and Welfare Casper Weinberger assigned this task to the Federal Interagency Commission (FIC). From this group would come, in 1977, the Office of Management and Budget's (OMB's) Statistical Directive No. 15, on which the current five-grid system of four racial groups and one ethnic group is based. The OMB accepted the FIC's suggestions almost verbatim, with the exception of East Indians, who were moved from the White category to the Asian and Pacific Islanders category. Directive No. 15 fostered the creation of compatible, unduplicated, and exchangeable racial and ethnic data for three reporting purposes: statistical, administrative, and civil rights compliance. The FIC admitted that the system it developed was not meant to be the final say about these matters. Nonetheless, it soon became just that, at least temporarily.

The ultimate effort was to provide a measure of civil rights compliance. But the OMB directive, with little political discussion, also shaped identity: the groupings in the grid system became political entities, with their own constituencies, lobbyists, and vested interests. People began to "find" and spawn identities based on these statistical artifacts. Before these official designations were created there was no Hispanic identity, only Dominican or Puerto Rican; no Asian American identity, only Americans who were Korean, Vietnamese, and Chinese.[5] Each of these new overarching "identities" was constructed out of experience and political expediency.

The groupings acknowledged by this effort were supposedly based on a process of self-selection, a reflection of self-identity. But given that the purpose of these data was to serve research and administrative goals, there is an inherent conflict between the state's definition of racial group membership and how group and individual identities are actualized, that is, a gap between administrative requirements and mass consciousness. States need statistical categories to measure things in comparable ways, to accurately track social trends over time, to identify groups along distinct boundaries. But these categories and their bureaucratic uses clash with individuals' experiences of race and ethnicity, their dynamic nature, and the slippery subjective indicators of that dynamism.[6] Administrative definitions are often meaningless to those they purport to represent. This is true in large part because they function to measure *groups of racial classes* by aggregating individual identities. The end result is to *erase individual identity.*[7]

With time, these racial categories have taken on broader implications for life in the United States. Directive No. 15 categories are now found on school enrollment forms, on job, scholarship, loan, and mortgage application forms, and in census materials. Every American must place himself or herself in one racial and one ethnic box. This information is used to monitor and enforce civil rights legislation, most notably, the Voting Rights Act of 1965, but also a smorgasbord of set-asides, entitlements, and affirmative action programs. The numbers drive the dollars. Racial groupings and issues of money, but also identity, are at stake.

Although the slipperiness of these concepts was apparent almost immediately, the move to have a separate multiracial box has drawn widespread public debate over the past ten years. The question is, why now?

HISTORICAL CONTEXT: THE CHANGING RACIAL ENVIRONMENT

At this writing, it is more than thirty years after the passage of legislation that fundamentally altered the composition of immigration to the United States—from European to primarily Asian and Mexican. Since the 1970s immigrants have settled primarily in non-White areas of major cities such as New York, Los Angeles, and Houston.[8] This "browning" of America has been part of record levels of population movement here and internationally. It has also escalated interaction among ethnic minorities and the number of people who are clamoring for their voices to be heard. This worldwide immigration is overwhelming our traditional racial distinctions, including those used for governmental purposes. As Sawyer has suggested, "The [racial] categories themselves inevitably reflect the temporal bias of every age. That becomes a problem when the nation itself is undergoing deep and historic diversification."[9]

This era has also witnessed an increase in another kind of border crossing, interracial marriages. Contemporaneous with new immi-

gration legislation, in 1967 the U.S. Supreme Court legalized interracial marriage. Since then, the number of these unions has grown
precipitously, from 310,000 in 1970 to 964,000 in 1990.[10]

Recent demographic trends have led to shifting meanings of race
and ethnic identification. One such development is the creation of
new, pan-ethnic identities. For example, an Asian American identity
has no counterpart elsewhere. Individual Asian groups now interact
as one, arguing that they share a common experience in U.S. history.[11]
This effort mutes significant cultural and linguistic differences, as,
of course, Asian America is not homogeneous.

ARGUMENTS FOR AND AGAINST AN AMALGAM RACE

Those who believe that the system of entitlements built over the past
thirty years has been predicated on clear, enduring, and monolithic
ethnoracial identities[12] are the most uneasy about the movement to
include a mixed race category in the census. For them, this movement will undermine years of civil rights work. They suggest that
multiracial advocates should understand that the United States has
a checkered history of dealing with racial minorities. Recent racial
categories in the census were a response to this history and sought to
ensure protection of all citizens. In this context, public authorities
were asked to facilitate and support affiliations based on racial ancestry. The five categories designating race or ethnicity get their integrity
not from biology or culture but from the dynamics of oppression in
U.S. society and the need for political tools to overcome the legacy
of that victimization. Any digression from this history invites a loss
of ground.

In the view of many advocates, if the census examines self-
identification, then multiracial people should be allowed to choose
for themselves—a choice that has been denied them.[13] I believe this
impetus stems in part from the personal experiences of multiracials
and their families but also reflects the tenor of our time. I see this
movement as part of the focus on identity politics, where affiliation
has become a preoccupation. This arises from successful efforts by
people of color to use racial group membership to bring about a
more equitable system. But more directly, the multiracial movement
follows in the footsteps of both the Black Power and multicultural
movements that used race as a guide for cultural identity and political

power. In this process labels are important, for they impute identity in a direct fashion. Like the Black Power movement, which displaced the word *Negro* with *Black*, a pejorative term then, those who advocate for a multiracial category seek to undermine the pejorative connotations of the word *multiracial* (mixed, mixed up, or impure) and make it something to be proud of. The multicultural movement influences this cause as well in its attempt to give full play to differentiated identities, in this case, those that fall along racial lines.

Thus the foundation of a significant part of this move for self-determination via the census (and government documents generally) appears to be to use "multirace" as an identity, a significant affiliation, to argue for its acceptance as an equal to its monoracial peers. For example, a guest commentary by Patrice Farmer in the newsletter the *Multiracial Activist* argued that multiracial people "do not have the choice to choose which heritage we want to identify with or the choice to be considered multiracial as a separate racial category, just as White, Hispanic, Asian and African American are. . . . This is a call to all multiracial/biracial families to declare war! We must fight for our rights to self-determine, categorize, define and classify ourselves."[14] Susan Graham, founder and executive director of Project RACE, has been on the forefront of advocacy for "the creation of an umbrella category for the multiracial, like those in place for Hispanics and Asians."[15] Project RACE and the Association of Multiethnic Americans (AMEA) seek to include a multiracial classification on all state and federal forms that request racial identification.[16] For the AMEA, an aim is to have the federal government correctly identify multiracials and not force them to choose a monoracial category, for to do so "interferes with personal dignity and interferes in a negative way with the development of self-esteem of multiracial/ethnic students."[17] Richard Miller wrote, in the multiracial newsletter *Interracial Voice:*

> Since "race" has no biological meaning but is a social construct, as mulattoes, we should see ourselves as a separate "race"—one with equal recognition as blacks, whites, Asians and Native Americans. After all, the Arabs and Latinos were able to pull it off. Instead of seeing ourselves as having "black blood" and "white blood" flowing through our veins, we should see ourselves as having one "type of blood" flowing through our veins— this blood is being 100% mulatto.[18]

This position also suggests that the traditional racialized system is a centrifugal force among multiracial people: it keeps them on the margin. Because traditional racial borders are based on outdated ideas about race, they do not parrot mixed racial realities. Asserting their own category is based on recognizing the centripetal forces that draw multiracials together. Respecting this, and if the census is truly asking for self-identity, so the argument goes, there should be a special box for their circumstances.

U.S. society, long hostile to talk of race mixing and skilled at denying its reality, is facing a growing community of avowedly multiracial people. In reality, current racial categories are filled with mixed race people, including Whites and Native and Latino Americans. However, confronting this view of race stirs muddied waters. The logic of multirace threatens to undermine the structure of state-defined racial identities.

While I will not examine in detail the views of the protagonists in this debate, I want to examine some of the implications of a successful push to institutionalize a multiracial category in government documents (in the 2000 census there was a "pick all that apply" approach). On the one side, the proponents of this position argue that they are only asking for what is fair in the context of the purpose of the census: the right to choose an identity that is appropriate for them. An added component of this argument is that multiracial people deserve this treatment because they have a unique identity that must be included if the census is a true representation of the diversity of the United States. Their assertion is predicated on the notion that there is an identity or experience common to all multiracials, very much like there is among Blacks or Asian Americans.

Those who argue against the multiracial category see little if any good coming out of this process. For them, the success of this effort will cause the sky to fall on the groups for whom the current racial categories have been used as powerful tools for equality. All the groundwork of our ancestors would be swept away by a new ethnic or racial category on government documents.

Taking each in turn, I show how each view presents a distorted reality in that each oversimplifies a complex set of issues. I argue that each view is deficient. And although the movement for official legitimation via the census is understandable, it would not leave us in a better place than where we are now.

"The Sky Will Fall"

The basic assertion here is that given the heavy reliance on racial and ethnic categories as they were originally established in 1977 for enforcing civil rights legislation, including another category, in essence another ethnic or racial group, would necessitate revamping twenty years of work and changing the institutions built up around this effort. According to Tanu Henry of Africana.com, many Black leaders and organizations pushed for Blacks to categorize themselves in a single racial category (Black or African American).[19] That many Black multiracials might choose something other than Black would do great harm given that Blacks are customarily undercounted and are less likely to participate in the census. For example, the undercounting of Blacks by more than 4 percent in the 1990 census means that some urban areas may have lost more than $11 billion in the past decade.

Reverend Norman Johnson of the Southern Christian Leadership Conference (SCLC) of Los Angeles argued, "We need to fill in the boxes with a historic understanding of who we are as African Americans. I have Indian in my family but that fact is more relevant in certain contexts than others." He argued further that misreporting the total number of Blacks would have repercussions in the distribution of funds to needy areas. Former U.S. Congressman Mervyn Dymally shared these concerns. He spearheaded a campaign, sponsored by churches, Caribbean organizations, the NAACP, the Urban League, the SCLC, and the state of California to ensure that Blacks in southern California check only the Black or African American option.[20]

Multiple options on the census would lead to shrinking numbers of "pure" racial minorities, the fear is, because a portion of these communities is expected to "change" identities, leaving traditional racial groups to check the new box, which in turn would force the reallocation of resources, away from these traditional groups to the new one. Tanya Schevitz reported that groups such as the Asian American Legal Defense and Education Fund (AALDEF) and the NAACP reached out to their communities to encourage them to check one box in the 2000 census to help these groups retain their clout.[21] Glenn Magpantay of the AALDEF asserted, "Nothing less than our civil rights, our schools, our health care, our housing, are at stake. It is a personal decision, but people should be fully informed that the census is not about affirming change in the very complex, dynamic notions of identity."[22]

A common estimate is that 75 to 90 percent of those who now check the Black category (the figure is usually used to describe how many Blacks are of multiple racial heritage, in most cases going back generations)[23] may choose the multiracial option. Roderick Harrison, head of the Census Bureau's Racial Statistics Division, believes it reasonable that a multiracial box would result in at least a 10 percent defection from the Black category (nearly 300,000 people).[24] If as few as 10 percent of Blacks checked the new box, legislative districts might need to be redrawn and the entire civil rights regulatory program reassessed. School desegregation plans would be cast into confusion. Of course, those currently in the traditional categories might not make this decision, but that they might suggests that complex issues of identity would emerge from institutionalizing a multiracial category.[25]

Black groups were particularly upset with these possibilities because what we now mean by Black would be gutted. Current definitions of Black unite a diverse group of people. The new category could divide Black communities. In Dymally's attempt to have people choose only the Black or African American option, his major targets were communities of African and Caribbean immigrants, many of whom, he argued, were more intent on identifying themselves as Jamaican or Senegalese than as Black or African American.[26] If this were not enough reason for concern, others pointed to the history of color prejudice in Black communities, which reflects wider social realities. The social and economic gap between light- and dark-skinned members remains as great as the gap between Blacks and Whites.[27] If Blacks of mixed heritage were to be considered part of the multiracial category, their already higher status (compared to their darker brothers and sisters) would be enhanced, and the rift between them and other Blacks deepened.

In addition, critics of the multiracial category suggested that since all people are mixed, with perhaps Blacks and Hispanics the most extreme cases, such a category would have no meaning. Anyone could choose the multiracial category, including Whites.[28] Given that scenario, what would this or the traditional racial categories mean?

Many of these fears may eventually turn out to be well founded, but some evidence suggests that a multiracial category should not have such dire consequences—at least not initially. The Current Population Survey, conducted in May 1995, sampled sixty thousand people and included multiracial panels. Only about 2 percent of the sample chose the new category. Those who were likely to do so were Hispanics and Whites, apparently because they viewed mixed ethnic heritage as multiracial heritage. The only groups who technically are multiracial and who chose the category (i.e., those whose parents were of different racial heritages) were American Indians/Eskimos. Most members of other identifiable multiracial groups passed on the multiracial option.[29]

In November 1996 the Census Bureau conducted a dress rehearsal to assess the effects of a multiracial category. The National Content Survey was mailed to ninety thousand households, approximately 1 percent of which chose the multiracial category. The highest response rates for this category were found in the 1994 census test of nearly three hundred households in Atlanta, Boston, and Chicago, in which respondents were given the revised Survey of Income forms that included a multiracial response. More than 7 percent chose the category; again Hispanics were most likely to do so. The mass exodus predicted by the critics of the new category did not appear.[30]

At least one observer, Stephan Thernstrom, suggested that this new category would have an enormous effect on American Indians. He argued,

> [Creating a racially mixed category would have its] most dramatic, indeed bizarre, effect on the enumeration of the American Indian population. A mere 2.1 million people checked the "American Indian, Eskimo, Aleut" box on the 1990 Census question. That is the figure everyone uses for the Indian population in that year. But the separate question about "ancestry or ethnic origin" on the same Census, on which multiple choices were possible, yielded a staggering 8.7 million people who claimed to have some Indian ancestors. If all of the additional 6.6 million identify themselves as both Indian and something else on the 2000 Census race question, now that multiple race choices are possible, the Indian-population figures used for purposes of civil-rights enforcement will suddenly quadruple. And most of these born-again Indians will be thoroughly assimilated Americans who have no contact or cultural connection to any Indian tribe today.[31]

These efforts might not reflect one other possibility. A recent paper on the open-ended question on ancestry or descent that appeared in the 1990 census underscores the fluid nature of ethnicity (here for Whites in particular but perhaps for others as well).[32] Whether or not a group appeared below the question as an example had a dramatic influence on responses. For instance, when Cajun was used as an example on the census ancestry question, their numbers jumped almost 6,000 percent compared to when it was not used. To remind people of a possibility is to encourage enormous change, which might suggest that if a multiracial box were made available, it would soon become a viable option for many people.

Perhaps a more valid concern with the growing support for institutionalizing a multiracial category in the census during the present era is related to the question of why many conservatives, those not normally supportive of efforts at self-determination among people of color, championed this cause. This advocacy is part of a conservative trend in racial issues in recent American life. This conservatism stands in sharp contrast to how we as a society once envisioned the role of race. In the 1960s, prejudice was always associated with discrimination against people of color; in some circles this was also tied to structural features of American society. Thus inequality was more related to environmental and institutional dynamics than to personal shortcomings. However, as Howard Winant suggests, while fundamentally accurate, its proponents reduced everything to race and ignored social class and gender.[33]

Part of the intellectual backlash against this view of the role of race went in the opposite direction, away from structural concerns toward reinforcing individualism, competition, and laissez-faire capitalism. Conservatives emphasized a color-blind society and in so doing undermined racial minority advancements and past achievements.[34] They used the language of integration and political rhetoric that is the opposite of that of traditional racial identity politics. This strategy taps into the multiracial movement because it sees its triumph as making race a less powerful political and legal tool, for if large numbers of people choose a multiracial category each racial category would lose whatever integrity it may have had. Newt Gingrich, at the time Speaker of the House, commented on the need for a multiracial category: "I don't believe any rational American can be comfortable with where we are on the issue of race. I think all of us ought to take on the challenge as leaders, beyond legislation, beyond our normal jobs, of asking some new questions in some new ways. After all, what does race mean when . . . many Americans cannot fill out their census forms because they're an amalgam of race?"[35]

Unique Identity

Perhaps the fundamental message of the effort to institutionalize a multiracial category is that it accurately reflects a group with its own ethnic identity, one that differs fundamentally from others, such that it should be seen to be like no other. Thus one well-known proposal calls for placing a multiracial category next to the traditional racial-ethnic selections. The respondent would also identify his or her parental racial groups.[36] What makes this effort unique is that this multiracial category is at its core, and by consensus, a combination of all racial groups. While the Hispanic designation in reality encompasses a very diverse racial group, the label itself is not racial but ethnic-cultural. This is an important distinction, which I will come back to, but suffice it to say here that advocates of a special multiracial box assume that knowing that one is of multiracial heritage is enough evidence to suggest that their experiences are essentially the same, and most of them must have similar identities. That they draw such a conclusion suggests that biology determines attitudes and culture. The evidence for such a view does not exist, especially with regard to non-Black–Black mixes.

But most of the discussion about multiracial identity arises from the assertion that it is different from others. What is highlighted is what separates multiracials from other racial groups, including those of their parents. What is rarely examined and what lies at the heart of an identity are a number of unanswered questions: What brings most multiracial people together such that they fit better together than in some other category? What is the core of their identification? After all, what should be important are not the group boundaries but its centers—ancestry, family, practice, and place.[37] What matters is what people share rather than the lines that divide them. If this is not the focus, then the multiracial category becomes a catchall for any group that does not fit comfortably into the other traditional categories. So the question remains: What about multiracials is consistently different as a group from other groups? Given the claim that they have a unique racial or ethnic identity, the key to answering this question lies in understanding the concepts of identity and ethnicity.

RACE VERSUS ETHNIC IDENTITY

Race is not a good proxy for ethnicity. Typically used interchangeably, race and ethnicity refer to different demographic attributes. Race is an idea that is created at the social level but transformed and experienced at the personal level. Race sets up certain expectations of experience and identity; but there is no automatic link. Race differences are given cultural explanations without obvious measures of experience or attitudes. Nevertheless, clearly race only approximates an individual's social location and acts as a proxy measure of experiences that people *may* encounter as a member of a group; it presumes that social expectations of group identity match personal experience. Based on racial stratification and the cultural aspects of ethnic group membership, there is no inherent association between race and ethnicity.[38]

If race provides indirect evidence of cultural heritage or ethnic identity, or is synonymous with either, then subgroup distinctions in the racial category are semantic. However, this is not the case. Within any racial group are several ethnic subgroups. Because Haitians and Jamaicans are termed Black, ethnic variations between them are assumed to be minor. Not appreciating the differences results in treating race as a self-explanatory variable and overlooks how it is connected to other indicators—actual bonds to the group or experience with intolerance—that are closer to assessing mixed racial life. Although the racial ideology treats them as uniform, races and the experiences within them are varied categories.

For example, West Indians are Black racially. But what does this tell us about their links to other Blacks? Assuming that race is paramount over ethnicity, they should feel special bonds with other native Black Americans; they should have substantively similar experiences due to their race. However, this assumption is inadequate. Whites see West Indians generally as more preferable than native Blacks as employees, coworkers, and neighbors. This is reinforced by their perception that Whites are treating them more favorably than they treat Blacks.[39] Moreover, West Indians, seeing the stigma attached to Blacks, are strongly motivated to maintain their own ethnicity and communities, despite pressures by the United States to classify themselves as Black.[40] West Indians are treated like Blacks in that they are denied access to White areas and are more likely to live near other Blacks than near any other group. Nonetheless, while living in Black areas, West Indians stay in ethnically isolated pockets, usually in higher-quality housing.[41] Thus, to equate a substantially similar existence based on race camouflages important subgroup (i.e., ethnic) distinctions. Furthermore, to have a Black identity means something very different for each group. Self-identity here, when based on ethnic identity, would be very different from one based on race. A similar pattern has been found among Black and White Hispanics.[42]

Clearly, advocates of a multiracial category interchange race and ethnicity: knowing one's race (here multiracial) presumably tells us something substantive about the experiences of most of the people in this category. It presumably tells us one's experience and how one feels about being a part of the group. Actually, ethnicity refers to a shared cultural identity, whereas race refers to inheritable biological and genotypic traits. Ethnicity contains dimensions of cultural socialization and expression. Within racial groups people are differentially exposed to ethnic socialization, and each type of socialization might have distinct implications for their group and individual or one-to-one behavior.[43] Thus knowing one's racial category does not necessarily predict one's identity; race is a given, with little personal choice. Not understanding this difference has meant that often the same person can identify his or her race and ethnicity in such a way that they seem to observers to be in conflict.[44]

An ethnic identity, at its core, comprises self-perception *and* other-perception. In other words, our link to others like ourselves is based in part on our *perceived* bond with them, which is to a great degree a matter of choice (the part we assert). Ethnic identity is also related to how and where other people place us in terms of group membership (our ascribed status). When self-description and the looking-glass self coincide (i.e., when we feel a bond with the group and that bond is reinforced by others), we have what Stephen Cornell and Douglas Hartmann term a thick identity, one in which our lives are organized heavily. For those who either do not feel close to their group or do not have institutional links to that group (via participation in its institutions or through encountering discrimination from outsiders), they are closer to what Cornell and Hartmann call a thin identity.[45]

Whether identity is thick or thin can be examined from personal experience, which includes how one feels about the bonds and how others (including institutions) react to you as a member of the group. Here identity involves both unique encounters as a multiracial (experience) and being perceived and treated similarly by outsiders. Experience and perceptions of others are part of the same picture. The debate on a multiracial category, however, tends to fall into either camp.

Personal Experience and Identity

To examine the first issue, personal experience, I focus on what Ian Lopez terms chance and choice in the makeup of an identity.[46] Identity is in part a matter of chance. This chance is based on biological heritage and is associated with morphology (i.e., physical features), which together play a key role in identity development. Not knowing the details of other lives, we examine a person's physical appearance looking for "White," "Black," or "Asian" features and from there assign them to racial categories on the basis of their most obvious characteristics, such as skin color, hair texture and color, eye color, and so on.[47] Multiracials share chance in that they often possess an ambiguous physical appearance. It is chance because how one looks "racially" still is mostly a result of coincidence, not subject to human will. Biology determines one's looks. But because race is socially constructed, morphology and ancestry gain importance on a social and not a physical plane. They are not entirely accidental, although one can alter looks in racially significant ways (e.g., hair straighteners, contacts, surgery).

Nonetheless, how one looks influences one's choice of identity. Choice comprises a crucial ingredient in the construction of racial identification and the fabrication of races. Choices occur on mundane and epic levels (what to wear, when to fight). They are made by individuals and groups, for example, deciding to pass or social movements deciding to protest. The effects may be minor or profound; they may slightly alter an affiliation or radically retain a community's identity. But in each circumstance choices are exercised not by free agents or autonomous actors but by people who are compromised and cramped by the social context. As Angela Harris explains, choice is not uncoerced or "freely given, but a 'contradictory consciousness' mixing approbation and apathy, resistance and resignation."[48] We constantly exercise choice in racial matters, sometimes in full aware-ness of our compromised position, though often not. As one Black–Asian American reported,

> When I was growing up, I tried to look White, I guess. I used hair straighteners, avoided the sun—wore hats and long sleeves even when it was hot. I was always afraid someone would find out that I was Black. I thought Black women were, while not ugly, not as attractive as Whites, who were also better looking than Asians. The only problem was, that I was not White. I would even avoid Black music. I felt I was on a treadmill, though I never questioned it until recently.[49]

Moreover, choice is linked to looks, for it limits the situations in which one can opt for one or another identity. The process of choice suggests that decisions are made in specific contexts rather than on neutral ground in American life.

The Looking-Glass Self: Context

Context is the social setting in which races are recognized, con-structed, and contested; it is the "circumstances directly encountered, given and transmitted from the past."[50] At a metalevel, context has both ideological and material components, such as entrenched cul-tural and customary prejudices and maldistributed resources, market-place inequalities, and skewed social services. These inherited social structures are constantly altered by anything from individual actors and community social movements to broad-based changes in the social, economic, demographic, and political landscape. Simultane-ously, context also involves localized settings. The systems of mean-ing regarding ancestry or morphology are unstable. These systems shift over time and across space and even across class and educational lines in ways that give to any individual different racial identities depending on his or her shifting social location.

Races are groups of people bound together by their historically contingent, socially significant morphology and ancestry. A race is not created because people share just any characteristic or just any ancestry, as is the case for multiracials. Instead, it is the social significance attached to certain features, like faces, and to certain forebears, like Africans or Asians, that defines races.[51] Context superimposed on chance largely shapes races in the United States. A multiethnic Black-Japanese man describes his experience:

> While at home it never really bothered or concerned me. When I went to college, it started to hit home. It was a period of Black Pride and anti-white and anti-black feelings. I was thrown into the middle. 'Cause I lived in a military environment, this was very strange to me. At first, I would identify as mixed; if asked I would not say black, but Indian and Japanese. It was, ironically enough, after I fell in love with a white girl who was very much into things in African history, that I first started to form a real identity—one with Africa.[52]

For many who advocate a special category, context, choice, and chance intersect in multiracials to create a central identity. Susan Graham argues that all multiracials feel a kinship through a set of shared historical, cultural, and social qualities.[53] Carlos Fernandez argued before a House subcommittee that multiracial people are a community deserving recognition like any other.[54] One wonders exactly what community this is. If it refers to specific mixes, such as Black-White, then the idea of community can perhaps be justified. But to suggest that there are substantive cultural and historical links between, for example, Black-Asian mixes and Latino-White mixes is much less convincing.

This is what advocates of a multiracial component in government documents do not want to address. Advocates argue that choice, context, and chance are equally problematic for most of the people in this grouping. Further, because they argue that there is a common multiracial identity, for most of them the external dynamics are such that most multiracials receive similar treatment by most outsiders (i.e., nonmultiracial people). It cannot be argued otherwise, for if, as a group, outsiders do not see them as more or less homogeneous, a key ingredient of identity—external reinforcement of the internal component—is lacking. If their argument that multiracials have a core experience is true, this suggests that there are major substantive internal similarities in the experiences of being of mixed racial heritage.[55]

Research on multiracials shows that there are parallel identities and that this is so across different mixtures.[56] However, this research also suggests that there is no multiracial racial identity per se or that there are many types of mixed identities that differ based on the racial mix at play.[57] Debate still exists in the literature about whether the similar experiences of individuals of mixed heritage are enough to create a separate cultural group. Generally, the literature supports the importance of recognizing multiraciality as a category and as a different experience but does not (yet) support describing multiracials as a separate cultural group by conventional definition.[58]

There is other evidence to suggest that within the so-called multiracial category lies a wide range of experiences. Much of the variation in choices available to multiracials has to do with their particular racial makeup. Studies on Asian-White combinations, the second largest mixed racial contingent, show that they generally have more options than their Black-Asian counterparts, which is supported by the fact that most of them do not see themselves as Asian.[59] Many White-Asians have racial-ethnic identities comparable to their White counterparts.[60] Cynthia Nakashima and Teresa Williams both found that among Asian Americans, those of mixed ancestry are ostracized from Asian American communities, especially if they are Black.[61]

Among Black mixtures choice is less optional, for they are invariably classified as Black by the larger society, a rule not generally applied to children of White-Native, White-Asian, and White-Latino couples, who are generally considered part Indian, Asian, or Latino.[62] Among interracial marriages with one Asian parent, the children of those who are married to Blacks are more constrained in their identity choices, for they are usually perceived as Black.[63] One Black-Asian informant suggested the range of difference across racial mixes:

When you have Black ancestry, you have to be more in tune to it. The world, thanks to history, has really put down Black people and anything associated with Africa so those of us who are mixed can't hide behind a mixed label to get away from it, even if we look [like] something else and get mistaken constantly for being a race that we aren't part of. I feel an extra "umph" when it comes to my Africanity. It's probably easier for me as an Asian/Black person to claim that I'm mixed because Black people don't mind mixing with other people of color, but I think the half-White mulatto kids have more issues of validation and legitimacy because they are kind of seen as being part of the oppressor and because the history of slavery and White people's deeds. In that sense, when you are a double minority mix, I think it's some ways easier.[64]

Thus various components of mixed ethnic identities are not equally prominent or important at all times. For many, identity is in part symbolic (or "thin"); for others, it is "thick" because of physical appearance. Usually for multiracial people the importance of multiple heritage is situational. And the tendency is to simplify, to emphasize one while holding on to the others. But the thickness of this identity is related to an individual's racial makeup. These results underscore the special salience of the particular racial mixture to understanding experience. Current evidence suggests that within multiracial populations, there is a racial hierarchy that mirrors one found among so-called monoracial populations. Thus, based on the evidence, although there may be important similarities among multiracials, there are substantive differences that reflect wider social dynamics. Most of all, this experience differs from the experience of other "racial" groups in that multiracials are not seen as one type of person by outsiders. It always depends on the mix and how obvious the mixtures are.

The 2000 census helps us begin to sort between these two interpretations, that which asserts the sky will fall and that which suggests there is a multiracial identity waiting to be tapped. It seems from the 2000 census data that the latter interpretation has more support than the former. About 2.4 percent of Americans noted having at least two racial backgrounds.[65] White–"some other race" was the most popular choice (32 percent of all multiracials), followed by White–American Indian/Alaska Native (16 percent), White–Asian American (13 percent), and Black-White (11 percent). The number of racial combinations was delimited, however. Of those choosing at least two races, 93 percent chose only two. Given the long history of mixing, for example, among Blacks and Native Americans, one would assume that the number of racial combinations would be higher. That it is not suggests that the cataloging of racial heritage in this way is limited to two groups, no matter how many are involved in reality.

These data suggest several other general patterns. First, when allowed to choose an identity, a relatively small number of Americans (2.4 percent) select multiracial heritage. Second, Native Hawaiian/ Other Pacific Islander, which is not traditionally considered a separate racial group, is one of the categories included in the racial mix. This also inflates the numbers identified as multiracial. Third, large numbers of Americans chose "some other race" that does not fit in the five already established categories. It was typically the second largest contingent of all groups. What those races might be is unclear. But more than 3 million Americans who identify as multiracial, almost 46 percent of the total multiracial population, selected "some other race" as part of their racial makeup. Deciphering what this "race" might be is important to understanding the extent of the multiracial phenomenon. It is safe to say that among those who chose this category are some who might more "objectively" fit into one of the monoracial groupings, which, along with the factors listed above, points to less than 2.4 percent of Americans as actually multiracial as we traditionally mean it.

Finally, those who argued that the sky will fall if racial choices were opened up may have some support when it comes to Asian American communities and less clear support when it concerns Black communities. More than 16 percent of Asian America reported being of more than one race. The proportion for Blacks is 5.1 percent. While this is well below the 75 to 90 percent figure typically given for the racial mixture found historically among Black Americans, it is two times larger than anticipated given precensus surveys that tried to ascertain what it might be. It is not a surprise that the figures for American Indians/Alaskan Natives and Native Hawaiians/Other Pacific Islanders indicate that for them multiracial status is the norm.

Altogether the newest census data suggest that choosing several racial heritages is still uncommon and probably occurs most often among first-generation multiracials. If this is the case, then it becomes even less clear what a multiracial ethnicity would look like. Because the census does not allow for an evaluation of what these choices mean to those who selected them, how thick or thin it is in their lives, and how the experiences differ by racial mix, we are left without answers to choice, context, and chance. Whether these choices of labels reflect a mere cataloging of racial histories or are an extension of an essential self is an unanswered question that makes premature any move to homogenize this diverse group of people.

In the final analysis, advocating for a multiracial category is an attempt to use racial identity politics to further the efforts of an amorphous group, one that knows that it does not fit easily elsewhere, that knows what it is not, but does not know what it is—yet. It remains, in the end, a racial project, which moves us farther from seeing ourselves as complex beings. It is not interested in reflecting commonalities of life and its completeness. In fact, this effort highlights differences much more than do other categories. While the movement may be admirable, the goals are not. The bigger issue may not be that current groupings are insufficient but that a multiracial category fosters a belief that there is something logical, necessary, and scientific about dividing people into groups called races.[66] And while the other categories do so as well, they are at least something we know about. A multiracial category has so many permutations that it does not offer clear advantages to anyone but those who choose this box.

So on one level the movement for a new racial category merely follows in the footsteps of those who used race as a means to achieve their goal of racial equality. But who exactly is this group of multiracials: everyone who ever had mixed "blood"? anyone who has multiple ethnicities? only those who are first-generation multiracial? The questions repeat themselves. Does it reflect a substantive category in U.S. society, one that, while not unique—after all, many of the census categories do not fit this requirement—does deserve the creation of a new race or ethnic group? And ultimately, is having this category an improvement over what we now have? At this time the answer to these questions is no.

Michael Omi and Howard Winant suggest that race is always in formation, the subject of constant struggle and contested at a social structural level, which includes racial dimensions of social stratification and distribution, institutional arrangements, political systems, and laws.[67] Race is also contested at the level of social signification, of production of meanings. The way race is culturally configured and represented, the manner in which race becomes a meaningful descriptor of groups and individual identities, is pertinent to social issues and experience.

The link between culture and structure is at the core of the racial formation process and gives racial projects their cohesiveness. Thus the currently popular argument that racial inequalities are merely differences in level of effort put into achieving economic success is closely succeeded by concomitant patterns of political orientation, economic and social programs, and other structural characteristics. Conservatives in the contemporary context react against movements for self-determination among the poor and people of color by using the ideas of the civil rights movement to reinforce individualism, competition, and laissez-faire policies. In the process, the idea of race is equated with ethnicity and, as Mary Waters found in her study on White ethnics, thus suggests that ethnicity (and thus racial identity) is optional.[68] The reverse is true too. When organizations, institutions, or the state advocate for and resist certain racial policies and practices and when they mobilize politically along racial lines, they implicitly, and perhaps explicitly, engage in racial signification. Featuring the idea of racial projects also refocuses our understanding of racism, for racism is seen as characterizing only some racial projects.

As Howard Winant suggests, a racial project is racist if it creates and/or reproduces hierarchical social structures based on essentialized racial categories.[69] The two key ideas here are essentialism and subordination. To identify a racial project as racist, one must link essentializing representations of race and hierarchical social structures that work together to protect dominant interests. Those who argue for a special multiracial category organize a racial project, for they essentialize and subordinate. They essentialize multiracial people by suggesting that most have similar experiences when the reality is that they probably do not. At this point, the idea that there is one common and unique experience that binds most multiracials together is more a wish than a fact. There may be as many multiracial experiences as there are racial and ethnic combinations within this group. More likely, major differences exist along particular racial combinations. The only common experience may have to do with feeling like an outsider or trying to identify with parents who have different backgrounds.

This essentializing is linked to subordination, to reinforcing or creating a hierarchy, although this may not be the intent. Most interracial couples meet at university, at work, or when serving in the military. There is some indication that having a multiethnic identity is related to having the opportunity to think about having choices (i.e., it is related to social class).[70] If this is the case, then creating a special category for already privileged people reinforces instead of tears down the social hierarchy. This social class dimension can also be seen in that light-skinned Blacks are already privileged by Whites over their darker counterparts.[71] Dark-skinned Blacks and dark-skinned Latinos would probably receive less favorable treatment regardless of whether there is a multiracial category. This intraracial divide, of course, reflects larger social dynamics surrounding race, which are in turn reflected in what appears to be a hierarchy within multiracial populations.

Racism is located in a fluid and disputed history of racially based social structures and discourses. There is no timeless or absolute standard for what constitutes racism, because social structures undergo reform (and reaction) and discourses are subject to rearticulation. Thus racism is provisional in appearance and changes with the property of political projects that link representation to the organization of race. On the surface, a multiracial category does not appear racist, but its implications are. It is a racial project that essentializes and will be used to subordinate.

Whatever comes of this social movement, we are involved in perhaps the most profound debate of racial questions in decades. Racial categories have been a significant part of redressing racial injustices, and even the multiracial movement uses race in its own self-interest. But as Sawyer has said:

> The dilemma we face is trying to assure the fundamental guarantees of equality of opportunity while at the same time recognizing that the population themselves are changing as we seek to categorize them. It reaches the point where it becomes an absurd counting game. Part of the difficulty is that we are dealing with the illusion of precision. We wind up with precise counts of everybody in the country, and they are precisely wrong. They don't reflect who we are as a people. To be effective, the concepts of individual and group identity need to reflect not only who we have been but who we are becoming. The more these categories

distort our perception of reality, the less useful they are. We act as if we knew what we're talking about when we talk about race, and we don't.[72]

Given the reality of race in today's world, we still need race to get beyond race. But focusing on race is not enough given the importance of color, social class, and gender issues that cut across all communities, not the least of which are communities of color. Any movement by people to overcome subordination must not come at the expense of other subordinated people. We must remember, as David Harvey has warned, "Politics which seeks to eliminate the processes which give rise to racism may turn out to look very different from a politics which merely seeks to give full play to differentiated identities once these have arisen."[73]

NOTES

1. I view each of these labels as cultural influences on my life. Nonetheless, in a real sense, I am American above all else, with "twists" due to my Japanese and Black linkages.

2. My focus here is on one segment of the movement for inclusion of multiethnic peoples in the census, those who advocate for the single box under any circumstance. As G. Reginald Daniel suggests in chapter 11 of this volume, there are actually several proposals for the format of a multiethnic category. At the federal level, AMEA and Project RACE activists supported a combined format (a multiracial box and allowing one to check all the categories that applied). Project RACE supported a stand-alone identifier at the state level for a variety of reasons. How much popular support any one category may have is not known.

3. Lawrence Wright, "One Drop of Blood," *New Yorker*, July 25, 1994, 46–50, 52–55.

4. Ibid., 46.

5. Before the Hispanic designation, however, there were official ways to aggregate Hispanics into one group, for example, "persons of Spanish mother tongue" or "persons of Spanish surname."

6. Michael Omi, "Racial Identity and the State: Contesting the Federal Standards for Classification," in *Race, Ethnicity and Nationality in the United States,* ed. Paul Wong (Boulder, Colo.: Westview Press, 1999).

7. Ellis Cose, *Color-Blind: Seeing beyond Race in a Race-Obsessed World* (New York: HarperCollins, 1997).

8. W. Frey and J. Tilove, "Immigrants In, Native Whites Out," *New York Times Magazine*, August 20, 1995, 44–45.

9. Wright, "One Drop of Blood," 46.

10. Michael Thornton and Suzanne Wason, "Intermarriage," in *Encyclopedia of Marriage and the Family*, ed. David Levinson (New York: Simon and Schuster, 1996), 396–402.

11. Yen Le Espiritu, *Asian American Panethnicity: Bridging Institutions and Identities* (Philadelphia: Temple University Press, 1992).

12. David Hollinger, *Postethnic America* (New York: Basic Books, 1995).

13. The inherent contradiction here is that bureaucratic mechanisms are not primarily about self-identification but aggregating identity for counting purposes. So advocating an identity through government involves conforming to specific, socially sanctioned boundaries. This process, too, ignores the fluid nature of identity. From my reading of the debate, it remains unclear what "multiracial" means in reality. If there are bureaucratic limitations of any sort, such as first-, second-, or even third-generation multiracials, how is that self-definition? Furthermore, at this point who would any label affixed to this group represent? Do we know how most multiracials or multiethnics feel about the choices? Unlike polls and surveys taken of the term "Black" since the 1960s, there seems little evidence to evaluate the popularity of any designation applied to multiracials. Unless the term chosen is supported by a significant portion of the target population, it will reflect most of all bureaucratic needs and activists' biases. Whose self-identification is it?

14. Patrice Farmer, "A Call for the End of the One Drop Rule: The Multiracial Community at War," *Multiracial Advocate* (March–April 2000). Found on www.multiracial.com/readers/farmer3.html.

15. Sara Cagno, "Race and Class: The 'Multiracist' Census 2000." Found on www.nyu.edu/gsas/dept/journal/race.class/census.html.

16. *Interracial Classified* (newsletter), August 1992, 3; Susan Graham, *Review of Federal Measurements of Race and Ethnicity, Hearings before the Subcommittee on Census, Statistics and Postal Personnel of the Committee on Post Office and Civil Service, House of Representatives, 103d Congress, First Session, June 30, 1993* (Washington, D.C.: U.S. Government Printing Office, 1994), 113, 115.

17. Carlos Fernandez, *Review of Federal Measurements of Race and Ethnicity, Hearings before the Subcommittee on Census, Statistics and Postal Personnel of the Committee on Post Office and Civil Service, House of Representatives, 103d Congress, First Session, June 30, 1993* (Washington, D.C.: U.S. Government Printing Office, 1994), 134.

18. Richard Miller, "Mulatto: A 'Race' of People," *Interracial Voice*, May–June 2000, www.webcom.com/~intvoice/warbird.htm.

19. Tanu Henry, "Counting Blacks in U.S. Census 2000," Africana.com/ index_2000530.htm.

20. Quoted in Henry, "Counting Blacks in U.S. Census 2000."

21. Tanya Schevitz, "Multiracial Census Form Poses Dilemma/Organizations Fear Dilution of Numbers," *San Francisco Chronicle*, March 11, 2000, A1.

22. Ibid.

23. F. James Davis, *Who Is Black? One Nation's Definition* (University Park: Pennsylvania State University Press, 1991).

24. Cited in Hanna Rosin, "Boxed In," *New Republic*, January 3, 1994, 16.

25. Reginald Daniel suggests that while most racial groups are in reality mixed race, people in traditional single-race categories have monoracial identities. Their identities do not embrace a kinship with those of multiple heritage. While true, I argue here that allowing them and so-called multiracials the opportunity to identify with all their backgrounds opens up a real possibility to claim a multiethnic heritage. We can see something comparable to this in the rejuvenation of Native American populations, an increase of more than 300 percent from 1960 to 1990.

26. Henry, "Counting Blacks in U.S. Census 2000."

27. Michael Hughes and Bradley R. Hertel, "The Significance of Skin Color Remains: A Study of Life Chances, Material Selection and Ethnic Consciousness among Black Americans," *Social Forces* 68 (June 1990): 1105–20.

28. Princeton University researchers suggest that many more people are likely to identify with more than one race than previously thought. Joshua Goldstein and Ann Morning estimate the number of Americans likely to mark multiple races at some 8 million to 18 million, several times greater than previous estimates. The vast majority of these chose "White" previously. See Web site: eurek.alert.org/releases/pu-mr005200.html.

As I was writing this chapter, the census suggested a partial answer to dealing with people choosing more than one racial category that included White. Those who did would be identified for census purposes as non-White. This decision, of course, continues the historical legacy that Whites are pure and racial minorities are anything but.

29. Ruth McKay and Manuel de la Puente, "Cognitive Testing of Racial and Ethnic Questions for the CPS Supplement," *Monthly Review* 119 (December 1996): 8–11; Clyde Tucker and Brian Kojetin, "Testing Racial and Ethnic Origin Questions in the CPS Supplement," *Monthly Review* 119 (December 1996): 3–7.

30. Ibid.

31. Stephan Thernstrom, "One Drop—Still: A Racialist's Census," *National Review*, April 17, 2000.

32. William Petersen, *Ethnicity Counts* (New Brunswick, N.J.: Transaction, 1997), 315–20.

33. Howard Winant, "Racism Today: Continuity and Change in the Post–Civil Rights Era," in Wong, ed., *Race, Ethnicity and Nationality*, 14–24.

34. Liberals were guilty of this as well. See, e.g., Michael Thornton and Hemant Shah, "U.S. News Magazine Images of Black-Asian American Relationships, 1980–1992," *Communication Review* 1 (summer 1996): 497–519; Hemant Shah and Michael C. Thornton, "Racial Ideology in U.S. Mainstream News Magazine Coverage of Black-Latino Interaction, 1980–1992," *Critical Studies in Mass Communication* 11 (June 1994): 141–61.

35. Cited in Angela Ards, "Whose Blackness Is This Anyway? The Multiracial Movement Raises Questions about Political Black Identity," *Village Voice* 42 (February 11, 1997): 36.

36. Carlos Fernandez, "Government Classification of Multiracial/Multiethnic," in *The Multiracial Experience: Racial Borders as the New Frontier*, ed. Maria P. P. Root (Thousand Oaks, Calif.: Sage, 1996), 15–36.

37. Paul Spickard and Rowena Fong, "Pacific Islander Americans and Multiethnicity: A Vision of America's Future?" *Social Forces* 73 (June 1995): 1378.

38. Doris Y. Wilkinson and Gary King, "Conceptual and Methodological Issues in the Use of Race as a Variable: Policy Implications," *Milbank Quarterly* 65, Supplement 1, (1987): 56–71.

39. Nancy Foner, "Race and Color: Jamaican Migrants in London and New York," *International Migration Review* 19 (fall 1985): 708–22; Mary Waters, "Ethnic and Racial Identities of Second-Generation Black Immigrants in New York City," *International Migration Review* 28 (winter 1994): 795–820; Milton Vickerman, "The Responses of West Indians to African Americans: Distancing and Identification," *Research in Race and Ethnic Relations* 7 (1994): 83–128.

40. Waters, "Ethnic and Racial Identities"; Nancy Foner, "The Jamaicans: Race and Ethnicity among Migrants in New York City," in *New Immigrants in New York*, ed. Nancy Foner (New York: Columbia University Press, 1987), 131–58; Philip Kasinitz, *Caribbean New York: Black Immigrants and the Politics of Race* (Ithaca: Cornell University Press, 1992); Vickerman, "Responses of West Indians"; Tekle Woldemikael, *Becoming Black American: Haitians and American Institutions in Evanston, Illinois* (New York: AMS Press, 1989).

41. Kyle Crowder, "Residential Segregation of West Indians in the New York/New Jersey Metropolitan Area: The Roles of Race and Ethnicity," *International Migration Review* 33 (spring 1999): 79–113.

42. Nancy Denton and Douglas Massey, "Racial Identity among Caribbean Hispanics: The Effect of Double Minority Status on Residential Segregation," *American Sociological Review* 54 (October 1989): 790–808; Douglas

Massey and Nancy Denton, "Hypersegregation in U.S. Metropolitan Areas: Black and Hispanic Segregation along Five Dimensions," *Demography* 26 (August 1989): 373–91; Douglas Massey and Nancy Denton, *American Apartheid: Segregation and the Making of the Underclass* (Cambridge, Mass.: Harvard University Press, 1993); Ira Goldstein and Clark White, "Residential Segregation and Color Stratification among Hispanics in Philadelphia: Comment on Massey and Mullan," *American Journal of Sociology* 91 (September 1985): 391–96.

43. Richard A. Kalish, "The Meanings of Ethnicity," in *European-American Elderly: A Guide for Practice,* ed. Christopher L. Hayes, Richard A. Kalish, and David Gutmann (New York: Springer, 1986), 16–34; Janet Helms and Regine Talleyrand, "Race Is Not Ethnicity," *American Psychologist* (November 1997): 1246–47.

44. Cynthia Pan, Robert Glynn, Helen Mogun, Igor Choodnovskiy, and Jerry Avorn, "Definitions of Race and Ethnicity in Older People in Medicare and Medicaid," *Journal of the American Geriatrics Society* 47 (June 1999): 730–33.

45. Stephen Cornell and Douglas Hartmann, *Ethnicity and Race: Making Identities in a Changing World* (Thousand Oaks, Calif.: Pine Forge, 1998).

46. Cited in Ian Lopez, "The Mean Streets of Social Race," in *The Social Construction of Race and Ethnicity in the United States,* ed. Joan Ferrante and Prince Brown Jr. (New York: Longman, 1998), 161–76.

47. Adrian Piper, "Passing for White, Passing for Black," *Transition* 58 (1992): 4–32.

48. Cited in T. J. Lears, "The Concept of Cultural Hegemony: Problems and Possibilities," *American Historical Review* 90 (June 1985): 570.

49. Michael C. Thornton, "A Social History of a Multiethnic Identity: The Case of Black Japanese Americans" (Ph.D. dissertation, University of Michigan, 1983), 183.

50. Karl Marx, *The Eighteenth Brumaire of Louis Bonaparte* (1963), quoted in Renato Rosaldo, *Culture and Truth: The Remaking of Social Analysis* (Boston: Beacon Press, 1989), 105.

51. Lopez, "Mean Streets of Social Race."

52. Thornton, "A Social History of a Multiethnic Identity," 124.

53. Graham, *Review of Federal Measurements of Race and Ethnicity,* 119.

54. Fernandez, *Review of Federal Measurements of Race and Ethnicity,* 127.

55. Furthermore, Cornell and Hartmann *(Ethnicity and Race,* 73) suggest there are several reasons for forming identities. Three are of particular importance in the present context: shared interests, culture, and shared institutions. Shared interests root many identities in political, economic, or status interests. In this case, what makes identity important to group members is the interests it serves in pursuit of political goals, in protecting rights and privileges,

and in achieving social status. To say that identities are rooted in group interests means that members see that they share issues at stake and that this perception is fundamental to group identity and solidarity. This type of identity is witnessed in the creation of an Asian American identity, created out of a belief that Asian immigrant groups have certain political interests in common.

Shared institutions involve identities that are bonded around organized institutions serving to pursue group interests. This usually involves creating (often exclusive) institutions that are sets of social relations organized specifically to solve the problems encountered by group members or to achieve their objectives. These might include extended families, educational systems, or even political parties. Group members are bound together in part by their dependence on and common participation in these institutions. This might describe the several multiethnic organizations that have been founded in the United States over the past decade.

Finally, a shared culture—shared understandings and interpretations that include ideas about what is important and what is real as well as strategic and stylistic guides to action—may bond one group to another. They may provide conceptual interpretations of the world at large and guides to action but also specify and exalt the identity of the group. From my reading of the multiracial movement, of the three underlying reasons Cornell and Hartmann mention for forming an identity, they highlight in a meaningful way only shared interests. Few would suggest that that is enough to form a meaningful identification.

56. Christine C. I. Hall, "The Ethnic Identity of Racially Mixed People: A Study of Black-Japanese" (Ph.D. dissertation, University of California, Los Angeles, 1980); L. Field, "Self-Concept and Adjustment in Biracial Adolescents" (Ph.D. dissertation, University of Denver, 1992); Thornton, "Social History of a Multiethnic Identity"; Teresa Williams, "Prism Lives: Identity of Binational Amerasians," in Root, ed., *Racially Mixed People in America*, 280–303; Nancy Brown and R. Douglas, "Making the Invisible Visible: The Growth of Community Network Organizations," in Root, ed., *The Multiracial Experience*, 323–40; Rebecca King and Kimberly DaCosta, "Changing Face, Changing Race: The Remaking of Race in the Japanese American and African American Communities," in Root, ed., *The Multiracial Experience*, 227–44.

57. Thornton and Wason, "Intermarriage."

58. Root, ed., *The Multiracial Experience*, xx.

59. Yu Xie and Kimberly Goyette, "The Racial Identification of Children with One Asian Parent: Evidence from the 1990 Census," *Social Forces* 76.2 (1997): 547–70; Rogello Saenz, Sean-Shong Hwang, Benigno Aguirre, and Robert Anderson, "Persistence and Change in Asian Identity among Children of Intermarried Couples," *Sociological Perspectives* 38 (summer 1995): 175–95.

60. Kwai Julienne Grove, "Identity Development in Interracial, Asian/White Late Adolescents," *Journal of Youth and Adolescence* 20 (1991): 617–28;

Ronald C. Johnson and Craig T. Nagoshi, "The Adjustment of Offspring of Within-Group and Interracial/Intercultural Marriages: A Comparison of Personality Factor Scores," *Journal of Marriage and the Family* 48 (May 1986): 279–84; James H. Jacobs, "Identity Development in Biracial Children," in Root, ed., *Racially Mixed People in America*, 190–206; Ana Mari Cauce, Yumi Hiraga, Craig Mason, Tanya Aguilar, Nydia Ordonez and Nancy Gonzales, "Between a Rock and a Hard Place: Social Adjustment of Biracial Youth," in Root, ed., *Racially Mixed People in America*, 207–22.

61. Cynthia Nakashima, "An Invisible Monster: The Creation and Denial of Mixed-Race People in America," in Root, ed., *Racially Mixed People in America*, 162–78; Teresa Williams, "Prism Lives: Identity of Binational Amerasians," in Root, ed., *Racially Mixed People in America*, 280–303.

62. Hollinger, *Postethnic America*.

63. Xie and Goyette, "Racial Identification of Children"; Saenz et al., "Persistence and Change"; Michael Thornton and Harold Gates, "Black, Japanese and American: An Asian American Identity Yesterday and Today" in *The Sum of Our Parts: Mixed Heritage Asian Americans*, ed. Teresa Williams-León and Cynthia Nakashima (Philadelphia: Temple University Press, 2001), 93–105.

64. Teresa Williams and Michael C. Thornton, "Social Construction of Ethnicity versus Personal Experience: The Case of Afro-Amerasians," *Journal of Comparative Family Studies* 29 (summer 1998): 263.

65. www.census.gov/population/cen2000/phc-tl/tab04.pdf.

66. Indeed, it is clear that for some the real goal is to abolish the idea of race altogether. See, for example, George Winkel, "Census 2000 Identity-Theft Targets Multiracial People," *Interracial Voice*, guest editorial, May–June 2000, www.webcom.com/~intvoice/gwinkel6.html; Thernstrom, "One Drop—Still."

67. Michael Omi and Howard Winant, *Racial Formation in the United States from the 1960s to the 1990s*, 2d ed. (New York: Routledge, 1994).

68. Mary Waters, *Ethnic Options* (Berkeley: University of California Press, 1990).

69. Winant, "Racism Today."

70. Thornton, "Social History of a Multiethnic Identity."

71. Hughes and Hertel, "Significance of Skin Color"; Denton and Massey, "Racial Identity among Caribbean Hispanics."

72. Wright, "One Drop of Blood," 55.

73. David Harvey, *The Urban Experience* (Baltimore: Johns Hopkins University Press, 1989), 154.

13

THE LANGUAGE OF *MESTIZAJE* IN A RENEWED RHETORIC OF BLACK THEOLOGY

ZIPPORAH G. GLASS

Recently, notable Black theologians met in Chicago to celebrate the thirtieth anniversary of James Cone's pivotal work, *Black Theology and Black Power*.[1] The skillful rhetoric of these theologians, including James Cone himself, resounded throughout the auditorium. But there was an uneasy feeling that the rhetoric of Black theology that found its impetus in the Black church to address the oppression of Black people in the 1950s and 1960s was not wholly adequate to redress the inequalities that plague the contemporary Black community in America.

Why was there uneasiness about the applicability of a Black theology that was so powerful to Black Americans fifty years ago? The answer to this question lies in the significantly changed U.S. context. Today, important shifts in the composition of the U.S. population and contemporary constructions and representations of biological and cultural mixture problematize the very nature of Black identity and the Black experience in America, the primary assets on which Black theology was founded.

Biological and cultural mixture are not new phenomena in the United States, and mixture of peoples and cultures is a known and accepted phenomenon in the American Black community. In my parents' household, my father, a mixture of American Indian and African, deplored my mother's habit of speaking Mexican Spanish in the house. He would warn her—in loud standard English—that it was not good to speak Spanish in the house for fear that their foreign-born, adopted children of German and African descent would not learn English well enough to pass their school subjects.

Despite historical mixing of racial groups in the United States, race remains a powerful metalanguage for constructing representations by which peoples are identified and identify themselves. It is predicated on signifying the Otherness in and among peoples to produce and maintain relations of power.[2] Recent constructions of "mixed race" and interracial categories have, however, raised questions about the signification of race, particularly Blackness, in the United States. These constructions are primarily the outgrowth of significant shifts in the racial composition of the country's population. Racial change in the population is being driven primarily by two factors: immigration and interracial marriage patterns.[3]

When one thinks back on the significant changes in the United States during the 1960s, the Civil Rights Act of 1964 immediately comes to mind. But it was the Immigration Reform Act of 1965 that overturned discriminatory provisions of earlier laws and can be linked to current changes in the racial makeup of the U.S. population.[4] The sponsors of the legislation may have envisioned increased immigration of persons from eastern and southern Europe and could not have anticipated the increased immigration from Caribbean, Central American, and the Latin American countries that has now dramatically altered the composition of the United States' population. In the 1980s, approximately fifty thousand persons immigrated to the United States from thirty-one nations, twenty-seven of which were Latin American, Caribbean, or Asian. Moreover, for the first time in U.S. history, large numbers of immigrants came from Central America.[5]

The immigration of persons from these countries and the continuing flow of persons, either "legally" or "illegally," from Mexico have dramatically increased the presence of persons of color and Hispanic/Latin heritage in the United States. Many of these immigrants are the very embodiment of biological and cultural mixture—Spanish, Indian, and African—yet are often treated as a monoracial group in the United States. They are projected to represent fully one-fourth of the U.S. population by 2050.[6] What is significant for Black American identity and experience is that many of these immigrants are of recognizable African descent, primarily from the Dominican Republic, Cuba, and the U.S. trust territory of Puerto Rico.

The U.S. context has significantly changed and is continually changing as a result of increased interracial marriage and the birth of mixed race children. Because of interracial marriage, there is now in the United States a multiracial population with clear patterns of identity. Expressions of mixture in the United States, particularly that of Black mixture, have inspired some of the most sophisticated sites on the Internet where social, political, and economic issues surrounding mixed race identities and experiences in America are debated on a daily basis.[7]

Mixture with Blackness, however, is a particular problem in a country that still adheres to a rigid binary racial classification of Black and White. American cultural logic still presupposes a biological basis for race. Race is perceived as being visibly evident, in what Frantz Fanon calls an "epidermal schema,"—skin color, hair texture, and facial structures.[8] But the multiplicity and content of electronic forums on issues of mixed race indicate that there is an escalation in the number of mixed race people who refuse to be diminished to a set of qualities as determined by the practice of Black or White essentialism. The famous U.S. golfer Tiger Woods is often held up as a model for fostering this resistance. Woods is identifiably Black by U.S. racial standards, but when he announced he was "Cablinasian" because his progenitors are European, African, Native American, and Thai, many African Americans were dismayed, as they saw Woods's recognition of his mixed heritage a rejection of Black identity.[9]

Changing population patterns and the insistence by persons of mixed biological and cultural heritage that they not be stereotyped within or by a binary racial classification of White or Black have now met at the federal level. The very nature of Black identity has been problematized by the federal government's initiative to give Black Americans who are of mixed biological and cultural heritage the option to identify themselves as *more* than just "Black" in the U.S. Census and on other federal documents beginning in 2000.[10] Crucial questions arise for Black theology when this new context is considered. How would a renewed Black theology include Black Americans who no longer wish to form their identity as "Black" but as mixed?

The rhetoric of Black theology as formulated in the 1950s and 1960s assumed a homogeneous Black people who shared a common identity and history in America. Black theology makes the disclaimer that Blackness does not refer to the color of one's skin but to one's disposition toward oppression.[11] However, when reading James Cone's writings, it is crucial to discern that the starting point of his theology is his own Black identity in a separate and supposedly equal America and that the basis for his formulation of Black theology is the Black American experience. Cone says it best when he argues that "it is this common experience among Black people in America that Black Theology elevates as the supreme test of truth."[12] Black theology was created to speak to and for a specific people of Black identity, in a specific context of struggle against structures of oppression, structures that Cone describes as "hovering over black being, stripping it of its blackness."[13]

Moreover, how would a renewed rhetoric of Black theology in today's context include Blackness as manifested in the increased presence of persons of Afro-Hispanic and Afro-Latin heritage? These immigrants, and many of their children who are born in the United States, embody Blackness through biological and cultural mixture but have no connection to a historical Black experience in the United States. The forebears of Afro-Latin and Afro-Hispanic peoples did not experience the harshness of slavery in the United States but in the African diaspora. Neither do they have a historical experience of the struggle for civil rights in the United States.

Afro-Hispanics and Afro-Latins are, however, identifiably "Black" under the starkly drawn dichotomous norms of race in the United States. These people, as do Black Americans, often live in a parallel world, living lives in American society but perceiving their reality in a manner different from the society in which they function. And, like Black Americans, they encounter similar forms of racism. In addition, some have the burden of a different language. But they do not process their experiences through a Black American perspective because their historical identity is different.

Given their historical difference, can a renewed Black theology simply afford to ignore these people? Latinos/as, including those of identifiable African descent, under the rubric Hispanic, are now the single largest minority group in the United States.[14] Blacks, or African Americans, are no longer the largest or the most important political minority group in America. This is a momentous shift in a country that is known as a melting pot of peoples but has denied the reality of biological mixture by imposing the racialized metalanguage of hypodescent to make all persons who have even one drop of African blood classifiable as Black.

The increased presence of Afro-Latins and Afro-Hispanics and the opportunity being given to Black Americans to opt for a more inclusive Black identity so as to make manifest their biological and cultural mixture have pluralized Black identity and are symptomatic of a broader occurrence in the U.S. politics on race. In recent history the notion of hypodescent worked in favor of the Black American community, helping to solidify its identity and increasing its numbers and political representation. Mixture and the construction of mixed race categories, however, now threaten these realities.

Contemporary manifestations of cultural and biological mixture in the United States are what I call *mestizaje*. Historically, *mestizaje* referred to the biological mixture of native Indians and Spaniards in Latin America. In the Caribbean, mestizaje was between Spaniards and Africans. But in its broader meaning, mestizaje refers to any biological and cultural mixture of peoples. Gloria Anzaldúa, in *Borderland/La Frontera*, offers a cultural and biological glimpse into mestizaje when she proclaims that she is not hispana, india, negra, española, or European; she is *mestiza,* one who is "caught in the crossfire between camps while carrying all five races on her back."[15]

Mestizaje is a formation that cannot be collapsed into a single essential category. But if one were to deconstruct the racial signifiers in Anzaldúa's mixed identity, one would find that each of the named identities has been manipulated in an American politics of race by means of tropes that configure each identity in American society. Negra or Black, and its characterization, however, is a primary racial signifier in Anzaldúa's mixed identity. As Lewis Gordon puts it, "[M]ixture is a function of colored realities, not white ones."[16] In addition, Lourdes Martinez-Echazabal, in her work on Afro-mestizo identity in the United States, says that Black signifies "todas las tonalidades cromáticas"—all the chromatic tonalities.

Mixture, then, in the American politics of race is not race neutral but loaded with racial values. These values, as Gordon believes, have less to do with becoming White than they do with distancing oneself from Blackness through mixture in order to gain better access to social, economic, and political resources.[17] This may very well be true for many who are now classified as Black by White society and have experienced limits in their access to resources and hence will decide to declare themselves "mixed" as a strategy for better access.

However, Gordon's argument is limited. He has not taken into account the increasing Afro-Latin/Hispanic population in the United States that recognizes its Black cultural and biological heritage but does not generally share a concept of—how shall I put it—"negative" negritude that in the American politics of race is implicit in Afro-mestizo identity. Moreover, Gordon misses vital and evolving manifestations of mixture in the United States. There is an increasing number of youth born of interracial marriages who are *not* interested in grounding their Blackness in an African identity in the attempt to create continuity with an ideal African past that predates colonized mixture. Instead, these young people do not believe their Blackness is thoroughly racial, but a complex historical identity formed through biological and cultural mixture and shaped through contact with contemporary contextual challenges.

There are also an increasing number of adults who are fully aware of how Black mixture and cultural ties can inhibit them but who themselves do not recognize this as a limitation, even in a country that still assigns inferior status to Blackness. Their orientation is quite the contrary: they believe their mixture with Blackness facilitates perspectives and affiliations that singularly self-understood Black or White identities may not venture into.

Mixture has taken on heightened awareness in the American politics of race and confronts this politics with the inevitability of a plurality that stretches beyond simple Black and White. The politics is now faced with a paradox. Black identity has become pluralized in the United States and is no longer reducible to a single inherent identity or experience that can be conveniently congealed under a criterion of hypodescent.

Lack of recognition of these trends leads some Black theologians to argue that the Black identity would only be diluted by the inclusion of a language of mestizaje in Black theology. For these theologians, the language of mixture fractures Blackness and provides no agenda for resistance based on an identity or a historical experience.[18] Such an argument, however, fails to perceive what Manuel Zapata Olivella has stated so eloquently, "America became black with the

African, not because of their black skin, but their rebelliousness, their antislavery struggle, their union with the Indian in order to combat the oppressor. . . . Mestizaje against racism has always been the formula of life against classist societies in the history of all the peoples of the world."[19]

The argument against the inclusion of mestizaje in Black theology falters on two points. First, *the* Black identity in the U.S. context no longer exists. This may worry some. As Gordon stated, "'The' black identity is the element that enters the room and frightens Reason out."[20] But there is no reason to worry about levels of Black frightening power. If, in the American politics of race, *the* Black identity could frighten Reason out of a room, then what are pluralized Blackened identities doing?

Black-White distinctions in the United States emanate from and are adapted to multiple uses of power premised on the notion that Whiteness is antithetical to mixture.[21] Moves at the federal and state levels to solidify, package, bundle, stamp, label, and classify mixture are implosive actions that solidify Whiteness against what is thought an exponential Blackness and presence of non-White, or colored, realities at all levels of society but particularly in the workplace and the market.[22]

Second, there is no substance to an argument that opposes the recognition of Blackness in mestizaje by grouping all those who lay claim to their mixed heritage as simply attempting to escape the realities of Blackness in the United States. This perspective does not take into account the reality that Blackness, when present, is the primary ingredient in mestizaje. Those who are mixed cannot and do not escape the reality of their Blackness; the American logic of race does not allow it.

Mestizaje neither denies nor precludes Blackness but rather expands the experience and the hue of Blackness. A renewed rhetoric of Black theology that seeks to be effective in redressing contemporary inequalities can no longer be premised on a particular Black identity or grounded in the historical experience of a singularly identifiable "Black" people.

Mestizaje itself is a politically charged cultural construct and has a long history of being a critical object of colonialism in the Western Hemisphere. Although the United States was not a colonizing force in the nineteenth century in the European sense, it nonetheless developed and profited from a system of internal colonial*ism* that included conquering indigenous lands, usurping Mexican territories, exploiting African labor, and constructing and privileging White identity over and against other identities. This internal colonialism, and all its other manifestations, brought into existence what Robert Blauner describes as "the present-day patterns of racial stratification in the United States."[23]

Mestizaje in America's early politics was a union to be avoided and denied. The contemporary American politics of race, however, does not outwardly expound avoidance, nor does it deny the existence of mestizaje. This does not mean, however, that the United States is following a race politics found in some Latin American countries where mestizaje is a buildup to *blanquemiento*—"Whiting"— where Blackness, Indianness, and other racialized identities are absorbed, giving rise to a Whitened mestizo nation. Black Americans who have suspicions about mestizaje and how it is being incorporated into the American politics of race are right to be suspicious. Moreover, Black theologians have reason to be concerned that mestizaje is being usurped and used to quantifiably reduce the presence of Blackness in the United States by institutionalizing a recognizable group of people into the racial hierarchy who are not White but who also are not Black.

It is seldom considered outside the Black community and other minority communities in America that Black Americans are extremely knowledgeable about White consciousness. Although the perceptions and writings of African Americans are often portrayed as subjective elaborations of what it means to be a "minority," it remains a fact of life in America that most Black Americans must on a daily basis enter the domains of White America to seek their livelihood; the reverse is seldom required.

Few African American writers have probed the depths of Whiteness as has James Baldwin. It is difficult to describe Baldwin's writing, in the sophisticated language of today, as a "social construction." Rather, Baldwin lays bear a simple truth: one's choice to be part of a biologically and culturally driven category of Whiteness is, he wrote, "absolutely a moral choice," since "there are no white people." Baldwin summed up just as succinctly the phenomenon of Whiteness in the United States: "No one was white before he or she came to America."[24]

Baldwin's words summon up Lewis Gordon's position on White-ness, when he argues that one is White only to the extent that one can delineate and separate oneself from Blackness. Both men may have hit on a tactical truth in the persistent being and nature of Whiteness in the United States. In the current context of composi-tional shifts in the U.S. population, White identity can only continu-ally re-create itself against a representation and categorization of non-White Others.[25]

Whiteness in the United States, however, is not coextensive with peoples of European descent, since the progenitors of many who classify themselves as White were African, Asian, or Indian. Hence it is curious why the U.S. Census has not yet included a dialogue on modifying, or even doing away with, the category of "White," but has centered on nomenclature for the category or categories for per-sons of visible and "colored" mixture—that is non-Whites—to place themselves within.

Under such a track, mestizaje does escape the political nature of social identity but becomes a racialized group identity. It can be rea-sonably argued that *una gente de la otrura*—a people of otherness— is being constructed and will function as an amalgamated third race mediating between Whiteness and Blackness. When translated into economic terms, a people of mestizaje would simply act as a buffer between privileged power and weakness.

It is impossible to imagine, at least at the theoretical level, engag-ing a hermeneutic of otherness that does not set up hierarchies and exclusionary categories as long as the U.S. political regime insists on racialized binary oppositions. Hence the task of a critical mestizaje is not only to appropriate the being and experience of otherness but also to separate it from the politics of subjugated, racialized cate-gories. When a hermeneutic of otherness is made the enterprise of a critical mestizaje arising out of a Black-affirming ideology of po-litical and cultural force and diaspora consciousness, mixture becomes a sign of a persistent Black aesthetic.

Mestizaje has always been a part of Blackness in the United States, but it was given a subaltern position vis-à-vis Blackness in tra-ditional Black theology in order to make Blackness the primary or-ganizing principle. A contemporary Black theology can no longer afford to construct Blackness in opposition to Whiteness but must incorporate the heterogeneous presence and experience of Blackness in mixture inside the borders of the United States.

Now, as odd as it may sound, Blackness must be subsumed in mixture, to make the pluralization of Black being and experience in the United States the broader principle by which to foster a resistant consciousness directed at challenging existing norms and practices of domination. A renewed Black theology must appropriate and articulate a language of mestizaje in order to elucidate Black identit*ies* and Black experience*s* to reflect the contemporary context of Black plurality. Resistance in a renewed rhetoric of Black theology will be found when creating and appropriating the language of mixture so that Blackness is affirmed in *el maridaje de las sangres y culturas*—the confluence of bloods and cultures.

A contemporary Black theology must practice a processual hermeneutic of otherness, whereby mixture is given the vantage point in meeting the challenges of social, political, and economic adaptation in the United States through what R. S. Sugirtharajah so eloquently describes as "unlimited alternative forms of group identity."[26]

Notes

1. James Cone, *Black Theology and Black Power* (New York: Seabury Press, 1969). The conference, "Black Theology as Public Discourse: From Retrospect to Prospect," was held at the University of Chicago, April 2–4, 1998.

2. See Evelyn Brooks Higginbotham, "African-American Women's History and the Metalanguage of Race," *Signs* 17.2 (winter 1992): 251–74.

3. Reynolds Farley, "One America in the 21st Century: The President's Initiative on Race, Presentation to the Race Advisory Board," October 1, 1997. Available at http://www.whitehouse.gov/Initiatives/OneAmerica/farley.html.

4. Ibid., introduction.

5. Ibid., Projections of the Population to 2050: Immigration Assumptions.

6. Ibid., conclusion.

7. See *Interracial Voice*, May–June 1999, at http://www.webcom.com/~intvoice. Additional citations are listed at http://www.webcom.com/~intvoice/add_site.html. See also "LatinoLink," May 1999, at http://www.latinolink.com; Roger Hernández, "February Is Black Hispanic Month, Too," February 9, 1997, at http://www.latinolink.com/opinion/opinion97/0209OROG.

HTM; Miguel Pérez, "Los Latinos de los Estados Unidos y del Caribe empiezan a enfrentarse a un asuntoprohibido," April 12, 1998, at http://www.latinolink.com/opinion/opinion98/0412HI1S.HTM.

8. Frantz Fanon, *Black Skin, White Mask,* trans. Charles Lam Markmann (New York: Grove, 1967), 112.

9. Ray Winbush, "Do We Really Want to Talk about Race," July 8, 1997, at http://www.fiskrri.org/home/articles/31rri/keynote.htm. See also Salli Richardson, "Regarding Tiger Woods Statement He's "Ca[u]bl[i]nasian," 1997, and various authors, "Tiger Woods You Are Soooooo Stupid," May 3, 1997–April 27, 1998, in *SPlusNet WWW Golf,* at http://www.splusnet.com/golf/golfboard/messages/93.html#followups.

10. Bob Taylor, "The Census 'Multicultural' Category: A Step Forward or a New Apartheid?" *Interrace* 7.4 (June 30, 1997): 14; Oralandar Brand-Williams, "Census Changes Stir Mixed-Race Debate," *Detroit News,* January 5, 1998; Gregory Kane, "Multiracial Category Raises Suspicions," *Baltimore Sun,* July 13, 1997.

11. James Cone, *God of the Oppressed* (Maryknoll, N.Y.: Orbis Books, 1997), 151.

12. Cone, *Black Theology and Black Power,* 120.

13. Ibid., 118.

14. "Maya Advertising and Communications Latino Fact Sheet," 1996, available at http://www.mayadc.com/maya96/Latino.htm.

15. Gloria Anzaldúa, *Borderland/La Frontera: The New Mestiza* (San Francisco: Aunt Lute Books, 1987), 194.

16. Lewis Gordon, *Her Majesty's Other Children: Sketches of Racism from a Neo-Colonial Age* (Lanham, Md.: Rowman and Littlefield, 1997), 56.

17. Lourdes Martinez-Echazabal, *Para una semiotica de la mulatez* (Madrid: José Porrua Turanzas, 1990), 19.

18. Here I am referring to some of the arguments and comments that I heard during Cornel West's brilliant "Black Theology at the Fourth Aims of Religion Address," at the University of Chicago's Rockefeller Memorial Chapel on the occasion of honoring James Cone's works, April 4, 1998.

19. Manuel Zapata Olivella, *Levantate mulato! Por mi raza hablara el espiritu* (Bogotá: Rei, 1990), 330; my translation.

20. Gordon, *Her Majesty's Other Children,* 53.

21. Higginbotham, "African-American Women's History," 253.

22. My use of the term "exponential" to describe Blackness borrows from Lewis Gordon's use of the term and his marvelous personal examples at Trinity College's first symposium on decolonization, "Border, Partitions, Statism" in Hartford, Conn., March 13, 1998.

23. Robert Blauner, *Racial Oppression in America* (New York: Harper and Row, 1972), 12.

24. James Baldwin, "On Being 'White' and Other Lies," *Essence* (April 1984): 90–92.

25. See Lewis Gordon, "On the Borders of Anonymity and Superfluous Invisibility," paper presented at Trinity College, Hartford, Conn., March 1998, 10.

26. R. S. Sugirtharajah, "Orientationalism, Ethnonation and Transnationalism: Shifting Identities and Biblical Interpretation," in *Ethnicity and the Bible*, ed. Mark G. Brett (Leiden: Brill, 1996), 427.

CONTRIBUTORS

Ralph Armbruster-Sandoval is Assistant Professor of Chicana and Chicano Studies at the University of California, Santa Barbara. His research interests include globalization, labor, social movements, race and ethnic relations, and Latin American studies. He is currently writing a book on globalization and the antisweatshop movement.

G. Reginald Daniel is Associate Professor of Sociology, University of California, Santa Barbara. He is the author of several seminal essays on racial theory, including "Passers and Pluralists: Subverting the Racial Divide," "Beyond Black and White: The New Multiracial Consciousness," and "Converging Paths: Multiracial Identity in Brazil and the United States." His book, *More Than Black? Multiracial Identity and the New Racial Order*, was published in 2002 by Temple University Press.

Zipporah G. Glass was educated at Indiana University, Wesley Theological Seminary, and Vanderbilt University. She has taught biblical languages, hermeneutics, and related subjects at several universities and seminaries, including Catholic University of America, Howard University, and the University of Sheffield in England. She is currently administrator at George Washington University.

Lori Pierce is Assistant Professor of American Studies at DePaul University. She was educated at Lake Forest College, Harvard University, and the University of Hawai'i, where she earned a Ph.D. in American studies. She is the author of articles on racial theory, race in Buddhism, and race in Hawaiian history and is currently working on a book on racial constructions in territorial Hawai'i.

Stephen A. Small is Associate Professor of African American Studies at the University of California, Berkeley. He is the author of many articles and papers on racial constructions in the United States and Britain and of *Racialised Barriers: The Black Experience in the United States and England in the 1980s* (Routledge, 1994). His most recent book is *Inside the Matrix of Miscegenation: Blacks of Mixed Origins under Slavery in Jamaica and Georgia* (New York University Press, 2003).

Paul Spickard is Professor of History at the University of California, Santa Barbara. He is the author or editor of eleven books, including *We Are a People: Narrative and Multiplicity in Constructing Ethnic Identity* (Temple University Press, 2000) and *Revealing the Sacred in Asian and Pacific America* (Routledge, 2003). He is currently writing a novel.

Michael C. Thornton is Professor of Afro-American Studies and the Asian American Studies Program at the University of Wisconsin–Madison. His Ph.D. from the University of Michigan is in sociology and Japanese studies. He is the author of many articles on racism, racial constructions, and the factors that explain when and why people cross so-called racial boundaries.

Hanna Wallinger is Assistant Professor of American Studies at the University of Salzburg. She was educated at Georgetown University and recently completed her Austrian Habilitation. She has written many articles and papers on Pauline Hopkins, Alice Dunbar-Nelson, and other figures in African American literature and is currently writing a book, *Pauline Hopkins: Negotiations in Life and Literature*.

William Wei is Professor of History and Director of the Sewall Residential Academic Program at the University of Colorado, Boulder, where he teaches modern Chinese history and Asian American studies. He received his Ph.D. in 1978 from the University of Michigan. Among his books are *Counterrevolution in China: The Nationalists in Jiangxi during the Soviet Period* (University of Michigan Press, 1985) and *The Asian American Movement* (Temple University Press, 1993). In summer 1997 he worked as a journalist covering the historic handover of Hong Kong to China.

INDEX

affirmative action, 158, 251, 285, 286
African Americans: and
  Afrocentrism, 221–28; and
  interethnic relations, 210–11; and
  multiracial identity, 103, 106–9,
  110, 114, 118, 277–304; passing,
  84–87, 90–92, 94, 99; political
  activism, 157–88; and Whiteness
  studies, 251, 257, 264. *See also*
  Afrocentrism; Asian Americans;
  Civil Rights movements;
  monoracial; multiracial;
  passing; Whiteness
Africans: enslavement of, 31–33,
  34–38, 253; and the
  Mediterranean world, 224, 225;
  and miscegenation laws, 60, 63,
  66, 71, 75. *See also* "Curse of
  Ham"; miscegenation;
  slavery
Afrocentrism, 222–42
Agricultural Workers Organizing
  Committee (AWOC), 175
agriculture, 24
aloha, discourse of, 124, 128, 144, 145
American College Testing Program
  (ACT), 294
"American dilemma," 284
American Friends Inter-Racial Peace
  Committee, 88, 91, 93
Americanization, 127, 131, 135, 147

anti-Semitism, 210
antiwar demonstrations. *See*
  Vietnam War
Arawaks. *See* Native Americans
Asian American Legal Defense and
  Education Fund (AALDEF), 318
Asian Americans: 257; development
  of pan-Asian ethnic identity,
  197–98, 201–2; and ethnic
  consciousness, 196; ethnic studies
  and, 204–5; ethnic violence
  toward, 208–9; formation of
  community organizations, 206;
  and gender inequality, 203–4;
  and interethnic relations, 209–10;
  and protest movements;
  198–200, 217; stereotypes of,
  201–2, 215; and Vietnam War,
  197–200, 208
assimilation, 129, 131–32, 134, 145,
  177, 222, 288, 301
Association for Asian American
  Studies (AAAS), 215, 216
Association of Multiethnic
  Americans (AMEA), 291, 300, 316
Attucks, Crispus, 312
Aztlán, 179–84

Balboa Day, 124, 125, 138
Baldwin, James, 348–49
Big Five, 130